CW00553720

THE CAMBRIDGE COMPANIC
ENGLISH LITERATURE, 1830-

The nineteenth century witnessed unprecedented ex
public and an explosive growth in the number of books and newspapers
produced to meet its demands. These specially commissioned essays examine
not only the full range and variety of texts that entertained and informed the
Victorians, but also the boundaries of Victorian literature: the links and overlap
with Romanticism in the 1830s, and the roots of Modernism in the years
leading up to the First World War. The *Companion* demonstrates how science,
medicine and theology influenced creative writing and emphasizes the
importance of the visual, in painting, in book illustration and in technological
innovations from the kaleidoscope to the cinema. Chapters also chart the
complex and fruitful interchanges with writers in America, Europe and the
Empire, highlighting the geographical expansion of literature in English. This
Companion brings together the most important aspects of this prolific and
popular period of English literature.

JOANNE SHATTOCK is Professor of Victorian Literature at the University of
Leicester. She is the General Editor of *The Works of Elizabeth Gaskell* (2005–6)
and edited *Women and Literature in Britain 1800–1900* (2001).

A complete list of books in the series is at the back of the book.

THE CAMBRIDGE
COMPANION TO

ENGLISH LITERATURE,
1830–1914

EDITED BY
JOANNE SHATTOCK
University of Leicester

CAMBRIDGE
UNIVERSITY PRESS

CAMBRIDGE UNIVERSITY PRESS
Cambridge, New York, Melbourne, Madrid, Cape Town, Singapore,
São Paulo, Delhi, Dubai, Tokyo

Cambridge University Press
The Edinburgh Building, Cambridge CB2 8RU, UK

Published in the United States of America by Cambridge University Press, New York

www.cambridge.org
Information on this title: www.cambridge.org/9780521709323

First published 2010

Printed in the United Kingdom at the University Press, Cambridge

A catalogue record for this publication is available from the British Library

Library of Congress Cataloging-in-Publication Data

The Cambridge companion to English literature, 1830–1914 / edited by Joanne Shattock.
        p.   cm. – (Cambridge companions to literature)
    ISBN 978-0-521-88288-0 (Hardback) – ISBN 978-0-521-70932-3 (Paperback)
 1. English literature–19th century–History and criticism. 2. English literature–20th century–
History and criticism. I. Shattock, Joanne.
                PR461.C35 2009
                820.9′008–dc22
                                                        2009036363

ISBN 978-0-521-88288-0 Hardback
ISBN 978-0-521-70932-3 Paperback

CONTENTS

CONTENTS

ILLUSTRATIONS

CONTRIBUTORS

BRIDGET BENNETT is Professor of American Literature and Culture at the University of Leeds. She has published a number of works related to the subject of her chapter in this volume. These include her recent monograph *Transatlantic Spiritualism and Nineteenth-Century American Literature* (2007) and her edited book (with Janet Beer) *Special Relationships: Anglo-American Affinities and Antagonisms, 1854–1936* (2002) as well as several essays. She is currently working on a monograph titled *Danger in the National Home*.

ALISON BOOTH is Professor of English at the University of Virginia. She is the author of *Greatness Engendered: George Eliot and Virginia Woolf* (1992) and *How To Make It as a Woman: Collective Biographical History from Victoria to the Present* (2004). In the digital project Collective Biographies of Women, and in her book-length study of literary tourism 'Homes and Haunts', she continues to pursue a historical interpretation of collective biographical discourses in Britain and North America since 1830.

PATRICK BRANTLINGER is James Rudy Professor of English (Emeritus) at Indiana University, where he edited *Victorian Studies* (1980–90). Among his books are *Rule of Darkness: British Literature and Imperialism 1830–1914* (1988), *The Reading Lesson: The Threat of Mass Literacy in Nineteenth-Century British Fiction* (1998) and *Dark Vanishings: Discourse on the Extinction of Primitive Races 1800–1913* (2003). *Victorian Literature and Postcolonial Studies* is forthcoming in 2009. With William B. Thesing, he co-edited Blackwell's *Companion to the Victorian Novel* (2002).

ALISON CHAPMAN is Associate Professor at the University of Victoria, Canada, and has co-edited (with Jane Stabler) *Unfolding the South: Nineteenth-Century British Women Artists and Writers in Italy* (2003) as well as writing several essays on the Victorians and Italy. She is currently completing a monograph on Elizabeth Barrett Browning's circle in Florence.

GOWAN DAWSON is Senior Lecturer in Victorian Literature at the University of Leicester. He is the author of *Darwin, Literature and Victorian Respectability* (2007) and co-author of *Science in the Nineteenth-Century Periodical: Reading the Magazine of Nature* (2004).

HILARY FRASER holds the Geoffrey Tillotson Chair of Nineteenth-Century Studies at Birkbeck College, University of London. She has written monographs on aesthetics and religion in Victorian writing, the Victorians and Renaissance Italy, nineteenth-century non-fiction prose, and gender and the Victorian periodical, and currently works on women writing about art. 'The Morals of Genealogy' (*Raritan*, Spring 2008) reflects on our own writing of the past via an intriguing personal encounter with Harriet Taylor and J. S. Mill.

JOSEPHINE GUY is Professor of Modern Literature at the University of Nottingham. She has published monographs on various aspects of nineteenth-century literary history as well as (with Ian Small) a study of the nature of English as a discipline of knowledge. Since 2000, she has been a contributing editor to the Oxford University Press edition of *The Complete Works of Oscar Wilde*. In 2007 she completed an edition of Wilde's critical writings (vol. IV) and she is currently editing a volume of some of his plays.

SUSAN HAMILTON is Professor of English at the University of Alberta. She teaches and researches in the area of nineteenth-century print culture, particularly women's journalism. Her recent publications include *Frances Power Cobbe and Victorian Feminism* (2006), *Animal Welfare and Anti-Vivisection, 1870–1910: Nineteenth-Century Woman's Mission* (2004), and (with Janice Schroeder) *Nineteenth-Century British Women's Education, 1840–1910* (2007).

MARY HAMMOND is Senior Lecturer in Nineteenth-Century Literature at the University of Southampton with a particular specialism in book history. Her publications include *Reading, Publishing and the Formation of Literary Taste in England 1880–1914* (2006), *Publishing in the First World War: Essays in Book History* (co-edited with Shafquat Towheed, 2007) and *Books without Borders* (co-edited with Robert Fraser, 2008).

SALLY LEDGER (1962–2009) held the Hildred Carlile Chair in English at Royal Holloway, University of London, and was the author of *Dickens and the Popular Radical Imagination* (2007), *The Fin de Siècle: A Reader in Cultural History* (with Roger Luckhurst, 2000), *Ibsen* (1999), *The New Woman: Fiction and Feminism at the Fin de Siècle* (1997) and *Cultural Politics at the Fin de Siècle* (1995).

KATHERINE NEWEY is Professor of Drama and Theatre Arts at the University of Birmingham. She is author of *Women's Theatre Writing in Victorian Britain* (2005), *John Ruskin and the Victorian Theatre* (co-authored with Jeffrey

Richards) and *Ruskin, the Theatre, and Victorian Visual Culture* (edited with Anselm Heinrich and Jeffrey Richards, 2009). She is co-editor of *Nineteenth Century Theatre and Film*.

JOHN PLUNKETT is Senior Lecturer in English at the University of Exeter. His publications include *Queen Victoria – First Media Monarch* (2003), and, co-edited with Andrew King, *Victorian Print Media: A Reader* (2005) and *Popular Print Media 1820–1900* (2004). He is working on a book on nineteenth-century optical recreations, including the panorama, diorama, stereoscope, magic lantern and peepshow, and directing an AHRC project, *Moving and Projected-Image Entertainment in the South-West 1820–1914*.

ANDREW SANDERS is Emeritus Professor of English at the University of Durham. He is the author of *The Victorian Historical Novel 1840–1880* (1978) and his studies of Dickens include *Dickens and the Spirit of the Age* (1999) and *Charles Dickens* (2003). A third edition of his *Short Oxford History of English Literature* appeared in 2004. He has written widely on Victorian culture and has edited a number of Victorian novels for various scholarly paperback series.

JOANNE SHATTOCK is Professor of Victorian Literature at the University of Leicester. She is General Editor of *The Works of Elizabeth Gaskell* (2005–6) and edited the volume on Gaskell's journalism. Her books include *Women and Literature in Britain 1800–1900* (ed. 2001), and the nineteenth-century volume of *The Cambridge Bibliography of English Literature* (1999), *The Oxford Guide to British Women Writers* (1993) and *Politics and Reviewers* (1989). She is co-editor of The Nineteenth Century monograph series for Ashgate, and is currently co-editing with Elisabeth Jay the *Selected Works of Margaret Oliphant* (2010–11).

JENNY BOURNE TAYLOR is Professor of English at the University of Sussex. Her books include *In the Secret Theatre of Home: Wilkie Collins, Sensation Narrative and Nineteenth-Century Psychology* (1988) and *Embodied Selves: An Anthology of Psychological Texts 1830–1890* (ed. with Sally Shuttleworth, 1998). She is editor of *The Cambridge Companion to Wilkie Collins* (2006) and co-editor, with Martin Ryle, of *George Gissing: Voices of the Unclassed* (2005). She is co-editing *Legitimacy and Illegitimacy in Law, Literature and History* (2009), and with John Kucich, the third volume of *The Oxford History of the Novel in English*.

CHRONOLOGY

	Contexts	Texts
1830	Accession of William IV Lord Grey prime minister *Fraser's Magazine* founded	Alfred Tennyson, *Poems, chiefly Lyrical*
1831	First meeting of the British Association for the Advancement of Science	
1832	Great Reform Bill *Chambers' Edinburgh Journal* established *Penny Magazine* begins *Tait's Edinburgh Magazine* founded	Harriet Martineau, *Illustrations of Political Economy* (1832–4) Tennyson, *Poems* Frances Trollope, *Domestic Manners of the Americans* Charles Lyell, *Elements of Geology* Charles Darwin, *Narrative of the Surveying Voyages of HMS Adventure and Beagle* (concl. 1836)
1833	Slavery abolished throughout the British Empire Oxford Movement begins with John Keble's sermon, 'National Apostasy'	Thomas Carlyle, 'Sartor Resartus' pbd in *Fraser's Magazine* *Tracts for the Times* begins, (concl. 1841) Charles Knight's *Penny Cyclopedia* (concl. 1844)
1834	Poor Law Amendment Act	
1835	Lord Melbourne prime minister	Charles Dickens, *Sketches by Boz*, 1st series
1836		Dickens, *Pickwick Papers*, in monthly parts 1836–7 A. W. G. Pugin, *Contrasts*

	Contexts	Texts
1837	Death of William IV; accession of Queen Victoria	Carlyle, *French Revolution*
	Bentley's Miscellany established	Dickens, *Oliver Twist* in *Bentley's Miscellany*, 1837–8
1839	Custody of Infants Act	Carlyle, *Chartism*
	Chartist Petition presented to Parliament	Edgar Allan Poe, *Tales of the Grotesque and Arabesque*
1840		Darwin, *Voyage of HMS Beagle*
1841	Robert Peel prime minister	Carlyle, *On Heroes, Hero-Worship and the Heroic in History*
	Punch founded	
1842	Copyright Act extends term to 42 years from publication or 7 years after author's death	Dickens, *American Notes for General Circulation*
	Illustrated London News begins	Tennyson, *Poems*
	Edwin Chadwick, Report, *On the Sanitary Condition of the Labouring Population*	
1843	Factory Act limits women and children under 18 to a 12-hour working day	Carlyle, *Past and Present*
		Thomas Babbington Macaulay, *Essays Critical and Historical*
	Wordsworth becomes Poet Laureate	John Ruskin, *Modern Painters*, vol. 1
1844		Robert Chambers, *Vestiges of the Natural History of Creation*
		G. W. M. Reynolds, *The Mysteries of London*, 1844–6
1845	Irish potato crop fails; Great Famine begins	Benjamin Disraeli, *Sybil*
		Friedrich Engels, *The Condition of the Working Class in England*
1846	Lord John Russell prime minister	Poems by Currer, Ellis and Acton Bell [Charlotte, Anne and Emily Brontë]
	Repeal of the Corn Laws	Marian Evans ['George Eliot'], trans. of J. F. Strauss's *Life of Jesus*
	Dickens starts *Daily News*	Richard Owen, *British Fossil Mammals and Birds*
1847	Chartist demonstration, Kennington Common, London	Anne Brontë, *Agnes Grey*
		Charlotte Brontë, *Jane Eyre*
	Ten Hours Act limits working day to 10 hours for women and children under 18	Emily Brontë, *Wuthering Heights*
		Tennyson, *The Princess*
		W. M. Thackeray, *Vanity Fair*, serialized 1847–8

	Contexts	Texts
1848	Revolutions in Europe	Karl Marx and Friedrich Engels, *The Communist Manifesto*
	Pre-Raphaelite Brotherhood formed	Anne Brontë, *The Tenant of Wildfell Hall*
		Elizabeth Gaskell, *Mary Barton*
		J. S. Mill, *Principles of Political Economy*
		J. H. Newman, *Loss and Gain*
		Thackeray, *Pendennis*, serialized 1848–50
1849		Charlotte Brontë, *Shirley*
		Macaulay, *History of England*, vols. I and II
		Henry Mayhew, *London Labour and the London Poor* begins in the *Morning Chronicle*
		Ruskin, *Seven Lamps of Architecture*
		Dickens, *David Copperfield*, monthly parts 1849–50
1850	Wordsworth dies	William Wordsworth, *The Prelude*
	Tennyson becomes Poet Laureate	Tennyson, *In Memoriam*
	Household Words launched by Dickens	Elizabeth Barrett Browning, *Poems*
	The Germ published, Jan.–April, by the Pre-Raphaelite Brotherhood	Carlyle, *Latter-Day Pamphlets*
		Nathaniel Hawthorne, *The Scarlet Letter*
	Roman Catholic hierarchy re-established in England	
1851	Great Exhibition at the Crystal Palace	Ruskin, *The Stones of Venice*, vol. I; concl. 1853
	Louis Napoleon becomes Emperor of France	Gaskell, *Cranford*, serialized 1851–3
1852	Rebuilt Houses of Parliament open	Harriet Beecher Stowe, *Uncle Tom's Cabin*
		Dickens, *Bleak House*, in monthly parts 1852–3
1853	Crimean War (1853–6)	Matthew Arnold, *Poems*
		Charlotte Brontë, *Villette*
		Gaskell, *Ruth*
1854		Coventry Patmore, *The Angel in the House* (completed 1856)

	Contexts	Texts
		Marian Evans [George Eliot] trans. of Feuerbach's *Essence of Christianity*
		Dickens, *Hard Times*
		Gaskell, *North and South*, 1854–5
		Tennyson, 'Charge of the Light Brigade'
1855	Lord Palmerston prime minister	Robert Browning, *Men and Women*
	Newspaper Stamp Tax abolished	Dickens, *Little Dorrit*, monthly parts
	Saturday Review founded	1855–7
		Tennyson, *Maud and Other Poems*
1857	Indian Mutiny	Elizabeth Barrett Browning, *Aurora Leigh*
	Matrimonial Causes Act	Gaskell, *Life of Charlotte Brontë*
		Anthony Trollope, *Barchester Towers*
		Eliot, *Scenes of Clerical Life* in *Blackwood's Magazine*
1858	*English Woman's Journal* established (1858–64)	R. M. Ballantyne, *The Coral Island*
1859	War of Italian liberation	Darwin, *On the Origin of Species*
	Langham Place circle and Society for Promoting the Employment of Women formed	Dickens, *A Tale of Two Cities*
		Eliot, *Adam Bede; 'The Lifted Veil'* (in *Blackwood's Magazine*)
	Second Palmerston administration	Edward FitzGerald, *The Rubáiyát of Omar Khayyám*
	All the Year Round begun by Dickens	Samuel Smiles, *Self-Help*
	Macmillan's Magazine founded	Wilkie Collins, *The Woman in White*, serialized 1859–60
		Mill, *On Liberty*
		Tennyson, *Idylls of the King*
1860	William Wilberforce and T. H. Huxley debate at British Association meeting, Oxford	Eliot, *The Mill on the Floss*
		Dickens, *Great Expectations*, serialized 1860–1
	Cornhill Magazine, ed. Thackeray, founded	Elizabeth Barrett Browning, *Poems before Congress*
		Essays and Reviews
		Trollope, *Framley Parsonage*, serialized 1860–1
1861	American Civil War begins (1861–5)	Ellen Wood, *East Lynne*
	Death of the Prince Consort	Isabella Beeton, *The Book of Household Management*
		Eliot, *Silas Marner*

	Contexts	Texts
1862		Mary Elizabeth Braddon, *Lady Audley's Secret*
		Collins, *No Name*
		Christina Rossetti, *Goblin Market and Other Poems*
		Elizabeth Barrett Browning, *Last Poems*
		Eliot, *Romola*, serialized 1862–3
		Ruskin, *Unto this Last* (in Cornhill Magazine)
1864	Contagious Diseases Acts	Robert Browning, *Dramatis Personae*
		Dickens, *Our Mutual Friend*, monthly parts 1864–5
		Gaskell, *Cousin Phillis*; *Wives and Daughters*, serialized 1864–6
		Tennyson, *Enoch Arden and Other Poems*
1865	*The Argosy, Fortnightly Review, Pall Mall Gazette* founded	Arnold, *Essays in Criticism*, 1st series
	President Abraham Lincoln assassinated	Lewis Carroll, *Alice in Wonderland*
		Ruskin, *Sesame and Lilies*
		Algernon Swinburne, *Atalanta in Calydon*
1866	*Contemporary Review, Aunt Judy's Magazine* founded	George Eliot, *Felix Holt*
		Christina Rossetti, *Prince's Progress and Other Poems*
		Poems and Ballads, 1st series
		E. S. Dallas, *The Gay Science*
1867	Second Reform Bill passed	Walter Bagehot, *The English Constitution*
	Women's Suffrage petition presented to Parliament	
1868	Gladstone prime minister (Dec.)	Robert Browning, *The Ring and the Book* (completed 1869)
		Collins, *The Moonstone*
		William Morris, *The Earthly Paradise* (completed 1870)
1869	*Nature, The Academy, The Graphic* founded	Arnold, *Culture and Anarchy*
	Suez Canal opened	Mill, *The Subjection of Women*
1870	Franco-Prussian War (1870–1)	Dickens, *Mystery of Edwin Drood* (unfinished)
	Elementary Education Act	
	Married Women's Property Act	D. G. Rosssetti, *Poems*
	Women's Suffrage Journal begins	
	Dickens dies	

	Contexts	Texts
1871	Religious Tests abolished at Oxford and Cambridge	Robert Buchanan, 'The Fleshly School of Poetry'
	Trade Union Act	Darwin, *Descent of Man*
		Eliot, *Middlemarch*, pbd 1871–2
		Thomas Hardy, *Desperate Remedies*
		Edward Lear, *Nonsense Songs and Stories*
		Lewis Carroll, *Through the Looking Glass*
		D. G. Rossetti, 'The Stealthy School of Criticism'
		Ruskin, *Fors Clavigera* (concl. 1887)
		Swinburne, *Songs before Sunrise*
1873		Hardy, *A Pair of Blue Eyes*
		Mill, *Autobiography*
1874	Disraeli prime minister	Trollope, *The Way We Live Now*, monthly parts 1874–5
		G. H. Lewes, *Problems of Life and Mind*, 1st series
		James Thomson, 'The City of Dreadful Night'
1876	*Mind* started	Eliot, *Daniel Deronda*
		Mark Twain, *Tom Sawyer*
1877	Queen Victoria proclaimed Empress of India	Harriet Martineau, *Autobiography*
	Nineteenth Century founded	
1878	Zulu War 1878–9	Hardy, *The Return of the Native*
	Second Afghan War	Swinburne, *Poems and Ballads*, 2nd series
	Matrimonial Causes Act	
	London University opens degrees to women	
	English Men of Letters series begins	
1879	*Boy's Own Paper* begins	Browning, *Dramatic Idylls*
		George Meredith, *The Egoist*
1882	Married Women's Property Act	R. L. Stevenson, *Treasure Island*
1884	Matrimonial Causes Act	George Gissing, *The Unclassed*
	Oxford English Dictionary begins (completed 1928)	Mark Twain, *Adventures of Huckleberry Finn*
	Society of Authors founded	Meredith, *Diana of the Crossways*, serialized 1884–5

	Contexts	Texts
1885	Criminal Law Amendment Act raises age of consent for girls to 16	H. Rider Haggard, *King Solomon's Mines* J. W. Cross, *George Eliot's Life* Walter Pater, *Marius the Epicurean* Stevenson, *A Child's Garden of Verses*
1886	Irish Home Rule Bill defeated Repeal of Contagious Diseases Acts *English Historical Review* founded	Stevenson, *Dr Jekyll and Mr Hyde* Hardy, *The Mayor of Casterbridge* Henry James, *The Bostonians* Tennyson, *Locksley Hall Sixty Years After*
1887	Queen Victoria's Golden Jubilee	Haggard, *She*; *Allan Quatermain* Hardy, *The Woodlanders* 'Mark Rutherford', *Revolution in Tanner's Lane*
1888	Matchworkers' strike 'Jack the Ripper' murders in London	Hardy, *Wessex Tales* Mary Ward, *Robert Elsmere*
1889	Net Book Agreement	Charles Booth, *Life and Labour of the People of London* (1889–97) Gissing, *The Nether World* Pater, *Appreciations* Twain, *A Connecticut Yankee in King Arthur's Court* W. B. Yeats, *The Wanderings of Oisin*
1890	*Review of Reviews* begins	William Booth, *In Darkest England* J. G. Frazer, *The Golden Bough* William James, *Principles of Psychology* William Morris, *News from Nowhere*
1891	International Copyright Act (Chace Act) William Morris founds Kelmscott Press	Arthur Conan Doyle, *Adventures of Sherlock Holmes* Gissing, *New Grub Street* Hardy, *Tess of the d'Urbervilles* Olive Schreiner, *Dreams* Oscar Wilde, *The Picture of Dorian Gray*; *Intentions*
1892	Gladstone prime minister Tennyson dies	Gissing, *Born in Exile* Rudyard Kipling, *Barrack-Room Ballads*

	Contexts	Texts
1893	Second Irish Home Rule bill defeated	Marie Corelli, *Barabbas*
		Gissing, *The Odd Women*
		Alice Meynell, *Poems*
		Wilde, *Lady Windermere's Fan*
1894	*Yellow Book* founded	George du Maurier, *Trilby*
		Gissing, *In the Year of Jubilee*
		Kipling, *The Jungle Book*
		George Moore, *Esther Waters*
		Wilde, *A Woman of No Importance*
1895	Trial and imprisonment of Oscar Wilde	Grant Allen, *The Woman Who Did*
		Joseph Conrad, *Almayer's Folly*
	Lord Salisbury prime minister	Corelli, *The Sorrows of Satan*
		Stephen Crane, *The Red Badge of Courage*
		Hardy, *Jude the Obscure*
		Max Nordau, *Degeneration*
		H. G. Wells, *The Time Machine*
1896	Alfred Austin Poet Laureate	A. E. Housman, *A Shropshire Lad*
		Arthur Morrison, *A Child of the Jago*
		Christina Rossetti, *Poems*, ed. W. M. Rossetti
		Wells, *The Island of Dr Moreau*
1897	Queen Victoria's Diamond Jubilee	Conrad, *The Nigger of the Narcissus*
	National Union of Women's Suffrage Societies formed	James, *What Maisie Knew*
		Kipling, *Captains Courageous*
		Bram Stoker, *Dracula*
		Wells, *The Invisible Man*
1898	Death of Gladstone	Hardy, *Wessex Poems*
		G. B. Shaw, *Plays Pleasant and Unpleasant*
		Wilde, *The Ballad of Reading Gaol*
		Wells, *The War of the Worlds*
1899	Boer War begins	Yeats, *The Wind among the Reeds*
		James, *The Awkward Age*
		Kipling, *Stalky & Co.*
		Margaret Oliphant, *Autobiography*
		Wilde, *An Ideal Husband; The Importance of Being Earnest* (acted 1895)
1901	Death of Queen Victoria	Hardy, *Poems of the Past and Present*
		Kipling, *Kim*

	Contexts	Texts
1902	Boer War ends	Conan Doyle, *The Hound of the Baskervilles*
		James, *The Wings of the Dove*
		Kipling, *Just So Stories*
1903	*Daily Mirror* started	Samuel Butler, *The Way of All Flesh*
		Conrad, *Typhoon*
		James, *The Ambassadors*
		Shaw, *Man and Superman*
1905		Conan Doyle, *The Return of Sherlock Holmes*
		E. M. Forster, *Where Angels Fear To Tread*
		James, *The Golden Bowl*
		Edith Wharton, *The House of Mirth*
		Wilde, *De Profundis*
1907		Hilaire Belloc, *Cautionary Tales for Children*
		Conrad, *The Secret Agent*
		Edmund Gosse, *Father and Son*
1908		Robert Baden-Powell, *Scouting for Boys*
		Arnold Bennett, *The Old Wives' Tale*
		Forster, *A Room with a View*
1910	Death of Edward VII, ascension of George V	Bennett, *Clayhanger*
		Forster, *Howard's End*
1911		Conrad, *Under Western Eyes*
		D. H. Lawrence, *The White Peacock*
		Katherine Mansfield, *In a German Pension*
1913	Robert Bridges Poet Laureate	Lawrence, *Sons and Lovers*
	New Statesman begins	Meynell, *Collected Poems*
1914	World War I begins	Hardy, *Satires of Circumstance*
		James, *Note on Novelists*
		James Joyce, *Dubliners*
		Lawrence, *The Prussian Officer*; *The Widowing of Mrs Holroyd*
		Meynell, *Collected Essays*
		Yeats, *Responsibilities*

JOANNE SHATTOCK

Introduction

This *Cambridge Companion to English Literature 1830–1914* comprises a series of newly commissioned essays that offer fresh perspectives on a literary period bounded at one end by the Romantic movement and by Modernism at the other. Debates about periodization, as we know, can be both intense and contentious. The parameters of what has become known as the 'long' nineteenth century and the divisions within it are regularly contested. Studies of Romanticism have variously adopted the 1770s or 1789 as their starting point, tracing the origins of the movement in the poetry of the late eighteenth century or highlighting the French Revolution as the context for an equally revolutionary period in literature. The transition to the Victorian period is generally marked by the end of the 1820s, the decade that witnessed the deaths of the second generation of Romantic poets, with 1832, the year of the first Reform Bill, sometimes chosen as the end date, rather than 1830.

The Victorian period has similarly porous boundaries. The dates of Queen Victoria's reign, 1837–1901, are sometimes adopted, as in the volume of *The New Cambridge History of English Literature*, which follows the divisions of the original *CHEL* (1907–27), although arguments about the artificiality of these dates are vigorous. The century (1800–1900) is sometimes used to circumscribe an area of study, as in the recent volume of the third edition of *Cambridge Bibliography of English Literature* (1999), which followed the pattern established by the original *CBEL* in 1940. Opposition to this particular arrangement turns on the differences between Romantic and Victorian writing and the need to recognize their distinctiveness as well as the unsatisfactory nature of century divisions in literary study.

The *Cambridge Companions* have set out to challenge conventional period boundaries. Thomas Keymer and John Mee's *Cambridge Companion to English Literature 1740–1830* (2004) emphasized the advantages of approaching the Romantic period from the longer perspective of the mid-eighteenth century, ending their study less controversially at 1830. Earlier, Stuart Curran's *Cambridge Companion to British Romanticism* (1993) focused on the forty-year period from 1785 to 1825.

This *Companion* begins with the 1830s, a formative and by definition 'pre-Victorian' decade, and one which has only recently begun to receive the attention it merits. The advantages of having more flexibility to consider the links and overlap with Romanticism and the transition from the Regency to the Victorian age are clear. The early work of Dickens, Tennyson and Carlyle, each of whom made his mark in the 1830s, features in several chapters, along with writers like Walter Scott, Frances Trollope, Harriet Martineau, Pierce Egan, Edward Bulwer-Lytton, Douglas Jerrold, Frederick Marryat and Catherine Gore, all of whom had an impact on later decades, and were shaped by earlier ones.

Several contributors to this volume emphasize the importance of the 1820s and 1830s to our understanding of the Victorian period as a whole. Katherine Newey sees Victorian popular culture as having been forged in these decades. Gowan Dawson identifies the beginnings of the popularization of science in the same period. John Plunkett, in his exploration of 'Visual culture', notes the growth of interest in physiological optics in the 1820s and 1830s, which led to a prevalence of optical and pictorial tropes in literature – part of the 'fascination for all things pictorial', he argues – which persisted throughout the century.

The advantages of carrying the discussion forward through the 'high Victorian' period of the 1870s and 1880s, and across the century divide to the First World War, are many. It facilitates a discussion of the emergence of Modernism in the last decades of the nineteenth century, a point made by Mary Hammond, who notes the growing division between 'good' and 'popular' literature in the perception of late nineteenth-century readers. She notes too the length of time it took for the works of Modernist writers like D. H. Lawrence, James Joyce and Virginia Woolf, all of whom wrote in the period covered by this *Companion*, to be published in formats which could be afforded by non-middle-class readers.

Recent nineteenth-century scholarship and criticism have seen a conscious widening of the focus from English metropolitan culture to include provincial cultures, and in particular the literature of Scotland, Ireland and Wales. Outside Britain, the geographical boundaries of literary study have been pushed even further to embrace the literature of the British Empire and its colonies as well as that of the United States. The interchanges between what might be called the 'centre' and the 'periphery' have become crucial to our understanding of the period 1830 to 1914, as have literary relations with continental Europe.

The impact and legacy of empire, the roots of which are in the eighteenth century, was felt from the mid-century onward. The concepts of empire and nation are central to both Romantic and Victorian writing, as Patrick Brantlinger points out. His chapter demonstrates the influence of the British Empire on writers as diverse as Walter Scott, Douglas Jerrold, Elizabeth Gaskell, Charles Kingsley and Wilkie Collins through to Kipling, Rider Haggard and Joseph Conrad, the last three writing well into the twentieth century.

Alison Chapman, in her chapter on 'European exchanges', notes the complex responses to European literature and culture, particularly to those of France and Italy, which developed throughout the long nineteenth century, and which challenge the 'Anglocentric disciplinary formations' of Victorian literature. She notes those points at which British national identity was seen to be challenged by continental Europe, while literary relations were close and reciprocal.

Nationhood and national culture are underlying themes of several chapters. Bridget Bennett, in her discussion of 'Transatlantic relations', argues that transatlantic approaches to literary texts can provide ways of challenging more nation-based definitions of writers and their work. There were cultural models constructed on both sides of the Atlantic, she suggests, that interacted with one another significantly throughout the period of this volume. In her chapter on 'Popular culture' Katherine Newey notes that while in the eighteenth century artists, critics and audiences shared a sense of a British national culture, by the time of Queen Victoria's accession in 1837 that national culture appeared 'fractured and contentious'.

The intellectual vigour of Victorian Studies, which first came to prominence in the 1950s, is in great part due to the way in which scholars and critics from a range of disciplines have engaged effectively with one another. Just as the nineteenth-century educated reader regarded works of history, philosophy, political economy, art, theology and science as 'literature' in its broadest sense, along with the traditional genres of poetry, the novel and drama, so the essays in this *Companion* demonstrate the fruits of an inter-disciplinary or multidisciplinary approach.

Gowan Dawson writes of the new cultural and political importance which science acquired during the nineteenth century, and of the consequences of this for other aspects of nineteenth-century culture. He argues that literature and science were more closely related between 1830 and 1914 than in subsequent periods, when the notion of 'two cultures' became entrenched. Jenny Bourne Taylor's chapter on 'Body and mind' shows the ways in which medical discourse, particularly that of the nascent science of psychology, influenced the work of novelists and also of poets, in their attempts to render legible the inner, emotional life. John Plunkett traces the impact of new modes of visuality in the period. He emphasizes the 'creative cross-over' between literature and painting, and the existence of a vastly enlarged visual field, 'created by the desire to be able to picture, and consequently observe, every detail of the physical environment'.

It would be 'wildly inaccurate' to describe Victorian Britain as multicultural, Andrew Sanders cautions, but in his chapter on 'Writing and religion' he argues that, as the result of a gradual evolutionary process, Victorian Britain could be described as a 'plural' society. He traces the fascination with 'the other' in terms of religion, a fascination that sometimes resulted in an 'open embrace', and he ranges widely over the representation of religious diversity in the nineteenth-century novel.

Hilary Fraser reminds us that 'the past as we know it was largely created by the Victorians', that historical terms and concepts and the idea of periodicity were invented in the nineteenth century. Our modern historical consciousness and historiographical methods were inherited from our Victorian predecessors, who first defined and professionalized the study of history. She considers the impact of the historical past on a variety of writers, from major figures such as Carlyle, Ruskin and Hardy, to the work of Vernon Lee, Alice Meynell and the late nineteenth-century poet 'Michael Field'.

Biography as we know it was largely the creation of Victorian biographers, as Alison Booth emphasizes, and it was the 'Victorian model' that was challenged by Modernists like Lytton Strachey. Booth emphasizes the variety of life writing in the period 1830–1914, from the multi-volume 'life and letters' to the family memoir, the diary, biographical dictionaries, 'brief lives' and travel writing. She notes too the close association of life writing with the stories of the rising professions, especially authorship.

The innovative approaches to literary studies offered by the History of the Book – the study of authorship, readerships, literary production and print culture in its widest sense – are reflected in several chapters of this *Companion*. Josephine Guy considers the status of authorship and the gradual professionalization of writing from the 1830s. She notes the emergence of literary lionism and celebrity culture, and she emphasizes the impact of new technologies on the process of writing.

Mary Hammond's subject is the reader and the consumption of literature in the period, beginning with the enormous growth in the numbers of readers and their expectations. Reading practices, solitary and shared, the physical conditions for reading, whether by candle, gas or electricity, and the stratagems adopted by publishers to reach the new, mass readerships are central to her chapter, as is the growth of public libraries.

Several contributors consider literary production in a period of technological change, the importance of serialization, the development of cheap reprints, and the emergence of an extensive and diverse periodical press. Susan Hamilton links the growth of periodical outlets with the increased opportunities offered to women writers, and the ways in which they used these to engage with political, legal and feminist issues. Joanne Shattock considers the changing life of the man (and woman) of letters, the emergence of a reviewing culture which enabled writers of both sexes to make a respectable living through journalism, and the consequent professionalization of literary criticism in the period.

The close connection between literature and politics is a common thread in several chapters: the impact of the Italian Risorgimento on English writers, the fears of invasion, literary responses to war, encounters with American democracy. Sally Ledger's chapter on 'Radical writing' explores three points in the century when political concerns were uppermost in writers' minds: the literature of the anti-Poor Law movement in the 1830s, the impact of Chartism and the debates surrounding the 'Condition of England Question' in the 1840s, and the emergence of the Socialist movement the 1880s.

In a period in which there are so many major literary figures, writing across all genres, and a period, too, in which so much has been done to reclaim less well known writers, women writers in particular, but also radical and working-class writers, and practitioners of other genres such as biographers, autobiographers, historians, scientists, travel writers and critics, it has not proved possible to devote chapters to individual writers or even to movements. Readers of the *Companion* will find fresh interpretations and perspectives on well-known authors and texts, together with an introduction to less familiar authors and writing in a range of genres, reflecting the constant revision and reconfiguration of the canon which has been, and continues to be, an ongoing process in nineteenth-century literary studies, and one which signals its intellectual health and vigour.

PART I

Modes of writing and their contexts

I

JOSEPHINE GUY

Authors and authorship

Nineteenth-century British historians tended to analyse historical causation in terms of the agency of individuals: in this historiography, then, events were understood as having been brought about by human actions rather than by large-scale impersonal forces. In keeping with this trend, literary historians writing during the same period also tended to understand authorship in relation to personal qualities which they attributed (accurately or otherwise) to a particular writer's character. This typically involved a delineation of what Edmund Gosse towards the end of the century termed (in his *A Short History of Modern English Literature* (1898)), in a comment made about Ben Jonson, 'temperament'; or, in Walter Pater's more famous definition made in the 1880s, 'soul': literary representation, Pater explained in his essay 'Style', could best be understood as the expression of 'a specific personality, in its preferences, its volition'.[1]

Such a view was not in keeping with contemporary European thinking, however. For example, in his widely read *Histoire de la littérature anglaise* (1863) the French critic and historian Hippolyte Taine elaborated a hereditary and environmental theory of authorship, defining creativity in terms of a conjunction of 'la race, le milieu, et le moment' – a proposition not dissimilar to that of Goethe's pithy injunction, as paraphrased by the English journalist John Morley, that to 'understand an author, you must understand his age'.[2] By contrast, even in a writer as self-consciously cosmopolitan as Matthew Arnold, who was famously critical of English parochialism, we find a residual belief in the power of the individual. So although Arnold argued that the critic should attend to the wider intellectual culture in which a writer was working, there is a pervasive sense that the creation of an Arnoldian 'master-work' required not just Taine's 'power of the moment', and the availability of appropriate intellectual 'materials', but crucially also the 'power of the man' to transform them.[3] Thus Arnold attributed the singular qualities of, say, Heinrich Heine's 'genius' not so much to the alleged 'wealth of ideas' and 'culture' of early nineteenth-century

Germany, but rather to a peculiarity in Heine's own 'character' – his want of 'self-respect' and 'true dignity'.[4] Looking back from the vantage-point of 1900, another critic and poet, Lionel Johnson, could sum up the significance of nineteenth-century poetry as having derived from an 'age of intense individuality', one which was 'rich in personalities'.[5] He could have been thinking here of the career of Oscar Wilde, one of the century's most notorious and iconoclastic writers who had also, unsurprisingly, insisted that 'art springs from personality'.[6]

A modern literary historian, however, would be inclined to look at matters in a different way: he or she is more likely to attempt to deconstruct this Romantic valorisation of individual expressivity by focusing instead on institutions, technologies and economics, such larger forces being viewed as more significant historical factors shaping the way individual writers were (and still are) able to express themselves. More precisely, a modern historian would be inclined to view this celebration of personal difference as itself the product of a growing institutionalization of authorship in the nineteenth century. 'Personality', in this argument, was merely an anxious defence against – or possibly, and more cynically, a valuable commodity to be exploited in – a pervasive process of professionalization and commerciali-zation in which authorship was being absorbed by an all-powerful culture industry. This context makes it easier to understand the protestations of one of the century's most seriously minded but (certainly in terms of sales) least successful literary authors: Henry James. In his 1884 essay 'The Art of Fiction' James drew a revealing comparison between literature and painting: the painter, he argued, is able to 'teach the rudiments of his practice' but the 'literary artist would be obliged to say to his pupil … "Ah, well, you must do what you can!"'. And what made literary author-ship unteachable, for James, was precisely the formative role of what he too termed 'temperament', a novel being in its 'broadest definition a personal … impression of life', one which required, for its execution, 'freedom to feel and say'.[7] The reality of nineteenth-century authorship, as James himself could not help but be aware, was that such 'freedom' was at best only partial or at worst only notional.

It is tempting to see in these different assessments an opposition between what might loosely be called an expressive and an institutional theory of literary authorship. However, and as I have already hinted, this opposition is more apparent than real, for in practice authorship involves a complex interplay between individuals and institutions. All writers who wish to place their work in the public domain have to negotiate with the institutional forces (whether legal, economic, social or religious) which have always controlled the process of publication. At the same time, however, it has also been the case that local circumstances have enabled individual authors to negotiate that relationship in a variety of different ways.

An author supported by private means, such as the poet and translator Edward FitzGerald, could be careless of issues such as sales figures or royalties, and therefore take risks with his material which authors who needed to earn their living with the pen could not. Such insouciance may explain why FitzGerald embarked on no fewer than three translations of medieval Persian poetry – he had both money and time to indulge an enthusiasm careless about whether or not it would be shared by the Victorian reading public (FitzGerald's translations of works by Jami and Attar today, as in the nineteenth century, are unknown by most admirers of his rendering of *The Rubaiyat of Omar Khayyam*). More exactly, and as I shall show in more detail below, the increasingly entrepreneurial elements taken to be characteristic of nineteenth-century publishing could result in a wide variety of authorial experiences and practices.

For a writer like Charles Dickens, they were liberating and empowering. Dickens's ambition to control both the production and the dissemination of his work (he co-owned and edited some of the periodicals in which his fiction was published, occasionally even ghost-writing contributions), together with his alertness to the value of self-promotion (as evidenced, for example, in his remarkably successful public readings of his work), seem strikingly modern: Dickens, we might say, was one of the first self-fashioned literary celebrities, exploiting the institutions of publishing to make of his writing a highly profitable business. Yet for a figure like George Gissing, similar conditions appeared debilitating: at least some of the failures which characterized Gissing's early career – such as his stubborn faith in an outmoded form of publication (the three-decker novel) and his misplaced loyalty to the under-capitalized publishing house of Lawrence and Bullen – can be attributed to his inability to understand or take advantage of the commercial realities of late nineteenth-century publishing. Finally, even when writers responded to publishing conditions in similar ways, achieving broadly similar successes, their efforts could elicit quite different reactions, a circumstance which also seems to owe something to their particular circumstances, to perceptions about their 'temperaments'.

For example, both Mary Ward and Marie Corelli achieved best-sellers with early works which are rarely read today, *Robert Elsmere* (1888) and *The Sorrows of Satan* (1895) respectively. Though at the time neither woman was poor, both needed the income from their writing to support increasingly costly life-styles. Both also showed evidence of a significant business acumen, not only in their negotiations with publishers, but in their ability to engage the interests of the general reading public. Yet where the well-educated and well-connected Ward (she was the niece of Matthew Arnold) was widely praised for the seriousness of her literary ambition, the illegitimate Corelli was derided as 'incurably common-place' appealing only to the 'unthinking classes'.[8] Corelli's assiduous self-promotion – she invented for herself both a name and a literary heritage, claiming affiliation with Shakespeare – appeared to many nineteenth- and early twentieth-century commentators as irredeemably vulgar; yet it is difficult to see how Ward's exploitation of her family connections, both in finding a publisher and in eliciting favourable reviews for *Elsmere*, was any less a self-conscious or self-interested manipulation of a career. What is significant here is not so much whether *Robert Elsmere* is a better literary work than *The Sorrows of Satan* (however we might define 'better'); but rather that each novel, as both women were well aware, owed some of its initial success less to the 'genius' of the author than to clever marketing.

The complexity of this interplay between individuals and institutions means that the historian must be cautious in making generalizations about the nature of nineteenth-century authorship. Those institutional forces – legal, economic, social or religious – referred to above are best understood as defining only the preconditions of writing, and not as determining the course of the career of any particular individual. Nonetheless as preconditions they are important, for they help us to understand in what ways the overall character of nineteenth-century authorship differed from that of previous centuries.

The author and the market

We can get a purchase on this difference by first considering some of the terms by which historians have typically described the nineteenth-century writing environment, that complex series of relationships between authors, publishers and readers. Of these, 'capitalism', and more especially 'consumerism', predominate, an indication that financial interests and an alertness to the economics of writing are being taken as the most important defining features of authorship in this period. (We might note here once more that, despite his celebration of the autonomy of intellectual life in works such as *Culture and Anarchy* (1869), Arnold's correspondence is peppered with anxieties about his earnings and with the financial, as opposed to intellectual, value of his works.) Confusingly, however, one will also find the term 'consumerism' being applied to writing conditions in other centuries, so it is not unusual for historians to claim to find evidence of consumerist attitudes in, say, eighteenth-century practices of book-buying. To understand the specificity of publishing conditions at any one moment it is thus also necessary to look at the raw facts and figures – what might seem, in Carlyle's phrase, to be 'dry-as-dust' evidence – which underwrite judgements about the character of patterns of production and consumption. For it is here, in the detailed empirical research of historians such as Simon Eliot and Alexis Weedon, that the real distinctiveness of nineteenth-century authorship emerges in what can be characterized as a step-change in the order of the numbers involved.

So although the number of titles produced by publishers in the eighteenth century has now been estimated to be higher than most modern readers would have thought, the average number of copies printed of each title was relatively low. By contrast there was a fourfold increase in book production – that is, in actual books printed – between 1846 and 1916.[9] Such numbers point to a dramatic enlargement of the reading public (which James referred to, somewhat disparagingly, as 'the multitude')[10] and so also of the potential market for books. During this same period the average price of books halved, making them affordable for a much larger proportion of an increasingly prosperous population. The forces which lay behind these changes were complex and involved a range of factors, most of which are not exclusive either to authorship or to publishing.

They include: an expanding population driven by patterns of sustained economic growth (of particular importance was the role of foreign trade and the export market for English-language books in Europe, in the USA and in British colonial territories); changes in work-practices and employment legislation which increased leisure time; improvements in education and literacy; structural changes in the mechanisms of distribution and in the selling of books; cheaper raw materials, particularly paper; and technological developments such as the mechanization of type-setting and printing which, by increasing the speed of production, lowered unit costs. Taken together, these phenomena made possible mass publishing, whereby a best-selling novel could mean tens and sometimes hundreds of thousands of copies sold. In the early 1800s first print runs for an average novel were around 1,000 copies; those for works by Walter Scott, one of the most popular authors at that time, were around ten times this figure. In 1886 Stevenson's *Jekyll and Hyde* sold 40,000 in six months, while *The Christian* (1897), by Thomas Hall Caine, was reported to have sold, within a year, over 150,000 copies in Britain and America. Writing at the century's close, in 1899, James described what amounted to a kind of publishing tsunami – a 'flood' of novels which 'swells and swells, threatening the whole field of letters with submersion'.[11]

Setting aside the inevitable exaggeration in James's polemic, we can nonetheless safely conclude that it was, in large part, sheer numbers, the temptation of exceptional profits as well as the ignominy of failure in such a buoyant though competitive market-place, which made nineteenth-century authorship, and in particular *literary* authorship, a singularly attractive if speculative business. As Weedon explains, when compared to other subjects, such as religion, mathematics or language, the market for literary works, and especially (as James notes) for the novel, required a high number of fresh titles – it had, that is, 'considerable "churn"', meaning quantity rather than quality seemed to dominate production.[12] Such an environment encouraged spectacular productivity among established authors. The prolific James Payn published some hundred novels in his lifetime, as well as several collections of critical essays and a volume of poetry; while Anthony Trollope, who never earned huge sums from any individual work, nonetheless produced some forty-seven novels while also working in the civil service. It also provided opportunities for new entrants to the market, particularly for women writers. (So towards the end of her career Elizabeth Gaskell was earning enough money from her novel-writing to buy herself a substantial house in the country.) There was, however, an important exception to this pattern, and it concerns the genre which nineteenth-century authors typically held in the highest esteem – poetry.

Throughout the century, but more particularly in the later decades, poets and publishers alike often complained about the meagre profits to be earned from books of poetry, and therefore the special difficulties which poets experienced in getting their work into print. Of course there were exceptions: sales of Tennyson's poetry increased as his career progressed and near the end of his life Macmillan offered him significant inducements to become part of their list. More typical was the experience of Thomas Hardy, who began his writing career as a poet, sending poems to publishers as early as the mid-1860s; but his signal lack of success led him to focus instead on fiction (only four poems had appeared in print before his 1898 *Wessex Poems*). In fact Hardy only concentrated fully on poetry when he had, by the time *Jude the Obscure* (1895) was published, earned enough money from novel-writing not to be concerned, at least financially, with the popularity of his poems.

It was not necessarily the case that sales of poetry had dropped in an absolute sense; rather, what in earlier decades had been considered a perfectly respectable print-run, of say 500–1,000 copies per title, had now become uneconomic owing to the lower profits earned per unit. From mid-century onwards economies of scale and competition exerted a constant downward pressure on prices. This meant that, as a general rule, to earn the same profit in absolute terms a particular title had to sell several times more copies than before.[13]

For example, in the 1830s to the 1840s demand for novels was dominated by the expensive three-volume novel priced between 30 and 40 shillings (the 'three-decker' I referred to earlier which was purchased largely by circulating libraries). By the mid-1880s, however, around 60 per cent of books were sold at 3s 6d or under to non-institutional purchasers. In this respect, the highest profits on literary works tended to lie with cheap reprints where large print-runs could compensate for the low profit margins per unit sold.[14]

On the whole, volumes of contemporary poetry did not generally command a readership large enough to support this practice. That said, anxieties about the declining readership for poetry in the late decades of the nineteenth century may have been exaggerated. Some literary historians, for example, have claimed to detect a poetry revival in the early decades of the twentieth century, one which is easier to appreciate when one looks at the range of poetry then being produced – that is, when one considers the Modernists alongside the Georgians and women poets.[15] Nonetheless it is still unclear whether this revival applies to the whole market for poetry (rather than for individual titles), and whether the proportion of volumes of poetry in relation to those published of fiction had undergone an increase.

These difficulties in the market for poetry are paralleled, to some extent, by that for volumes of essays or criticism. In the early decades of the nineteenth century the essay, as Lee Erickson has argued, had evolved from the 'modest' experiments in 'scepticism and judgment' by authors such as Joseph Addison and Samuel Johnson to become the 'dominant form of intellectual discourse'.[16] This situation had changed dramatically, however, by the last quarter of the century, when the publisher William Blackwood can be found complaining, in 1889, that 'volumes of reprinted . . . essays are not remunerative to either publisher or author'.[17] Such genres, as I explain in more detail below, did not seem able to compete in the high-volume, quick-turnover and high-risk market-place of leisure reading which catered largely for a mass taste in fiction.

The scale of the financial returns which flowed from mid and late nineteenth-century publishing enterprises (as opposed to those in the early decades), and particularly from certain forms of literary publishing (such as the novel), required in their turn new forms of institutional arrangements to manage the manufacture and selling of books as well as the financial relationships between authors and publishers. Of crucial importance was the introduction of more systematic and transparent accounting practices, not least so that authors could see more clearly the profitability of their work, essential when payment was by royalty. Legislative reform, such as changes in copyright law and the Net Book Agreement (1889), was enacted to help protect the financial interests of authors and publishers. Of particular significance was the securing of international copyright agreements, notably with the United States. The possibilities offered by foreign publication and translation as well as syndication – typically of serialized fiction – meant that authors could have multiple contracts, and therefore multiple earnings, for a single work.

The greater commercial opportunities for authors thus inevitably brought in train a growing professionalism in which author–publisher relations became more formalized. Indeed it is possible to see the setting up of institutions such as the Society of Authors (1884) and the growth, in the late decades of the century, of literary agents who specialized in negotiating terms in an increasingly complex literary market-place (A. P. Watt and J. B. Pinker were among the first to make successful careers from this business) as indicative of a breakdown in trust between author and publisher, or at least of a perception that the two sets of interests were not necessarily compatible with each other.

Here it may be significant that towards the end of the century the magazine of the book trade, *The Bookman*, recorded evidence of a certain disquiet about the introduction of literary agents, blaming them for what was perceived as a gross inflation in the advances being offered to authors, particularly young or first-time writers. The consequent 'puffing' or 'booming' of their reputations before they had properly mastered their craft was seen as compromising creativity by encouraging formulaic writing. Whether such concern was genuine or merely sour grapes is hard to tell; John Feather, for example, notes that the arrival of literary agents was initially greeted with hostility within the trade, with publishers such as William Heinemann refusing to deal with them.[18]

At any rate, the kind of intimate relationship which, say, Charlotte Brontë had enjoyed with George Smith, where a publisher acted as a friend and mentor, as well as businessman and occasionally banker, became somewhat less common as the century progressed. (As I noted earlier, a writer like Gissing, who did treat his publisher as his friend, left himself open to being exploited.) Surviving correspondence between nineteenth-century authors and publishers is often fraught with tension, with disagreement typically centring on such issues as the relationship between pricing and print-runs – given the tendency to equate economic with literary worth, some authors were hostile to low pricing – or the amount of money a publisher would be prepared to invest in the materials and design of a book.

Another factor which contributed to a distancing in the relationship between publisher and author was the practice, common-place from the middle decades of the century onwards, of employing professional or semi-professional readers (few were full-time employees of publishing houses) to assess the literary and commercial value of manuscripts. The sheer volume of material publishers received, particularly in the genre of prose-fiction, had demanded this sort of paid help. These anonymous, behind-the-scenes figures could wield enormous, and for certain authors what must have appeared arbitrary, power over their careers.

As I noted above, authors have of course always been central to the business of publishing; in the nineteenth century, however, that business was undergoing rapid change, and so participation in it was bringing about subtle but significant changes in the author's conception of his or her craft, as well as in the relationship between, on the one hand, author and pub-lisher and, on the other, author and reading public. Some of the most commented upon of these changes, at the time, were the consequence of a more explicit and systematic use of advertising and mass retailing techni-ques, as publishers competed to secure customer loyalty. The creation of special 'series' and uniform editions, together with the use of publishers' 'lists', tended to brand authors with particular identities, packaging their writing into preconceived categories.

Commenting on the standards of contemporary critical writing, Wilde, for example, complained bitterly about the restrictive format of such series as Macmillan's English Men of Letters and the Great Writers series by the Edinburgh publisher Walter Scott, accusing them of being 'cheap criticisms' in 'cheap books'.[19] Moreover, as publishing houses became increasingly aware of the need also to brand themselves – as, say, the producers of finely printed books or of popular classics – so to choose a particular publisher, and to be associated with other authors on that publisher's list, was also to be branded as a particular sort of writer.

In the nineteenth century, as today, the most prestigious publishing houses (certainly for literary works) tended to be those that were well established, such as that of Macmillan (the business was set up in 1843 when the brothers Alexander and Daniel Macmillan bought out the Cambridge bookseller Richard Newby). Large commercial houses could, however, be quite conservative, especially when they also had a reputation (as Macmillan did) for publishing family journals and children's books. For this reason some of the more risqué literary works were often published by smaller houses; for example, in 1891 Hardy's *Tess of the d'Urbervilles* and Wilde's *Intentions* both appeared on the list of the newly founded, and short-lived, firm of Osgood, McIlvaine.

Likewise, if publishers felt that a work was in danger of compromising their reputation they did not hesitate to withdraw it, regardless of the consequences for the author. This, for example, was the fate of Algernon Swinburne's controversial *Poems and Ballads* (1866); withdrawn by

Moxon & Co. (the leading publisher of new poetry in the middle decades of the century), it was re-issued by John Camden Hotten, a publisher who had a reputation for publishing unsavoury work, some of which was considered by his contemporaries to be pornographic. Fisher Unwin, disturbed by the conviction and imprisonment of Oscar Wilde in 1895, refused to honour their contract to publish Edward Carpenter's proposed collection of essays entitled *Love's Coming of Age* while also withdrawing his *Towards Democracy*, then in its third edition. Meanwhile Wilde's own publisher at the time, the Bodley Head, also refused to honour a contract drawn up in 1893 for the book version of 'The Portrait of Mr W. H.'.[20] Moreover, when Wilde was looking for a publisher after his disgrace and imprisonment, he too had to resort to the less than respectable Leonard Smithers.

An awareness of how choices about publication could contribute to the perceived value of a work may go some way to explaining the weak sales of poetry and criticism (compared to fiction) in the later decades of the century, which I alluded to earlier. Contemporary commentators like Swinburne or Pater were apt to explain the limited appeal of poetry in terms of an alleged lack of refinement and education in the average fiction-reader – the Jamesian 'multitude' was ill-equipped to appreciate the complexity and subtlety of a higher art-form. However, there is evidence that some mid and late nineteenth-century poets resisted publishing their work in the media where the average fiction-reader was most likely to encounter it – newspapers and magazines (here it is worth recalling how the taste for novel-reading was cultivated via periodical serialization). Poets appeared to fear that their artistic integrity, and thus their identity as a poet, might be compromised by association with the popular press. The Brownings, in particular, were notably hostile to what Elizabeth Barrett rather pompously referred to as 'the periodical vehicle of publication'; and Robert Browning, certainly in the early stages of his career, had held it to be something of a badge of honour that his sales were so poor.[21]

It seems to have been the case, then, that poetry, as a form, was resistant to mass-marketing strategies which, by encouraging quantity over quality, tended to equate literary with economic worth. This does not mean that poetry was *not* marketed, only that different techniques were needed. Thus John Lane and Elkin Matthews of the Bodley Head tried in the 1890s to turn this situation to advantage by recasting the limited appeal of poetry as an indicator of rarity, one which could command, and was underwritten by, a higher market-price. Oscar Wilde encapsulated the problem rather neatly when he complained to Smithers that the attempts to market his poem *The Ballad of Reading Gaol* through advertisements were making him feel like 'Lipton's tea', an image which could hardly be further from that Romantic individualist whom he propagandised in his critical writing.[22] Of course not all poets took this view. Rudyard Kipling and Henry Newbolt were happy to have their poems printed in the popular press: many of the poems in Newbolt's *Admirals All and Other Verse*s (1897) and *The Island Race* (1898) had been first published in British and American periodicals; likewise, several of the poems in Kipling's *Barrack-Room Ballads* (1892) first appeared in W. E. Henley's *Scots Observer*. Such exposure may have contributed to the strong sales of these volumes (together with Newbolt's appeal to patriotism and Kipling's use of popular iconography and verse forms).

The author as commodity

It is interesting here that what Wilde objects to is the commodification of himself rather than of his poetry: it is he, as a person, who feels like a popular beverage. Literary advertising, in the nineteenth century, was not just a matter of how books themselves were marketed. Creating consumer demand also required the selling of the author, a process which we have already glimpsed in Dickens's career, and the origins of which can be traced back even earlier, to figures such as Chatterton and Byron – namely the development of the author as a media celebrity, and the explicit practice of selling a work by selling its author, or, more precisely, a carefully cultivated image of its author. This phenomenon was widespread in the nineteenth century, to the extent that there seems hardly a career untouched by it. For even those who attempted to resist, such as James or Pater, found it necessary to construct an alternative image to hide behind, as it were, such as the ivory-tower recluse in the intellectual prison-house described by Pater in the controversial conclusion to *The Renaissance* (1873). In practice, this was just as much an artifice as Wilde's more flamboyant persona.

Nineteenth-century interest in the personal lives of authors, whether details of their 'actual' biography or a biography carefully constructed for public consumption, can be traced back to the first quarter of the century and was, as I have hinted, in part a legacy of the Romantic emphasis on an intimate connection between expressive authenticity and felt experience. A related phenomenon was that of literary tourism, an industry generated by readers' desire to immerse themselves in the landscapes and environments – most notably the Lake District, the Yorkshire Moors and, of course, the Scottish Highlands – which had, apparently, inspired their favourite authors.

Moreover such selling was also, like the book-trade in general, dependent on nineteenth-century technology (particularly the development of the railway system) and involved some of the same paradoxes. So John Ruskin could celebrate the value of the Lake District scenery to its poets and artists while at the same time deprecating the coming of the railways which made access to the Lakes, and thus an appreciation of their expressive potential, increasingly possible for mass tourism. *Punch* was quick to respond to such apparent hypocrisy, publishing a witty cartoon (in the 5 February 1875 issue) in which Ruskin (with paint-tube for body) was depicted wielding a sword against a train threatening to run over a flower-clad 'Lady of the Lake District'.[23]

By positing such a close identification of the author with his or her work, Romanticism appeared to suggest that biography, a deep knowledge of how and where an author lived, was a crucial element of literary appreciation. Some nineteenth-century critics had seen in the Romantic preoccupation with self a dangerous solipsism, what was termed a propensity towards 'egotism' and disregard for 'civic life'.[24] However, such distrust did not extend to personality per se; it was rather a case of defining what constituted an appropriate authorial life. It is perhaps unsurprising, then, that the nineteenth century also witnessed a growth of interest in several forms of life writing – in the publication, invariably posthumous, of writers' letters, diaries and reminiscences, as well as in autobiographies and particularly in biographies. Demand was sufficient to generate a figure such as John Forster who fashioned a successful career in biographical writing, producing lives of Jonathan Swift, Oliver Goldsmith, Walter Savage Landor and most famously Dickens, as well as numerous biographical essays on political figures. Such productivity has led him to be judged by some historians to be the first professional literary biographer.

Whether such works really vouchsafed that access to the psychology of the author was, however, a moot point. Although Boswell's *Life of Samuel Johnson* (1791) was acclaimed by early nineteenth-century critics, who tended to see Boswell as a mere stenographer, the publication of Charles Rogers's *Boswelliana: The Commonplace Book of James Boswell* (1874) permitted later readers to appreciate the extent of Boswell's artifice and invention. Moreover, as most biographies and collections of letters were produced by, or published only with the permission of, friends or family members, they were hardly exercises in candour or objectivity. Thus Forster's *Life of Charles Dickens* (1872–4) was silent about Dickens's relationship with the actress Ellen Ternan (Forster was both Dickens's friend and his literary executor); while Elizabeth Gaskell's *Life of Charlotte Brontë* (1857) exaggerated the deprivations and eccentricities of the Brontë household in order to throw into sharper relief the marvel of her achievements.

Moreover, when biographers did include less savoury or glamorous elements of a writer's life, it was typically via a comfortingly familiar arc of tragedy. So John Gibson Lockhart's documentation in his *Memoirs of the Life of Sir Walter Scott* (1837–8) of the financial over-reaching and bankruptcy which characterised his father-in-law's late career could be troped as a heroic struggle against the frailties of old age, as Scott tried desperately to recover his fortunes though writing.[25]

In all these cases the life being shaped was one in accord with the work or, to be more precise, with a particular view of the sort of identity and value attached to it. It is possible to interpret this aspect of nineteenth-century biography more cynically, that the life was written with an eye to selling the work by producing an acceptable image of authorial endeavour and integrity. In this inevitable fashioning of the self we see a gap opening up between Romantic ideologies of individualism and the way in which individuality – or authorial personality – was typically being constructed for public consumption. The 'author' became, in a sense, as much an artifice or creation as his or her work.

An awareness of the role which an author's identity played in the valuation (and thus sales) of a work also lay behind another pervasive nineteenth-century marketing phenomenon: the use of pseudonyms. Although it has been traditional for modern critics to focus on the use of male pseudonyms by women writers (the Brontës, Mary Ann – later Marian – Evans (George Eliot) and Violet Paget (who wrote as Vernon Lee) being among the best-known examples), it was also the case that men, on occasion, saw advantage in adopting a female name (so the poet and essayist William Sharp wrote romantic fiction under the pen-name Fiona Macleod).

The construction of such identities, whether female of male, or vice versa, is typically attributed to deeply entrenched prejudices about the gendered nature of creativity (and this is certainly how Eliot saw the practice in her 1856 essay 'Silly Novels by Lady Novelists'). What is sometimes lost, however, in this focus on the sexual-political dynamic of the practice is the sheer suggestive power of the name in itself – the desire, that is, of the reading public to put a face or a personality to a work. So even anonymously published novels, such as Gaskell's *Mary Barton* (1848), were greeted with a feverish guessing game about their authors. The culmination of this process can be seen much later in the century, when Oscar Wilde, who was by now a social outcast, lamented, once again to Smithers (who was trying unsuccessfully to syndicate *The Ballad of Reading Gaol* in the United States), 'I see it is my *name* that terrifies.'[26] The poem was eventually published with the author's name replaced by the gnomic 'C.3.3.', Wilde's prison number. (After his release from prison in 1897, and to protect his identity, Wilde had assumed the pseudonym of Sebastian Melmoth.)

As the example of Wilde usefully reminds us, the nineteenth-century public's appetite to 'know' their authors was very much a double-edged sword. Eliot's publisher, Blackwood, panicked when rumours began to circulate concerning her real identity, and eventually dropped the planned serialization of *The Mill on the Floss* (1860) in *Blackwood's Magazine*, fearing that the revelation of her true identity, and so too her unorthodox private life, might damage sales. Here 'George Eliot' (like 'Currer', 'Ellis' and 'Acton Bell') was nothing but a name – a straightforward, rather 'thin', and therefore vulnerable marker of maleness (some reviewers postulated that 'he' might be a clergyman). By the end of the century, however, the 'name' could be but one aspect of a complex, multi-layered authorial identity constructed via a variety of media (which then included photography and so dress) in the expectation of, and in order to exploit, unrelenting public scrutiny.

The distinction I am drawing is between an authorial persona understood solely or primarily as a textual construct, and an authorial persona which is actively performed. If Wilde, at the close of the century, provides the most dramatic example of the latter practice, then Walter Scott, whose career precedes and just overlaps with the Victorian period, exemplifies the former. Scott, it is worth recalling, published most of his work anonymously, and insisted upon so doing even when it became something of a public joke, earning him the nickname of the 'Great Unknown'. It was not the case, as Bradley Deane argues, that his original readers literally knew nothing about the 'Author of *Waverley*', for Scott's opinions and philosophies were exhaustively discussed in the introductions to his works and in contemporary reviews. However, they had no ability to map that 'textual construction' onto a named 'biographical individual' (and this in turn perhaps explains why Lockhart's biography was so eagerly read by later Victorians).[27]

In between these two extremes it is possible to trace a progressive desire on the part of nineteenth-century readers to flesh out authorial names (whether real or invented) into fully realised personalities, and thus to posit a continuity between such factors as early and mid-nineteenth-century literary hagiography and the use of pseudonyms, on the one hand, and the late nineteenth-century cult of literary celebrity on the other. But there is also an important difference: the public gaze under which late nineteenth-century authors laboured to sell themselves and their works was both wider and more penetrating than that which Eliot (and her publisher) had feared. This in turn may explain why protestations of authorial privacy among late nineteenth-century writers are just as vehement as those made by Walter Scott. Moreover, for some of the writers concerned there was a great deal more at stake at the century's end, in that revelations about the sexual lives of figures such as Pater, J. A. Symonds, Wilde, A. E. Housman and also (as some biographers allege) Henry James threatened not just to make them pariahs in the world of literature, but to criminalize them as well.

The problem for those nineteenth-century authors who wished to maintain their privacy was that the very individualism which was seen as a marker of expressive authenticity was also, in part, a motor of public curiosity. One way through this paradox was to insist upon a distinction, as writers associated with the Aesthetic movement tried to do, between the man (and they were usually men) and the artist: the only aspect of an author's 'personality' which in their view the public was entitled to know about was that which was revealed via the work of art itself. In the view of the Aesthetes the quintessential image of the nineteenth-century literary artist was that of the French novelist Gustave Flaubert. Although Flaubert's fiction, particularly *Madame Bovary* (1857), became identified with sexual immorality, little taint was applied to the author himself (who apparently lived quietly, principally with his mother). By contrast, the most famous victim of the British tendency to identify the man and the work was once again Wilde; in the trial of Lord Queensberry, Queensberry's counsel Edward Carson persistently tried to equate Wilde's private life with the 'sins' of the hero of his novel, *The Picture of Dorian Gray*.[28]

Authorship and technology

This purist image of Flaubertian artistry, of a writer preoccupied above all else with questions of literary style, was also attractive for another reason: by isolating the artist from the mechanisms and institutions of publishing, it disguised the extent to which creativity was also formed, at least in part, by changes in technology. Here a second issue which arises from the advent of mass publishing concerns the way in which specific elements of technological innovation – particularly, as I have noted, the mechanisation of typesetting and manufacture of type, and, later in the century, the invention of the typewriter – altered the very manner in which authors composed and thus how they conceptualized the creative process itself.

Writing, it is possible to argue, became over the course of the century a different sort of physical and mental activity as the mechanisms by which thought could be converted into print underwent fundamental changes. In the first decades of the nineteenth century all type was set by hand, a letter at a time; and type itself, made of lead, was expensive. The consequence was that a publisher could afford to set and keep in type only relatively small portions of a work at any one time, a circumstance which severely restricted an author's ability to correct and revise his work. (He or she might typically have to correct proofs and thus finalize the text for one portion of a work before having seen a later part even set up in type, and in some instances, particularly with serialized fiction, later portions may not even have been composed.) For novelists this constraint could lead to errors and confusions, which could be further exacerbated by the fact that, when checking proofs, they probably did not have to hand a manuscript of the work (fair-copy usually remained in the hands of the printer, and was often destroyed as type was set by more than one compositor). Such a set of events explains, for example, the inconsistent use of names and incorrect positioning of two paragraphs in chapter 59 of W. M. Thackeray's *Vanity Fair*.[29]

As Allan C. Dooley has argued, this situation only began to change in the late decades of the century, in part because the introduction of new technology did not bring about immediate changes in long-established print practices.[30] Thus although typecasting machines were in use from the 1850s and 1860s, and their introduction was quickly followed by that of stereotyping and electrotyping (which freed up type immediately upon completion of proofing), up until the 1870s (and even, in some instances, into the mid-1880s) for nearly all printed books proof sheets came to an author not as a complete set, but only a few at a time which had to be corrected and returned before the next batch arrived, and often under the pressure of time. Only the most distinguished writers, such as Tennyson, could persuade their publisher to keep type standing while they sought the advice of literary friends.

After the 1870s, however, authors were able to work with much longer portions of proof text, particularly following the introduction of galley proofs which were typically issued as an intermediary stage before page proofs. Galleys had been common for newspapers and magazines since the early decades of the century, but were not used in book-work till the last quarter. A further advantage of galley proofs was that they were relatively cheap to print, and were thus often issued in duplicate on thin paper, providing authors with the opportunity to experiment with different revisions before returning a marked-up fair-copy to the printer.[31] We can best grasp the significance of this change by examining the physical opportunities which proofs provided for authors.

Even in fair-copy, manuscripts typically included numerous deletions and emendations, themselves often difficult for the compositor to decipher. Consequently non-authorial elements of composition could figure quite strikingly in the printed text. Thus idiosyncrasies in nineteenth-century novels typically attributed to authorial agency were more often the result of the imposition of a printer's house-style; and on some occasions, they were due to simple errors brought about by haste. (One of the most famous examples can be found in the first edition of Emily Brontë's *Wuthering Heights* (1847) where modern editors find it difficult – in the absence of any surviving manuscript – to draw a line between printing errors on the one hand and, on the other, the peculiarities of Brontë's style, particularly her use of dialect words.) As Dooley notes, nineteenth-century writing manuals repeatedly drew attention to the inadvisability of submitting ill-prepared manuscripts, complaining about cramped and illegible hand-writing as well as confusing pagination.[32] For example most of the surviving manuscripts which Wilde gave as printer's copy were composite documents, made up of various drafts collated with each other and interleaved with further fair-copy and corrected pages, which in turn led to a complex process of numbering and renumbering; unsurprisingly type-setters frequently made errors in setting his texts, some of which turned out to be too expensive to correct.[33]

The transposition of hand-writing to print thus inevitably involved a process of clarification and objectification in which the product was distanced from its creator. Moreover that distancing involved not just what we might call the formalization that appearance provided by type represented,[34] but also the intervention of other hands. As I noted above, typesetters or compositors would routinely standardize accidentals, such as spelling, punctuation, capitalization and italicization, and house-readers or editors might also impose cuts or changes to phrasing.[35]

There is, then, abundant evidence that many nineteenth-century writers viewed first proofs as a crucial moment in a work's genesis because it gave them the first real sense of how their work was, and would be, perceived – it helped, that is, to reify it. This in turn explains why, despite the costs (in time and money), they typically treated proofs not as a type-setter might have wished, as an opportunity to 'correct' a work to conform to some notional original (we should remember that they rarely had to hand the fair-copy manuscript from which the text was set), but rather as an opportunity for further creation and revision, changing as much, and as often, as they felt they could get away with.

Moreover, it seems that some publishers were prepared to indulge this desire, at least with their better-known and most profitable authors. For example, when George Eliot lost confidence part way through writing *The Spanish Gypsy*, her publisher, Blackwood, by way of encouragement, offered to set what she had completed in type, a gesture which she gratefully accepted.[36] A somewhat more extreme example of the effect of seeing one's thoughts in print is provided by Pater. Following the success of the first edition of *The Renaissance*, Pater proposed to Macmillan a second collection of essays, provisionally entitled *The School of Giorgione and Other*

Studies (later changed to *Dionysus and Other Studies*), to be published, according to notices in the *Academy* and *Athenaeum*, in early 1879. Although the pieces collected in the volume had already appeared in print (as separate essays in periodicals such as the *Fortnightly Review*), they had not before appeared together, as a collection. Pater received proofs of the volume in November 1878. Halfway through correcting them, however, he lost confidence in his project, writing to Alexander Macmillan: 'I find more and more, as I revise proofs of my essays, so many inadequacies that I feel compelled, very reluctantly, to give up the publication of them at present.' The disgruntled publisher asked Pater to reconsider, pointing out the 'awkwardness' of having to explain 'Why ... Mr Pater's book is not forth-coming' (we might recall here the importance publishers attached to crea-ting a coherent and prestigious list). But Pater was resolute: the type was broken up and Pater, who was by no means a wealthy man, was sent the bill to cover the printer's considerable expenses.[37]

Some years later, in 1897, Wilde, finding (as usual) writing difficult, requested as 'a great favour' that Smithers 'have the poem [*Reading Gaol*] ... type-written' and 'sent by post'; Wilde continued, '[i]t is not yet finished, but I want to see it type-written. I am sick of my manuscript.'[38] On this occasion Wilde was referring not to proofs, but to the provision of a typed copy of his manuscript. He had made a similar request a few months earlier when he asked Robert Ross to make 'two type-written copies' of his prison manuscript – the document now known as *De Profundis* – presumably, as Ian Small has argued, because he intended to revise it for publication.[39] The dates here are significant: until the early 1890s there is no evidence that Wilde used typescript drafts as part of his compositional practices; on the contrary, surviving manuscripts of works such as 'The True Function and Value of Criticism' (1889) and 'The Soul of Man under Socialism' (1890) suggest that he submitted as printer's copy hand-written (and often, as I noted above, messy) manuscripts. A surviving typescript draft of the first, periodical version of *The Picture of Dorian Gray* (1890) was probably prepared by his American publisher from the manuscript which Wilde handed over as printer's copy in the spring of 1890.[40]

Yet for works composed after 1890 – most notably the society comedies which are also Wilde's most commercially successful achievements – numerous typescript drafts do survive. The initial reason may have been the need to provide multiple legible copies for use in the theatre, but for Wilde the 'discovery' of the typewriter, and the provision of typed copies of manu-script drafts, quickly became a crucial element of the writing process. The first commercially successful, mass-production typewriter was the 1873 Remington design; there is little evidence, though, of writers using such machines themselves; Wilde, for example, in common with many other late nineteenth-century authors, such as Mary Elizabeth Braddon, made use of professional type-writing agencies, such as that run by a Mrs Marshall in the Strand.

By giving an author the ability to generate his or her *own* typed drafts, type-writing dramatically enlarged the possibilities for revision, particularly for writers (like Wilde) who earned their living by the pen, and who were always under pressure to meet deadlines. A typescript allowed the author to see a work in that distanced way previously associated only with proofs, but without the necessity of involving either type-setter or publisher (and therefore the problems of cost and time encountered by Pater). Most typists would also produce carbon copies, allowing writers to retain a copy of the original in a way not possible with a manuscript.

The significance of this development is immediately apparent when we consider the numerous cases of lost or accidentally destroyed manuscripts: Carlyle's first manuscript of *The French Revolution* when on loan to John Stuart Mill was used by a maid to light a fire (Carlyle with characteristically Puritan perseverance re-wrote it from scratch); Tennyson absent-mindedly left the only manuscript of *In Memoriam* in a lodging house (and had to send Coventy Patmore to retrieve it); while Oscar Wilde claimed that he left the only fair-copy manuscript of his unpublished play *La Sainte Courtisane* in a cab in Paris.[41] The production of typed carbon copies also of course allowed for the circulation of drafts of a work, and thus for the prospect of collaboration. (The most famous such example is perhaps the typescript of T. S. Eliot's *The Waste Land*; but similar examples exist for nineteenth-century authors, notably, as I suggested above, for Wilde.)

Unfortunately there is not the space in this chapter to attempt to analyse in full the formative or dynamic relationships between printing technology and literary creativity. Nonetheless, it is difficult to ignore the fact that one of the most striking instances of stylistic experimentation, that associated with some early Modernist works, followed the revolution in print culture which I have described. It has been commonplace to explain the difficulties and obscurities of early Modernist works in terms of a reaction against the encroachment of mass culture, including the appetite, systematically cultivated in the Victorian period, for biographical knowledge of authors. By contrast, a relatively unexplored area has been the way in which the technological innovations that produced mass culture in the first instance could also have had a formative influence on the writing practices of those authors, beginning with Wilde but including also and most notably Joyce and Eliot (both of whom worked extensively with typescript drafts), often supposed to be most hostile to it.

Notes

1 See Edmund Gosse, *A Short History of Modern English Literature* (London: William Heinemann, 1898), p. 137; and Walter Pater, *Appreciations with an Essay on Style* (1889; London: Macmillan, 1912), p. 10.

2 John Morley, *Studies in Literature* (London: Macmillan, 1891), p. 219.

3 Matthew Arnold, 'The Function of Criticism at the Present Time', in *Essays in Criticism* (1865; London: Macmillan, 1889), p. 5.

4 *Ibid.* p. 192.

5 Lionel Johnson, *Post Liminium: Essays and Critical Papers by Lionel Johnson*, ed. Thomas Whittemore (London: Elkin Mathews, 1912), p. 120.

6 Oscar Wilde, 'The Critic as Artist', in *The Complete Works of Oscar Wilde*, vol. IV: *Criticism*, ed. Josephine M. Guy (Oxford: Oxford University Press, 2007), p. 166.

7 Henry James, 'The Art of Fiction', in *The House of Fiction: Essays on the Novel by Henry James*, ed. Leon Edel (London: Hart-Davis, 1957), pp. 29–30.

8 Quoted in Marie Corelli, *Wormwood*, ed. Kirsten McLeod (Toronto: Broadview Press, 2004), pp. 9–10.

9 See Alexis Weedon, *Victorian Publishing: The Economics of Book Production for a Mass Market, 1836–1916* (Aldershot: Ashgate, 2003), p. 57.

10 Henry James, 'The Future of the Novel', in *The House of Fiction*, ed. Edel, p. 49.

11 *Ibid.* p. 48.

12 Weedon, *Victorian Publishing*, p. 92.

13 Calculating the profitability of print-runs is complex because not all costs in book production went down at the same rate.

14 See Weedon, *Victorian Publishing*, pp. 103–7.

15 See e.g. Peter Howarth, *British Poetry in the Age of Modernism* (Cambridge: Cambridge University Press, 2005) and Jane Dowson, *Women, Modernism and British Poetry: 1910–1939* (Aldershot: Ashgate, 2002).

16 Lee Erickson, *The Economy of Literary Form: English Literature and the Industrialization of Publishing: 1800–1850* (Baltimore: Johns Hopkins University Press, 1996), p. 73.

17 See *The Complete Letters of Oscar Wilde*, ed. Merlin Holland and Rupert Hart-Davis (London: Fourth Estate, 2000), p. 405 n.

18 See *The Bookman*, 14, 79 (April 1898), pp. 9–10, and John Feather, *A History of British Publishing*, 2nd edn (London and New York: Routledge, 2006), p. 140.

19 See e.g. his unsigned reviews, 'Great Writers by Little Men' and 'A New Book on Dickens', in the *Pall Mall Gazette*; repr. in *The Collected Works of Oscar Wilde*, vol. XIII: *Reviews*, ed. Robert Ross (London: Methuen, 1908), pp. 135–44.

20 For details, see Josephine M. Guy and Ian Small, *Oscar Wilde's Profession* (Oxford: Oxford University Press, 2000), pp. 172–7.

21 Elizabeth Barrett Browning's comment is quoted in Alison Chapman, '"Vulgar Needs": Elizabeth Barrett Browning, Profit, and Literary Value', in Francis O'Gorman (ed.), *Victorian Literature and Finance* (Oxford: Oxford University Press, 2007), p. 74.

22 *Complete Letters*, ed. Holland and Hart-Davis, p. 1043.

23 The cartoon is reproduced in Jeffrey L. Spear, *Dreams of an English Eden* (New York: Columbia University Press, 1984), p. 192.

24 See W. J. Courthope, 'Wordsworth and Gray', *Quarterly Review*, 137 (1874), pp. 389–415.

25 See Bradley Deane, *The Making of the Victorian Novelist: Anxieties of Authorship in the Mass Market* (London and New York: Routledge, 2003), pp. 1–26.

26 *Complete Letters*, ed. Holland and Hart-Davis, p. 1011.

27 Deane, *The Making of the Victorian Novelist*, p. 2.

28 See Merlin Holland, *Irish Peacock and Scarlet Marquess: The Real Trial of Oscar Wilde* (London: Fourth Estate, 2003).

29 The paragraphs in question were misplaced in the first and all succeeding editions of the novel; see Gordon N. Ray, *Thackeray: The Uses of Adversity 1811–1846* (London: Oxford University Press, 1955), pp. 495–6.

30 See Allan C. Dooley, *Author and Printer in Victorian England* (Charlottesville and London: University Press of Virginia, 1992), pp. 42–5.

31 *Ibid.* pp. 24–34.

32 *Ibid.* pp. 8–15.

33 The most problematic concerns a misplaced paragraph in 'The Soul of Man under Socialism'; for details see *Complete Works of Oscar Wilde*, vol. IV, ed. Guy, pp. lxii–lxxv.

34 We also need to take account of book design and layout – the significance of a text's iconic or graphic status. The interpretive effect of typography, layout and colour of ink has been discussed in Donald F. McKenzie, *Bibliography and the Sociology of Texts* (London: British Library, 1986) and Jerome J. McGann, *The Textual Condition* (Princeton: Princeton University Press, 1991).

35 Again Wilde's texts provide good examples: *Intentions* uses italicization for emphasis, yet manuscript evidence suggests that decisions about what to italicize changed when the work passed through proofs; Wilde also quarrelled with the editor of the *Nineteenth Century* over cuts to 'The True Function and Value of Criticism' (see *Complete Works of Oscar Wilde*, vol. IV, ed. Guy, pp. xlix–liv).

36 Dooley, *Author and Printer*, p. 44.

37 The relevant correspondence is reprinted in Robert M. Seiler, *The Book Beautiful: Walter Pater and the House of Macmillan* (Cambridge: The Athlone Press, 1999), pp. 87–8.

38 *Complete Letters*, ed. Holland and Hart-Davis, p. 931.

39 *The Complete Works of Oscar Wilde*, vol. II: *De Profundis. 'Epistola: In Carcere et Vinculis'*, ed. Ian Small (Oxford: Oxford University Press, 2005), p. 21.

40 See *The Complete Works of Oscar Wilde*, vol. III: *The Picture of Dorian Gray*, ed. Joseph Bristow (Oxford: Oxford University Press, 2005), p. lxii.

41 Another version of the loss blames Wilde's friend More Adey. See Karl Beckson, *The Wilde Encyclopedia* (New York: AMS Press, 1998), p. 324.

2

MARY HAMMOND

Readers and readerships

The 'reading revolution'

The period 1830–1914 saw some of the greatest changes in readerships and the types and availability of reading material ever experienced in the Western world. These changes had already begun by the late eighteenth century, but the majority of them only came to fruition during the Victorian era; it was only after progressive nineteenth-century legislation had finally over-ruled the preceding generation's fears of a print-fuelled social revolution that real and lasting changes in reading patterns became possible.

The shift from eighteenth- to nineteenth-century reading habits has often been characterized as a shift from 'intensive' to 'extensive' reading: a change, that is, from the regular, repeated reading of a few expensive texts by a few privileged readers to the rapid consumption of a wider range of cheaper ones by a broader audience. It is certainly irrefutable that reading matter gradually became far cheaper and more plentiful between 1830 and 1914, and that there were more readers to enjoy it. The numbers of books and newspapers produced more than quadrupled across the century. The population of England, Scotland and Wales more than trebled from 10.5 million in 1801 to around 37 million by 1901.[1] Literacy rates in England and Wales increased from about 60 per cent of men and 45 per cent of women in 1800, to 94 and 93 per cent respectively by 1891.[2] This was due both to industrialization and to a concomitant demand for a more literate workforce, and to parliamentary reform which speeded up the increase with successive compulsory education acts after 1870. Overall, the effect was more readers at the end of the nineteenth century than at the beginning, and more printed matter to satisfy their demands.

There is, though, a problem with the intensive/extensive model and its assumption of a simple correlation between industrial and social progress and new modes of reading. It tends to obscure the individual experience and the differences between classes, regions, sexes and various points on the colonial map. The truth is that the spread of literacy and cheap, readily available mass publications varied widely according to where one lived and how. For one thing, there were regional variations in the pace of these social changes. Scotland's literacy rate was a few percentage points higher than that of England and Wales throughout the century, largely owing to its progressive education system, while Ireland's overall population actually decreased during this period through famine and emigration. Urban centres gained efficient centralized lighting systems (first gas, then electricity) far more quickly than rural areas, so first upper- and middle- and then finally working-class readers in cities could read after nightfall far more easily than their contemporaries in the country who continued to rely for much longer on candlelight. The coming of the railways in the 1840s brought great changes to the lives and possibilities of potential readers, enabling news-papers, books and letters to be delivered more quickly and cheaply, and people themselves to travel easily between towns and cities (and often, of course, to read while on those journeys). But these changes came to the urban centres first; bookstalls were set up by W. H. Smith's in London in the 1840s and then at stations between London and the larger Northern cities, reaching more remote stations only later.[3]

The slow spread of change in reading practices across social strata over time has often tended to be downplayed by literary historians. Only recently has scholarship effectively begun to demonstrate that 'revolutionary' or 'ground-breaking' literature can take years – sometimes generations – to achieve its intended effects. It has recently been demonstrated by William St Clair, for example, that the Romantic poets Byron, Shelley and Keats, so often considered the best-sellers of their age, were prohibitively expensive for the majority of the population and did not reach the lower classes until well into the nineteenth century when cheaper editions became available.[4] These and other initially expensive texts must therefore be seen as very much a part of what was being circulated and read long after 1830, despite their first publication years earlier.

This slow trickle-through effect according to which new works reached different social sectors at different rates continued well into the twentieth century, at the opposite end of our period. Recent scholarship has also shown us that the Modernist works of D. H. Lawrence, James Joyce and Virginia Woolf from the 1910s and 1920s took well over a generation to filter down to the working classes owing to the deliberately high cost of early editions set by these authors' publishers,[5] to widespread perceptions that experimental literature was beyond – or irrelevant to – the working and lower-middle classes,[6] and (in the case of Lawrence) to censorship. The history of reading in this period is in reality a rich and complex mixture of the old and the new.

The spread of certain types of literature varied equally widely across the British Empire. The school 'readers' on history and geography that were so much a feature of late nineteenth-century British and colonial school-rooms continued to do service in post-independence Africa and to influence African authors well into the twentieth century,[7] and Victorian best-sellers whose star had fizzled out in Britain by the First World War continued to be regularly borrowed from libraries in Calcutta until the 1940s.[8] To these variations by class and region we also need to add variations by age and gender; Victorian attitudes towards certain types of literature (particularly novels) were by no means always positive, and they changed at different rates among different reading communities. Fiction reading by middle-class Victorian women and children was frequently disapproved of by the heads of households, and it was discouraged by most public libraries at least until the turn of the century.[9] For women and children, religious texts were the recommended literary diet, with perhaps the addition of some poetry, languages, history and biography.

Fiction, it was thought, was likely to lead to moral laxity, so while women certainly read (and wrote) fiction in ever-increasing numbers, in the face of widespread cultural disapproval in the first half of the century in particular they often had to do so in secret, writing anonymously (like Jane Austen) or under pseudonyms (like the Brontës and George Eliot), and reading surreptitiously when parents were away. In the attempt to protect the nation's daughters from corruption through fiction, several Victorian publishers (of whom Emile Zola's publisher Henry Vizetelly is only the most famous) suffered imprisonment at the hands of the moral majority, just as others would suffer on the outbreak of war in 1914 when the Defence of the Realm Act once more enacted a perceived necessity to keep readers in the dark.

A reading revolution there certainly was between 1830 and 1914. But it was slower and more sporadic than most other revolutions. It affected different people in different ways at different times, and quite apart from the material factors such as price affecting accessibility, there were ideo-logical forces at work which often determined whether or not a given reader was permitted or even wanted such access. Thus, while it is possible to generalize quite usefully about available reading matter based on known facts about print-runs and prices, these details tell us only what readers may have bought, not whether they ever read it. In what follows I will be building on the traditional starting points for readership analysis grounded in material facts (often called 'quantitative book history'), by using further evidence gleaned from the autobiographies, journals and letters of real historical readers, to whose testimony we have only recently begun to pay serious attention.[10]

1830–1865

Certain types of reading in 1830 were very much – although certainly not exclusively – the preserve of the upper and middle classes. Books, still made out of paper produced from rags and bound in leather (until new and cheaper methods were developed between 1840 and 1860), were durable enough to last through many repeated readings, but new ones were extremely expensive. The labour-intensive processes used to make them were partly to blame for this, but another reason for their prohibitive cost was the so-called 'taxes on knowledge', namely Stamp Duty (applied to newspapers and not abolished until 1855) and paper taxes (only finally repealed in 1861). Both taxes were instigated in the eighteenth century and designed to keep the cost of printing high, and so prevent the working classes from getting hold of inflammatory (or simply informative) literature which might incite them to revolution of the kind France had seen in the 1780s and 1790s.

In fact, even among the middle classes prices affected the ways in which reading took place. Owing to the cost of postage (which until the advent of the penny postage in 1840 was charged at the rate of both distance and number of sheets, and therefore all but impossible for the lower classes), letters were frequently written, not just on both sides of a sheet of paper, but also often a second time on each side, the handwriting threading its way through or between previously written lines. Even wealthier readers frequently shared texts, either by passing on a book after reading or by reading aloud to one another.

This makes it difficult to get a sense of how many readers there actually were based on book sales alone, but the practice was so common that we can easily assume that for every print-run of a given book there were at least twice or even three times that number of readers. There was another alternative to passing on whole books; the construction of 'common-place books', blank volumes into which individuals or whole families copied out favourite quotations from poetry, history, drama or prose, was also normal in this period. Indeed, it has been suggested recently that some readers encountered literature almost exclusively in this form, seldom seeing a full published book apart from the Bible.[11]

The sharing of print as a way around high prices also extended to other forms such as newspapers. At the beginning of the nineteenth century new copies of *The Times* catered for a small, select group of middle- and upper-class readers, its circulation amounting to only around 2,000. It was read by many more people than this, however, by being passed between family members (even those living some way apart) or levels of the household, and also by the renting out or resale of used copies to the less affluent middle classes via coffee houses, pubs and street barrows. A newspaper might thus be a week or more out of date by the time a reader got hold of it. This was made possible, of course, by the more durable rag paper on which the news was printed. But it meant the idea of 'news' had a different meaning in the 1830s than it does now. The attention-grabbing headline and the 'scoop' were still some way in the future; the problem facing many newspaper readers in this period was not how to ingest gobbets of news rapidly, but how to catch up. Of course, a paper might also be read aloud to an assembled company; in fact this was so common an event that reading silently in such a situation could be thought rude: 'Noticed at dinner time the improper conduct of Mr Slyfield he having taken the paper and not reading aloud', recalled one Joseph Jenkinson of Nottingham, anxious to get a peek at the *Morning Chronicle* in September 1839. 'I kindly requested him to read the city article and sat 1/4 of an hour thinking he would look at it in a while, he however continued reading to himself and deigned not to answer me or to comply with my request or to give up the paper but sat as if he were the only person who had a right to know any of its contents.'[12]

For readers in the lower classes, new novels were out of the question unless borrowed from a generous employer, newspapers were likely to be shared or second-hand, and letters were sporadic. If they were themselves illiterate (or if they were too busy to read), working-class people and artisans were frequently dependent on friends and neighbours to write or read on their behalf, a process that could prove slow and frustrating depending on the reader's proficiency and the listeners' powers of comprehension. William Edward Hickson, an artisan, records attempting to read articles from *The Times* to some labourers in his village in the 1830s: 'I found that we did not get on at all; and upon cross-examination of some of my auditors afterwards, I discovered, to my surprise, that I could not read 20 lines of the leading article of the "Times" without finding that there were 20 words in it which none of my auditors understood.'[13]

Similarly, English compositor Charles Manby Smith remembers that at the publishing house where he worked in the 1830s, '*The Times* newspaper was taken in daily, and it was the office of each compositor in town to read the debates and leaders aloud for the benefit of the rest. When it came to my turn, they could never understand my "professional" mode of reading, and made me many humble requests for explanation.'[14]

It is noteworthy that the publishing house in this last example chose to take in the politically conservative *Times* rather than the *Manchester Guardian* (established 1821), renowned for its radical politics. Fears of worker unrest were still rife among employers, and as long as newspapers were prohibitively expensive for the working classes the reach of their contents could be in some measure controlled. The fears were genuine; the labour movement known as Chartism climaxed in demonstrations, petitions and strikes in the 1840s, and were characterized by – for employers – the dangerous precedent of workers co-operating for the common good. Chartist newspapers such as the *Northern Star* (1838–52) were run by working-class editors and subsidised by working men clubbing together to raise capital. Only when Chartism had been crushed and conditions in factories and mines gradually began to improve did the paper fold. By this time the cat was out of the bag: after the repeal of Stamp Duty in 1855, the *Manchester Guardian*'s price dropped to a penny and it became a daily, almost rivalling *The Times* in circulation.

New novels might be out of their reach in the 1830s, 1840s and 1850s, and newspapers sometimes hard to get hold of, but the lower classes had accessible to them a range of other types of reading matter such as popular ballads and poems peddled by itinerant travellers, religious tracts distributed by groups such as the Society for the Diffusion of Useful Knowledge, and 'broadsides', typically cheaply printed tales of recent murders or hangings.[15] Cheap reprints of popular dramas were also available to all but the very poorest readers, and serialized fiction at around a penny per instalment was very much a feature of lower-class life in the 1830s and 1840s, with those who could not themselves afford a penny a week frequently clubbing together. The kinds of stories found at this price were often of dubious quality and as a result became popularly known as 'Penny Dreadfuls'. Generally revolving around the exploits of contemporary criminals or legendary heroes, they did also encompass some new fiction such as G. W. M. Reynolds's *The Mysteries of London* (begun in 1844), which explored the sordid underworld of the nation's capital and, like most of these serialized pieces, ran for as long as it could find an audience. In fact, such literature was as flexible as it was disreputable and driven solely by reader demand: if a serial ceased to find buyers it would be discontinued without being concluded. Among these readers, excitement was apparently rated above closure.

Concerns about the effects of this kind of reading matter inevitably accompanied its success. Between the 1830s and the late 1840s, journalist Henry Mayhew interviewed several groups of young 'vagabonds'. He reported that their only reading matter consisted of Penny Dreadfuls, and felt that these were frequently responsible for the boys' moral decline: 'Numbers avowed that they had been induced to resort to an abandoned course of life from reading the lives of notorious thieves and novels about highway robbers.'[16] This concern about the effects of fiction on the lower classes – culturally allied to women and children in terms of their susceptibility – was to have far-reaching consequences, and to inhibit its general availability to them for some years to come.

Somewhat paradoxically, Dickens's successful arrival on the publishing scene in 1836 owed everything to his emulation of lower-class serial-reading habits. But he managed to re-package them for the middle classes by weaving his complex dramatic tales around a moral frame, and by raising the price. Dickens, in effect, made the penny serial respectable and hugely widened its audience. Despite his popularity with the working classes, however, Dickens was not always easily accessible to them, and there were those to whom he was all but out of reach. As Jonathan Rose reports: 'George Acorn, growing up in extreme poverty in London's East End, scraped together 3½d to buy a used copy of *David Copperfield*. His parents punished him when they learned he had wasted so much money on a book.'[17] While Acorn's parents later learned to enjoy Dickens, the price and the punishment seem to have been retained in his memory as vividly as the conversion.

Even Dickens's public readings of the 1850s and 1860s, while occasionally performed free for working people, were after 1853 usually priced at a shilling even for the cheapest seats, and were therefore commonly out of the reach of the very poor.[18] But for the lower middle classes and above, Dickens's brand of serial publication – full of cliff-hanging excitement like the Penny Dreadful, but morally improved and formally more sophisticated – was a revelation, and it was for them that he founded the weekly publications *Household Words* (1850) and its successor *All the Year Round* (1859). These periodicals cemented both the serial as a widely popular form across class lines, and his own – and several other authors' – success in writing effectively for it. Several of the best-sellers of this period, such as Wilkie Collins's *The Woman in White* (1860) and Elizabeth Gaskell's *North and South* (1855), first appeared in these periodicals, and several other of the period's now well-known names such as Leigh Hunt and Elizabeth Barrett Browning contributed regularly.[19]

The experience of reading a novel in serial form was crucially different from the ways in which these authors are typically read today. Each instalment had to be complete in itself, and yet also encourage readers to buy the next. For this reason, novels from this period tend to be both lengthy (if they were successful) and filled with 'peaks and troughs' of suspense at roughly regular intervals. These characteristics mark nineteenth-century novels out as unique in ways that have less to do with authorial heavy-handedness than they do with readers' demands.

Technical and other factual material was available to skilled workers at adult evening classes in the mechanics' institutes, founded in the 1820s but thriving and spreading steadily throughout the nineteenth century, as some wealthy industrialists realized the value of a workforce well versed in information pertinent to their trades. The institutes regularly ended up supplying quantities of fiction as well as factual reading, as Durham collier Jack Lawson, having discovered fiction at the Miners' Institute at age fourteen, testifies: 'I was tireless … once I started. Scott; Charles Reade; George Eliot; the Brontes; later on Hardy; Hugo; Dumas and scores of others. Then came Shakespeare; the Bible; Milton and the line of poets generally. I was hardly sixteen when I picked up James Thomson's Seasons, in Stead's "Penny Poets".'[20]

Poetry, in fact, played a prominent role in most reading communities up to and beyond the First World War, with recitations in both community and domestic settings extremely common. Poetry that was easy to memorize was thus at a premium, and this might help to explain the success of Alfred (later Lord) Tennyson whose poems, composed almost entirely in his head because of his chronic shortsightedness, naturally tended towards memorable forms. All but unknown in the 1830s, by the 1840s Tennyson was such a popular favourite that he was granted a Civil List pension, and by 1850 had been made Poet Laureate. He had a remarkable ability to appeal across class lines; at one end of the social scale were working-class readers such as collier Jack Lawson, above, and at the other were Prince Albert and Queen Victoria. Tennyson is a poet of his time: one of his most famous poems, 'The Charge of the Light Brigade' (1854), owed everything to the increasing circulation of newspapers; he lifted several of its most famous phrases from the dispatches printed in *The Times*.

Tennyson also heralded a new generation of poets such as Coventry Patmore, whose 'Angel in the House' sequence (1854–63) provided a model of idealized middle-class feminine domesticity throughout the century and beyond, to the extent that in 1931 Virginia Woolf made it part of her mission to kill off this paragon in order to free the woman writer from domestic incarceration.[21] Other poets such as Robert Browning had an influence almost as long: author John Masefield was still citing him as one of his formative 'masters' in the 1890s.[22] More topical poets, such as the 'Corn Law Rhymer' of the 1840s, Ebenezer Elliott, lasted a shorter time, their popularity apparently tied to the issues they highlighted. Other poets had more exclusive readerships; the Pre-Raphaelite poets Swinburne, Morris and the Rossettis depended largely upon patronage, rather than sales, for their livelihoods, and (owing largely to a tendency towards sexual frankness) were not widely circulated among the lower classes until the end of the century, and were an equal cause of concern for the patriarch anxious to safeguard his family's innocence. Such frankness was deliberate and pointed, meant to shock its readers; indeed, in the 1860s, according to one contemporary account, the young Swinburne set out to scandalize his fellow dinner guests, Thackeray's two daughters and the Archbishop of York, by reading aloud from his work at the table.[23]

In the absence of organized compulsory education, self-help – in addition to the help provided by benevolent employers – was a prominent feature of the middle of the century. Appealing to literate artisans and the lower middle classes for whom further education was impossible, self-help books were designed and priced accordingly. The most successful of these – and one which, like poetry, appealed across class lines – was Samuel Smiles's *Self-Help* (1859). It sold 20,000 copies in its first year and was still selling well forty years later, though by the end of the century (as we will shortly see) the autodidact was being increasingly attacked as an inferior type of scholar.

Also available in cheap editions throughout the century was Charles and Mary Lamb's *Tales from Shakespear* (1807), originally designed to introduce young children to the nation's premier dramatist by turning dramatic dialogue into simple prose, modernizing the Elizabethan language, and editing out anything indelicate, but also reaching many new adult readers for whom Shakespeare in the original was overly challenging. Sir Walter Scott's novels and poems, though prohibitively expensive when new at 31s 6d for a three-volume set, filtered down through the price strata as the century wore on, not losing their appeal until its very end.

Copies of the Bible and Bunyan's *Pilgrim's Progress* were to be found in most working-class (as well as middle- and upper- class) homes in the first half of the century; indeed, the nineteenth-century publishing history of Bunyan's allegory demonstrates that it was one of the era's most successful books, available in a wide range of formats from the parson's pulpit version to the edition designed to be read aloud to servants or children. Jonathan Rose records that Bunyan played a prominent part in the otherwise severely limited reading opportunities of the working-class poet Gerald Massey as he was growing up in Middlesex during the 1830s. Thanks to the care of his mother, who had sent him to the penny school, he had learnt to read, and the desire to read had been awakened. Books, however, were very scarce. The Bible and Bunyan were the principal texts; he committed many chapters of the former to memory, and accepted all Bunyan's allegory as bona fide history. Afterwards, he obtained access to *Robinson Crusoe*, a few old Wesleyan magazines and some battle histories. These constituted his sole reading, until he came up to London, at the age of fifteen, as an errand boy.[24] Massey's experience of the widening of his horizons by moving to the city in this period is fairly typical as Britain's industrial growth demanded more and more labour. But the 1840s also saw two further vital new developments for readers: the arrival of the railway and the establishment of the cheap circulating library.

It is impossible to over-emphasize the impact that the arrival of train travel had on readers and the distribution of print. Newspapers, growing ever cheaper between 1830 and 1865, could be transported from one end of the country to the other in a single day, as could letters. Even before W. H. Smith hit upon the idea of opening bookstalls at stations (his first opened at Euston station in 1847), various individuals had been running stalls containing old newspapers and second-hand books (often pornography). W. H. Smith cleaned up the railway stalls, providing them with reputable new fiction, newspapers, maps, travel guides and magazines.

Cheaper even than the stage coach, trains made travel possible for an ever-increasing number of people of all classes except the very poorest, and while new reading material might still have been prohibitively expensive for third-class travellers, for the slightly wealthier dozens of new possibilities opened up. The bulky three-volume novel was too big for the limited storage space available at bookstalls and too heavy for passengers to carry, so the shorter cheap reprint came into its own. Ever since the first eighteenth-century copyright enforcement, publishers had realized the potential of out-of-copyright reprints, and more and more of these began to appear as production costs decreased and new opportunities for small cheap books opened up. Soon, readers could purchase out-of-copyright literature organized in themed 'series' or 'libraries' ranging from *Aesop's Fables* and *Pilgrim's Progress* to Milton, Pope, Fielding and a number of lesser-known novelists. They were available in a range of colours and sizes, some designed for self-education, some for entertainment, and their quality varied enormously; the best were attractive and durable, the worst flimsy and barely legible. Routledge's Railway Library was one of the most famous of the better sort. Known as 'yellowbacks' because of their binding, these books made all sorts of literature available for a few shillings. The railway – and the cheap reprint that went with it – enabled even living authors to gain new markets; one of the most successful authors of the 1840s and 1850s was Charles Lever, whose works quickly found their way into cheap formats to suit almost every pocket. This success in a range of prices was matched by that of Charles Reade, whose novels *It's Never Too Late To Mend* (1856) and *The Cloister and the Hearth* (1861) were among the best-sellers of their time, and particular favourites at bookstalls.

Realising the opportunities their bookstall empire provided, in the 1860s Smith's started a circulating library which enabled members to borrow a volume at one station and return it at another. The library included all the authors mentioned above, along with others such as 'Ouida' (the pseudonym of French/English novelist Marie Louise Ramée), whose romantic novels of high society were considered indecent by most moralists of the time and frequently denied to young women. While conservative Smith's hung on to their reputation for wholesome literature, embroiling themselves in a number of legal battles with authors or newspaper proprietors (particularly socialist ones) whose works they refused to stock, they were nonetheless forced by reader demand to hover fairly close to the respectability line. As a result, 'railway fiction' retained its taint of seediness well into the twentieth century.

The railway did not just affect the price of fiction; it also had a profound impact on its form. Reading while travelling was not the same thing as reading in the quiet of a parlour; train travel meant noise, disruptions and tension, particularly in the early years when accidents and assaults were fairly frequent. The result was new types of reading matter geared towards the distracted reader. In mid-century 'sensation fiction' emerged, its first exponent being Wilkie Collins whose tale of stolen identity *The Woman in White* (1860) was such a page-turner it was said to have kept Gladstone from a theatre engagement. Sensation fiction was characterized by its breathless, spine-tingling plots and its combination of Gothic adventure and real-life drama set in realistic contemporary settings, perfect for taking the reader's mind off the discomforts of travel. Short stories and detective fiction, equally dependent upon a limited attention span alongside the need to keep the reader's eye fixed on the page, are both creations of the railway age towards the close of the century, with Sir Arthur Conan Doyle's Sherlock Holmes stories in the *Strand* magazine only the most famous of these.

In addition, the small newsprint and long articles representative of established publications like *The Times* and of static reading situations gradually gave way to larger print, shorter articles, more illustrations and adverts, and the miscellany format of periodicals like the *Pall Mall Gazette* (1865, reformatted for a modern commuting audience by W. T. Stead in 1883) and *Cassell's Family Magazine* (1867) which provided something for everybody in an easily digestible form. It is worth mentioning, too, that railway and underground stations (the first of which opened in 1863) were plastered with adverts; some readers got their entertainment for free.

The second great breakthrough of mid-century was Charles Mudie's Circulating Library (in its heyday 1842–94). Built along the lines of the eighteenth-century subscription library for the wealthy but with crucial differences, the secrets of Mudie's success were cheapness and moral conservatism. For a mere guinea (21 shillings) a member could borrow up to twelve volumes a year (each one of which would cost 10s 6d new) of the latest fiction, poetry and drama, and even the most prudish parent could not object to the carefully pre-scrutinized book list.

1865–1900

Mudie's dominated the fiction market until 1894 through the discounts they negotiated with publishers which kept the price of new novels artificially high. In that year, finally giving in to pressure from authors and readers, publishers began publishing new fiction in relatively cheap, single-volume form. From around 1870 on, however, readers increasingly had other choices available to them.

The year 1870 saw the first in a series of Education Acts designed to make primary education compulsory, and to meet the demands of a new age with a newly literate workforce fit to compete in Britain's colonies overseas. The Acts did not fundamentally alter, though they did add impetus to, the prevailing trend of increasing literacy. Parents initially had to pay a nominal fee of up to ninepence weekly to allow their children to attend the new Board Schools, and for many both the financial outlay and the loss of a child's earning power were simply not possible. It was not until the 1891 Education Act that elementary schooling became free.

The result of the establishment of nationwide schools, however, had a profound impact on publishing, on the availability of reading material, and on the establishment of the idea of a 'national canon' of works which everyone ought to have read. Publishers such as Nelson's and Oxford University Press became specialists in providing Board School readers and exam papers, and other publishers specialized in producing books to give as prizes. Building on the earlier success of Sunday school prizes given away by charitable institutions, school prize books did much to spread reading matter and a taste for reading among otherwise bookless households.

George Gregory, the son of an illiterate Somerset miner and a servant who read only the Bible, recalled that growing up at the end of the nineteenth century he had access only to a few school prizes: '*Jack and the Ostrich*, a children's story; *The Crucifixion of Philip Strong*, a gripping tale of labour unrest; and the verses of Cornish poet John Harries – and the family read a weekly serial, *Strongdold the Gladiator*. Having left school at twelve to work in the mines, Gregory had no access to serious reading matter until mid-adolescence, when a clerk introduced him to Smiles's *Self-Help*'.[25]

Other publishers branched out into equally specialized markets. Ever since the popular success of Dickens's Christmas stories, starting with

A Christmas Carol (1843), the idea of a midwinter 'publishing season' had begun to take hold, and by the second half of the century readers could purchase a wide range of books with Christmas themes, or designed to give as gifts. Children's publishing also burgeoned, with the appearance of a vast array of stories, anthologies and periodicals aimed at younger readers. At the same time, niche marketing and its varied pricing structures began to demonstrate the first signs of a division between 'serious' and 'leisure' reading, and (perhaps inevitably in a class-bound society) between readers who recognized and valued the former and those who did not. The serious realist novels of mid to late century which we tend to think of as representative of this period – novels by George Eliot, Thomas Hardy, Olive Schreiner, Henry James, George Gissing and French novelists such as Zola – appealed largely to the middle classes, with lower-class readers either denied them as a result of the cost or the occasionally contentious contents, or perhaps even bored by their earnestness.

One institution which now came into its own as a disseminator of fiction – and as a cementer of this division between 'good' and 'bad' reading material – was the public library. The Act which enabled city councils to charge ratepayers for the establishment of a free library had been passed in 1850, but most towns did not exercise their right until twenty or more years later. Gradually, however, readers in almost every town were able (theoretically at least) to borrow books for free, and numerous memoirs testify to the advantages this gave to those on lower incomes.

This was not, though, the unmitigated blessing it first appears. In the early part of the period even councils prescient enough to have built a library frequently found they could not afford to stock it properly. And even into the twentieth century, city councils still anxious about the effects of reading on untutored (and particularly female) minds policed their catalogues with the same rigour as Mudie's had done, banning contentious books (such as those by Thomas Hardy and Ouida) and instructing their users to borrow less fiction and concentrate on more instructive reading, even as – paradoxically – they supplied newspapers and magazines to attract them. Library committees also worried about their new building being used by loafers and their books being damaged, and positively discouraged working-class readers from using it because of their perceived idleness, or their dirty hands and clothes. Recalling the experience of borrowing books for her family in the first decade of the twentieth century, factory worker Alice Foley recalls that 'After the selection I usually crept upstairs to the reading-room trying to still the clatter of clogs on stone steps, but on settling down with a picture magazine, up came the irate caretaker, and I was shunted out like an unwanted animal.'[26]

It is hardly surprising that extant library borrowing records show that, ultimately, the movement did not significantly increase working-class access to literature. Libraries were used primarily by the lower middle classes – particularly clerks – who found in them a means to better themselves. This class also became an important part of the book and periodical buying public. Review journals aimed at a middle-class readership had been a feature of the publishing scene since the monthly magazines and reviews of the 1860s, with periodicals such as *Macmillan's Magazine*, the *Cornhill*, and later the *Fortnightly Review*. In emulation of this mixture of criticism and review, a new cheaper type of periodical emerged in the 1880s and 1890s, designed both to entertain the newly literate lower-class reader and to guide him or her through the minefield of new books on offer. W. T. Stead's *Review of Reviews* (1890), full of digestible criticism and sensational journalism, is a classic example, but by the 1890s most cheap periodicals contained advice on what to look out for at the bookstall and there were dozens of advice manuals devoted to helping the aspirational reader to make the right choice in everything from clothes to party food. There was, however, no easy way for a clerk to rise through the ranks of taste. Provided for with cultural know-how as never before, paradoxically, the figure of the autodidact bent on social climbing became one of the most ridiculed figures in late nineteenth- and early twentieth-century literary criticism at the hands of a new brand of aesthetic purism which, though it took several forms, had at its root a profound fear of the petite bourgeoisie.

There were further ideologically inflected variations in novels and their readerships in Britain during this dynamic period. Fiction in cheap instalments gradually declined after 1870 with the death of Dickens, and after 1894 when the three-decker novel was finally killed off by the agreement between Mudie's and the major publishers, and new novels suddenly became cheaper. In addition, although in real terms rising wages had not kept pace with inflation and the cost of living was higher at the end of the nineteenth century than at the beginning, there was a steady increase in disposable income and – equally important – in leisure time. With fiction available to almost everyone in this most socially mobile (and socially anxious) of centuries, there began to be a marked difference in its types, and in deepening contemporary perceptions of the difference between 'literary' and 'popular' works. Indeed, it became a critical commonplace that a novelist in vogue with many readers could not, almost by definition, be 'good'.

Certain works had by now been labelled as 'classics' by publishers anxious to attract readers to an authenticated list of 'must read' works, and these were commonly taught in schools and, later in the century, in universities. These inevitably included Shakespeare, Chaucer, Milton, Dryden, Swift and Pope; George Eliot and Jane Austen were usually included, but many series were male-dominated. For example Grant Richards's World's Classics Series (founded in 1901, taken over by Oxford University Press in 1905) numbered only four women among its initial list of forty-three titles. Just as importantly, contemporary best-sellers were firmly excluded. This did not prevent their appeal to readers, however; the end of the nineteenth century represents the first concerted effort by authors and publishers (and increasingly agents) to advertise their wares, to market the author as a commodity, and thus to sell vast numbers of copies, and it succeeded.

Popular authors such as Marie Corelli and Hall Caine, both of whom wrote melodramatic romances that broke all sales records in the 1880s and 1890s, were constantly interviewed in periodicals such as the *Bookman*, and Stead's *Review of Reviews* made celebrity profiles – including those about journalists – a regular feature. Readers of novels such as *A Romance of Two Worlds* (1886), *Vendetta* (1886) and *The Sorrows of Satan* (1895) by Corelli and *The Shadow of a Crime* 1885), *The Bondman* (1890) and *The Manxman* (1894) by Caine could thus regularly read about their favourite authors' life-styles and opinions. They could also often buy 'theatrical versions' of their favourite novels such as the *Daily Mail*'s 'theatrical version' of Hall Caine's *The Bondman*, published in 1906; the theatre was too expensive for the lowest classes, but theatre-going was popular (if sometimes frowned upon for women) among most other classes, and popular novels were prime targets for adaptation. Groups of readers could, and did, then act out the plays for themselves at home, or read them aloud to one another. In the age before television, the art of declamation lingered a surprisingly long time among many reading communities.

Building on the success of the 'miscellanies' of the 1860s, new sensational periodicals such as *Tit-Bits* (started 1881) specialized in dramatic stories, competing with niche-targeting publications such as the *Boy's Own Paper* (1879), the *Women's Penny Paper* (1881), the *Girl's Own Paper* (1880), and a vast array of still more specialist publications catering for interests ranging from the *British Women's Temperance Journal* (1883–92) to *Cycling* (1891). British novels, newspapers and periodicals circulated freely overseas; British officials and troops administering and fighting for the Empire throughout the nineteenth century were regularly supplied with news and books from home, and in some corners formed a publication's most regular readership. *Blackwood's Magazine* (started in Edinburgh in 1817) had a declining circulation in Britain by the 1890s, but it still had a dedicated following in the colonies, reflecting this readership by the inclusion of non-British authors such as Joseph Conrad, whose *Heart of Darkness* appeared there in 1899.

In Britain, the outpouring of review journals was tempered with comedy in the shape of comics such as the weekly *Ally Sloper's Half Holiday* (1884), which initially attracted a working-class male readership, but quickly established a cult following among the middle classes. After 1891, when international copyright agreements were ratified, British readers also had access to a wide range of reasonably priced reading matter, both popular and literary, that was not home produced. The global age of print had very much arrived. The last decades of the century had seen the most rapid growth, and by 1900 the pattern of variegated readerships, niche publishing and a distinct ideological divide between 'art' and 'the market' that was to dominate until almost the middle of the twentieth century was already in place.

1900–1914

Surprisingly little changed for some reading communities between 1900 and the First World War. As a child growing up in Suffolk before 1914, V. S. Pritchett remembered that his passion for reading – fostered by the Board School – was answered by a miscellaneous collection of reading material that owed everything to nineteenth-century tastes: 'I had read every line of several volumes of the "Home Magazine"', he recalls, 'especially a grotesque serial called "The Wallypug of Why", an enjoyable fantasy about the plots of a cathedral gargoyle: also bits from the "Children's Encyclopaedia", "Hereward the Wake", comics and "Marriage on Two Hundred a Year", one of the popular handbooks of the period.'[27] Indeed, for the lower classes, now comfortably settled into a reading habit and well supplied with fiction and periodicals, innovation was not considered necessary: Harry Burton, growing up in London in the same period, remembers that his father, an irregularly employed housepainter, liked a 'stirring novel' but nothing more challenging than Conan Doyle: 'He had no use whatever for anything remotely approaching the spiritual in art, literature or music.' In fact, while the whole family enjoyed reading aloud to each other, they did so from the *Family Reader*, the *Daily Chronicle*, *Lloyd's Weekly News*, the tales of Jules Verne and children's comics such as *Chips* – all nineteenth-century publications, some of them of long standing.[28]

Popular fiction went through its cycles; Corelli and Caine, though still publishing, went slowly out of fashion in Britain though they remained popular in the colonies where new books, particularly indigenous ones, were harder to come by. The exotic adventure tales of Rider Haggard,

Kipling and Stevenson continued to find audiences even as a new generation of adventure novelists sprang up which included John Buchan, Edgar Wallace and G. K. Chesterton, who began to imagine equally thrilling adventures at home. Outside of the thriller and adventure genres, new popular novels were split between the racy (Elinor Glyn's *Three Weeks*, 1907) and the Evangelical (Florence Barclay's *The Rosary*, 1909), both of which became publishing sensations. *The Rosary* was even described by Barclay's daughter, her effusive biographer, as suddenly to be seen in the hands of every reader in the land.[29]

This was not, however, strictly true. The notional division between 'good' and 'popular' literature deepened and further sub-divided, rather than disappeared, in the first decade of the new century. For the lower classes, as the above examples attest, a diet of tried and tested Victorian favourites, leavened now and then with some lightweight new fiction, was the norm. Indeed, sales of the late Victorian poet A. E. Housman actually increased during this period, particularly once war broke out. For the more aspirational (and we should not forget that these often also came from the working classes), new novels might help to while away the leisure hours, but there was also available a new and more scholarly dedication to cheap reprints of classics in the shape of the Everyman series (1906) and Oxford World's Classics (started, as we have seen, in 1901; purchased by OUP in 1905). Cheap enough for every pocket and eclectic enough to introduce a whole new generation of readers to world literature, these series professionalized the reprint phenomenon, eventually appealing to the student market that replaced the culture of autodidacticism. Some readers from the newly literate classes began to turn writer, too; Robert Tressell's novel of working-class life, *The Ragged Trousered Philanthropists* (1906–8), did not appear until 1914, after his death, and even then its radical politics were cut and its circulation was interrupted by the war, but it later became one of the most influential working-class novels of the century and a testament to the ways in which the nineteenth century's new readers, in entering the literary market-place, had begun to change the face of literature itself.

More widely read than Tressell, though possibly less so than Glyn or Barclay, were the 'middlebrow' offerings of authors such as Arnold Bennett who, while committed to helping the lower classes to educate themselves and writing popular journalism and best-selling lightweight fiction such as *The Card* (1911), also wrote serious realist novels and criticism. These include the four *Clayhanger* books (1910–18), and many critical articles on literature for *The New Age*. Although it had started in 1894, *The New Age* took a significant new direction from 1907 and (with Bennett's help) was to become one of the most influential literary journals of the day, particularly in providing an outlet for Modernism. Bennett was not alone in this capacity to please several different publics. John Galsworthy was both a best-seller with works such as *The Forsyte Saga* (1906–21) and also a serious man of letters, eventually winning the Nobel Prize for literature. Both these authors appealed to a wide readership, excepting perhaps the least adventurous, but by far their greatest number of readers came from the vast, growing and multi-layered middle class created by nineteenth-century progress.

Another reading community, separating itself from the herd by dint of its appreciation for the avant-garde, began to form at around this same time. Victorian realism, while still alive in the works of Bennett and Galsworthy into the new century, was being challenged at least as early as the 1890s by the more free-flowing narrative style of some 'New Woman' fiction and the darkly contemplative tales of Conrad. By the dawn of the new century, experiments with narrative form which embraced the new technological age were being tried out by poets such as Ezra Pound, whose Imagist movement (1910) became the backbone of what was later called Modernism, a movement that eventually dealt the death blow to the realist prose and sentimental poetry of the Victorians.

But not, for most readers, before 1914. The men who joined up in their thousands on the outbreak of war were still reading adventure stories, comics, technical manuals and popular novels. Throughout the war they would continue to read these alongside letters, cartoons, journalism, stories and poetry, some of it of their own devising. Modernism was barely on their horizon. D. H. Lawrence's ground-breaking novels *The White Peacock* (1911) and *Sons and Lovers* (1913) were deemed pornographic and were expurgated or banned outright until long after his death in 1930. Other Modernist works were published in specialist magazines or limited editions. They were not meant for – indeed, they were expressly constructed to alienate – the general reader for whom the rest of the publishing industry now so comprehensively catered. The movement's main early readers, indeed, were each other.

In these decades, as in previous ones, change came slowly, and new readerships perhaps still more so. But on the eve of the First World War British readers could, if they so wished, look back on almost a century of revolution that was to shape the face of literary production for the next seventy years.

Notes

1 Richard D. Altick, *The English Common Reader: A Social History of the Mass Reading Public 1800–1900* (Chicago and London: University of Chicago Press, 1963), pp. 70, 81.

2 Simon Eliot, 'From Expensive and Few to Cheap and Many', in Simon Eliot and Jonathan Rose (eds.), *A Companion to the History of the Book* (Oxford: Blackwell, 2007), p. 293.

3 Charles Wilson, *First with the News: The History of W. H. Smith 1792–1972* (London: Guild Publishing, 1985).

4 William St Clair, *The Reading Nation in the Romantic Period* (Cambridge: Cambridge University Press, 2004).

5 Lawrence Rainey, *Institutions of Modernism: Literary Elites and Public Culture* (New Haven: Yale University Press, 1998).

6 Jonathan Rose, *The Intellectual Life of the British Working Classes* (New Haven: Yale University Press, 2001).

7 Robert Fraser, 'School Readers in the Empire and the Creation of Postcolonial Taste', in Robert Fraser and Mary Hammond (eds.), *Books without Borders*, vol 1: *The Cross-national Dimension in Print Culture* (Basingstoke: Palgrave Macmillan, 2008), pp. 89–106.

8 Priya Joshi, *In Another Country: Colonialism, Culture, and the English Novel in India* (New York: Columbia University Press, 2002).

9 Mary Hammond, *Reading, Publishing and the Formation of Literary Taste, 1880–1914* (Aldershot: Ashgate, 2006), pp. 23–50.

10 This kind of information is currently being collected by the Reading Experience Database (www.open.ac.uk/Arts/RED/).

11 Stephen Colclough, 'Readers: Books and Biography', in Simon Eliot and Jonathan Rose (eds.), *A Companion to the History of the Book* (Oxford: Blackwell, 2007).

12 Joseph Jenkinson, *The Diary of Joseph Jenkinson of Dronfield*, ed. K. Battye (Chesterfield: Derbyshire Record Society 1987), p. 56, www.open.ac.uk/Arts/reading/recorddetails.php?id=9860, accessed 18 January 2008.

13 Parliamentary Papers, Select Committee on Newspaper Stamps [Commons] 1851 (facsimile edn, Shannon: Irish University Press, 1969), p. 468, www.open.ac.uk/Arts/reading/recorddetails.php?id=1561, accessed 10 January 2008.

14 Charles Manby Smith, *The Working Man's Way in the World* (London: Cash, 1857), p. 188, www.open.ac.uk/Arts/reading/recorddetails.php?id=6582, accessed 5 January 2008.

15 Altick, *The English Common Reader*, p. 271.

16 Henry Mayhew, *London Labour and the London Poor* (London: Charles Griffin & Co., 1861), vol. 1, p. 416, www.open.ac.uk/Arts/reading/recorddetails.php?id=1314, accessed 7 January 2008.

17 Rose, *The Intellectual Life of the British Working Classes*, p. 111, www.open.ac.uk/Arts/reading/recorddetails2.php?id=2368, accessed 2 July 2009.

18 Helen Small, 'A Pulse of 124: Charles Dickens and a Pathology of the Mid-Victorian Reading Public', in James Raven, Helen Small and Naomi Tadmor (eds.), *The Practice and Representation of Reading in England* (Cambridge: Cambridge University Press, 1996), p. 273.

19 Anne Lohrli, *Household Words: A Weekly Journal 1850–1859 Conducted by Charles Dickens – Table of Contents, List of Contributors and Their Contributions Based on The Household Words Office Book in the Morris L. Parrish Collection of Victorian Novelists, Princeton University Library* (Toronto: University of Toronto Press, 1973), p. 33.

20 Rose, *The Intellectual Life of the British Working Classes*, p. 52, www.open.ac. uk/Arts/reading/recorddetails.php?id=1422, accessed 10 January 2008.

21 Virginia Woolf, 'Professions for Women', in *Collected Essays* (London: Hogarth Press, 1966), p. 285.

22 Muriel Spark, *John Masefield* (London, 1953; rev. edn 1992), p. 41, www.open. ac.uk/Arts/reading/recorddetails.php?id=5949, accessed 8 April 2008.

23 Philip Waller, *Writers, Readers, and Reputations: Literary Life in Britain 1870–1918* (Oxford: Oxford University Press, 2006), p. 365.

24 Gerald Massey, *Poetical Works*, ed. Samuel Smiles (1861), p. xi, www.open.ac. uk/Arts/reading/recorddetails.php?id=5379, accessed 5 January 2008.

25 From an unpublished memoir. Cited in Rose, *The Intellectual Life of the British Working Classes*, p. 69, www.open.ac.uk/Arts/reading/recorddetails.php?id= 1473, accessed 11 January 2008.

26 Alice Foley, *A Bolton Childhood* (Manchester: Manchester University Extra Mural Department and the Northwestern District of the Workers' Education Authority, 1979), p. 25.

27 V. S. Pritchett, *A Cab at the Door: An Autobiography: Early Years* (Chatto and Windus: London, 1968), p. 83, www.open.ac.uk/Arts/reading/recorddetails. php?id=2624, accessed 18 January 2008.

28 Rose, *The Intellectual Life of the British Working Classes*, pp. 87–8, www.open. ac.uk/Arts/reading/recorddetails.php?id=1823, accessed 18 January 2008.

29 *The Life of Florence Barclay*, by One of her Daughters (London and New York: Putnam's, 1921), p. 213.

3

ALISON BOOTH

Life writing

Although Edmund Gosse (1849–1928) was raised to follow a divine calling in the Plymouth Brethren and strove to be a great poet, he is most remembered today for the vivid memoir *Father and Son* (1907). His father Philip Gosse (1810–88) was a popular zoologist and fundamentalist pastor whose ill-received book, *Omphalos* (1857), sought to forestall the theory of evolution by reconciling fossil evidence with the account of creation in Genesis (it was published two years before Darwin's *Origin of Species*). *Father and Son* vividly evokes Edmund's childhood with his dying mother and grieving father. It is a narrative of self-development, capturing a characteristically Victorian loss of faith in established authorities. Edmund Gosse's own authority as a critic and biographer was challenged by the standards of the new era, but in the early twentieth century few people appeared more representative of the literary establishment. And for our purposes, Gosse effectively introduces the changing aims of life writing as it developed from 1830 to 1914.

In the year of Queen Victoria's death (1901) Gosse wrote a pivotal article, 'The Custom of Biography'.[1] It begins with a satire on Victorian funereal biographies: 'there must be a pall, two volumes of biography, and a few wreaths of elegant white flowers'; the life writing section of the library resembles a bourgeois cemetery (195). Gosse urges some ambitious young man to write the neglected 'History of Biography in England'. Only around 1750 did the English overcome their distrust of 'memoirs' as fiction or falsehood and gain an 'interest in the life of an individual … In the vast flight of locusts … how can one care to take up a solitary insect and study its legs and wings?' Few biographies of 'private people' could be written before 'the ages settled down to some personal comfort, and the movements of kings began to be regulated' in modern times (196). Gosse's metaphor of scientific examination of a natural specimen aligns his father's collecting of insects, birds or marine life in Newfoundland, Jamaica or Dorset with the son's own profession. Gosse is right that biography as we know it required both a clearer line between fact and fiction and a curiosity about individuals. Hagiography, or legends of saints, belonged with 'the rhetorical bondage of the Middle Ages' (196) – that is, actual details subordinated to ideal patterns to guide the audience. Though biographies continued to model their subjects for the 'edification' of readers (199–200), critics should value particular truths instead of ideal consequences.

As Gosse tries to sort biographies written by spin doctors from the genuine article, however, he also seeks to raise the status of biographers, who until the late eighteenth century had been footmen 'in the house of literature' (202–3). James Boswell in his 1791 *Life* of Samuel Johnson (1709–84), the biographer and creator of the monumental English dictionary, proved that the life of a great man of letters could be a literary undertaking in its own right. Yet the nineteenth century fell into a habit of amateur life writing. 'The Widow' (or someone else delegated by the family of the deceased) spread 'the worst of all the diseases of biography. She is the triumph of the unfittest' (205). Gosse's allusion to Darwinian natural selection suggests that many Victorian biographies were unfit to survive. The Widow (i.e. the Victorian biographer) creates a perfect effigy for Madame Tussaud's waxworks. 'She dwells on instances in which he was "a help to others," and a "wonderful example to the young" … carefully suppress[ing] all evidence of his being unlike other men, or having any oddities' so as not to 'scratch the flawless pinkness of his wax' (206).

Notice Gosse's assumptions about gender and class. The proper subject of biography, it seems, is a man who has some role in public life, while the biographer should be neither a lackey nor a devoted woman but a professional man of letters not unlike Gosse himself. He acknowledges a few well-proportioned Victorian biographies, including the *Dictionary of National Biography* edited by Leslie Stephen and Sidney Lee and the series of compact volumes, English Men of Letters, edited by John Morley (204). Yet most biographies since 1830 are encumbered by unedited documentary material and 'decency and reticence' (207): too much and yet not enough of the truth, too much or too little sense of the consequences.

To younger writers, Gosse was ironically associated with the vulgar sentimentality he sought to eliminate from life writing. In 1926, the novelist Virginia Woolf (1882–1941) described in her diary a literary lecture at which Gosse presided over rows 'of old stout widows whose husbands had been professors, beetle specialists doubtless'; Gosse behaved like a 'little dapper grocer' and seemed 'to be drawing round … them … the red plush curtains of respectability … Gosse will survive us all.'[2] Woolf dismisses Gosse as a servile Victorian, a survival of the unfit. Nevertheless, the Bloomsbury group of Woolf and her friends adopted Gosse's perspective on life writing. When in 'The New Biography' (1927) Woolf called for a fusion of 'rainbow' and 'granite', the art of fiction and the craft of fact, in concise lives expressive of personality and experience instead of public events,[3] she might be interpreting the principles that her father Leslie Stephen had laid down in 1885 for articles in the *Dictionary of National Biography*.

The Modernists dismissed the pomp and circumstance of many things Victorian, yet in life writing they continued Victorian tendencies. Woolf's friend Lytton Strachey echoed Gosse's mortuary metaphors for Victorian biography in the preface to his unflattering collective biography *Eminent Victorians* (1918): the 'two fat volumes … with their ill-digested masses of material … [and] tedious panegyric … as familiar as the *cortège* of the undertaker'.[4] Advocates of a new mode of life writing sought to detach the genres from their ancient functions of honouring the dead and modelling character – from consequences of all sorts. Yet they continued to ask life writing to instruct the reader. They insisted on the truth, no matter how it hurts. But not too much of the truth in undigested masses; there must be discrimination. Not every grocer should get his massive monument. Death and biographies are all too common.

Historical perspectives on the genres of life writing

These retrospectives on conventional life writing are revealing, though largely through what they magnify or overlook. Victorian 'lives' appeared in many varieties besides the corpulent two-volume 'life and letters'. And the Modernist models of life writing grew from Victorian roots. With greater distance, the achievements in Victorian life writing have stood out more clearly; after the Second World War, renewed interest in Victorian literature focused not only on the novel but on non-fiction prose. Yet there was relatively little discussion of the forms of life writing. In general, criticism of life writing has lagged behind that of other genres, just as Gosse suggested in 1901. If Victorian life writing was studied at all, the focus was on a few eminent subjects such as Thomas Carlyle, John Ruskin, John Henry Newman or John Stuart Mill. In the 1970s a new focus on autobiography emerged from France, influenced by the ground-breaking *Confessions* of Rousseau and by new theories of language and subjectivity. This turn to first-person narrative coincided with the rise of feminist studies in the 1980s and renewed historical investigation of Victorian culture, introducing life writing by women as well as men. It is true that such studies still tend to focus on a few select subjects, contributors to 'literature' more than science, politics or other fields, with Elizabeth Gaskell, Harriet Martineau or Margaret Oliphant standing in.[5]

Only recently has the concept of nineteenth-century life writing taken into account subjects of all social and economic positions and the formal variety of texts.[6] For a long time, critics of life writing, like those writers of 'lives' whom they recognized, were chiefly professional men of letters.

The culture of the Victorian period can scarcely be comprehended if its outpouring of 'lives' is overlooked; it has been called an 'age of biography'.[7] This chapter could resemble a stroll through an overcrowded cemetery (in Gosse's image), reading aloud row after row of names and dates. Instead, like other critics I select a few largely literary representatives, omitting or abridging many presences. As I argue, life writing is never a solitary or individual practice. Even my opening glance at Gosse has involved a network of associated figures. And this glance has perceived a bewildering formal variety: the family memoir, the diary, the dictionary, the collection of brief lives, the series of volumes, and more.

The scope of writings that represent real people is so vast that 'life writing' is the preferred term to cover 'autobiography and biography' and various subgenres. More significantly, 'life writing' avoids the false impression that it is easy to tell who is telling and who (or what) is the subject, no matter what the title or the 'byline'. Life writing always entails a network of positions (which may be occupied by more than one person): authors (or presenters, since this role often includes executors, illustrators, publishers, etc.), subjects (whether focused on one person or more) and readers (or audience, since again lives may be received in various media). The full-length monograph about a single person is outnumbered by other forms. Life writing continues to be a communal occasion not unlike a funeral oration, no matter how impious or individualist.

Inevitably, writing (*graphy*) the life (*bio*) of one's self (*auto*) impinges on the representations of others. Autobiography may be disguised as biography by using the third person or putting a proxy author's name on the title page, as Thomas Hardy wrote most of the words in the two-volume biography of Hardy (1928–30) 'by' his second wife, Florence. Autobiography also frequently masquerades as fiction; some classic Victorian novels take the form of first-person life writing, such as Charlotte Brontë's *Jane Eyre* (1847), first published as *Jane Eyre: An Autobiography* edited by Currer Bell. Elizabeth Barrett Browning transposed the life of a woman poet in the autobiographical epic poem *Aurora Leigh*, with a plot echoing that of *Jane Eyre*. (Autobiography and memoir frequently appear in poetry, as in Tennyson's *In Memoriam*.) Life writing in the third person may be self-reflexive, as when Walter Pater (1839–94), aesthetic critic and Oxford professor (and teacher of Oscar Wilde), experimented in fictional lives slightly distanced from his experience: *Imaginary Portraits* (1887) and *The Child in the House* (1894).

Self-portraiture emerges as well in third-person biographies, especially when quoting the subject's own words. Official or authorized biographies as well as family memorials resemble self-portraits of the famous person. Conversely, a presenter of someone else's life to some extent portrays him- or herself, though not necessarily as part of the action. Life writing triggers identification (sometimes through aversion); it has the power to make everyone involved, including the audience, begin to trade places. Although in this chapter I focus largely on prose 'literary lives' in book form, it is important to note other collaborative modes and media, including magazine articles, portrait galleries, names and statements on buildings and monuments, tours to homes and shrines, and even coins, stamps and souvenirs.

Before turning to some of the multifarious forms of nineteenth-century life writing, a bit of historical perspective will help. Written records of individuals have existed since the dawn of writing. Margaret Oliphant (1828–97), novelist, leading reviewer and autobiographer, pointed out that 'the art of biography is one of the oldest in the world … primitive story-telling is always a kind of biography'.[8] It was not until 1683 that John Dryden coined the term *biography* in his 'life' of the Greco-Roman bio-grapher Plutarch, defining it as 'the history of particular men's lives', and only in 1813 that a book-length study of the genre appeared.[9] *Autobio-graphy* is a more modern genre (the term itself is newly coined at the beginning of the nineteenth century). The preconditions for paying attention to the individual locust in the swarm – as Gosse would have it – included not only the formation of nations but also the mobility associated with capital-ism, exploration and empire; as people other than monks and scribes learned to write, their chronicles began to record personal experience of such movement. The Protestant Reformation with its emphasis on the Bible sponsored both literacy and printing, fostering conceptions of public and private life. The solitary act of reading contributed to a sense of unique interiority, a realm of experience known through introspection and revealed by confession or publication. Significantly, many early diaries, letters or memoirs had vanished until antiquarian societies printed them in the nine-teenth century, thus influencing Victorian life writing. Letters and diaries often have such a delayed release when later centuries take an interest in lives of the obscure; thus documentation of nineteenth-century women and workers is now being recovered.

Varieties of early life writing continued to be vital as the borders between fact and fiction were negotiated. Printers and booksellers blended legends, histories and memoirs in such hagiographies as Foxe's *Book of Martyrs*. What Max Weber called the Protestant ethic, middle-class values of self-discipline and investment, generated new stories of triumph over adversity rather than sin, adapting the quest of Christian in John Bunyan's *Pilgrim's Progress*. Recent lives, cross-checked with facts, in a sense came down to earth, admitting various kinds of 'worthies' – men and women of learning or good deeds. Not that the unworthy were neglected: in addition to confessional broadsides, the *Newgate Calendar* collected ostensibly true lives of criminals in London's Newgate prison; reaching a new edition in the 1820s, it was considered suitable reading to warn children against crime. The perennial interest in *error* or wandering, growing out of epic and picaresque traditions, informed new fiction as well as nonfiction. Daniel Defoe's novels intertwined first-person forms in the travels of *Robinson Crusoe* (1719), the confessions of *Moll Flanders* (1722). Similarly, Samuel Richardson adapted letters in *Pamela* (1740) and *Clarissa* (1747–8). Just as life writing influenced the origins of the novel, the nineteenth-century novel's realistic representation of characters, setting and action in turn shaped life writing.

In this brief chapter, I can only mention some strains of life writing that deserve more discussion. One of the oldest narrative forms, travels, thrived with the development of railroads and steam ships, as well as the postal service and the telegraph. One of the most famous explorers, Sir Richard Francis Burton (1821–90), infiltrated the Islamic pilgrimage to Mecca and Medina; in his *Personal Narrative* (1855), his trustworthy narrative persona conflicts with his act of passing as an Afghan doctor. Isabella Bird was no doubt the most famous woman traveller, whose feats of venture tourism on several continents became best-selling personal narratives; Mary Kingsley gained comparable renown for her travels in Africa, while a series of Englishwomen from Frances Trollope to Harriet Martineau found a wide audience in Britain for sharp observations of the (raw) state of society in America. It is not too much to say that life writing engineered a transformation of the known world in the nineteenth century, at least in that many voyages of exploration, archaeology and the sciences as well as tourism were financed by the sales of 'travels' upon return. Just as British colonialism provided occasions for life writing, so did political and religious movements at home and overseas, as in the much reprinted lives of founders of the Salvation Army or suffragettes, or the autobiography of Annie Besant, radical, advocate of birth control, and ultimately leader of the Theosophical Society in India.

The avalanche of records of individuals between 1830 and 1914 has confounded critics. In a landmark essay, 'Biography' (1832), Thomas Carlyle lamented the dearth of good biographies other than Boswell's *Life of Samuel Johnson*. In 1916, Waldo H. Dunn, a New England professor of English, in only the second book to be written about English biography, claimed that 'during the last half of the nineteenth century, no language surpassed English in the importance and number of biographies'.[10] Turbulent times generated eventful lives in which the end was far from the starting point – and hence highly narratable. A chorus in the great drama of Britain's industrial and imperial expansion, the publishing industry documented British lives as never before. Among many causes of this boom was the removal – between 1836 and 1861 – of limitations on the popular press (the so-called 'knowledge taxes') imposed in the aftermath of the French Revolution. Although the novel gained status during the century, nonfiction still dominated the stock of the lending libraries (only 20 per cent of books were novels as late as 1850).[11]

In general, the 'business' of life writing shifted towards the private, idiosyncratic and common. New disciplines of observing the natural and social worlds contributed to life writing, eventually leading to recognition of impulses and contradictions within the normal mind: psychology as terrain to be explored. The Gossean themes of faith and education featured as sources of the development of adult character and vocation. The noun 'career,' once referring to the course of a race or a planet, came in the early nineteenth century to refer to the shape of one's 'course or progress through life' (*Oxford English Dictionary*). Newly educated women and working-class men pursued newly opened careers, made something of themselves, and warranted memorials of success. Further, the norm of the self-determining public man met its counterpart in the sensitive child. Childhood might be said to have been the invention of nineteenth-century literature, and life writing was a key source of authentic early impressions. All such individual claims of recognition implied rights to greater freedoms. Life writing, rousing sympathies, was the main melody as well as the accompaniment of change in nineteenth-century Britain.

Lives en masse

Though individual rights may suggest autonomous narratives, life writing is a collaborative social exchange, as I have indicated, and many lives appeared in collective forms. The nineteenth century developed new ways to produce multiple lives much as it enhanced industrial production of other items. I have already mentioned long-standing varieties that came into their own in the nineteenth century: collective biography (*Eminent Victorians*), the biographical reference work (*Dictionary of National Biography*) and the series of volumes on a category of subjects (English Men of Letters). The illustrated 'gallery' of celebrities (with prose sketches) became a feature of periodicals and books in the 1830s, capitalizing on new engraving and printing techniques, for example in *Heath's Book of Beauty* (1833). *Fraser's Magazine*'s monthly series 'Gallery of Illustrious Literary Characters' (1830–8), short illustrated biographies of living writers, continued to be collected and reprinted until the end of the century.[12] The 'Gallery' had the appeal of a newspaper's 'society' page, implying fellowship in clubs and salons.

Then as now, the public was fascinated by privileged personalities, from royalty downward. When Victoria became queen in 1837, an apparatus of celebrity reproduced her image and story, from her strict private upbringing with a German governess to the night-time scene of the ministers kneeling before the young girl just roused from her sleep and about to become sovereign. Fashionable women seemed for once to dictate national politics: *The Book of the Boudoir; or, The Court of Queen Victoria*, W. and Edward Francis Finden's engravings of 'portraits of the British nobility', appeared in 1839, the same year as the 'Bedchamber Crisis', when Queen Victoria refused Sir Robert Peel's demand that she dismiss ladies in waiting who belonged to the opposing Whig party; her insistence on the privacy of the boudoir brought the return of Lord Melbourne's ministry. Prestige beyond the court produced a demand for 'lives', as women who edited the best-selling literary annuals or gift books themselves became the subject of biographical interest. Lady Blessington, who edited *Heath's Book of Beauty* and appeared in *Fraser's* 'Gallery', became the subject of Richard Robert Madden's three-volume *The Literary Life and Correspondence of the Countess of Blessington*.[13]

Far from being confined to fashionable circles, successful careers were the more remarkable when there were class disadvantages to overcome. Romantic poetry and fiction had cast a glamour over the rural poor, contributing to the celebrity of such poets as Robert Burns and James Hogg, whose differing careers were widely retold in shorter or longer biographies. Certain poor women of 'noble deeds' or pious service became popular subjects in collective biographies. Grace Darling (1815–42), a lighthouse keeper's daughter in the Farne Islands, rowed out in a perilous storm to rescue the survivors of the shipwrecked *SS Forfarshire* in 1838. This feat made her famous long after her death from tuberculosis in 1842, with biographical fiction, a poem by Wordsworth, folk ballads, at least fifteen appearances in collective biographies of women before 1940, and full-length biographies as recently as 1998; around the English-speaking world, young women who performed feats of rescue became known as the 'Grace Darling' of their region. Sarah Martin (1791–1843), literate, less dramatic and less famous than Darling, was the orphaned daughter of a tradesman who earned her living as a seamstress in Yarmouth, and who organized

Bible classes and other instruction in prisons and workhouses. She is all but forgotten today, and I know of only six existing copies of *A Brief Sketch of the Life of the Late Sarah Martin*.[14] Martin was reluctant to appear 'egotistical' in writing her own life, though others requested it; on her deathbed she revised the narrative to emphasize her youthful error and her reliance on divine agency rather than her own (36). The drab little volume, compiled by her executor Mrs Glasspoole, prints letters, an oration that she left to be read at her funeral, and other samples of her vivid writing. It is as if her sharp management, and her alert, honest warmth, cannot be submerged in the saintly type; Martin inspired as many as twenty versions of her life in collections up until 1900.

Some collections offered a cultural history for the educated, as in William Hazlitt's *The Spirit of the Age* (1825), a keynote for the century's tendency to attribute collective progress to the 'hero' or originating genius. The social canvas is more crowded and detailed in a sequel, Richard Henry [later Hengist] Horne's *The New Spirit of the Age* (1844), including groups of emerging writers, women and men. By mid-century a demand for information about the living exceeded the scope of Hazlitt or Horne, requiring alphabetical reference works anticipating *Who's Who* (1899). *Men of the Time* (1852) answered demand for sketches of leaders in various spheres; this had evolved into *Men and Women of the Time* by 1889. Contribution to life writing was one leading factor in whether one was listed in such a record.

Encyclopedic projects promulgated 'lives' as instruments of reform, whether religious, educational, economic or electoral. George Craik and others in 1830 illustrated *The Pursuit of Knowledge under Difficulties* with individual 'Memoirs' as guides to the rewards of good conduct. The Society for the Distribution of Useful Knowledge produced a biographical dictionary in 1842, and lives frequently appeared in such venues for the working classes as the *Penny Cyclopedia* and *Penny Magazine*. Producers of such literature were often just a few steps ahead in self-improvement – in middle-class status – than their readers. Like several comparable literary families, William and Mary Howitt participated in periodical life writing, editing of annuals and journals, and any other literary labour that would answer. William Howitt published series of topographical essays about English houses and landscapes, blending these in a new genre of auto/biographical anthology, *Homes and Haunts of the Most Eminent British Poets* (1847) – with hundreds of imitators in later decades. Quakers and later spiritualists, outsiders in the metropolitan, university-educated elite, the Howitts were nevertheless international literary personalities who surfaced in records of the period – including Horne and *Men of the Time*. Not so the servants who made the writers' soirées possible. A few documents of working-class lives have been preserved, most notably the diary of Hannah Cullwick (1833–1909), a literate domestic servant who clandestinely married her middle-class employer and fellow diarist, Arthur Munby.[15]

A standard form of advice literature was established in 1859 with Samuel Smiles's international best-seller, *Self-Help*. Smiles (1812–1904), a Scotsman raised in strict Calvinism and trained as a medical practitioner, shifted to a career in journalism and adopted the rationalist outlook of the Unitarians. *Self-Help*, which began as a lecture to a working-men's association, spins a web of exemplary careers of men, mostly working class, many in the textile industry, who through thrift, hard work and perseverance become wealthy industrialists. Any reader adopting these characteristics might grow up to become a subject, and perhaps to present further examples as Smiles and others did. It was the life writing of praiseworthy consequences more than harsh truths, and it dominated life writing until the end of the nineteenth century. It was accompanied by a small portion of negative models of crime or failure, along with 'eccentric biographies' that might be viewed as predecessors of illness, disability or recovery narratives today.[16] Towards the turn of the century, the taste for good people gave way to an increasing appetite for adventurers, scandalous women and widely errant tales.

Thomas Carlyle, hero worship and the 'ethics of biography'

If any one person represents life writing in the Victorian age – and it is very *Victorian* to personify cultural history – it is Thomas Carlyle (1795–1881). A historian and biographer who had the podium of public debate for decades, Carlyle subscribed to the idea that individuals can stand for the spirit of an age. It was Carlyle who, in the first lecture collected in *On Heroes, Hero-Worship, and the Heroic in History* (1841), wrote, 'the history of what man has accomplished in this world, is at bottom the History of the Great Men who have worked here'.[17] Although Carlyle undoubtedly shaped life writing in the period 1830–1914, he nevertheless serves as a warning against placing heroes on pedestals in a hall of history. The 'great man' model of historiography fell out of favour in the twentieth century. Before the nineteenth century was quite over, Carlyle himself was no longer so 'great' a man.

Ironically the sage was deposed by his own devotees, and largely by his own words and precepts. Carlyle had ordained James Anthony Froude as posthumous spokesman, and Froude dutifully issued a four-volume biography, *Thomas Carlyle* (1882–4), along with correspondence and a memoir of Carlyle's wife Jane Welsh Carlyle. Although this famous couple of Scottish intellectuals, at the centre of many networks of well-known Victorians in Chelsea and London, initially wrote many of the words reprinted in these volumes, Froude was held accountable for their self-revelation: that Thomas indulged his peevish ailments and phobias; that he harried Jane, whose talent was spent in maintaining the household and coping with her own illness while Carlyle flaunted his infatuation with Lady Harriet Ashburton; that he was impotent.[18] Margaret Oliphant denounced the exposure of the Carlyles: 'Can nothing be done to prevent this system of desecration?'[19] In 'The Ethics of Biography' (1883), Oliphant hails Carlyle as practitioner of traditional eulogistic biography in his lives of Cromwell and Frederick the Great. Deplorably, he was subjected instead to a new, 'cynical' or debunking mode. The modern way of indelicately revealing private life, if it had been applied to saints and heroes of earlier ages, would have extinguished 'every noble name', leaving 'the past as naked of all veneration or respect as is the present'.[20] Both Carlyle and Oliphant maintain that biography should improve the living community through habits of venerating the dead. Like most Victorians, they associate the private, the privileged and the sacred; the consequence of life writing, then, is conservative. Many Victorians denounced the publication of correspondence and family concerns. Yet the value of truth led life writing to be an influence of change and exposure of the privileged. By the early years of the twentieth century, the public was sure of its right to know the details.

Perhaps Carlyle – the hero as man of letters – was a victim of his own demand for the historical truth about lives. He was certainly contradictory on the worship of heroes. As early as 1833–4, in his fictional, satiric biography *Sartor Resartus*, he exhibited profound scepticism about coherent identity, heroic motives and the power of language. And his works reveal awareness that history is the aggregation of innumerable biographies of unknown people, and that any one life is impossible to record in full. In short, Carlyle epitomizes tensions in nineteenth-century life writing; as a biographical subject, he marks a turning point to modern codes of ethics; and philosophically he anticipates postmodern views of identity as a social construction rather than an innate essence.

The hero as men of letters

The story of nineteenth-century life writing is inseparable from the stories of the rising professions, in particular of authorship and academic disciplines.[21] Most of the Victorian 'lives' still prominent today present subjects who published something. Literature itself was a broader field than it has become in the era of college English courses; these notable men and women may have published life writing, descriptive essays, treatises on mathematics or art, travels, philosophy or history, as well as poetry, drama or fiction.

Alongside the growing field of collective biography, the two- or three-volume 'life and letters' of the great male author by an affiliated male writer, the Boswellian tradition, entered the nineteenth century with two international celebrities, Lord Byron, the libertine poet (1788–1824), and Sir Walter Scott, the upstanding historical novelist. Each had his first official posthumous 'life' written by a companion writer, and the result has become part of the canon, to the lasting renown of all concerned. Thomas Moore, Byron's executor, compiled *Letters and Journals of Lord Byron, with Notices of His Life* (1830); Moore (1779–1852) was a prominent Irish poet and musician, and friend of his subject, who, willingly or not, participated in burning the all-too-revealing memoirs that Byron left in his hands. A year after Moore died in his turn, his close friend Lord John Russell published *Memoirs, Journal, and Correspondence of Thomas Moore* (1853), and others wrote short biographies for new editions of Moore's poetry in later decades. (The controversy of Byron's incestuous relationship with his half-sister Augusta, his miserable marriage, and his notorious affairs and debts continued to rage, stirred up by Harriet Beecher Stowe, the celebrated author of *Uncle Tom's Cabin*, in *Lady Byron Vindicated* (1870).) A similar nest of life writing – though not of scandal – surrounds Scott. John Gibson Lockhart (1794–1854), active in the influential Edinburgh magazine *Blackwood's* (and held responsible for its attacks on the Romantic poets), wrote the definitive biography of his father-in-law, likewise a Scotsman trained in the law: *Memoirs of the Life of Sir Walter Scott, Bart.* (1837–8). Another prolific Scots writer, Andrew Lang, known today as a pioneering folklorist, issued the *Life and Letters of J. G. Lockhart* in 1897. These intertwined memorials set the standard for Carlyle's lives (those he wrote and those about him) and many others. In 1892, the critic George Saintsbury upheld the ideal biography as the meeting of two (literary) men of genius, and hence a small canon of good biographies: 'Boswell's *Johnson*, Moore's *Byron*, Lockhart's *Scott*, Carlyle's *Sterling* ... and ... Trevelyan's *Macaulay*' – the latter the two-volume *Life and Letters* (1876) of the great Whig historian Thomas Babington Macaulay by his nephew, Sir George Otto Trevelyan, author and politician.[22] True enough, these are major achievements in life writing, but they form a coterie gallery rather than individual monuments. The canon of Victorian biographies creates a hero as *men* of letters, alerting us to the networking of all life writing. And even the monument to the eminent man showed cracks, hints that a self is an ongoing negotiation.

Lives of profession: autobiographies

Autobiographies would seem to be less multiple. At the time they are written, autobiographies appear to be the direct expression of a living person who knows more than anyone else about the subject. Of course it must be a selective story – as the life writer often admits – while it concerns much beyond the name on the title page: other people, public issues, occupations and roles. The nineteenth century produced memorable autobiographies as never before, responding to transformations in types of experience.

Few autobiographies ever have received more attention than the *Auto-biography* of John Stuart Mill (1873). Yet the philosopher of liberalism gave a rather muted sales pitch for 'a memorial of so uneventful a life as mine'. Unlike a twenty-first-century autobiographer, Mill avoids intimacy with his reader. Instead of curious details about himself, he exhibits an example of modern education; those not interested in this theme need read no further. Like Gosse, Mill acquaints the public with a remarkable father whose son became an experiment in upbringing according to irreconcilable principles – in Mill's case, Utilitarianism and Romanticism. James Mill, disciple of Jeremy Bentham, pressed his son through a rationalist education, producing a prodigy (learning Greek from the age of three) who contributed to political discourse in his twenties. A turning point comes dramatically at chapter 5, 'A Crisis in My Mental History': one day, in 'a dull state of nerves' resembling that of 'converts to Methodism ... when smitten by their first "conviction of sin"', he asked himself whether the achievement of his goals for reform would bring him happiness. 'And an irrepressible self-consciousness distinctly answered, "No!" At this ... the whole foundation on which my life was constructed fell down ... I seemed to have nothing left to live for' (ch. 5). Mill's dialogue of the soul drives him to seek solace in rereading literature. William Wordsworth's poetry, with its response to nature, helps to restore him whereas Byron's poetry only worsens his depression. Interestingly, Mill writes as if his childhood were a duet with his father (his mother and siblings are scarcely mentioned), whereas his account of adulthood reveals a symbiosis with Harriet Taylor, whom he loved for twenty-one years before she, newly widowed, could marry him in 1851. For generations, experts on Mill expressed dismay that he credited the love of his life with some of his best insights in *On Liberty* and *The Subjection of Women*. In his respect for women's intellects, education and rights – in his willingness to concede shared inquiry rather than unique genius – Mill was an exception, though not alone in reforming circles.

Mill's life of unconversion and conversion has counterparts in other self-authored career narratives of the period, such as John Henry Newman's

Apologia pro Vita Sua (1864). Cardinal Newman had been part of a religious revival at Oxford University (an arm of the Church of England), but in the 1840s he converted to Catholicism – deeply threatening in light of England's history of anti-Catholic wars. Well after leaving the university and becoming a cardinal, Newman wrote the autobiography in the form of a public quarrel as well as a contribution to theology and institutional history. Charles Kingsley has attacked Newman, thereby attacking Catholicism, as treacherous, according to 'the common English notion of Roman casuists and confessors' (ch. 1). Newman's 'apology' or defence avers that he is the soul of reasonable truth; 'I have no romantic story to tell … it is my duty to tell things as they took place' (part iv). His own clear-minded probity – he is neither the 'knave' nor the 'fool' Kingsley says he must be – fuses with Catholicism itself. To submerge personality in an institution may seem to readers today to evade autobiography's task of self-understanding, but Newman makes his representative role the strongest argument on the side of his church.

Although the novelist – and Post Office official – Anthony Trollope contended less with ideological affiliations than Gosse, Mill or Newman, his posthumous autobiography (1883) threatened a different sort of belief. Ironically, he wrote this engaging, even-keeled book in part to gain respect for the novelist's vocation, but he revealed it instead as the 'trade' that his own mother had resorted to as a fifty-year-old with children and a ne'er-do-well husband. (The second chapter of the autobiography is a portrait of Frances Trollope, beginning with a rediscovered bundle of love letters between his mother and father.) Although Carlyle calls writers of fiction liars and fools, they are actually preachers who must simultaneously charm their audience (ch. 12). But this ministry is also a business. Serving the Post Office, Trollope travelled many hours on the new railways: 'to make a profitable business out of my writing … I made for myself a little tablet, and found after a few days' exercise that I could write as quickly in a railway-carriage as I could at my desk' (ch. vi). Revealing that he struck hard bargains with publishers and measured his daily output of words, Trollope demystified genius too much. It took decades for his reputation as a major novelist to recover.

One of the most intimate and beautiful autobiographies, John Ruskin's *Praeterita* (1885–9) ('praeterita' means 'of things past'), sets aside the usual themes of a life, from career to relationships. He reminisces 'at ease … of what it gives me joy to remember, at any length I like … passing in total silence things which I have no pleasure in reviewing' ('Preface'). Ruskin (1819–1900), the only child of a wine merchant, whose mother wished to dedicate him to the Church, instead dedicated himself to European art and architecture. His thunderous books denounced the conventional taste and unethical materialism of industrial Britain, and sparked an international revival of Gothic designs and handicrafts still felt today. Yet he could never reconcile his ideal of woman with an accessible, adult partner; his six-year marriage to his cousin Effie Gray was unconsummated and annulled, and he later became obsessed with a little girl, Rose La Touche, thirty years younger than he. Written in lucid intervals as he was going insane, his autobiography resembles spiritual exercises in memory. *Praeterita* directly influenced the French Modernist Marcel Proust in his autobiographical cycle of novels *In Search of Lost Time*.

Other Victorian self-portraits create indelible impressions. I will simply mention two that are still read because of their contributions to new fields: the lives of Charles Darwin (1809–82) and Harriet Martineau (1802–76). Part of Darwin's and Martineau's initial renown was based on fact-finding travels only indirectly autobiographical: Darwin's record of his experiences in the Galapagos, *The Voyage of the Beagle* (1839), and Martineau's *Society in America* (1837), with its observations of democracy and slavery. The naturalist and the social scientist both challenged Victorian beliefs in later works: Darwin's *The Origin of Species* and Martineau's defences of atheism and mesmerism. Posthumously published 'lives' served as interpretive guides to these controversial careers. Martineau prepared her two-volume *Autobiography* (1877) in 1855, convinced that she would die soon; it is a rare contribution to the classic form by a woman, and offers a compelling sense of a suffering childhood and of Martineau's unvarnished criticism of family and friends. Like Martineau's remains, Darwin's were edited with additional material when finally published, though Darwin's were more third- than first-person: *The Life and Letters of Charles Darwin, including an Autobiographical Chapter* (1887).

The emergence of women's lives

Martineau's full-fledged 'autobiography' was a rarity. Although literate women had now and then left records, only in the mid-eighteenth century did third-person lives of women other than saints, rulers or companions of great men begin to appear, with a marked increase after 1830. Anna Jameson (1794–1860), like Lady Blessington one of *Fraser's* circle of literary women, launched her career with an anonymous fictional travel memoir, *The Diary of an Ennuyée*,[23] a sort of prose remake of Byron's *Childe Harold's Pilgrimage* uniting European tourism with a disillusioned spiritual journey. The 'ennuyée' or alienated young woman dies of a broken heart in the end; readers were dismayed when it was learned that the author was alive. The unhappily married daughter of an Irish portrait painter, Jameson became an acclaimed authority on European art, while much of her work took the form of lives of women, from *Memoirs of the Loves of the Poets* (1829) to *Memoirs of Celebrated Female Sovereigns* (1832) to *Characteristics of Women*, later known as *Shakespeare's Heroines* (1832). (Biographies of fictional characters became a minor industry.) When Jameson died, her niece Gerardine Macpherson prepared *Memoirs of the Life of Anna Jameson* (1878), which was finally brought to press after Macpherson's early death by a mutual friend, Margaret Oliphant. Jameson had sponsored initiatives for women's opportunities that shaped pioneering careers, including those of Barbara Bodichon and Florence Nightingale.

One of the finest biographies published in the nineteenth century, by long-standing acclaim, was *The Life of Charlotte Brontë* by Elizabeth Gaskell (1857). Both presenter and subject, friends, were famous women novelists from the North of England who married clergymen. *Jane Eyre* (with its autobiographical subtitle) had stirred rumours that 'Currer Bell' had been in love with a married man; perhaps she had been a governess in the household of William Makepeace Thackeray, to whom Brontë dedicated the third edition of her novel without knowing that he had an insane wife. The false rumours and the general opinion that the Brontës' novels were coarse led Brontë's father to ask Gaskell to improve the record. Gaskell's two-volume text divides Charlotte Brontë into two figures, the good domestic woman and the inspired writer. It reproduces so much of Brontë's correspondence that at times it reads like autobiography. Gaskell creates a novelistic sense of the Yorkshire environment and the pinched life of the isolated clergyman's daughter who was also a genius. Like Gaskell's novels, the biography created a scandal. Brontë had indeed been in (unrequited) love with a married man, her teacher in Belgium. Gaskell hides this humiliating episode by playing up Charlotte's brother Branwell's affair with Mrs Robinson in the household where he served as tutor. For her attack on Mrs Robinson and on the director of the school that the little Brontë sisters attended – the original of 'Lowood' in *Jane Eyre* – Gaskell and her publishers faced lawsuits, and a revised edition was necessary. This one biography generated countless other fictional and factual accounts of the gifted and blighted Brontë family and brought pilgrims to their home in Haworth.

Harriet Martineau was also a literary friend of Charlotte Brontë who wrote a key obituary of the novelist in 1855, later collected in *Biographical Sketches* (1869). She and Charlotte Brontë had become estranged when Martineau criticized the all-consuming passion in Brontë's last novel, *Villette*; 'her heroines love too readily … after a fashion which their female readers may resent'.[24] Martineau was very severe on women who showed any relish for public recognition, but Brontë impressed her as suitably impervious to flattery. Although 'morbidly sensitive', 'in her high vocation she had, in addition to the deep intuitions of a gifted woman, the strength of a man, the patience of a hero and the conscientiousness of a saint' (45). Martineau can conceive of Brontë's private and public life as a combination of gendered virtues rather than a schism.

Other memorable lives of women tend to focus on interrelations among writers, the usual divisions between private and public personae widened by the expectations of gender. The eminent novelist George Eliot (1819–80) was included (with a handful of other women) in Morley's English Men of Letters series – a biography by none other than Leslie Stephen, who also wrote the entry on Mary Ann Cross published in his *Dictionary of National Biography* in 1888.[25] These were narratives about the same woman; the married name and the pseudonym were symptomatic of the perceived contradiction between authorship and a conventional woman's life. In *George Eliot*, Stephen wrote in praise: 'no novelist of note ever possessed a wider intellectual culture. With all her knowledge, she attended to the ordinary feminine duties' (197). Marian Evans had been ostracized because she lived with a married man, the writer and critic George Henry Lewes (author of a *Biographical History of Philosophy* and a classic biography of Goethe). She published some of the greatest novels of the nineteenth century, and after Lewes's death in 1878 she married a much younger man, John Walter Cross. After her death in 1880, Cross assembled *George Eliot's Life as Related in Her Letters and Journals*, hailed as 'to all intents an autobiography'.[26] The problem was that most readers did not like the woman in her own voice, preferring the great author of the novels. Alice James (1848–92), talented invalid sister of the novelist Henry James and the philosopher William James, wrote in the diary she began in England in 1889 (published posthumously) that Eliot's *Life* gave an 'impression … of mildew, or some morbid growth – a fungus of a pendulous shape'.[27] Alice James was disillusioned that the writer of masterpieces could be prone to hypochondria and depression. James ought to have questioned whether Cross's editing and Eliot's self-censorship presented the entire story.

Edith Simcox, a close associate of Eliot and Lewes, recognized Cross's *Life* as management of his wife's reputation; Simcox was also a keeper of that flame. The *Life* did not 'give a very true or complete picture … it gives the world as much as it deserves and is not likely to misuse'.[28] Simcox's journal, written from 1876 to 1900 without the prospect of publication, tells the story of a cause – her work running a shirt-making co-operative to employ poor women – and of an unrequited love. Most of her diary records visits and conversations with or about George Eliot amid her devotees: 'There is no one who loved Her so well for whom She cared so little' as Simcox (221). Simcox is an unacknowledged Boswell, devoted, jealous, humble. The diary was long lost, and only published in full in 1998 because of continuing interest in George Eliot as well as a desire to retrieve the lives of Victorian women.

Margaret Oliphant shared some of Alice James's dismay in reading Eliot's *Life*: 'she must have been a dull woman with a great genius distinct from herself'.[29] But whereas James is appalled by a self-pitying fellow invalid, Oliphant is troubled by a triumphant fellow novelist. The fragments of Oliphant's autobiography, rearranged and edited by nieces, her companions and assistants, had been prompted by different occasions: the death of her eldest child, Maggie, in 1864; the hope of leaving a memoir to her sons, whom she outlived; the 'involuntary confession' provoked by reading Eliot's enviable *Life* (and recollection of Trollope's autobiography, which she reviewed sympathetically in 1883). Widowed early, Oliphant produced some 120 books. Writing was a natural 'pleasure … like talking or breathing' (14); she kept at her 'trade' to support an extended family, and laughed off 'compliments about my industry' with a bit of the Scots pride of Mrs Carlyle (15). 'Should I have done better if I had been kept, like [George Eliot], in a mental greenhouse and taken care of?' (14–15). If she had written less, she might have 'done better work' (16). But perhaps she had never had the requisite genius. 'No one even will mention me in the same breath with George Eliot.' 'I wonder if I will ever have time to put a few autobiographical bits down before I die. I am in very little danger of having my life written' (16–17). As now printed, these are ironic statements. She is often mentioned in comparison with Eliot; Oliphant has become the subject of biographies and studies as one of the major Victorian novelists as well as life writers. And this entry is followed a week later, on 8 February 1885, by her first organized 'try at the autobiography' (18). Oliphant wished to protect Carlyle from public scrutiny as Lewes and Cross protected Eliot or Gaskell defended Brontë, all in the effort to reconcile the flawed private person with the heroic public persona. But in a sense Oliphant's autobiography, with its powerful feeling and honest self-questioning, has restored her reputation as a heroic woman of letters.

The story of life writing 1830–1914 risks being the story of everything in the period, as the period revealed that everyone has a life to tell. I have suggested that life writing not only documented change but promoted it. At the same time it can retard development, in spirit and form deeply conservative – the pieties that made the Modernists itch to smash the church window. Quite literally, life writing is late, allowing earlier times to live on. Hidden letters and diaries may wait centuries, while memoirs often wait most of a lifetime to be recorded. Up until the First World War, reminiscences about Victorian childhoods or the eminent people one met at London parties in the eighties continued to be published. The general trends in the matter of life writing – from consequences to truth, from public to private, from high rank to low – permitted 'psychobiography' and tell-all confessions in the twentieth century that lead us to the vanishing threshold of privacy in talk show confessionals, blogs, and other means of broadcasting instantaneous experience. The push towards individual recognition remains less individual than it appears, however, as social networking affirms mutual likenesses (identity as a linked list of media favourites and 'friends'). The examples of life writing 1830–1914 signal that the subject is never solitary, never unitary, even in the classic monograph on the eminent man. The exposure of flaws in authorities or celebrities today is only an intensification in a long-standing relish for anti-heroes and grotesques. True, the new online *Oxford Dictionary of National Biography* (2004), the most delightful of databases, includes criminals and other figures once thought unfit to survive in the national mausoleum. Life writing will flourish with new technologies and new visions of identity and society. It will always put names and faces on the spirit of the age.

Notes

1 Edmund Gosse, 'The Custom of Biography', *Anglo-Saxon Review*, 8 (March 1901), pp. 195–208. Further citations appear parenthetically in the text.

2 Virginia Woolf, Saturday, 30 October 1926, in *The Diary of Virginia Woolf*, ed. Anne Olivier Bell, 5 vols. (New York: Harcourt Brace Jovanovich, 1980), vol. III, p. 115. The lecturer on this occasion, Woolf's aristocratic lover Vita Sackville-West, was promoting the modern poetry of T. S. Eliot, for which Gosse had no appreciation.

3 Virginia Woolf, 'The New Biography', *New York Herald Tribune* (30 October 1927), repr. in *The Essays of Virginia Woolf*, ed. Andrew McNeillie, 4 vols. (London: Hogarth, 1994), vol. IV, pp. 473–80.

4 Lytton Strachey, *Eminent Victorians* (1918; New York: Penguin, 1986), p. 10.

5 See for example George P. Landow (ed.), *Approaches to Victorian Autobiography* (Athens, Ohio: Ohio University Press, 1979); Linda H. Peterson, *Victorian Autobiography* (New Haven: Yale University Press, 1986).

6 See for example David Amigoni (ed.), *Life Writing and Victorian Culture* (Aldershot: Ashgate, 2006).

7 Richard D. Altick, *Lives and Letters* (New York: Knopf, 1966), pp. 77–8, 87–8. Virginia Woolf, *A Room of One's Own* (1929; repr. New York: Harcourt, 2005), p. 85.

8 Margaret Oliphant, 'The Ethics of Biography', *Contemporary Review*, 44 (July 1883), pp. 76–93; repr. in Ira Bruce Nadel (ed.), *Victorian Biography* (New York and London: Garland, 1986), p. 76.

9 See *Oxford English Dictionary*; Waldo H. Dunn, *English Biography* (London: Dent, 1916), p. xii. James Field Stanfield, *An Essay on the Study and Composition of Biography* (Sunderland: Printed by G. Garbutt, 1813).

10 Dunn, *English Biography*, pp. 250–1.

11 Simon Eliot, 'Some Trends in British Book Publishing, 1800–1914', in John O. Jordan and Robert L. Patten (eds.), *Literature in the Marketplace* (Cambridge: Cambridge University Press, 2003), pp. 47, 58.

12 William Bates (ed.), *The Maclise Portrait Gallery of Illustrious Literary Characters* (London: Chatto and Windus, 1898). See Alison Booth, 'Men and Women of the Time: Victorian Prosopographies', in Amigoni (ed.), *Life Writing and Victorian Culture*, pp. 41–66.

13 Richard Robert Madden, *The Literary Life and Correspondence of the Countess of Blessington* (London: Newby, 1855).

14 *A Brief Sketch of the Life of the Late Sarah Martin* (London: Religious Tract Society, 1847).

15 *The Diaries of Hannah Cullwick* (London: Virago, 1984). See Julia Swindells, *Victorian Writing and Working Women: The Other Side of Silence* (Oxford: Polity, 1985); John Burnett, *Useful Toil: Autobiographies of Working People from the 1820s to the 1920s* (London: Allen Lane, 1974).

16 James Gregory, 'Eccentric Biography and the Victorians', *Biography*, 30 (Summer 2007), pp. 342–76.

17 Thomas Carlyle, 'Lecture I: The Hero as Divinity [1840]', in *On Heroes, Hero-Worship, and the Heroic in History* (Project Gutenberg, November 1997), www.gutenberg.org/dirs/etext97/heros10.txt, accessed 23 April 2008. See also The Literature Network, www.online-literature.com/thomas-carlyle/heroes-and-hero-worship/1/, accessed 23 April 2008.

18 Trev Lynn Broughton, *Men of Letters, Writing Lives* (London: Routledge, 1999).

19 Oliphant, 'The Ethics of Biography', p. 93.

20 *Ibid.* p. 77.

21 David Amigoni, *Victorian Biography* (London: Harvester Wheatsheaf, 1993). See also chapters 1 and 4 in this volume.

22 George Saintsbury, 'Some Great Biographies', *Macmillan's Magazine*, 66 (June 1892), p. 97.

23 Anna Jameson, *The Diary of an Ennuyée* (London: Colburn, 1826).

24 Harriet Martineau, *Biographical Sketches* (London: Leypoldt and Holt, 1869), pp. 45–6. The collection reprints periodical obituaries of literary and political figures as well as writers (including Anna Jameson and John G. Lockhart).

25 Leslie Stephen, *George Eliot* (English Men of Letters, London and New York: Macmillan, 1902). Further references appear parenthetically.

26 'Cross's *Life of George Eliot*', *New York Times* (16 November 1884), p. 4. John Walter Cross, *George Eliot's Life*, 3 vols. (New York: Harper; Edinburgh: Blackwood, 1885).

27 *The Diary of Alice James*, ed. Leon Edel (New York: Library of America, 1984), p. 1010, quoted in Rosemarie Bodenheimer, *The Real Life of Mary Ann Evans: George Eliot, Her Letters and Fiction* (Ithaca, NY: Cornell University Press, 1994), pp. 1–2. Four copies of Alice James's journal were printed posthumously (Cambridge, Mass.: John Wilson, 1894), and it was published in Anna Robeson

Brown Burr, *Alice James, Her Brothers – Her Journal* (New York: Dodd, Mead, 1934).

28 Entries on 31 January and 3 February 1885, in Edith J. Simcox, *Autobiography of a Shirtmaker*; repr. in Constance M. Fulmer and Margaret E. Barfield (eds.), *A Monument to the Memory of George Eliot* (New York: Garland, 1998), p. 211.

29 See Deirdre D'Albertis, 'The Domestic Drone: Margaret Oliphant and a Political History of the Novel', *Studies in English Literature*, 37, 4 (1997), pp. 805–29. *The Autobiography of Margaret Oliphant: The Complete Text*, ed. Elisabeth Jay (Oxford: Oxford University Press, 1990), p. 17. Further references appear in the text.

4

JOANNE SHATTOCK

The culture of criticism

> Perhaps there is no single feature of the English literary history of the nineteenth century, not even the enormous popularisation and multiplication of the novel, which is so distinctive and characteristic as the development in it of periodical literature . . . Very large numbers of the best as well as of the worst novels themselves have originally appeared in periodicals; not a very small proportion of the most noteworthy nineteenth-century poetry has had the same origin; it may also be said that all the best work in essay, whether critical, meditative or miscellaneous, has thus been ushered into the world . . . and though there is still a certain conventional decency in apologising for reprints from periodicals, it is quite certain that, had such reprints not taken place, more than half the most valuable books of the age in some departments, and a considerable minority of the most valuable in others, would never have appeared as books at all.

This passage from George Saintsbury's 1896 *History of Nineteenth-Century Literature* highlights one of the most remarkable publishing phenomena of the period 1830–1914, the proliferation and predominance of the periodical press. As he notes, many novels were first published in magazines and then issued in volume format. Individual poems first appeared in reviews and magazines. Many influential prose works were published serially, along with scholarly work in emerging academic disciplines.

Saintsbury was well qualified to comment. Until his recent appointment to the Regius Chair of English at the University of Edinburgh in 1895 he had spent nearly a quarter of a century as a journalist, writing and reviewing with frenetic energy for *Macmillan's Magazine*, and the *Fortnightly*, the *Academy* and the *Saturday* reviews among others, covering contemporary English and French literature as well as current politics. He once claimed he could earn on average £3 10s for an evening's reading and a morning's writing.[1]

His comment is simultaneously celebratory and somewhat apologetic. He celebrates the diversity and range of the periodical press but at the same time emphasizes its status as a transitional if not a transitory medium. Had reprints from periodicals not taken place, 'more than half the most valuable books of the age' would never have been published. He is here, I take it, endorsing what Lee Erickson has called 'the intellectual hierarchy of written formats' – books, magazines, newspapers – which assumed its present form in the early nineteenth century.[2]

In *The Economy of Literary Form* Erickson argues that the essay was *the* dominant literary form in the 1830s and 1840s, and the periodical the dominant publishing format. He takes as his starting point the decline in the publishing of poetry at the end of the Romantic period, and the rise of the periodical. From 1802 through to the 1830s, quarterly reviews like the *Edinburgh*, the *Quarterly* and the *Westminster*, and their younger competitors and imitators, and magazines like *Blackwood's*, *Fraser's*, the *New Monthly*, the *Metropolitan* and *Tait's Edinburgh Magazine* had proved commercially so successful for the publishers who promoted them that other publishing houses followed suit. One source estimated that between the years 1815 and 1832 more than twenty new journals were established.[3] The number was possibly even higher. The genre which developed and flourished with the proliferation of reviews and magazines was the essay.

Such was the circulation of these periodicals amongst the growing middle-class readership, Erickson argues, that an essay in any major periodical could be guaranteed a wider circulation in this format than could be expected by collecting and reprinting them in volume form. There is evidence, he suggests, that readers preferred reading essays in a periodical context, combined, as they were, with articles on other subjects, and often with serialized fiction, poetry, and political news and analysis.[4]

The 'profession' of letters

The writing of essays paid well, and formed the staple of what was increasingly coming to be regarded as a professional writing life. G. H. Lewes, in an article on 'The Condition of Authors in England, Germany and France' in *Fraser's Magazine* for March 1847, declared that 'Literature has become a profession. It is a means of subsistence, almost as certain as the bar or the church.' 'The real cause', he argued, was 'the excellence and abundance of periodical literature'. In England a journalist of 'ordinary ability' could hope to earn between £200 and £1,000 a year, a sum beyond the expectation of his counterparts in Germany and France where payments for articles were much smaller, and where the range of weekly, monthly and quarterly publications open to the English journalist did not exist.[5]

'Professional' was a term which would have been incomprehensible to writers for the periodical press in the earlier decades of the nineteenth century. To the contrary, the early contributors to the *Edinburgh* and *Quarterly* reviews prided themselves on their amateur status. Francis Jeffrey's determination, in 1802, that the writers for the *Edinburgh* should be 'all gentlemen and no pay' gave way to his colleague Sydney Smith's argument that the best contributions would be secured through generous payments. Notwithstanding the financial rewards, the early reviewers for the *Edinburgh* and the *Quarterly* on the whole regarded writing for reviews as a gentlemanly occupation. The same was not true of writing for the newspaper press, which from the outset carried with it tradesman-like connotations.

Patrick Leary has described the first phase of *Fraser's Magazine for Town and Country*, between its establishment in 1830 and the point when James Fraser relinquished the proprietorship in 1847, as 'standing astride a fault line in conceptions of what constitutes the literary life'.[6] In the early years its contributors, who included Thackeray, Carlyle, James Hogg, John Galt and Lewes, experienced the precarious existence of all 'literary workmen' of the day, offering an article to a succession of editors in the hope that one of them would accept it, or waiting for an invitation to write for a particular publication. None of the reviews or magazines employed writers on a full-time basis. Even editors were uncertain of an adequate stipend. Throughout the 1840s there was an increasing concern that writers were denied the security and respectability of a professional life.

It was precisely this concern that Lewes's article was addressing. In his view it *was* now possible for a writer to earn a living by reviewing, writing articles, essays and encyclopedia entries, compiling anthologies, editing the works of the past, and contributing to various book series. More importantly, this way of life was now regarded as socially acceptable.

The residual anxiety of the first generation of reviewers – Jeffrey and his colleagues in the *Edinburgh*, and their counterparts John Gibson Lockhart, Robert Southey and Walter Scott of the *Quarterly* – that editing or writing for a quarterly review or a monthly magazine might not quite be the role of a gentleman gave way to a mid-Victorian assumption that writing for the periodical press was both respectable and adequately paid. The new mood was epitomized by a modern, self-confident generation of reviewers, men like Lewes, David Masson, Walter Bagehot, John Morley, Leslie Stephen and Richard Holt Hutton, most of them middle class and university educated. It included a small number of women writers – among them Marian Evans, Harriet Martineau, Margaret Oliphant – for whom book reviewing provided an essential and regular source of income.

Christopher Kent has termed the 'higher journalism', represented by mid-century reviews like the *Fortnightly*, the *Contemporary*, the *Nineteenth Century*, the *Saturday* and the *Academy*, as 'one of the most characteristic cultural manifestations of nineteenth-century Britain'. Increasing numbers of graduates, looking for opportunities beyond the traditional ones of the law, the church and the universities, or in combination with them, seized the opportunities provided by the newly established periodicals of the 1850s and 1860s. As a result, the same 'profession-consciousness',[7] as Kent has termed it, attached itself to the world of reviewing as to other professional occupations. Literary critics – and the term was now being used self-consciously in preference to 'reviewers' – began to see themselves as professionals, and the production of literary criticism as a professional as opposed to an amateur occupation.

David Masson's *Memories of London in the 'Forties* (1908) provides an insight into the early career of the new-style, mid-Victorian 'man of letters'. Born in Aberdeen, the son of a stonemason, Masson's entry into metropolitan literary circles was initially through his fellow Scot Carlyle, on whom he paid the obligatory call when visiting London in 1844. Carlyle offered an introduction to the proprietor of *Fraser's Magazine*, who promptly accepted an article by Masson and published it within a period of six weeks.[8]

G. H. Lewes proved to be another important contact, introducing Masson to a literary club at which he met T. K. Hervey, the editor of the *Athenaeum*. Hervey's advice to the novice was unequivocal: 'When I send you a book, say exactly what you think of it and if you don't like it, if you think it bad, say so – even if it should be my own brother's.' The consequence was, Masson recounted, 'that I became a regular contributor to "The Athenaeum", hardly a week passing in which I did not have something or other in that paper so long as T. K. Hervey continued to be editor, after which time I did little or nothing for it'.[9] Such were the conditions of editorial patronage.

During the same visit to London in 1844 Masson met George Lillie Craik, who was then involved with the publishing ventures of the popular educational publisher Charles Knight. Craik introduced him in turn to the Scottish publishers William and Robert Chambers, and as a result Masson began to write for *Chambers's Edinburgh Journal*, and later for *Papers for the People*.

It was through these important early contacts that Masson's career as a reviewer and critic began. He went on to write for the *British Quarterly* and *North British* reviews. He succeeded Arthur Hugh Clough in the chair of English at University College London and wrote a biography of Milton. At the invitation of his publisher Alexander Macmillan he became the first editor of *Macmillan's Magazine* in 1859 and later the editor of the *Reader*, a literary weekly also published by Macmillan. In 1865 he was appointed professor of Rhetoric and English Literature at the University of Edinburgh, from where he continued to write for the periodical press. Masson's career, like Saintsbury's, who succeeded him, is a good example of what Grevel

Lindop has termed the 'fluid' frontier which existed in Scotland between the academic and journalistic worlds, where authors, editors, publishers and professors easily exchanged roles.[10] The same was true, although perhaps less obvious, in England and in Ireland, supporting Kent's point about the hybrid careers of many mid-Victorian men of letters.

Equally impressive and more typical of the metropolitan literary world was the career of G. H. Lewes. Unlike many of his colleagues he was not a 'university man', but voraciously self-educated. He spent some of his formative years in France, where he became fluent in the language, and acquired an intense enthusiasm for and knowledge of French literature and culture. At the time of writing his 1847 article for *Fraser's* and his meeting with David Masson, he had contributed to *Bentley's Miscellany*, *Blackwood's*, the *British and Foreign*, the *British Quarterly*, the *Edinburgh*, the *Westminster* and the *Foreign Quarterly* reviews, and the *Monthly Chronicle*. He would later add the *Leader*, the *Cornhill*, the *Fortnightly* and the *Pall Mall Gazette* to his list. At one point, he told fellow journalist and reviewer Francis Espinasse, he had had an article in every major publication 'except the d – d old Quarterly'.[11] When he and Thornton Hunt established the weekly *Leader* in 1850, Carlyle, once suspicious of Lewes, dubbed him 'the Prince of Journalists'. It was meant as a compliment.[12]

Women of letters

Women writers engaged with the periodical press through a number of less public routes. Opportunities for networking of the kind experienced by David Masson, and a vital aspect of masculine literary life, were limited. The world of clubs and editors' dinners was an almost exclusively male one, as Margaret Oliphant wistfully recalled in the first of her 'Old Saloon' pieces in *Blackwood's Magazine* in 1887.[13] The 'Old Saloon' of the title was the Edinburgh publisher's George Street premises, the meeting place in the early days for the magazine's contributors, almost all of whom were men.

But for women writers too, possibilities of a professional writing life had begun to emerge as early as the 1820s. Linda Peterson has shown how Harriet Martineau redefined authorship away from the Romantic notions of originality, genius and inspiration, towards a more pragmatic and 'Victorian' engagement with editors and book publishers. Martineau began her literary career by writing for the Unitarian *Monthly Repository*, under the aegis of its editor W. J. Fox, who as R. K. Webb notes, was her 'main point of entry to intellectual circles'.[14] She also wrote for the *Westminster*

Review, both publications being linked to the radical groups with which she had family connections. Following a rift with the *Westminster* she shifted her allegiance to the *Edinburgh Review* after her cousin Henry Reeve became its editor in the 1850s. She also wrote for the *Athenaeum*, and for Dickens's *Household Words*. In 1852 Frederick Knight Hunt, the editor of the *Daily News*, suggested she contribute two or three leaders a week to the paper, beginning an association which was to last for the rest of her life. Her *Biographical Sketches* collected from the *Daily News* were republished in 1869.

Margaret Oliphant's association with *Blackwood's Magazine* began in the 1850s and continued until her death in 1897. Her last article was published posthumously in the July 1898 number. In the last decade of her life she wrote three regular columns: 'A Fireside Commentary' in the *St. James's Gazette* (January–June 1888), 'A Commentary from an Easy Chair' in the *Spectator* (December 1889–November 1890) and 'The Old Saloon' series (which ran in *Blackwood's* from January 1887 to December 1892). Interspersed with these, she wrote for *Atalanta*, the *Contemporary Review*, the *Cornhill*, the *Edinburgh*, *Fraser's*, *Good Words* and *Macmillan's*.

Marian Evans began her association with the press by writing for the *Coventry Herald and Observer* in the late 1840s. On moving to London she began work on the *Westminster Review* under John Chapman's proprietorship, becoming the de facto editor between 1851 and 1854. From 1855 to 1857 she had responsibility for the 'Belles Lettres' section of each quarterly issue. Following the establishment of her permanent union with G.H. Lewes in 1854, her engagement with the press was greatly shaped by his connections. She wrote for the *Leader*, for the *Saturday Review*, with which they were both involved from its establishment in 1855, for *Fraser's*, and for the *Fortnightly* during Lewes's brief term as founding editor (May 1865–December 1866). She also contributed to her publisher George Smith's *Pall Mall Gazette* under the pseudonym 'Saccharissa'.

Martineau, Oliphant and Evans were competent professional reviewers, like their male counterparts, each financially dependent at certain points in their writing lives on the earnings from the periodical press, and contributing extensively to a culture of reviewing and an evolving sense of what constituted literary criticism.

Criticism comes of age

The self-confidence of the new generation of reviewers was never more obvious than in their estimates of their predecessors. Prompted by a spate of republished essays between 1843 and the mid-1850s by Francis Jeffrey, Sydney Smith and Francis Horner, three of the four founders of the *Edinburgh Review*, and, most celebrated of all, by the historian and essayist Thomas Babington Macaulay, one of its star reviewers, the modern generation of critics and reviewers were quick to assert their own superiority. 'The sketchy "beauty and blemish" species of criticism in which Jeffrey had excelled, has now passed out of date', according to David Masson, 'and has been succeeded in all our higher periodicals by a kind of criticism intrinsically deeper and more laborious.'[15]

Reviewing the collected letters of Macvey Napier, Jeffrey's successor as editor of the *Edinburgh* in 1878, Leslie Stephen wrote: 'Everyone who turns from the periodical literature of the present day to the original "Edinburgh Review" will be amazed at its inferiority. It is generally dull, and when not dull, flimsy. One may most easily characterise the contents by saying that few of the articles would have a chance of acceptance by the editor of a first-rate periodical today.' Stephen no doubt saw himself as just such an editor, presiding as he did over the *Cornhill Magazine*. It had been an enormous leap to the present system, he went on, 'the system according to which much of the most solid and original work of the time first appears in periodicals'.[16]

Walter Bagehot, reviewing several collections of essays reprinted from the *Edinburgh Review* by Jeffrey and his colleagues in 1855, coined the phrase 'the review-like essay and the essay-like review' to denote a typical article in the early quarterly reviews. The review essay, as he described it, was discursive, extending to forty or more octavo pages, sometimes rich in information, often prodigal of quotation. Some reviewers used the book under review as a peg, in the jargon of the day, on which to hang a much broader discussion.

'Review-writing', Bagehot observed, 'is one of the features of modern literature. Many able men really give themselves up to it.' But the modern reader, he went on, does not have the leisure of his predecessors. 'People take their literature in morsels as they take their sandwiches on a journey.' And review-writing also 'exemplifies the casual character of modern literature. Everything about it is temporary and fragmentary.'[17]

What Bagehot did not say directly, but what his references to the modern reader implied, was that the modern reader was also less well educated, and in need of instruction. The usefulness of reviewing was obvious: 'The modern man must be told what to think – shortly, no doubt – but he *must* be told it. The essay-like criticism of modern times is about the length which he likes. The Edinburgh Review, which began the system, may be said to be, in this country, the commencement on large topics of suitable views for sensible persons.'[18]

The mid-Victorian generation of reviewers, of which Bagehot was one, were confident that their reviewing was superior to that of an earlier generation, but at the same time they acknowledged the challenge of writing for a new and quite different reading audience. Just as the quarterly reviews, with their 250 pages per number, had come to be regarded as outmoded, not what the age required, so too their forty-page review-essays, came under scrutiny.

Bagehot's coinage of the terms 'review-like essay' and 'essay-like review' emphasized the slipperiness of the distinction between essays and reviews. In essence, a self-effacing or indeed a cynically slick writer who focused on the work, either summarizing it or describing it, was considered to have written a 'review'. The more reflective, imaginative and independent the writing, the more likely the product was to be seen as an essay. The mid-century retrospective on the work of Jeffrey and his colleagues was in fact part of a much larger and searching discourse about the nature of criticism, and about the role and authority of the critic in the second half of the nineteenth century.

None of Jeffrey's articles had been written with a view to immortality. He would never have reprinted them of his own accord, in the view of Whitwell Elwin, the editor of the *Quarterly*, reviewing Cockburn's *Life of Jeffrey* in 1852. 'The majority of his articles are strictly reviews, and not essays; and if a work has dropped out of notice, the criticism must possess some extraordinary qualities of thought or style to maintain an interest of its own.'[19]

So the 'review' was coming to be regarded as a summary, a descriptive and emphemeral account of a book or a topic, whereas an essay was a more considered, comprehensive and enduring treatment of the same book or topic. To Frederick Oakley, reviewing a collection of essays by the notable Roman Catholic churchman Nicholas Wiseman in the *Dublin Review* for 1853, the essay was *the* genre of the present times. The age preferred it to books and treatises. The essay was a form which shared 'the character of earnest conversation' and one which more than any other literary form could be regarded as 'a simple transcript of the writer's mind'.[20]

The discussions about what differentiated a review from an essay overlap with concerns about the nature of criticism, and the distinctions between reviewers and critics. The 'profession-consciousness' which Kent identified in the world of reviewing is reflected in the self-conscious use of the term critic in preference to reviewer at mid-century.

Several modern critics have identified a point at which Victorian literary criticism changed both its style and its focus. Isobel Armstrong, in *Victorian Scrutinies: Reviews of Poetry 1830 to 1870*, identifies the 1860s as the point when criticism of poetry underwent a significant development, one which she links to the critics' belated adoption of Coleridgean ideas and terminology. Ian Small, in *Conditions of Criticism*, argues that in the twenty-five years between 1865 and 1890 the nature of critical writing underwent profound changes. Distinctive academic disciplines were emerging, and specialist journals like the *English Historical Review* and its counterparts would soon siphon off academic criticism. John Gross, in *The Rise and Fall of the Man of Letters*, has identified the 1870s as the period when criticism ceased to be driven by moral, political or religious concerns. 'By the end of the 1870s', he maintains, 'the winds of doctrine were dying down, the lay sermon was giving way to the causerie, the emphasis had shifted to Appreciation.'[21]

John Woolford, in an essay entitled 'Periodicals and the Practice of Literary Criticism 1855–64', sees a change occurring in the decade between the reviews of Browning's *Men and Women* and his later volume *Dramatis Personae*. During this ten-year period, he suggests, critics' conception of their own role in relation to the poet and to the reader altered perceptibly. During those years, literary criticism moved from what he terms 'adjectival' criticism, characterized by self-display and superiority on the part of the critic, to more analytical criticism, in which the critic positioned himself in the role of advocate and interpreter, and indeed reader, rather than judge of his subject. In adjectival criticism, it is the critic's personality that dominates, rather than the writer's work. Woolford emphasizes the role of anonymity and the use of the ubiquitous 'we' in promoting an assertiveness on the part of the critic. His virulence of language, Woolford argues, 'stems from the enormous and overbearing authority he derives from his position of anonymous reviewer'.[22] The period 1855–64 witnessed the final rejection of the methods of Romantic reviewers like Francis Jeffrey.

In the 1860s practitioners and readers alike were conscious, if not of a change of direction, at least of the importance of criticism. To Matthew Arnold, writing his essay 'The Function of Criticism at the Present Time' in 1864, criticism is wrong-headed, and in need of reform, but there is no doubt of its urgency, and of its significance and relevance. Arnold was by no means alone in his assumption. The general confidence in current criticism is endorsed in a letter written by the scholar and reviewer Harriet Grote in 1865, on having read an article published by Bulwer-Lytton in 1834:

> Such a production would never go down now. Surprising how exigent the present race of readers has become. The competition among writers of passing criticism seems to have sharpened up the quality of periodical writing to a degree of which one is really not always conscious, unless you recur to things of 30 years ago. Modern writing is, now, so able, that I begin to tire of cutting out articles![23]

The confidence of the new generation of critics of the 1860s was palpable. But by the 1880s there were anxieties about the direction it was taking. These related to the number of outlets for criticism: the new monthlies like the

Fortnightly, the *Contemporary*, the *Nineteenth Century* and the *Academy* (later a weekly), and more specifically the new weeklies, with their shorter articles and their shortened timescales. Writing in the *Fortnightly* in 1882, prompted by a recent article in the *Revue des Deux Mondes* about the 'decay' of French criticism, the novelist and critic Grant Allen pronounced English criticism as coming into its own: 'Just at the moment when the critical impulse is dying out in France, it has begun to live in England.' English critics owed much to their French colleagues: 'they have learnt much from the Villemains and the Sainte-Beuves on the one hand, from the Taines, the Renans, and even the Gautiers on the other'. But the current demand for shorter articles and the time limits imposed by the daily and weekly press were posing a serious threat to the authority and the integrity of criticism:

> The state of the periodical press makes serious criticism an absolute impossibility. Journalism no longer demands either special aptitude, special training, or special function. Nowadays, any man can write, because there are papers enough to give employment to everybody. No reflection, no deliberation, no care: all is haste, fatal facility, stock phrases, commonplace ideas, and a ready pen that can turn itself to any task with equal ease because supremely ignorant of all alike.

There were far too many publications producing reviews, far too many books being published. As a result 'critics' were becoming 'reviewers', forced to provide summaries of books and snap judgements:

> Look at the space placed at the disposal of each reviewer . . . does not the mere word 'reviewer' call up a wonderfully different mental concept from the word 'critic'? Well, the reviewer has to say what he has got to say in some two or three short columns at the outside. How absurdly inadequate for anything like real criticism![24]

But the discursive essay, like the expansive quarterlies which nurtured and developed it, was no longer what the modern reader wanted. The weeklies which had sprung up after the removal of the stamp duties in 1855 – the *Saturday*, the *Reader*, as well as longer-lived publications like the *Athenaeum*, the *Spectator* and the *Economist* – were joined by W. E. Henley's *Scots* and later *National Observer* (1885), the *British Weekly* (1886), the *New Review* (1889) and the *Bookman* (1891).

Allen's argument, however, was not just with the demise of the essay, but rather with the conditions of criticism at the present time. The authoritative and intellectual role which he envisaged for literary criticism could not, in his view, be delivered by the shorter review articles now in fashion, and the time frame in which the critic was required to write. But the alternative, a more specialized, scholarly criticism based in the universities, whose end product was the lengthy monograph, was equally detrimental to the health of criticism. Specialism was rampant in the universities, he argued, and it was a 'second-hand German specialism'. There was a danger that English critics were 'a little over-anxious to convert ourselves forthwith into the image of the fashionable Teutonic monographist'.[25] The process was a gradual one, but Allen's concern about the current malaise of criticism in the press and his dismay at the possibility of criticism in the form of turgid monographs was, in 1882, far-sighted.[26]

Anonymity versus signature

The new generation of critics – those writing from the late 1850s onward – differed from their predecessors in an important respect. They were writing in an era in which anonymity, which had been universal up to the end of the 1840s, was gradually being eroded. Not all were convinced of the advantages of signature. The arguments were finely balanced. But most of the new generation had had some of their work published under a form of signature.

The gradual abandonment of anonymity in the 1860s was linked to new attitudes to criticism and to the role of the critic. According to the editors of the *Wellesley Index to Victorian Periodicals*, nearly 97 per cent of articles before 1865 in the publications it indexed were anonymous. The figure dropped to 57 per cent for the period 1865–1900.[27] Anonymity was absolute in the quarterlies until mid-century – the *Edinburgh Review*'s articles remained unsigned until 1912 – and for the most part in the magazines and weeklies, although some contributions carried an initial or occasionally a pseudonym.

The well-rehearsed defences of the old system, that it enabled editors to establish a unified, corporate voice for their journals, that it provided opportunities to little-known reviewers whereas signature demanded established names, that it offered protection and freedom to eminent public figures, no longer stood up in the new reviewing climate.

The discussion had been ongoing for more than a decade.[28] Some converts to signature found themselves arguing, paradoxically, that signature would force critics to produce what was expected of them, whereas anonymity would provide the truest freedom of expression. Experienced editors like John Morley when taking over the *Fortnightly* in 1867 found themselves genuinely divided on the issue, even though the *Fortnightly* had made signature one of its most important innovations.[29]

In practice, authorship had always been a badly kept secret, and gossip in literary and political circles was full of revelations of who was responsible for the latest articles and reviews. John Mullan, in his book *Anonymity: A Secret History of English Literature*, suggests that the perpetual 'author-spotting' which went on in most reviewing circles was a way of claiming a literary 'kinship' amongst critics and readers. He instances the satisfaction which Marian Evans's mentor, the Coventry manufacturer Charles Bray, felt when he had correctly identified her as the author of an article on 'Evangelical Teaching: Dr Cumming' in the *Westminster Review* for October 1855. Mullan sees this as an example of provincial intellectuals being made to feel like 'insiders' in metropolitan literary life.[30]

The anonymous system was also open to abuse. It was not unusual for reviewers to review the same book more than once, making minor adjustments, or adroitly cutting and pasting to produce a 'new' article in a different journal. De Quincey was adept at making the most of his material in order to accommodate the several periodicals to which he was committed. Coventry Patmore, who undertook extensive reviewing of modern poetry for the *Edinburgh*, the *North British* and *Macmillan's* in the 1850s, cynically plagiarised one of his own articles. Marian Evans reviewed some of the same books in the *Leader* as she was to review in the *Westminster*.[31]

Anonymity also enabled authors to contribute to several periodicals at the same time, including those with opposing political or sectarian affiliations. The only contract was the fee, and many reviews and magazines shared contributors: among them the *Edinburgh* and the *Foreign Quarterly* in the 1830s and *Blackwood's* and *Fraser's* in the same decade. De Quincey began his career with *Blackwood's,* whose conservative politics were closest to his own, moved to the radical *Tait's Edinburgh Magazine* in 1833 when Blackwood rejected one of his articles, and kept both in play over a period of nearly twenty years, along with *Hogg's Instructor* and *Titan* in the 1850s.

Anonymity also enabled writers to promote the work of friends, and to orchestrate a favourable reception for their own works. As Mullan has shown, Marian Evans offered her services or those of Lewes to review her friend Sara Hennell's *Christianity and Infidelity* for the *Leader* in 1857. In the end Lewes wrote the review.[32] As 'Vivian', his signature in the *Leader*, he promoted the works of his friends R. H. Horne and Herbert Spencer. Marian Evans, too, reviewed Lewes's biography of Goethe (1855), a work for which she had done some of the research during their visit to Weimar in 1854, in the *Leader*, of all places.

Marian Evans, who had not yet adopted her celebrated pseudonym of George Eliot, proved to be a canny manipulator of the conventions of anonymous reviewing. She wrote in the first-person plural, as was customary, and had no scruples about feigning masculinity. 'We read the Athenaeum askance at the tea-table and take notes from the Philosophical Journal at soirees; we invite our friends that we may thrust a book into their hands, and presuppose an exclusive desire in the "ladies" to discuss their own matters, that we may crackle the Times at our ease', she wrote characteristically in her essay 'Woman in France: Madame de Sablé' published in the *Westminster* for October 1854, giving clear signals that a masculine pen was at work. But in the main body of the review, and especially in its emotive ending, she projects an ungendered and at times a personal voice, which undercuts her masculine persona.

The book which John Chapman had asked her to review, Victor Cousin's *Madame de Sablé: études sur les femmes illustres de la société du XVIIe siècle*, came at a propitious time. Reading Cousin's account of the role of women in seventeenth-century French intellectual life while in Weimar during the first month of her 'marriage' to Lewes, she was struck by the freedom enjoyed by French women, and their influence on intellectual as well as political life. 'In France alone', she contended, 'woman has had a vital influence on the development of literature; in France alone the mind of woman has passed like an electric current through the language, making crisp and definite what is elsewhere heavy and blurred; in France alone, if the writings of women were swept away, a serious gap would be made in the national history.'[33] But the 'superiority of womanly development' in France is not only of historical interest: it has a bearing 'on the culture of women in the present day':

> Women became superior in France by being admitted to a common fund of ideas, to common objects of interest with men; and this must ever be the essential condition at once of true womanly culture and of true social well-being . . . Let the whole field of reality be laid open to woman as well as to man, and then that which is peculiar in her mental modification, instead of being, as it is now, a source of discord and repulsion between the sexes, will be found to be a necessary complement to the truth and beauty of life. Then we shall have that marriage of minds which alone can blend all the hues of thought and feeling in one lovely rainbow of promise for the harvest of human happiness.   (36–7)

That uncharacteristically lyrical ending to her review is undoubtedly linked to the period of intense personal happiness in which it was written. But the passage is also related to her own predicament, as often the sole woman in the *Westminster Review* circle, surrounded entirely by intellectually able, often brilliant men, but with no female companionship. When such companionship existed it was fraught with jealousy. Weimar had begun to introduce other possibilities into society. Reading Cousin's book had persuaded her that circumstances had always been different in France, even during the present century, beginning with Mme de Staël, followed by George Sand and their contemporaries.

'Woman in France' bears the same relationship to her developing career as a writer as the later, better-known essays, 'Silly Novels by Lady Novelists' and 'The Natural History of German Life', both published in 1856. In the reflections on women's role in intellectual and cultural life, the perceived need for a recognized equality with men, the crippling effect of imitation or assumed masculinity, there are anticipations of 'Silly Novels by Lady Novelists'. Of all the journalism written in 1854–5 her essay 'Woman in France' stands out, a reflection on the role of women in the wider world of literary, political and scientific culture, as well as part of her self-conscious preparation for her future novel-writing career.

Marian Evans's anonymous essays in the *Westminster Review* of the 1850s were some of the last manifestations of the old-style 'review-like essay and essay-like review' identified by Bagehot as characterizing a bygone age of criticism. Her fellow reviewers and critics were soon writing shorter critical articles for the newly founded *Cornhill* and *Macmillan's* magazines, and for monthly publications like the *Fortnightly* and the *Nineteenth Century*, and articles shorter still for the *Saturday Review*, the *Reader* and the weeklies of the 1880s. Meanwhile a strand of more scholarly articles was beginning to emerge in publications like the *Academy* which would eventually result in literary criticism becoming a more specialist and academic pursuit.

Book making

George Saintsbury's feeling, in 1896, that there was still need to apologize for reprints from periodicals belies the ubiquitous practice among mid to late nineteenth-century critics, of collecting and republishing their periodical essays as books. The phenomenal success, in terms of sales, of Macaulay's *Essays Critical and Historical* collected and republished from the *Edinburgh Review* in 1843 set a trend which was copied by his *Edinburgh* colleagues in the 1840s and 1850s, and became the norm for most reviewers from the 1860s onward.

Erickson's argument that an essay in any of the periodicals of the 1830s and 1840s could be guaranteed a wider circulation in this format than could be expected by collecting and reprinting them in volume form assumes that the anonymity practised almost without exception at this time was only the thinnest of veils, and that most people knew the authors of the essays. This may have been true of Macaulay's *Edinburgh* essays, which attained an unprecedented celebrity beginning with his first, on Milton, written and published in 1825 at the age of twenty-five. It was probably true of many of Carlyle's essays published in the *Edinburgh*, in *Fraser's*, and elsewhere, given his idiosyncratic and recognizable style. Some contributors to the magazines of the 1820s and 1830s were identifiable by an initial, a pseudonym or a soubriquet, as with De Quincey's self-projection as the 'English

Opium Eater' in the *London Magazine*, and later in *Tait's Edinburgh Magazine*. The acquisition of well-known contributors was often an open secret in the 1830s, in publications like *Fraser's* and *Blackwood's*, leading to an early version of the celebrity or star system which became a feature of late nineteenth-century journalism. Erickson's conjecture may well be right, when applied to these well-known figures.

But why did reviewers and critics collect and republish their periodical essays and why did publishers encourage the practice? One obvious answer is the anxiety shared by essayists and reviewers about the ephemeral nature of the periodical press. 'A periodical production must be read the next day, or month, or quarter, otherwise it will not be read at all. Every motive, therefore, which prompts to the production of anything periodical, prompts to the study of immediate effect, of unpostponed popularity, of the applause of the moment', the historian James Mill wrote in the opening number of the *Westminster Review* in 1824.[34] 'The public judges and ought to judge indulgently of periodical works. They are not expected to be highly finished. Their natural life is only six weeks', Macaulay commented to Macvey Napier, the editor of the *Edinburgh Review*, as an argument for not republishing his essays.[35] In his 1847 article Lewes had deplored 'declamations uttered against the so-called disease of our age [writing for the press]; how it fosters superficiality – how it ruins all earnestness – how it substitutes brilliancy for solidity and wantonly sacrifices truth to effect'.[36] Bagehot's reflections on the temporary and fragmentary nature of modern reviewing were also part of this collective concern.

Anxiety about ephemerality was at its most acute with De Quincey. In the preface to *Selections Grave and Gay*, a collection of his periodical publications promoted by his American publisher James T. Fields in 1853, he insisted that 'by the ordinary standard of what is understood by *publication*, it is probable that, in many cases, my own papers must have failed in reaching even this. For they were printed as contributions to journals … Here, at home, they may be regarded as still unpublished'.[37]

This was a disingenuous disclaimer from one of the most wayward, erratic and yet prolific writers for the periodical press, a writer constitutionally unsuited to the discipline required for periodical publication. At the time of his death in 1859 De Quincey could legitimately claim to be the author of scarcely more than three conventionally published books. Yet he wrote over one hundred essays and articles for *Blackwood's*, and more for *Tait's*, *Hogg's Instructor*, *Titan* and the mid-century quarterly *North British Review*. Fields's collected edition of *De Quincey's Writings* published between 1851 and 1859 and comprised mainly of his periodical articles ran to twenty-two volumes.[38]

The professional generation of critics at mid-century had none of Macaulay's reluctance to republish. For a group who were quick to condemn the work of their predecessors as unworthy of republication, they showed no uncertainty about the worthiness of their own. Leslie Stephen and John Morley between them published five multi-volume series of their periodical essays. Richard Holt Hutton, a prolific reviewer and critic of the same generation, produced six collections of his essays during his lifetime, and four editions of the periodical writing of his friends Walter Bagehot and W. C. Roscoe. There were also two posthumous collections of his work. And there are many more examples of critics republishing their periodical essays. David Masson's *Essays Biographical and Critical: Chiefly on English Poets* appeared in 1856, followed by *British Novelists and Their Styles* (1859), *Wordsworth, Shelley, Keats and Other Essays* (1875) and *Edinburgh Sketches and Memories* (1892).

Given the scale of his critical writing, G. H. Lewes's collections were modest. *On Actors and the Art of Acting*, articles republished from the *Pall Mall Gazette* in 1875, was a highly regarded collection of his theatre criticism. *The Times*'s theatre critic William Archer edited some of his drama criticism from the *Leader* along with essays by John Forster in 1894.[39] Lewes also republished a short series from the *Fortnightly*, *The Principles of Success in Literature* (1885). He was more proactive in collecting and republishing his non-literary essays, as in his *Sea-Side Studies* reprinted from *Blackwood's* in 1856–7, his *The Physiology of Common Life*, 2 volumes, 1859–60, also republished from *Blackwood's*, and *Studies in Animal Life* reprinted from the *Cornhill Magazine* in 1862.

It was as though this later generation, however self-confident about the quality of their criticism, remained ever mindful of the 'intellectual hierarchy of written formats'. They may have benefited from the system 'according to which much of the most solid and original work of the time first appears in periodicals', as Leslie Stephen put it, but they were keen to secure their reputations by republishing that 'solid and original work' in the more enduring volume format.

As to what efforts, if any, they made towards republication, practice varied. Most seem to have made few revisions to individual essays and paid scant attention to the collections. The prefatory material was perfunctory and there was often little if any sense of a structure to the volumes. Some inserted footnotes to identify the first publication of the essays, or to make an occasional correction. The titles given to the collections were often chosen, as John Gross has observed, to convey scholarly leisure and forethought, as if to counter the haste and hand-to-mouth circumstances of original publication. Stephen's *Hours in a Library* (1874) and *Studies of a Biographer* (1898) and Morley's *Studies in Literature* (1891) are cases in point.

In contrast, Matthew Arnold took particular care in assembling his *Essays in Criticism* published in volume form in 1865. Several of the essays had been given as lectures in his capacity as Professor of Poetry at Oxford, and then revised for periodical publication. R.H. Super in his edition of Arnold's *Complete Prose Works* shows how detailed was his involvement in the process of republication, down to suggesting a price of five shillings (it became six shillings), advocating paper covers rather than boards, and even determining the colour of the wrappers. Arnold deliberated about the order of the essays, supplied a preface and rewrote the influential first essay 'The Function of Criticism at the Present Time' in which he lamented the sectarian affiliations of much current criticism.[40]

Laurel Brake has interpreted Arnold's efforts as part of a strategy by which he engaged with the world of journalism, but at the same time declared himself firmly to be a man of literature. She has also demonstrated the attention both Walter Pater and Oscar Wilde paid to their own collected essays, in particular Pater's *Appreciations* (1889) and Wilde's *Intentions* (1891), and how they subtly responded to Arnold.[41] I interpret the practice of republishing essays by Leslie Stephen, John Morley, David Masson, Richard Holt Hutton and their colleagues as similarly declaring themselves to be men of letters, and endorsing the literariness and durability of the 'essay' as opposed to the brevity and the damaging time-constraints of the 'review'.[42]

The conditions for criticism, to adapt Ian Small's phrase, underwent a series of changes from the early nineteenth century through to the beginning of the twentieth. The personality-driven reviewing of Francis Jeffrey and his colleagues, anonymous, opinionated, at times politically motivated, gave way in the middle decades of the century to a more modulated, reflective and professionally delivered critical discourse, disseminated through an increasingly varied and mainly non-politically aligned periodical press. Its non-specialist practitioners were secure in their role as critics, prepared and indeed eager to sign their work, and confident that criticism had reached a new level of maturity. The challenge to this mid-Victorian generation of critics would come from two directions: from the weekly and later the daily press, with its pressure for shorter review articles, which, as Grant Allen claimed, made reflective and discursive criticism difficult if not impossible; and from a growing scholarly community, located mainly in universities, which would produce a critical discourse which was specialized and exclusive. The culture of criticism, as it had emerged in the mid-nineteenth century, would never be the same.

Notes

1 See John Gross, *The Rise and Fall of the Man of Letters: English Literary Life since 1800* (London: Weidenfeld and Nicolson, 1969; rev. edn Penguin, 1991), p. 154, and *ODNB*.

2 Lee Erickson, *The Economy of Literary Form: English Literature and the Industrialization of Publishing, 1800–1850* (Baltimore: Johns Hopkins University Press, 1996), p. 13.

3 According to *Poole's Index to Periodical Literature*, quoted by Erickson, *The Economy of Literary Form*, pp. 27–8.

4 Erickson, *The Economy of Literary Form*, p. 94.

5 [G.H. Lewes], 'The Condition of Authors in England, Germany and France', *Fraser's Magazine*, 35 (March 1847), pp. 285–95; see p. 288.

6 Patrick Leary, 'Fraser's Magazine and the Literary Life, 1830–1847', *Victorian Periodicals Review*, 27, 2 (Summer 1994), p. 106.

7 Christopher Kent, 'Higher Journalism and the Mid-Victorian Clerisy', *Victorian Studies*, 13 (December 1969), p. 181.

8 David Masson, *Memories of London in the 'Forties* (Edinburgh and London: Blackwood, 1908), p. 56.

9 *Ibid.* p. 214. Hervey edited the *Athenaeum* between 1847 and 1854.

10 Grevel Lindop, 'De Quincey and the Edinburgh and Glasgow University Circles', in Jeremy Treglown and Bridget Bennett (eds.), *Grub Street and the Ivory Tower: Literary Journalism and Literary Scholarship from Fielding to the Internet* (Oxford: Clarendon Press, 1998), pp. 41–57; see p. 45.

11 Francis Espinasse, *Literary Recollections and Sketches* (London: Hodder and Stoughton, 1893), p. 276. Quoted by Rosemary Ashton, *G. H. Lewes: A Life* (Oxford: Clarendon Press, 1991), p. 4.

12 Espinasse, *Literary Recollections and Sketches*, p. 282.

13 'In Maga's Library: The Old Saloon 1', *Blackwood's Magazine*, 141 (January 1887), pp. 126–53.

14 Linda Peterson, '(Re)inventing Authorship: Harriet Martineau in the Literary Marketplace of the 1820s', *Women's Writing*, 9, 3 (2002), pp. 337–50. R.K. Webb, 'Harriet Martineau', *ODNB*.

15 [David Masson], 'Lord Cockburn's *Life of Jeffrey*', *North British Review*, 17 (August 1852), p. 322.

16 Leslie Stephen, 'The First Edinburgh Reviewers', *Cornhill Magazine*, 38 (August 1878), pp. 269, 243, 248.

17 Walter Bagehot, 'The First Edinburgh Reviewers', in *Literary Studies*, ed. R.H. Hutton, 2 vols. (London: Longmans, Green, and Co., 1884), vol. 1, p. 2.

18 *Ibid.* pp. 3, 6.

19 [Whitwell Elwin], 'Lord Cockburn's *Life of Jeffrey*', *Quarterly Review*, 91 (June 1852), p. 152.

20 [Frederick Oakley], 'Periodical Literature', *Dublin Review*, 34 (June 1853), p. 544.

21 Isobel Armstrong, *Victorian Scrutinies: Reviews of Poetry 1830 to 1870* (London: Athlone, 1972); Ian Small, *Conditions of Criticism* (Oxford: Clarendon Press, 1990); Gross, *The Rise and Fall of the Man of Letters*, p. 145.

22 John Woolford, 'Periodicals and the Practice of Literary Criticism', in Joanne Shattock and Michael Wolff (eds.), *The Victorian Periodical Press: Samplings and Soundings* (Leicester: Leicester University Press, 1982), p. 113.

23 Quoted by Walter Houghton in 'Periodical Literature and the Articulate Classes', in Shattock and Wolff (eds.), *The Victorian Periodical Press*, p. 25 n. 28.

24 Grant Allen, 'The Decay of Criticism', *Fortnightly Review*, 31 (1882), pp. 342, 344, 347.

25 *Ibid.* pp. 350–1.

26 For an account of a celebrated controversy highlighting these tensions, see Valentine Cunningham, 'Darke Conceits: Churton Collins, Edmund Gosse, and the Professions of Criticism', in Treglown and Bennett (eds.), *Grub Street and the Ivory Tower*, pp. 72–90.

27 W. E. Houghton, 'Introduction', in *The Wellesley Index to Victorian Periodicals 1824–1900*, 5 vols. (Toronto: University of Toronto Press, 1968–89), vol. II, p. xvi.

28 See Oscar Maurer, 'Anonymity vs Signature in Victorian Reviewing', *Texas Studies in English*, 27 (June 1948), pp. 1–28, and Dallas Liddle, 'Salesmen, Sportsmen, Mentors: Anonymity and Mid-Victorian Theories of Journalism', *Victorian Studies*, 41 (Autumn 1997), pp. 31–68 for the arguments on each side.

29 See Kent, 'Higher Journalism', pp. 195–6.

30 John Mullan, *Anonymity: A Secret History of English Literature* (London: Faber and Faber, 2007), p. 202.

31 Joanne Shattock, 'Spreading It Thinly: Some Victorian Reviewers at Work', *Victorian Periodicals Review*, 9, 3, (1976), pp. 84–7; Mullan, *Anonymity*, p. 204.

32 *The Leader*, 28 February 1857. Mullan, *Anonymity*, p. 205.

33 'Woman in France: Madame de Sablé', *Westminster Review*, o.s. 62, n.s. 6 (October 1854), pp. 448–73; repr. in *George Eliot: Selected Essays, Poems and other Writings*, ed. Antonia Byatt and Nicholas Warren (London: Penguin, 1990), pp. 8–37. See p. 9.

34 James Mill, 'Periodical Literature: Edinburgh Review', *Westminster Review*, 1 (January 1824), p. 207.

35 *The Letters of Thomas Babington Macaulay*, ed. T. Pinney, 6 vols. (Cambridge: Cambridge University Press, 1974–81), vol. IV, pp. 40–1.

36 Lewes, 'The Condition of Authors', p. 288.

37 Thomas de Quincey, Preface to *Selections Grave and Gay* (Boston: Ticknor and Fields, 1853).

38 *De Quincey's Writings*, ed. J. T. Fields (Boston: Ticknor, Reed and Fields, 1851–9). The most recent scholarly edition is *The Works of Thomas de Quincey*, 21 vols., gen. ed. Grevel Lindop (London: Pickering and Chatto, 2000–3).

39 *Dramatic Essays by John Forster and George Henry Lewes*, ed. W. Archer and R. W. Lowe, 3 vols. (London: Walter Scott, 1894–6).

40 The *Complete Prose Works of Matthew Arnold*, ed. R. H. Super, vol. III: *Lectures and Essays in Criticism* (Ann Arbor: University of Michigan Press, 1962), p. 399 *et seq.*

41 Laurel Brake, 'Culture Wars? Arnold's *Essays in Criticism* and the Rise of Journalism 1865–95', in Dinah Birch and Mark Llewellyn (eds.), *Conflict and Difference in Nineteenth-Century Literature* (London: Palgrave, 2009); Laurel Brake, *Subjugated Knowledges: Journalism, Gender and Literature in the Nineteenth Century* (London: Macmillan, 1994), ch. 4.
42 But see chapter 1, p. 15 above, for a publisher's view of the sales of volumes of essays.

5

SUSAN HAMILTON

Women's voices and public debate

> Journalism will, no doubt, occupy the first or one of the first places in any
> future literary history of the present times, for it is the most characteristic
> of all [our] productions.
> 'Journalism', *Cornhill Magazine*, 1862

Since the 1970s, the recuperation of women's voices has made the work of novelists and poets of tremendous power and accomplishment available for scholarly and teaching purposes. New editions and collections of women's writing, scholarly monographs and essays, academic journals and professional associations devoted to women's writing, biographies of key figures – the extraordinary outpouring of such resources since the 1970s has ensured that nineteenth-century women's writing is securely part of this period's writing canon. Women's writing in the periodical and newspaper press, however, has not yet undergone so comprehensive a reclamation as the preferred genres of novels, poetry and life writing, despite scholarship that argues persuasively that the periodical was 'the most significant organ for disseminating knowledge, information, and social attitudes';[1] despite the long-standing centrality of such figures as Matthew Arnold, Thomas Carlyle and John Ruskin, whose writings first appeared primarily in the periodical press, to our sense of this period; and despite long-standing interest in what the Victorians called 'the Woman Question', a periodical debate of great vigour and range. In this context, the *Cornhill Magazine*'s certainty about the place of journalism in English literary history is arresting, striking the twenty-first-century reader as somehow misplaced, a quaint reminder about the vast differences in critical sensibilities between then and now.

This chapter takes up the *Cornhill*'s certainty as an invitation to consider women's participation in the 'most characteristic' of nineteenth-century productions. Using the writings of five prominent and successful women writers in this period, this chapter explores the ways in which nineteenth-century women writers engaged with the established periodical press as reviewers, essayists, polemicists and political campaigners. It focuses on the shaping relation between Victorian writing on 'the Woman Question', with its concern for women's education, employment and 'influence', and the ways in which women writing in the periodical press grasped the multiple opportunities of periodical signature in order to present 'women' – their voices, perspectives, experiences, knowledge – as critically vital, relevant and representable subjects for, and agents of, periodical debate. In a period when press conventions for author signatures ranged from anonymity, through initialled contributions, to full signatures (and combinations of the above), the idea of a press signature is necessarily complex. I use it here to denote writing in the nineteenth-century context that combines rhetorical attributes (ethos, persona) and recognizable and repeated stylistic and analytical flourishes with an individual's professional identity. Such writing presents a 'voice' that is distinctive, recognizable and marketable. Women like Anna Jameson (art critic and social commentator), Margaret Oliphant (novelist and literary reviewer), Frances Power Cobbe (journalist and political essayist), Eliza Lynn Linton (novelist and political commentator) and Mona Caird (novelist and political essayist) developed distinctive press signatures in a period when to write as, on behalf of or about 'women' from a range of political positions and across a sweep of genres (leader, newspaper report, review, serialized novel, essay) was one of the principal ways in which women addressed the substantial, established periodical press readership. Their careers saw them offering monthly reviews of novels and assessments of trends in contemporary literature, and daily newspaper leaders on women's education, employment and civil rights, through to controversial 'open platform'[2] exchanges on women as domestic versus political agents, and excoriating social commentary on changing definitions of marriage.

Writings of these kinds have not yet been at the centre of sustained research on women's voices in the nineteenth century. But such a focus holds out the promise of rethinking how different sources allow us to tell different stories about the means through which women engaged with and shaped the literary and cultural landscape of the nineteenth century. In order to give some sense of the changing modes in which women wrote as periodical writers throughout the long nineteenth century, I will focus on specific ways in which women exploited the possibilities of press signature. From Anna Jameson's *Athenaeum* report on the Children's Employment Commission and Margaret Oliphant's writing on 'the Woman Question' for *Blackwood's Magazine* and other periodical titles, to Frances Power Cobbe's newspaper editorials on domestic violence and women's civil rights in the *Echo* and Eliza Lynn Linton's and Mona Caird's 'Wild Women' exchange for *Nineteenth Century*, these writers explored the opportunities of writing in the periodical press in compellingly diverse ways.

Anna Jameson (1794–1860)

When Anna Jameson detailed the report of the Children's Employment Commission in her 1843 article 'The Milliners' for the weekly *Athenaeum*, she was the celebrated author of such work as *Diary of an Ennuyé* (1826), a fictionalized travel biography, and *Memoirs of Celebrated Female Sovereigns* (1831), a very popular book of travel writing and art criticism, amongst many other works. She has been acclaimed as the first professional art historian and her importance as a popularizer and compiler of knowledge about art is well established.[3] Born in Dublin, Anna became a governess at the age of sixteen, continuing in this line of work for fifteen years. She left governessing to marry the barrister Robert Jameson in 1825, but was separated from her husband for much of their married life. During her marriage Jameson's literary reputation grew exponentially. She was a vital role model for a generation of women writers and activists at a time when the accustomed institutions for professional development and networking were simply unavailable to women. Men's university connections, gentlemen's clubs and other professional organizations ensured innumerable opportunities for professional development and networking. Women writers created more informal networks through which to pass along vital information about professional life. Jameson's stature as a mentor was legendary. She was a 'tower of strength to the girl-editor and writers'[4] and had benefited from such informal mentoring herself, learning for example about the importance of retaining copyright from the writer Maria Edgworth.[5]

By 1843, when she was writing for the *Athenaeum*, Jameson was a writer with a transatlantic stature. In significant ways, her work on the Children's Employment Commission is anomalous. Her writing success was grounded in a meticulously presented feminine voice addressing an audience of primarily female readers. That voice stressed the careful cultivation of taste and due regard for women's proper sphere as both the source and site of women's cultural power. The voice made no overt claim for women's political rights. As Jameson wrote in the preface for *Memoirs of Celebrated Female Sovereigns*, 'the power which belongs to [women] as a sex, is not properly, or naturally, that of the sceptre or the sword'.[6]

The article for the *Athenaeum* appeared anonymously, as was customary for periodical contributors at this time. It was the only occasion on which Jameson presented her writing voice as masculine, using the default masculine anonymity that periodical writing offered throughout her article. 'The Milliners' is the third in a series of articles on the findings of the *Report* that the *Athenaeum* ran in 1843, and was Jameson's first attempt at using a kind of pamphlet style, with all of its political import, to offer an argument about the need to improve women's rights. She repackaged the material three years later in *Memoirs and Essays*

(1846), when a version of the article, drawing attention to its work as political commentary, appeared as 'Women's Mission and Women's Position'.

The differences between Jameson's art writing and her foray into the periodical press are important, but the article also repeats signature writing strategies that characterized Jameson's art criticism. If that work popularized the writings of 'experts' as a way to provide access to art for an expanding middle-class audience, her review article on the *Report* similarly distilled and interpreted the imposing findings of the Commission for an audience eager to know more. Interestingly, the *Athenaeum* had favourably reviewed Jameson's *Handbook to the Public Galleries of Art in or near London* (1842) in its previous month's leading article, indicating that Jameson's stature as an art writer professionally facilitated the circulation of her piece on children's and women's employment, and signalling that the professional networks a well-established writer like Jameson cultivated and maintained are an integral component in our understanding of women's writerly success. Significantly, 'The Milliners' uses the strategies of Jameson's popular travel and art criticism to voice (and answer) the question: what should a cultivated person in 1843 know?

The fit between Jameson's repertoire of art writing strategies and the *Athenaeum*'s press signature is striking. Founded in 1828, the weekly *Athenaeum* subtitled itself a 'Literary and Cultural Journal'. With its combination of original reviews and articles of interpretation, a feature commonly associated with the monthlies and literary reviews of this period, and its claim to topicality, reflected in its weekly date stamp, the *Athenaeum* is what Laurel Brake has termed a 'hybrid' form. The exclusion of news proper from its columns meant that it was not classified as a newspaper for tax purposes. Less pragmatically, the exclusion of political news from its pages was also a marketing strategy to appeal to multiple political persuasions. The weekly arrangement of pressing topicality (the engagement with news on a regular basis) and reflection (a kind of urgent thoughtfulness that a week's distance from events might enable) was enormously successful.

Writing in the *Athenaeum*, Jameson used her critical strategies to represent political knowledge and the response to political events as necessary *cultural* knowledge and cultivated affect rather than political analysis. As Oz Frankel has shown, Royal Commissions and other kinds of government inquiries were an important new form of reading matter for the Victorian public, a form aimed at what Frankel terms the 'voter–reader'. Such reports performed multiple tasks as part of governance.

In their ability to convey investigative range, they testified to the governmental power to probe, analyse and dissect. In bringing 'marginal' or less powerful groups to the voting–reading public in such forms as witness statements, testimonials and illustrations, they offered 'enlightenment' and 'knowledge' to the voter–reader as a way to manage public debate and perception about pressing social questions. They were an integral element of the print-based public sphere, garnering ample coverage in daily newspapers, periodicals and magazines from the time of the first inquiries on the workings of England's Poor Laws. Jameson's reports to the *Athenaeum* are part of this larger print phenomenon. Written between the great Reform Bills of 1832 and 1867, which expanded the electorate, Jameson's reports addressed voter–readers in the making at a time when the size – and civility – of the electorate was a topic of constant political discussion.

'The Milliners' opens with an exclamation that the world of the seamstresses, its 'pain, toil, disease, and vice', is little known, and a declaration that 'graphic narratives and discoveries of horror' documented in the *Report* 'ought to have been long since known and remedied' (4 March 1843). In Jameson's article, the untutored reader, like the seemingly untutored writer of the article, confronts the mass of information that the *Report* presents, consults the experts as to the meaning of that information, and cultivates a proper understanding and response as a result. Making clear that its purpose is 'to pourtray [*sic*], and not to philosophize', the article culls extensively from the *Report*, presenting the selected evidence of seamstresses and medical practitioners as 'the most striking and interesting of the descriptive passages' contained within it. Evidence taken by many expert witnesses, along with diverse witness statements from 'the girls themselves', is presented to the *Athenaeum* reader for consideration.

Such substantial extracts are a conventional feature of reportage in this period. Government relied on papers like the *Athenaeum* to circulate findings from its inquiries, even though the reports themselves were available for purchase. Here the reporting strategy is also a powerful enactment of the cultural importance of dissemination. In her critical writing, Jameson's persona was that of an almost overwhelmed middle-class female traveller, consulting experts to guide her through the maze of artistic artefacts to proper cultivation. In this *Athenaeum* piece, cultural dissemination is a political act with significant consequences. '[T]he most striking and interesting of the descriptive passages' of the *Report* that Jameson disseminates are those that demand a particular affective response, which is presented in turn as the culturally and politically 'literate' response of the proper reader.

Jameson marks the connection between knowing and feeling forcefully in the opening of her article. By quoting with 'appreciation' the response of a person 'acquainted with the facts', Jameson's article is immediately framed by the political necessity of a new response to pain and toil: 'I shall', asserts the well-acquainted person, 'have no more pleasure [at the Court Fancy Ball]: I shall have before my eyes a score of the makers of those gay dresses in their coffins'. Linking knowledge with feeling in this way, Jameson's article rehearses a dynamic central to the state inquiry's form, one that, in 1843, had its detractors. Critics suggested that inquiry reports, and so the newspapers that offered heavy extractions as part of their coverage, presented as vigorous scientific 'inquiry' the very conclusions that policy-makers had already determined to adopt. Jameson's response, in such critics' views, runs the risk of constituting political response to the social and economic conditions the *Report* details as based entirely on sympathy.

Despite such criticism, the anonymous voice of the *Athenaeum* review is grounded in a cultivated affective response to the 'outpouring of facts', and is confident both that such a response is significant and that the political judgements it offers to a newspaper's readers is valuable. In key passages, Jameson's anonymous speaker, bolstered by proper feeling, moves past the mere dissemination of the contents of the *Report* to offer political judgements on the conditions of women's labour in terms that require no supplementary 'expert' opinion to authorize its analysis. When a dressmaker and proprietor proposes 'the restriction of the work of young persons under 18 to 12 hours a-day, to be taken between half-past 5am and half-past 8pm, which would not interfere with the efficiency of the business' the assured response of the speaker, offered as guide to the reader's own responses, is excoriating:

> We dare say not. The question which the humanity of this country has to settle, is how far it may interfere with the health, for a young girl, under 18, to be confined at work for 12 hours a-day to a close sedentary occupation. Where really humane employers deem this 'moderation,' it is manifest that less moderate mercies must interpose to save the victims.   (4 March 1843)

The slightly acid tone of this interjection brooks no argument; or, rather, takes as its starting point the tacit agreement of readers. Having been guided through the maze of witness statements and expert testimonies, the reader, like the speaker, knows there is only one valid response.

Jameson's affective response to the *Report* may or may not constitute acceptable politics as some activists might have defined them. Nevertheless, the apparent ease with which Jameson's writing persona takes up the position of Frankel's 'voter–reader', and addresses that potential constituency, compels our understanding. The political efficacy of this response is but one concern. Party political identities aside, Jameson's writing voice is that of a political subject who recognizes herself (and her readers) in the invitation to assess, react to and process the 'facts' of government inquiry. Modelling the ability of the voter–reader to acquire knowledge, Jameson's anonymous *Athenaeum* voice identifies itself as sufficiently 'expert' to form judgements on political questions. In other words, Jameson's signature marks the voice of a competent political agent who can take in and respond to political experts, and in so doing, model the process of political adjudication for voter–readers, including women. Though Jameson rarely entered into such overt political territory in the course of her writing career, her ability so smoothly to take up that vantage point, and to pull the professional strings to make it happen in the pages of the *Athenaeum*, testifies to the capaciousness of an elsewhere feminized press signature to address overtly political matter.

Margaret Oliphant (1828–1897)

Born Margaret Oliphant Wilson in Scotland, married to her cousin Francis Oliphant in 1853, but widowed early, Oliphant's position and power as a 'general utility woman' for *Blackwood's* is evident in the masses of novels, reviews, biographies, histories and other writing. Ambivalent about the amount of writing she produced in the name, as she always insisted, of the many children for whom she was responsible, Oliphant worried about the effects of familial and financial pressures on her writing. Reading about George Eliot's relationship with G. H. Lewes, she exclaimed 'How I have been handicapped in life! Should I have done better if I had been kept like her, in a mental greenhouse and taken care of?'[7] Certainly, Oliphant never received the editorship of a periodical, a key sign of professional accomplishment in the world of Victorian letters which her singular professional success would seem to warrant. Salaried positions, such as editorships, were the most secure journalistic positions. During the 1860s and 1870s, when Oliphant was at her peak, such positions went overwhelmingly to men. But important work, including *Annals of a Publishing House* (1897), continued to appear until her death. She died at home in Windsor in 1897, having outlived all of her children.

For all of her doubts about the deleterious effects that financial need had on her craft, Oliphant's was a professional name to contend with. Though she was never a salaried employee, instead arranging payments for each piece and regularly asking for advances, Oliphant's reviewing and piece-work was clearly a staple for *Blackwood's*, and she remained a primary literary reviewer for that journal from 1854 to near her death.

Nearly twenty years after her death, Henry James lamented that 'No woman had ever, for half a century, had her personal "say" as publicly and irresponsibly' as Oliphant.[8] His derogatory assessment reminds us of the influence of the kind of reviewing at which Oliphant excelled, and it registers the very real dismissals of critical relevance with which she grappled as a woman writer. But James's sneer also points to an integral component of her writing in her approach to overtly political questions that is worth exploring. Again and again, in her reviews and critical essays on the Woman Question, from her 1856 'Laws concerning Women' (*Blackwood's Edinburgh Magazine*, 79) to her 1869 review of Mill's *Subjection of Women* and Josephine Butler's *Woman's Work and Woman's Culture* (*Blackwood's*, 130) through to her reassessment of 'The Grievances of Women' (1880) for *Fraser's Magazine*, Oliphant as 'general utility woman' formulated a press signature of the 'everyman' (or everywoman) who had sufficient, if not specialized, knowledge to have her 'say', or rather to form political opinion.

Oliphant wrote the short article 'Laws concerning Women' in response to a request to sign a petition calling for revision of property laws affecting married women. These laws were at the centre of a prolonged legal debate between those who argued that married women were sufficiently protected through the legal representation of their husbands, and those who sought direct political representation for women. Oliphant's article takes up Barbara Bodichon's *A Brief Summary in Plain Language of the Laws Affecting Women* (1854), the first salvo in the campaign to reform married women's property law that would eventually lead to two important legal reforms, the Married Women's Property Acts of 1870 and 1882.[9]

Blackwood's Magazine, which published 'Laws concerning Women', was overwhelmingly against the kinds of women's political rights that Bodichon advocated. In the review, unsigned as was usual for *Blackwood's* and written in an anonymous masculine voice, Oliphant takes up a signature dislike, the insistent voicing of political grievances, using it to frame her analysis and shape reader response. Her first characterization of the pamphlet is important. *A Brief Summary* is a 'very serious and well-meaning pamphlet' (379), a 'quiet summary of real laws and positive (apparent) injustices' (379). Taking the pamphlet's own 'quiet' tone as a value to conjure with, Oliphant requests her readers to pause and reflect. There is much that the review rejects in Bodichon's analysis, including what Oliphant reads as the supposition of a 'natural antagonism' between men and women. However, Oliphant finds Bodichon's summary of the laws affecting women 'somewhat humiliating' (380), and concludes her article with tepid support for the call for married women's property rights, noting as she does so that such a reform would be a 'very easy and unimportant concession' (385).

On the one hand, representing reform as 'unimportant' may stem from Oliphant's need to have her review of this pamphlet accord with *Blackwood's* overarching rejection of women's political rights, but there is an ambivalence in this review that is not fully explained by Oliphant's agreement with or dissent from *Blackwood's* policy. Arguing that the majority of women 'know nothing of these laws [summarized in the pamphlet] and are entirely unmoved by their action' (384), Oliphant at once makes Bodichon's case for her and denies the full charge of Bodichon's political premise. *A Brief Summary* was written, after all, because married women's property law reformers argued that women did not *know* the laws affecting them, and therefore needed the summary to be galvanized into action. The 'unknowing' woman is precisely one of the pamphlet's targeted readers. But through her suggestion that most women do not know and are not affected by the laws, Oliphant points to the world of the 'everyday' in order to ground the political efficacy of her position, which insists that legal reform is of little value in marriage. For her, the meaning of legal reform is effortlessly transparent. If property law is reformed, 'every one must see at a glance how superficial this manner of reformation is' (385).

The connection between everyday lives and the 'everyman' perspective rehearsed in this early article is more central to Oliphant's view in the substantial thirty-page review of John Stuart Mill's *Subjection of Women* and Josephine Butler's *Woman's Work and Woman's Culture* published in 1869. Oliphant begins with her distinctive disavowal of all that is extreme in argument. Condemning the 'wild statement[s] on both sides' of the Woman Question, Oliphant poses a problem: 'What is the puzzled spectator to do?' (573). The answer is immediately forthcoming. The puzzled spectator rejects the metaphor of slavery, in which Mill grounds his plea, primarily because of its excess.

The language of rejection permeating the review is particularly important. Oliphant is at pains to lament that so revered a figure as Mill should err in the vociferousness of his argument – what she calls his 'unevenness of tone' (577). But it is Mill's stature as a philosopher that also legitimates her critique. Unlike many philosophical questions demanding the rarefied expertise of a Mill, the question of women in society, the review contends, is 'a matter on which we are all qualified to form an opinion' (577). If Jameson's review in the *Athenaeum* models the voter–reader's competency to assess political arguments, a similar strategy is at work here. It will be 'common experience, common eyesight' (577), available to reviewer and reader alike, that will repudiate Mill's argument most effectively.

The legitimacy of common experience is everywhere evident and requires no rational explication or defence. '[A]ny candid reader can fairly look the question in the face' (582), assures the reviewer. Again and again, reliance on what 'any reader' can know, not the skewed eyesight of the rarefied expert, is stressed. '[W]e have but to look' (583), urges the reviewer. 'Every observer, whose eyes are open to the common facts about him' (585), who uses 'daylight' not 'philosophical spectacles' (588) to see, will come to proper conclusions. Indeed, the value of everyday instinct over expertise is paramount: 'We cannot explain how it is', says the reviewer about the ideal of unity in marriage, 'but we know that it is' (589).

The certainty attached to the everyday is used to different political ends in Oliphant's 'Grievances of Women', published in 1880 in *Fraser's Magazine*. Invited to address a meeting in support of women's suffrage, Oliphant declines to participate, but determines to query her decision. The resulting article is written with a visible feminine signature that, based in a writer's knowledge of journalism, critiques the press's treatment of women in politics, and conveys her own sense of press standards and ethics. In so doing, Oliphant presents the 'common' everyday exchanges of readers and her own voice as deserving respect, and worth a hearing.

Beginning her piece with a self-characterization as a woman too cowardly to brave the public platform, Oliphant's writing voice as the anonymous voice of the everyday is galvanized to reclaim the debate on the Woman Question from the many 'newspapers and public speakers of the coarser sort' (231) who have commandeered discussion by ridiculing opponents. The consequence has been 'to quash the honest opinion of a great many women whose views on the subject might be worth knowing perhaps, being the outcome of experience and average good sense, if no more' (231). Oliphant frames her analysis of the dampening effects of ridicule on debate by a call to the reader: 'I wish to ask the reader his and her opinion', presenting her own position as simply the first statement in what should be a shared exchange: 'This is mine to start with' (234).

Oliphant uses press coverage of responses to women medical students as a case in point. Accusations 'in a very well known and influential English paper' that women sought medical education only from 'prurient curiosity and the foulest of motives' (241) are greeted with outraged astonishment: 'This was said in English print in full daylight of the nineteenth century, and nobody, so far as I can remember, objected to it. The journalist was not denounced by his brethren, and public opinion took it quite coolly, as a thing it was no shame to say. I ask the reader . . . what is his opinion on the subject?' (241). Oliphant insists on the disgrace of a debate in which there is no expectation of fair play: 'that nobody cared, that there was no protest, no objection, and that this was thought quite a permissible thing to say and to publish . . . is the extraordinary point in the matter' (242).

Oliphant's 'everyday' voice calls here for adjudication, insisting as it does so that the reader is competent to assess the proper protocols of public exchange. As elsewhere in her journalism, that voice does not object to the rejection of feminist claims; Oliphant makes clear that the stuff of political differences is not the issue. Rather, her press signature is used to respond to the ungenerous tenor of public discussion fostered by newspaper practices, a tenor that so jeopardizes the assumptions of rational and useful debate that the voices of average good sense, which she and others may offer, are lost in favour of more attention-getting representations of political women from all corners of the field.

Frances Power Cobbe (1822–1904)

If Oliphant's press signature insists upon the political validity of an everyday voice, whether progressive or conservative, writers like Frances Power Cobbe engaged the press to challenge 'everyday' understandings of women's lives, using press interest in the Woman Question to promote feminist causes. Born in Dublin to a prominent Anglo-Irish family, Cobbe was one of a handful of women making a living in the newspaper press. A feminist journalist and activist, she argued for women's increased educational and employment opportunities, was a vocal critic of marriage, and was involved in the women's suffrage campaign. She was instrumental in the passage of the 1878 Matrimonial Causes Act, which made domestic violence grounds for legal separation. She was also a leader in the Victorian anti-vivisection movement. Cobbe's writings on feminist topics in established periodicals and for daily newspapers, like the first halfpenny evening paper, the *Echo*, earned her about £300 a year, substantially less, as she often pointed out, than the £5,000 per year her eldest brother earned from the family estate. Her writings also offer one way to explore how a feminist writer brought feminism to the broader public. Here we will consider how Cobbe used the conventions of anonymous masculine signature in the newspaper leader to transform 'everyday' understandings of domestic violence. Her anonymous press signature insisted on the fair exchange of ideas and, in doing so, claimed the relevance and competence of feminist analysis of everyday political questions.

An 1870 *Echo* leader, titled 'The Right to Beat a Wife' (17 January 1870), written a year into Cobbe's seven-year tenure at the newspaper, addresses legal responses to domestic violence, inaugurating what becomes a signature analysis of domestic violence in her writing. With this leader, Cobbe explores what the serial form of the newspaper offers Victorian feminist analyses of domestic violence, using the first of what will be another signature component of her leader writing on domestic violence, the semi-dramatized account of the larger social patterns she sees promulgated by domestic violence, and their effect on perpetrators, witnesses, the legal system and the readers of the *Echo*. 'The Right to Beat a Wife' takes up the case of a police officer who had intervened in the battery of a woman by her husband in the street only to be charged with assault upon the husband. Railing against a system that would lay such charges, the leader represents the officer's actions as socially necessary in a way that the legal system is unable to comprehend: 'In these days of the "decay of public sentiment" he actually thought and felt as brave men used to feel at the sight of a trampled woman, and he laid Mr. Macgovern in the same mud wherein that meek and unoffending person had rolled his wife.' Cobbe's approval of the officer's action is part of her broader concern with public indifference to domestic violence, which she pursues relentlessly in her leader writing for the *Echo*. Here, she analyses a comment made by the magistrate presiding over the case, who reiterates an accusation lodged by the defendant against the police officer. The magistrate concurred with the defendant that '[t]he assault was unprovoked, brutal, and unjustifiable'. The ominous implications of this statement are made strikingly clear in the leader: 'The sight of a woman in the gutter is ... henceforth to be understood to be no "provocation" at all to the passers by; nor the brutality of the man who thrusts her there any "justification" of the Quixote who may be so foolish as to take her part.' When magistrates agree with violent husbands, the leader writes, 'women's claims to protection from violence in the streets are of the most doubtful kind'. If 'English magistrates and English public opinion' conspire to suggest that husbands have the right to beat their wives, England's single women are similarly vulnerable: 'Are single women who may need at any moment the aid of a constable to set up flags in their bonnets ... inscribed with the word "Unmarried," so that the police may know that nobody has the right to knock them down ... ?'

The incongruity of the image points to Cobbe's determination to jolt her readers into new ways of reading domestic violence by assuming their agreement with the analysis she proposes. Her editorials repeatedly emphasize the lurid strangeness of reports of domestic violence, and the degree to which they require perpetrators, bystanders and readers to depart radically from the everyday scripts shaping relationships and social justice that would ordinarily lead them to oppose it. The serial form of the newspaper is part of this work. Cobbe takes care to present the sensationalist details of legal reports as part of a narrative script she presents as all too everyday, and one which she strives to identify as aberrant. Approaching the same dissonance between everyday expectations about safety and public responses to domestic violence, Cobbe labels as 'unEnglish' the social laws which allow witnesses to violent assaults to stand by and do nothing: 'Week after week we record stories of husbands beating their wives, and often actually killing them, and dragging their corpses about while the neighbours stand by quiescent, as if a wife came under the old Mosaic law concerning slaves, and her master was not to be punished for killing her, "for she is his money".'

Another 1870 *Echo* leader, 'Even-Handed Justice', compares the wildly disproportionate punishment of a young carter found guilty of gaming on a Sunday (two months' hard labour) to a man who beats his wife so severely that she dies days later in the workhouse (eight months' imprisonment). The leader stresses the jarring dissonance of a judge hearing about a woman '"on her hands and knees, moaning fearfully, bleeding from the mouth and eyes"' (18 August 1870) from her husband's assault, who is able to conclude that 'he "has no doubt he did not intend to kill his wife"'. The leader's fury is palpable: 'In Heaven's name, we ask, what does a man intend to do, who stamps on a woman's breast and assaults her afresh while she is vomiting blood?' Again and again, the leader intervenes in the story told by the court transcripts of the trial to question interpretation. 'We read', Cobbe points out, 'he was "seen dragging his wife by the hair of her head" – does anybody quite realise what this process means?' Other interjections clarify the full horror of what the transcript presents as the facts of the case: the beating appears to have taken place in public; despite the woman being near death, neighbours did not intervene.

In these leaders, as in the dozens she wrote on domestic violence, we see Cobbe using the daily newspaper's formal properties – its serial form and anonymous editorial voice – to reframe public debates about domestic violence. Exploiting the leader's anonymous masculine voice and its capacity to interrupt and challenge legal and popular narratives surrounding domestic violence in the moment of their circulation; reframing court transcripts; re-creating the drama of the assault from written records; insistently intervening in the legal narrative lines that yield inadequate punishment, Cobbe's leaders challenge a cultural apparatus that fails to protect women from bodily assault, and seek to demonstrate a world in which everyone realizes vividly what it means to attack a woman, and knows the appropriate punishment to be meted out.

Eliza Lynn Linton (1822–1898) and Mona Caird (1854–1932)

Writers like Cobbe had a sharp but nuanced eye for the possibilities and opportunities that the press offered their positions. As the press underwent profound change through the course of the century – from changes to tax regimes and technological improvements to massive expansion of titles and readers – the press opportunities for women writers also underwent profound change. One of Cobbe's fellow pioneers, journalist and novelist Eliza Lynn Linton, eyed the same press landscape and saw rather different possibilities for women's voices in the newspaper press.

Born Eliza Lynn in Cumberland, Linton left home at twenty-three to become a writer in London. Her first publications were historical novels. She never abandoned novel writing entirely, publishing *The Autobiography of Christopher Kirkland*, a novel espousing the sensationalist and antifeminist aesthetic of her successful journalism, at the height of her journalistic career in 1885. Like Oliphant, Eliza Lynn Linton was a novelist and journalist admired in her day primarily for her journalism, becoming one of the first women to be elected to the governing council of the Society of Authors, and the first salaried woman journalist in Britain. Her journalism – exhilarating, excoriating and often vituperative in its tone – took as its primary subject the threat to domestic womanhood represented by a series of inappropriate women, from aging coquettes to the 'shrieking sisterhood', Linton's phrase for feminists.

Much critical attention on Linton has focused on the perceived gap between such writings as 'The Girl of the Period' (1868), which attacks 'independent' women who smoke, talk loosely, and otherwise act too much like men, and Linton's own life as an independent, wage-earning, married but separated woman who devoted substantial amounts of her professional time to helping other women become the independent individuals her journalism pilloried. The tension does appear insurmountable. Yet, attention to her writing, not as seemingly 'hypocritical' content but as a particular kind of press writing with specific strategies and formal properties, offers a more productive framing that eliminates what can seem a critical impasse. As Andrea Broomfield argues, Linton's writing is moulded not simply by questions of her political allegiances, but also by her role as a popular journalist whose work gained a massive audience.[10] In this critical framework, anti-feminism is a popular press strategy for creating audience demand. Linton's press signature or voice uses the strategies of popular journalism – from extreme rhetoric and ad hominem attacks to sensationalism, assertion and a kind of zealous reductionism – to create scandal, and gain an audience.

Her primary employer, the *Saturday Review*, used such tactics in a bid to gain success by combining popular journalistic techniques with the kind of weighty political articles that signalled a serious, intellectual journal. Linton's press signature fitted the journal's editorial and stylistic remit profitably. Appealing to and reinforcing masculine prejudices, her 'Girl of the Period' essays – the series draws its name from the first article – were part of the journal's 'middle' section designed to be lighter and more controversial in tone. The series, written anonymously, was enormously successful, with a *Girl of the Period* journal launched, and spin-off stage comedies and farces performed.[11] Linton did not claim authorship of the series for sixteen years, but when she did she was unrepentantly controversial: 'I neither soften nor retract a line of what I have said.'

Though Linton's pieces for the *Saturday Review* were anonymous, her professional reputation was highly distinguished. When the *Nineteenth Century*, an 'open platform' journal that published controversial pieces on social and political topics, sought to re-ignite the Woman Question in the 1890s by publishing an exchange between explicitly feminist and non-feminist writers, Linton's controversial press signature seemed an almost natural fit. The overt marketing of controversy, which the *Nineteenth Century* journal packaged as traditional debate in serial form, offered yet another press opportunity for women journalists and the full range of their political voices.

Linton's series 'The Wild Women', published in 1891, made use of her signature style, beginning with characteristic resolution: 'All women are not lovely, and the wild women never are.' The series is a combination of a breathtaking romp through every stereotype used to vilify political women and the occasional interesting critique of such trends as Victorian feminist orientalism. Whether castigating wild women for travelling or for playing golf and cricket, Linton relishes the extreme image. A sportswoman is compared to a '"butching" woman, nursing her infant child with hands red with the blood of an ox she has just poleaxed' ('Wild Women as Social Insurgents', 200). On the question of political representation, Linton offers a curt and marketable aphorism: 'The cradle lies across the door of the polling-booth and bars the way to the senate' ('Wild Women as Politicians', 188).

At a time when controversial signatures and tone were highly profitable, Linton's press signature was compelling and enormously successful. But hers was not the only signature to embrace the periodical press's popular style to address an audience. Mona Caird, responding to Linton's series, also flourished some of the signature components of popular journalism to circulate an opposing political analysis. Born on the Isle of Wight, Caird was a novelist and essayist active in the National Society for Women's Suffrage and the Women's Social and Political Union. She was a charter member of the Women Writers Suffrage League founded in 1908 and active in the anti-vivisection movement. She was also well known beyond activist circles for her writings on marriage, particularly her 1888 article 'Marriage', published in the *Westminster Review*. Her feminist colleague Annie Swan called that article a 'flaming bomb'.[12] The article was taken up in the popular daily press, one newspaper, the *Daily Telegraph*, asking its readers: 'Is Marriage a Failure?' The response to that question filled editorial pages for months, prompting the paper to refuse to accept any further letters. A selection of letters was quickly assembled and published by Harry Quilter, barrister and editor of the *Universal Review*, in the same year.

As a controversially feminist writer, Caird is a calculated choice to square off against Linton for the *Nineteenth Century*'s open platform exchange on political women. Importantly, if earlier writers like Cobbe and Oliphant built their press signatures (whether feminist or conservative) largely around the display of fair and rational exchange, Caird's press signature is predicated on a rather different mix of rational argument and popular extremism. In her signed retort to Linton's wild women excesses, Caird claims the high ground of reasoned response and objective analysis. She opens 'A Defence of the So-called Wild Women' with an extended presentation of the position Linton's opponents find themselves occupying. Since Linton 'gives them nothing to answer' (287); since responding to her is 'undignified and futile' (287); and since '[i]t is of no real moment whether Mrs. Lynn Linton's unfavourable impression of the women who differ from her ... be just or unjust' (287), Caird identifies her task as answering the question: are progressive views on women's roles 'nearer or farther from the truth than the doctrines from which they dissent?' (287).

Despite this strategic dismissal of Linton's relevance, and the article's focus on a progressive representation of women's social roles, Caird allots ample space to her opponent's style of argument, using the same cutting strategies that characterize Linton's three-part serial, yet distinguishing her writing by a series of decorous slights that disparage whilst claiming fair play. Caird imagines constructing a table of the charges Linton lays against women, suggesting that, though the resulting 'sad list' (288) would 'lack the eloquence and literary quality of Mrs. Lynn Linton's arguments' (288), it would not 'yield to them in cogency' (288). Caird homes in on Linton's style of attack, characterizing her writing as 'taunts and accusations against her sex' (297) which Linton 'hurls ... as if it pleased her to add another insult to those which the literature of centuries' (297) has directed at women.

In contrast, Caird associates her own writing, and so her progressive views on women, with rational inquiry. It is the mind that 'consider [s] principles not persons' (287), that 'inquire[s] into ... real causes' (298), that turns to research not hyperbole for its political analysis, which best responds to the challenges of women's new social role. The mind, like

Linton's, that 'prefers the simple finger of scorn, the taunt, the inexpensive sneer' (298) and depends upon 'decaying institutions' (305) is not worth engaging.

The turbulent 'Wild Women' exchange is an orchestrated battle between political positions embodied in distinctive press signatures. Caird's signature – assessing relevant research and rejecting extravagant press gestures – claims authority against the uncommon success of Linton's popular press persona. Erudite and acerbic, Caird's press signature takes its place alongside those of Jameson, Oliphant, Cobbe, Linton and the many other women journalists who knew how to exploit the various opportunities of an ever-competitive press to voice a sweeping range of political and professional goals.

Notes

1 Hilary Fraser, Judith Johnston and Stephanie Green, *Gender and the Victorian Periodical* (Cambridge: Cambridge University Press, 2003), p. xi.
2 'Open platform' was an editorial policy that, modelled on the idea of the debate, brought together writers with different positions on a topic of social or political interest. The policy encouraged debate on controversial topics, especially between writers presented as well-known or 'star' contributors.
3 Adele M. Holcomb, 'Anna Jameson: The First Professional English Art Historian', *Art History*, 6, 2 (1983), pp. 171–87.
4 Barbara Onslow, *Women of the Press in Nineteenth-Century Britain* (New York: Palgrave Macmillan, 2000), p. 28.
5 *Ibid.*
6 Quoted in Clara Thomas, *Love and Work Enough: The Life of Anna Jameson* (Toronto: University of Toronto Press, 1967), p. 55.
7 Margaret Oliphant, *The Autobiography of Margaret Oliphant*, ed. Elisabeth Jay (Peterborough, ON: Broadview Press, 2002), pp. 49–50.
8 Quoted in Deirdre D'Albertis, 'The Domestic Drone: Margaret Oliphant and a Political History of the Novel', *Studies in English Literature*, 37, 4 (1997), p. 824.
9 Property law reform began with Barbara Bodichon's campaign to add married women's property rights to the 1857 Divorce Act. That campaign had limited success, and was followed by the establishment in 1868 of the Married Women's Property Committee, headed by Elizabeth Wolstenholme Elmy. See Mary Lyndon Shanley, *Feminism, Marriage and the Law in Victorian England, 1850–1895* (London: I. B. Tauris, 1989).
10 See Andrea L. Broomfield, 'Much More than an Antifeminist: Eliza Lynn Linton's Contribution to the Rise of Victorian Popular Journalism', *Victorian Literature and Culture*, 29, 2 (2001), pp. 267–83.
11 For further discussion of the 'Girl of the Period' phenomenon, see Nancy Fix Anderson, *Woman against Women in Victorian England: A Life of Eliza Lynn Linton* (Bloomington: Indiana University Press, 1987).
12 Ann Heilmann, *New Woman Strategies: Sarah Grand, Olive Schreiner, Mona Caird* (Manchester: Manchester University Press, 2004), p. 4.

6

HILARY FRASER

Writing the past

The past as we know it was largely created by the Victorians. Historical terms and concepts such as the Renaissance, the Augustan, Modernity, the Zeitgeist – indeed, the very coinage 'Victorian', and even the idea of period-icity itself, were nineteenth-century inventions. Moreover, we have inherited from the nineteenth century a modern historical consciousness, and his-toriographical methods, for it was during this period that the modern discipline was defined and professionalized, that the counterclaims of empiricists and idealists were first articulated. This was when the German empiricist Leopold von Ranke introduced the methods of 'objective' history, the French republican Jules Michelet those of 'total' history, and the Swiss historian of art and culture Jakob Burckhardt those of *Kulturgeschichte*, and when Hegel and Marx shifted the focus of historical study away from the rise and fall of rulers and nations to the analysis of social change, together revolutionizing the historical sciences across Europe; while, in Britain, Carlyle and Macaulay presided over an efflorescence of narrative history and in 1886 the professional journal the *English Historical Review* was founded.

Nineteenth-century historiography is sometimes represented as somewhat monolithic, comprising predominantly grand narratives of great men, and celebrating nationalist and imperialist ideologies within either the progres-sivist paradigm of Whig history or the cyclic model of history favoured by conservatives. However, it is on the contrary precisely because history writing in an age described by Nietzsche in *On the Use and Abuse of History for Life* (1873) as suffering from a consumptive 'historical disease'[1] was so rich and various, and took so many literary forms beyond that of the formal academic treatise, that modern cultural historians, critics and theor-ists so often turn to it, as a source or model, or as offering exemplification and elaboration of modern methods. It is exactly because the multifarious nineteenth-century understandings of history included an acknowledgement that the historical is always defined and constituted by its opposite – the past by the present, the historical by the unhistorical, the real of history by its fictional or mythic representation – that it continues to be of such interest to modern scholars. We are haunted equally by Carlyle's heroes and Vernon Lee's ghosts, our historical imaginary shaped by the tropes of the nineteenth-century museum and arcade, by Victorian romance and necromancy, and by the Victorians' own sense of belatedness.

Hence Walter Benjamin's historiographical method for his materialist 'primal history' of the nineteenth century in *The Arcades Project* is that of the nineteenth-century collector of antiquities and curiosities, or the ragpicker of the 'refuse' and 'detritus' of history.[2] Hayden White's thesis on the interplay of the historical and literary imagination in *Metahistory* (1973) is proved on the pulse of nineteenth-century historical narrative and discourse. The 'Annales' School looked to Michelet, Foucault to Nietzsche. New Historicist critics in the 1980s, in the spirit of Stephen Greenblatt's professed desire to 'speak with the dead',[3] produced a rush of books on nineteenth-century historicism that reflected, and reflected on, the Victorians' own 'mirror of history',[4] while modern novelists write historical fiction about the Victorians' encounters with the past, from evolutionary biology to Pre-Raphaelitism. Today's feminists and historians of gender and sexuality find nineteenth-century prototypes as well as subjects in early experimental women's histories and revisionist queer readings of the classical past, and it was in the nineteenth century also that working-class subjects began to be written, and to write themselves into history. We are intrigued and inspired by the intricacies, contradictions and huge diversity – generic, stylistic, methodological, ideological – of the Victorians' writing of the past, and it is these qualities of nineteenth-century historicism that this chapter will explore.

Modernity and loss

Why were the Victorians so drawn to the past? Was it in part a paradoxical consequence of their acute consciousness of their own modernity? There was a new awareness of the historical moment of the present (Richard D. Altick reminds us that '[s]ignificantly, the Victorian period was the first in English history to be christened while it was still in progress'[5]), but also of its contingency, of its place in the linear history by which the past becomes the future – and nineteenth-century writers were also, remember, notable for imagining utopian and dystopian futures. Of course, as Benjamin observes, 'Every epoch appears to itself inescapably modern';[6] neither is it unusual for modern cultures to celebrate, make capital of, and appropriate the alien materials of their received past, rendering it an embodiment of present concerns. Nevertheless, in the middle of the nineteenth century, a number of circumstances conspired to make people differently and more urgently conscious of their place in history. The emergence at mid-century of evolutionary theories about the prehistory of life on the planet opened up unimaginably huge vistas of time, and it must have seemed all the more important to recover a sense of human history amidst such temporal vastness. Amidst this recalibration of human time itself, more recent and localized social and political events reinforced the sense of the nineteenth century as inaugurating a new modern era in European history. In the wake of the French Revolution, the Industrial Revolution and various nationalist movements for political reform across Europe, the Victorians were conscious to an unprecedented degree of a radical discontinuity between past and present. As Benjamin notes, 'The feeling that an epochal upheaval had begun with the nineteenth century was no special privilege of Hegel and Marx.'[7]

Such seismic change explains the intensity of yearning and regret for a vanishing past experienced by some, who felt that the old ways of life seemed to be disappearing before their very eyes. Ruskin's *Fors Clavigera* (1871–84), for example, includes records of anguished correspondents who had witnessed within their lifetime the ruination of their environments, and seen ancient links with the past heedlessly severed. In his 'Letters to the Workmen and Labourers of Great Britain', Ruskin himself laments the changes that have taken place within just a few decades, and directly links the demolition of the past with the encroachment of modern life. Letter XX, from Venice, dated 3 July 1872, for example, is prefaced by an engraving showing 'Part of the Chapel of St. Mary of the Thorn, PISA, as it was 27 years ago. Now in Ruins.'[8] He tells us that he watched the old marble cross of the thirteenth-century chapel, for centuries a beacon to Pisan oarsmen, and since the fifteenth century a shrine for a branch of Christ's crown of thorns brought there by a returning merchant, being 'struck … to pieces' by a shamefaced workman:

> The last quarter of a century has brought changes, and made the Italians wiser. British Protestant missionaries explained to them that they had only got a piece of blackberry stem in their ultramarine box. German philosophical missionaries explained to them that the Crown of Thorns itself was only a graceful metaphor. French republican missionaries explained to them that chapels were inconsistent with liberty on the quay; and their own Engineering missionaries of civilization explained to them that steam-power was independent of the Madonna. And now in 1872, rowing by steam, digging by steam, driving by steam, here, behold, are a troublesome pair of human arms out of employ. So the Engineering missionaries fit them with hammer and chisel, and set them to break up the Spina Chapel.[9]

Ruskin maps a direct correlation between the so-called missionaries of Modernity – German biblical criticism, republicanism, post-industrial capitalism – and the fate of the medieval chapel; the values of the past are implicitly defined and brought to life as the very contrary of those of the present day.

Interestingly, the accompanying illustration of the church itself bears witness to a historical moment of technological transformation. Ruskin notes that, having drawn it in 1840, he 'daguerreotyped the eastern end of it some years later, (photography being then unknown), and copied the daguerreotype, that people might not be plagued in looking, by the lustre'.[10] The frontispiece is engraved from the drawing. In the period between his first capturing an image of the chapel, 'then as perfect as when it was built',[11] and his memorializing of it, 'Now in Ruins', photography has been invented, and has superseded the daguerreotype. Indeed, in another letter, photography itself is made to signify modern loss:

> You think it a great triumph to make the sun draw brown landscapes for you. That was also a discovery, and some day may be useful. But the sun had drawn landscapes before for you, not in brown, but in green, and blue, and all imaginable colours, here in England. Not one of you ever looked at them then; not one of you cares for the loss of them now; when you have shut the sun out with smoke, so that he can draw nothing more, except brown blots through a hole in a box.[12]

Like the railroad 'enterprised' through what was once a lovely rocky valley between Buxton and Bakewell, 'divine as the Vale of Tempe', photography, a scientific instrument for the representation of that landscape, though some day it 'may be useful', signifies for Ruskin a rupture between ways of seeing 'then' and 'now' that can never be healed.[13]

Past and present

Modern commentators have suggested that, in the context of a widespread withdrawal of confidence in the present, the Victorian historical imagination was a means for the individual to transcend the fractured contemporary world and to rediscover lost continuities with the past by forging new mythic connections. The past offered the chance to address and reconcile the tensions engendered by the rapid material advances that characterized the age. One explanation for this retrogressive tendency in a century of unprecedented change is, then, that it was a reaction to progress and its problems. It is undoubtedly the case that the vaunted Victorian faith in progress was chronically beset by anxieties, the fast-moving trajectory of modernity shot through by ambivalently retrospective cross-currents. Yet the appeal of the past for Victorians was not just a reactionary and conservative 'dream of order' amidst the speedy disorder of modernity.[14] England's medieval inheritance, for example, appealed as strongly to the industrial, liberal, nonconforming, middle-class population as it did to those opposed to progress; Gothic could, as readily as ancient Greek polity, be found to signify democratic values, such as liberty, idealism, creative individualism and co-operation. Whilst it was no doubt true that some Victorians with democratic leanings felt, as Matthew Arnold contended in *Culture and Anarchy* (1869), a '[v]iolent indignation with the past',[15] and by the same token for others their preoccupation with history signified a disaffection with their post-industrial world and its capitalist values and a longing for stability and continuity in times of change, others appropriated the past to legitimate a decidedly modern ethos. For example, the decoration of Manchester Town Hall celebrates through historical references such modern values and concepts as parliamentary rights, municipal autonomy, industry and free trade. What we read there is not nostalgia for a lost past, but provincial and national civic pride, and a display of a cultured appreciation of the history of civilization to counter any prejudiced image of Northern philistinism that might prevail in the South.

This example reminds us that the Victorians were not only writing, but also building, painting, reading, translating, excavating, restoring, collecting and displaying the past, and their relationship to the various historical cultures with which they engaged is often ambivalent and conflicted. Newly exposed, as they were, to the dizzyingly rich repository of material culture of the past in museums and galleries and special exhibitions up and down the country, as well as throughout continental Europe (thanks to the greater ease of the modern steam-driven travel so loathed by Ruskin), it was not unusual for Victorian writers to access the past and build their readings of history around an intense personal encounter with a historical artefact. This enabled them to reflect not only on the past culture that is embodied in the artefact but also on the meaning of their encounter with it; it enabled them to explore, that is, larger questions of history and historical consciousness.

Dante Gabriel Rossetti's poem 'The Burden of Nineveh' (1856, revised 1870) begins with just such an encounter. Rossetti's personal immersion in the past was unusually profound and formational; he was baptized into it when he was named after Dante Alighieri; he mythologized his own life around the Italian poet's mystical love for Beatrice; and his founding association with Pre-Raphaelitism, dedicated to the renovation of modern art according to the principles of painting before Raphael, meant that both his art and his writing were saturated in an idea of early Italian culture. He was, moreover, a painter/poet who habitually wrote poems about visual images, and made pictures of and within framing texts, in an extraordinarily symbiotic and intensely sensuous way. Jerome McGann has observed that Rossetti's 'Sonnets for Pictures' typically bring together three 'aesthetic events': namely, the ekphrastic poem, the painting that elicits it, and 'the liminal event that emerges from their dialectical relation'.[16] In this poem too Rossetti's encounter with the 'wingèd beast from Nineveh', being hoisted into the British Museum at the very moment he 'made the swing-door spin/ And issued', constitutes exactly such a constellation of events, enacting a transitional moment and a liminal space for dialectical reflection upon the ancient artefact, his own 'living eyes' in this modern museum to the dead, and their complex and dynamic relationship.[17]

Sir Austen Henry Layard had completed his excavation of the ruins of Nineveh in 1851, and in 1849 had published an account of *Nineveh and Its Remains*, which Rossetti must have known, that highlights the winged bull as his most significant acquisition. The [hi]story is told and retold, and in Rossetti's poem given a dramatic *mise en scène* at the threshold of the museum, the very heart of empire. Thomas Hardy was later to write in 'The Fiddler of the Reels' (1893), a story set during the Great Exhibition, of the year 1851 as 'a precipice in Time', when, '[a]s in a geological "fault," we had presented to us a sudden bringing of ancient and modern into absolute contact',[18] and it is just such a vertiginous museum moment that Rossetti's poem, begun in 1856, captures. Time and space are (ironically, given its archival role and the historicist and classificatory principles that underpin it) collapsed in the museum, historical and geographical difference erased in a site characterized by Foucault as 'heterotopic'; that is, 'capable of juxtaposing in a single real space several spaces, several sites that are in themselves incompatible'.[19] Abstracted from its historical setting, the winged beast is paradoxically consigned to this random collection of synechdochal cultural samples along with all the other gods – Greek, Roman, Egyptian, Assyrian – 'All relics here together'. 'Nay, but were not some/Of these thine own "antiquity"?' asks the speaker, reasserting a sense of historical lineage; and, he adds disconcertingly, situating himself and Victorian London in the same historical process, might the winged creature one day be borne off to distant lands, 'a relic now/Of London, not of Nineveh!'[20] It is an alternative, less bleak, vision of the future of the Victorian museological project than the one H. G. Wells would later predict in *The Time Machine* (1895) in his portrayal of the Time Traveller amidst the derelict remains of the South Kensington Museums, but it suggests notwithstanding that the burden of Nineveh is the burden of history.

Brief encounters

It is striking how often for Victorian writers an image or a material object becomes an intensified site for historical realization. Benjamin privileges the dialectical image, 'the image in the now of its recognizability', and the arrested moment, 'dialectics at a standstill', in the writing of history.[21] His articulation of how such fleeting images of the past, such moments of tension and change, must be caught, seized, at the instant of their legibility, so that 'what has been comes together in a flash with the now to form a constellation', seems to capture what happens not only in Rossetti's poem but also in writing by authors such as Robert Browning, Ruskin and Vernon Lee, where an image is made to speak dialectically for the past. Sometimes, as in the case of 'The Burden of Nineveh', such images are fulfilled by narrativization, so that the historical snapshot afforded by the artefact or the event is worked into a historical story. Browning's 'Fra Lippo Lippi', 'Andrea del Sarto' and 'The Bishop Orders His Tomb' are all examples of how the poet conjures a period (the Italian Renaissance) from his face-to-face encounters with its artworks, but also goes on to create historical narrative out of static paintings and tomb sculpture – not only biographical narratives around the artists and the subjects of their portraits, but narratives of patronage and commercial transaction, of the social production and consumption of art, generational histories of the emergence and decline of schools and styles of art, of the rise and fall of the Renaissance itself.

Likewise Ruskin builds his history of the Middle Ages and the Renaissance in *The Stones of Venice* (1851–3) around his own highly idiosyncratic and physical encounters with, for example, sepulchral monuments; climbing ladders to peer behind the visible façade, examining facial features in close focus, to discover what each particular sculpture reveals about its subject, its maker and the culture that produced it; then weaving from these emblematic cultural signs of the times a counter-narrative to those mainstream histories which viewed the High Renaissance as the zenith of culture, to produce his own story of spiritual purity overtaken by pride as thirteenth- and fourteenth-century sanctity degenerated into fifteenth- and sixteenth-century decadence. Ruskin's account is itself overturned by Vernon Lee, who parodically deploys his own methods of reading funerary sculpture to propose an alternative history again. In the Middle Ages, she writes, 'The sculptor's work was but the low relief on the church flags, the timidly carved, outlined, cross-legged knight or praying priest, flattened down on his pillow as if ashamed even of that amount of prominence, and in a hurry to be trodden down and obliterated into a few ghostly outlines.'[22] She has no time for Ruskin's appreciation of the spiritual humility of medieval tomb sculpture, or for his denigration of the coarseness and pride of the Renaissance sarcophagus, typified for him by the fact that 'the figures which before had been laid at rest upon the tomb pillow, raised themselves on their elbows, and began to look round them', signifying that 'The soul of the sixteenth century dared not contemplate its body in death.'[23] Instead, she celebrates the fact that 'to this humiliated, prostrate image, to this flat thing doomed to obliteration, came the sculptor of the Renaissance, and bade the wafer-like simulacrum fill up, expand, raise itself, lift itself on its elbow, arise and take possession of the bed of state'.[24]

Vernon Lee's writing on the Renaissance is full of examples of direct, visual and tactile examples of her encounters with the past. She was to write in 1897, in her volume *Limbo and Other Essays*, of her powerful 'sense of being companioned by the past, of being in a place warmed for our living by the lives of others'.[25] She describes hurrying through narrow Venetian streets, and feeling 'that I am in contact with a whole living, breathing thing, full of habits of life, of suppressed words; a sort of odd, mysterious, mythical, but very real creature; as if, in the dark, I stretched out my hand and met something (but without any fear), something absolutely indefinable in shape and kind, but warm, alive'.[26] But it is in her very first book, *Studies of the Eighteenth Century in Italy* (1880), written when she was only twenty-four, in which she figuratively evokes her recovery of the past as 'the play instinct let loose in a lumber-room', a place of 'discarded mysteries and of lurking ghosts', that she is most literally in touch with the past of which she writes.[27]

She describes the moment of eighteenth-century scholarship of which she writes as a pivotal time, when 'The men and things of the Italian eighteenth century have not yet been exhumed and examined and criticised and classified; they have not yet been arranged, properly furbished and restored, like so many waxwork dolls decked in crumbling silk and lace, like so many pretty, quaint, or preposterous nicknacks in the glass cases of our historical museum.' They remain still, but only for a very short time, just within imaginative reach. For that 'volume of Gozzi's plays was probably touched last by hands which had clapped applause to Truffaldino-Sacchi or Pantalone-Darbes; the notes in the book of cantatas may last have been glanced over by singers who had learned to sing them from Porpora himself'.[28] We have never known the people of the eighteenth century, she says, 'but we have met occasionally men and women who have': the lady 'whose hand, which pressed ours, had pressed the hand of Fanny Burney', and the old musician 'who had sung with boyish voice to Cimarosa and Paisiello those airs which he hummed over for us in faint and husky tones'.[29] It is this intense desire for tactile contact with a past world about to move beyond her grasp, for the faintest echo of performances which can never again be heard, before its men and women are 'exhumed, restored, put into glass cases and exhibited mummy-fashion in our historical museums',[30] that defines the particular quality of Lee's approach to the eighteenth century.

We are invited to picture her wandering through the streets and rediscovering an eighteenth century that is more authentic because its traces, fragments of a world that has not quite passed away, may still be found in a kind of metonymics of history that is not yet circumscribed by the museum; in dusty volumes rummaged from market stalls, like Browning's 'old yellow book' that became the basis of his monumental dramatic poem *The Ring and the Book* (1868–9), or in forgotten little archives; in sudden encounters with faded portraits; in the street theatre and puppet shows which are all that remain of a rich indigenous heritage; and in neglected gardens and ramshackle rooms that once were the venues of august cultural gatherings. Throughout her life, Vernon Lee was obsessed with the idea of the 'genius loci', the way history is embodied in place, and places are invested with the spirit of the past, and made into sites of intensified experience and meaning. Decayed and ruined buildings – such as the Bosco Parrasio in Rome, the former meeting place of the Arcadians, or the home of the old Philharmonic Academy in Bologna – tell stories of glorious pasts and cultural decline and fall or, like the Paduan home of the formerly great but now forgotten singer Pacchierotti, summon a fanciful memory 'that we ourselves must once, vaguely and distantly, have heard that weirdly sweet voice, those subtle, pathetic intonations'.[31] Paintings are made to provide the basis for an imagined historical scenario, as when the concert pictures of Niccolò Abati and Leonello Spada are invoked to bring to life a scene of players and singers on stage sitting around the harpsichord. Lee recalls one such picture in which 'a musician has left the harpsichord and is pacing the boards, plumed hat in hand, with solemn gesture', and wonders 'Is he reciting, or is he singing? Is this a rudimentary opera or merely a play interlarded with concerts?',[32] thus dramatizing the pivotal moment of the birth of the opera as she has been describing it, and making the static painting tell a narrative of musical history.

History and narrative

There are countless examples in Victorian historical writing, both fictional and nonfiction, where an author's personal encounter with a historical image is thus narrativized in a way that captures at once the material object that speaks of a historical moment and the modern experience of looking at it – or even of not looking at it, as was the case when George Eliot visited

San Marco as part of her research for *Romola* in 1860, and was denied access, as a woman, to the cells decorated by Fra Angelico on the first floor of the cloisters, including those of Savonarola, who is such an important figure in her novel. She had to rely on notes taken on her behalf by her partner George Henry Lewes for her own description of the interior of the monastery. Eliot was, though, permitted to enter the Chapter House, where she saw Fra Angelico's large Crucifixion, which she admired enormously, singling out the group of grieving women at the foot of the Cross for special praise. She wrote in her journal, 'The frescoes I cared for most in all Florence were the few of Fra Angelico's that a donna was allowed to see in the Convent of San Marco. In the Chapter-house, now used as a guard-room, is a large crucifixion, with the inimitable group of the fainting mother, upheld by St. John and the younger Mary, and clasped round by the kneeling Magdalen.'[33]

Eliot alludes to her female experience of exclusion from the cells, as well as to the painting in the Chapter House, in *Romola* to reinforce the heroine's own grief at the deathbed of her brother Dino, a Dominican monk. Romola, we are told, 'was conducted to the door of the chapter-house in the outer cloister, whither the invalid had been conveyed; no woman being allowed admission beyond this precinct'. As she tends to her brother she is 'just conscious that in the background there was a crucified form rising high and pale on the frescoed wall, and pale faces of sorrow looking out from it below'. As the scene progresses, 'the pale faces of sorrow in the fresco on the opposite wall seemed to have come nearer, and to make one company with the pale face on the bed'.[34] In another chapter, Romola's own pale face is explicitly compared by one of the characters with 'that fainting Madonna of Fra Giovanni's'.[35] It is interesting to think about the tensions of time- and space-based media in Eliot's narrative technique here both in light of early Italian fresco series that tell biblical stories in panels that the viewer must put together, like a cartoon, and in terms of proto-cinematic effect and montage. And it affords a nice example of how a still image is engaged by her at once to conjure an authentic cinquecento scene in a particular time and place, and to situate the heroine both in a history of suffering women stretching back to the Madonna and in the evolving history of the Renaissance, at the very centre of the conflicting paradigms represented by the old medieval religious order and modern humanism.

Romola was published in serial parts in the *Cornhill Magazine* in 1863, and illustrated by one of the up-and-coming historical painters of the day, Frederic Leighton, who had established his reputation in the previous decade with numerous canvases depicting Italian Renaissance scenes. Visualisation was an important dimension of Eliot's fictional representation of the past. She was later to write in her notebook about what she hoped to achieve through the kind of imaginative 'historical picturing' we find in *Romola*:

> The exercise of a veracious imagination in historical picturing seems to be capable of a development that might help the judgment greatly with regard to present and future events. By veracious imagination, I mean the working out in detail of the various steps by which a political or social change was reached, using all extant evidence and supplying deficiencies by careful analogical creation.[36]

Wishing to steer a judicious path between history proper and romance, she declares:

> I want something different from the abstract treatment which belongs to grave history from a doctrinal point of view, and something different from the schemed picturesqueness of ordinary historical fiction. I want brief, severely conscientious reproductions, in their concrete incidents, of pregnant movements in the past.[37]

For Eliot, then, 'historical picturing' sits somewhere between 'grave' unadorned history and the formulaic picturesque banalities of historical romance, which Lewes had disparagingly described, in an article of 1848 in the *British Quarterly Review* on Alexandre Dumas, as a genre for which 'a writer only requires a reasonable fund of historical ignorance, and, with a dashing pen, he is sure to succeed'.[38]

Lewes is referring to a popular vogue for escapist historical romance in the 1830s and 1840s that was already on the wane by 1848. The historical novel even at this time, though, ranged across a much wider spectrum than his generic description suggests, taking in historical romance at one end, to be sure, but equally fictional realism, which was more closely allied to the more literary forms of history writing practised by Carlyle and Macaulay, at the other. Indeed, historical novelists from Sir Walter Scott to Eliot herself often combined realism and romance in their fictional representations of the past, using romantic and sensationalist plotting to engage their readers with more serious ideas relating to the dilemmas of their own times. *Romola* (1863) is Eliot's most obviously 'historical' novel, but in fact all of her novels, with the exception of *Daniel Deronda* (1876) (and even that deals centrally with an archaic form of Judaism), are set more than a generation in the past, and turn on the profound connections between the past and the present – one thinks particularly of *Adam Bede* (1859), *The Mill on the Floss* (1860) and *Middlemarch* (1871–2). Although some, like Edward Bulwer-Lytton and Charles Reade, took a longer historical perspective and explored the more distant past in their fiction, many Victorian novelists, in the tradition of Scott's subtitle to *Waverley* (1814) ''tis sixty years since', made use of a comparable retrospective to reflect upon the recent history that had been responsible for forming their own generation. Dickens's *A Tale of Two Cities* (1859), for example, is set at the time of the French Revolution; Thackeray's *Vanity Fair* (1848) against the backdrop of the Napoleonic Wars.

Dickens was a friend and admirer of Carlyle, dedicating his novel *Hard Times* (1854) to him, and when he was writing *A Tale of Two Cities* he immersed himself in Carlyle's epic history *The French Revolution* (1837), a revised edition of which had been published in 1857. Not only did he share Carlyle's political sympathies, viewing the Reign of Terror as an inevitable consequence of the poverty and oppression of the people, but the style of his novel recalls the dramatic immediacy of Carlyle's history, a work described by John Stuart Mill in his review of it as 'not so much a history, as an epic poem; and notwithstanding, or even in consequence of this, the truest of histories'.[39] The performative aesthetic of this history in which, as John Rosenberg argues, Carlyle 'co-opts' his readers by supplying 'the script and stage directions, as it were, and we enact the scene in our heads' clearly appealed to Dickens's own sense of theatre, and so did the author of *Past and Present*'s 'power of endowing the past with extraordinary "presence"', and 'his complementary genius for undermining the actuality of the here and now'.[40]

There are many scenes in Carlyle's history where we see these qualities displayed: in his account of the Fall of the Bastille, for example, and his descriptions of the public execution of Louis XVI and Robespierre. The use of the present continuous tense and the first-person plural produces a sense of immediacy, as if he and we the readers are eye-witnesses to these scenes on the streets of Paris, figures in the crowd, caught up in the drama of these cataclysmic events. It is about as far removed from the contemporaneous ideal of objective history as it is possible to be. Here is his rendition of the death of Robespierre by guillotine:

> All eyes are on Robespierre's Tumbril, where he, his jaw bound in dirty linen, with his half-dead Brother and half-dead Henriot, lie shattered, their 'seventeen hours' of agony about to end. The Gendarmes point their swords at him, to show the people which is he. A woman springs on the Tumbril; clutching the side of it with one hand, waving the other Sibyl-like; and exclaims: 'The death of thee gladdens my very heart, m'enivre de joi'; Robespierre opened his eyes; 'Scélérat, go down to Hell, with the curses of all wives and mothers!' – At the foot of the scaffold, they stretched him on the ground till his turn came. Lifted aloft, his eyes again opened; caught the bloody axe. Samson wrenched the coat off him; wrenched the dirty linen from his jaw: the jaw fell powerless, there burst from him a cry; – hideous to hear and see. Samson, thou canst not be too quick![41]

Our visual perspective, as readers, shifts from the viewpoint of 'all eyes' present at this public spectacle to Robespierre's own eyes, as first they open on the Sibyl-like woman baying for his blood, and then catch sight of the 'bloody axe', to a close-up as he must have appeared to the ironically named executioner Samson, 'hideous ... to see'. It is a compellingly realized scene that, again, has proto-cinematic qualities, and is a striking demonstration of what Roland Barthes coined 'l'effet de réel'.[42]

Nietzsche wrote that it is 'only perhaps if history suffer transformation into a pure work of art' that it can 'preserve instincts or arouse them'. Such historical writing, however, he adds, 'would be quite against the analytical and inartistic tendencies of our time, and even be considered false'.[43] Carlyle's *French Revolution* is an interesting test case. Highly rhetorical, allusive and metaphorical, yet well researched and historically accurate, much of its power derives, as Rosenberg argues, from 'the shock of its transpositions, the explosive interpenetration of modern fact and ancient myth, of journalism and Scripture'.[44] These different discursive registers are readily apparent in Carlyle's description of the start of the revolt led by women on the morning of 5 October 1789:

> The young woman seizes the drum; sets forth, beating it ... Descend, O mothers; descend, ye Judiths, to food and revenge! All women gather and go; crowds storm all stairs, force out all women ... and so, like snowbreak from the mountains, for every staircase is a melted brook, it storms; tumultuous, wild-shrilling, towards the Hotel-de-Ville.[45]

In just a few lines the language moves between a sonorously biblical call to arms, stark journalistic reportage and lyrical Romantic metaphor.

The lives of others

Carlyle not only wrote remarkable narrative histories but also reflected upon historiography in his critical essays. In his essay 'On History' (1830), for example, he draws attention to the importance of linearity in narrative. Narrative, he proposes, 'travels towards one, or towards successive points', thereby enabling a person to feel part of a teleological historical order, and to 'unite himself in clear conscious relation ... with the whole Future and the whole Past'.[46] In the nineteenth century in England, the need to feel connected in this way with the past and the future reflected a more general cultural condition, arising from the sense of historical dispossession felt by many in a world secularized and temporally redefined by Darwin. In order to recover a sense of human historicity, it was necessary to rewrite the human story. This, Peter Brooks has intriguingly suggested, is the explanation for 'the enormous narrative production of the nineteenth century'. Brooks has observed that a widespread cultural 'anxiety at the loss of providential plots' may explain 'the nineteenth century's obsession with questions of origin, evolution, progress, genealogy, its foregrounding of the historical narrative as par excellence the necessary mode of explanation and understanding'.[47]

Some nineteenth-century writers, though, eschewed narrative in their writing of history, preferring to cast their own representations of the past as images, fragments, intuitions – abstract, suggestive renditions of historical persons and events and issues in brief essays and sketches and lyrical poems that do not pretend to linearity but rather directly, sometimes shockingly, collapse time to confront us with the past. Alice Meynell, for example, gives us her own version of the heroism of women in the French Revolution at the end of her essay 'The Colour of Life', in her final paragraph on the actress Olympe de Gouges who, in her *Declaration of the Rights of Women and Citizenesses* (1791), had movingly called for the inclusion of women in the totalizing revolutionary agenda, and was tried and executed in 1794. What begins as a prose meditation on colour modulates into a final powerful statement about female political agency, whereby the colour red with which the essay opens, 'the colour of violence, or of life broken open, edited, and published', is made figurative in the broken body of a woman. Red is made to signify, ironically, both the 'flush' of a properly modest woman and the violent death by guillotine of Olympe de Gouges, when 'The blood wherewith she should, according to Robespierre, have blushed to be seen or heard in the tribune, was exposed to the public sight unsheltered by her veins', Meynell's description of her violent and bloody death, her body viscerally displayed, retrospectively colouring the entire piece.[48]

However, if Meynell's historical work does not conform to Carlyle's ideas about linear narrative, she did appear to share his belief in the close connection between history writing and biography, indeed his view that history should be 'the essence of innumerable Biographies'. 'Of History', he declares, 'the most honoured, if not honourable species of composition, is not the whole purport Biographic?'[49] But where Carlyle wrote great tomes on great personages – his six-volume life of *Frederick the Great* (1858–65), for example – and where he assembled the events of a person's life into a historical narrative, Meynell produced brief sketches of unhistorical figures, generally women, to restore them to public memory, to illuminate shadowy corners of the past and thicken our historical understanding of the more famous people and times with which they were associated. She recuperates for the historical record such elusively intimate areas of experience as private suffering. 'By far the greater number of human sufferings have been forgotten by man as purely and freshly as by nature', she wrote.

> Of a few, that fictitious memory which is history and tradition renews the report with so much attention as to preserve something like the unity of time. To read of them and to think of them is nearly as long as it was to endure them. But of others again we have the brief record that shows long hollow spaces of time, perfectly dark and indescribed.[50]

It is these of whom she writes, such as 'the bitter life and death of Arabella Stuart, told by our popular historians in a short paragraph that ends with her death of a "broken heart" – the extravagant phrase interrupting the historical style and making the page conspicuous to childish learners'.[51] But she commemorates also happier women who have been passed over or misrepresented by history. She writes of the women in Jonathan Swift's life 'a paper of reparation to Mrs. Dingley', for example (noting 'We cannot do her honour by her Christian name'), who made, with 'Stella', his friend Esther Johnson, 'the two-in-one whom Swift loved "better a thousand times than life, as hope saved"'. Admittedly 'Forgotten Dingley, happy in this, has not had to endure the ignominy, in a hundred modern essays, to be retrogressively offered to Swift as an unclaimed wife', but Meynell seeks to redress the historical neglect that has for two hundred years 'stripped her of so radiant a glory as is hers by right'.[52]

Meynell, in such essays, thinks about historiographical issues that have affected how the past, and especially the history of women, has been written. She questions the distortions of history that have, for instance, condemned 'Steele's Prue' to 'eternal silence' for the simple reason that 'Prue kept all the letters that Steele wrote to her from their marriage-day onwards, and Steele kept none of hers.'[53] And she finds the letters of another woman, Mary Wollstonecraft, whose revolutionary feminist work had been retrospectively discredited as a consequence of revelations about her unconventional private life in her husband William Godwin's biography (so that even her most serious and moral writings appeared to the next generation somehow 'reprehensible', as George Eliot was wryly to observe), 'quick with the feelings of the personal and intense woman' and 'with charity towards the individual, with philanthropy towards the race'.[54] A number of other writers interested, like Meynell, in casting light on those 'long hollow spaces of time' that constitute the unwritten histories of the past, turn to letters as offering a more personal and intimate insight into public lives and historical events. Julia Cartwright, for example, in her books on *Beatrice d'Este* (1899) and *Isabella d'Este* (1903), both audaciously subtitled 'A Study of the Renaissance', brings together for the first time 'the vast number of letters which passed between [Isabella d'Este] and the chief artists of the day', which have 'hitherto lain buried in foreign archives or hidden in pamphlets and periodicals, many of them already out of print'.[55] She draws attention not only to the fact that our perspective on the past depends on which archival sources the historian uses, but also to the silences in the historical record, noting '[t]his is especially the case with the women of the Renaissance'.[56] Her own work on the correspondence of Isabella d'Este, in the Gonzaga archives at Mantua, throws, she says, '[a] flood of light … on the history of Italy in the fifteenth and sixteenth centuries; public events and personages have been placed in a new aspect; the judgments of posterity have been modified and, in some instances, reversed'.[57] It is a new aspect that takes us from the masculine history of the public arena into the feminine private sphere: 'We see now, more clearly than ever before', she writes, 'what manner of men and women these Estes and Gonzagas, these Sforzas and Viscontis, were … We follow them from the battlefield and council chamber, from the chase and tournament, to the privacy of domestic life and the intimate scenes of the family circle.'[58]

With the heightened awareness of history in the nineteenth century, then, came also a sense of who and what had been left out, or misrepresented in the official record, and efforts were made to recuperate the 'unhistorical' stories of the unexceptional, and the private and domestic histories behind the public face of the past. It began to be recognized that the past existed for the present only as a collection of fragments, a partial record characterized by absences and gaps that could be entered and reclaimed. This is something that poets and playwrights Katharine Bradley and Edith Cooper – aunt and niece, devoted lovers – writing under the signature Michael Field, did quite literally in the case of their translation and elaboration of the Sapphic fragments in a volume entitled *Long Ago* (1889). Their adaptation of Sappho's lyrical remains, written in an ancient and other language, for a late nineteenth-century Anglophone readership has been read by some as an intriguing and (for the times) audaciously explicit celebration of love between women, a project that enabled these two women to articulate their lesbian experience. Like those Oxford classicists such as Walter Pater who, as Linda Dowling has demonstrated, reinterpreted the Hellenic tradition as a way of articulating and authorizing male homosexual and homosocial identity at this time,[59] Bradley and Cooper writing as Michael Field explored the modern resonances of Sapphic love, and identified with classical bacchants and maenads, locating themselves as poets within an alternative and even more subversive classical tradition. And like other late Victorian female writers, such as Amy Levy and Emily Pfeiffer, they engaged critically with ancient Greek texts as a way of enhancing and legitimating the cultural position of modern women, with a view, not least, to authorizing their own status as writers.

That they did so in a context that was ostensibly 'long ago' is crucial to their enterprise. Michael Field's ancient Greece, like Pater's, was an ambivalent gesture to a pre-sexological age before modern sexual categories existed; as such, it was a compromised or transposed Greece, appropriated for modern ends. But so – equally albeit differently inflected – was mainstream Victorian Hellenism such as Benjamin Jowett's. Hellenism, like other historicist projects, was a manoeuvre consciously employed for contemporary cultural and political reasons. The cultural capital offered by the classical was unparalleled, but other cultures of the past – Ancient Rome, the Middle Ages, the Renaissance, Romanticism – often Anglicized and anachronistically updated to suit Victorian needs, were also invoked to serve modern purposes. History and historicism, looking to and writing the past, were always and profoundly connected to the textures of Victorian thinking and Victorian politics: classicism with late nineteenth-century definitions of sexuality and theories of civic republicanism; medievalism with modern social and religious thought; the Italian Renaissance with Victorian sympathy for contemporary republican politics in Italy and with modern civic sensibility. And beyond such specific entanglements of the now and then, we might wish to agree with Foucault that history itself, that 'great obsession of the nineteenth century ... with its themes of development and of suspension, of crisis and cycle, themes of the ever-accumulating past, with its great preponderance of dead men and the menacing glaciation of the world', provided a discourse for the period's deepest preoccupations.[60] We may also, though, want to acknowledge other historical patterns than the developmental, cyclical and cumulative narratives that Foucault invokes, other historical agents than his 'dead men', and other governing paradigms than that of the second law of thermodynamics. What I have tried to convey in the foregoing discussion is something of the range of ways in which that profound historical sensibility and impulse, that 'obsession' with history, so variously inflected and so fundamental to what it meant to be a Victorian, was textually realized in the writing of the past.

Notes

1 *On the Use and Abuse of History for Life* (1873), in *The Complete Works of Friedrich Nietzsche*, ed. Oscar Levy, trans. Adrian Collins, 18 vols. (Edinburgh and London: T. N. Foulis, 1909), vol. v, p. 96.
2 Walter Benjamin, *The Arcades Project*, trans. Howard Eiland and Kevin McLaughlin (Cambridge, Mass. and London: Harvard University Press, 2002), p. ix.
3 Stephen Greenblatt, *Shakespearean Negotiations: The Circulation of Social Energy in Renaissance England* (Oxford: Clarendon Press, 1988), p. 1.

4 A. Dwight Culler, *The Victorian Mirror of History* (New Haven and London: Yale University Press, 1986).

5 Richard D. Altick, *The Presence of the Present: Topics of the Day in the Victorian Novel* (Columbus: Ohio State University Press, 1991), p. 8.

6 Benjamin, *The Arcades Project*, p. 546.

7 *Ibid.* p. 156.

8 John Ruskin, *Fors Clavigera: Letters to the Workmen and Labourers of Great Britain*, ed. Dinah Birch, The Whitehouse Edition of John Ruskin (Edinburgh: Edinburgh University Press, 2000), p. 80.

9 *Ibid.* pp. 91–2.

10 *Ibid.*

11 *Ibid.*

12 *Ibid.* pp. 26–7.

13 *Ibid.* p. 27.

14 Alice Chandler, *A Dream of Order: The Medieval Ideal in Nineteenth-Century English Literature* (London: Routledge and Kegan Paul, 1971).

15 Matthew Arnold, *Culture and Anarchy*, ed. R. H. Super (Ann Arbor: University of Michigan Press, 1965), p. 109.

16 Jerome McGann, *Dante Gabriel Rossetti and the Game That Must Be Lost* (New Haven and London: Yale University Press, 2000), p. 71.

17 'The Burden of Nineveh', in *The Collected Works of Dante Gabriel Rossetti*, ed. William Michael Rossetti, 2 vols. (London: Ellis and Elvey, 1897), vol. I, pp. 266–71 (at p. 266).

18 'The Fiddler of the Reels', in *Selected Stories of Thomas Hardy*, ed. John Wain (London: Macmillan, 1966), pp. 134–53 (at p. 134).

19 Michel Foucault, 'Of Other Spaces', trans. Jay Miskowiec, *Diacritics*, 16, 1 (Spring 1986), p. 25.

20 Rossetti, 'The Burden of Nineveh', pp. 269, 271.

21 Benjamin, *The Arcades Project*, pp. 462–3; Walter Benjamin, 'Theses on the Philosophy of History', in *Illuminations*, ed. Hannah Arendt, trans. Harry Zohn (London: Fontana, 1973), pp. 255–66 (at p. 257).

22 Vernon Lee, *Euphorion; being Studies of the Antique and the Mediaeval in the Renaissance*, 2 vols. (London: T. Fisher Unwin, 1884), vol. II, p. 17.

23 *The Works of John Ruskin*, ed. E. T. Cook and Alexander Wedderburn, 39 vols. (London: George Allen, 1903–12), vol. XI, pp. 109–10.

24 Lee, *Euphorion*, vol. II, p. 17.

25 Vernon Lee, *Limbo and Other Essays, to which is now added Ariadne in Mantua* (London: John Lane at the Bodley Head, 1908), p. 29.

26 *Ibid.* p. 31.

27 Vernon Lee, *Studies of the Eighteenth Century in Italy* (London: Satchell, 1880), pp. xvi, xxi.

28 *Ibid.* pp. 293–4.

29 *Ibid.* p. 294.

30 *Ibid.* p. 295.

31 *Ibid.* p. 121.

32 *Ibid.* p. 160.

33 *The Journals of George Eliot*, ed. Margaret Harris and Judith Johnston (Cambridge: Cambridge University Press, 1998), pp. 356–7.

34 George Eliot, *Romola*, ed. Andrew Brown (Oxford: Clarendon Press, 1993), pp. 155, 162.

35 *Ibid.* p. 395.

36 *Essays of George Eliot*, ed. Thomas Pinney (London: Routledge and Kegan Paul, 1963), p. 446.

37 *Ibid.* p. 447.

38 George Henry Lewes, 'The Art of Historical Romance', in *A Versatile Victorian: Selected Writings of George Henry Lewes*, ed. Rosemary Ashton (London: Bristol Classical Press, 1992), pp. 202–16 (at p. 208).

39 J. S. Mill, 'The French Revolution', in *Literary Essays*, ed. Edward Alexander (Indianapolis: The Bobbs Merrill Company, 1967), pp. 132–51 (at p. 132).

40 John D. Rosenberg, *Carlyle and the Burden of History* (Cambridge, Mass.: Harvard University Press, 1985), pp. 77–8, 24.

41 Thomas Carlyle, *The French Revolution: A History*, ed. John D. Rosenberg (New York: The Modern Library, 2002), p. 743.

42 Roland Barthes, 'L'effet de réel' (1968), trans. as 'The Reality Effect', in *The Rustle of Language*, trans. Richard Howard (Berkeley: University of California Press, 1989), pp. 141–8.

43 Nietzsche, *The Use and Abuse of History*, p. 58.

44 Carlyle, *The French Revolution*, p. xviii.

45 *Ibid.* p. 212.

46 *The Works of Thomas Carlyle*, ed. H. R. Traill, centenary edn., 30 vols. (London: Charles Scribner's Sons, 1896–1901), vol. XXVII, pp. 88–9.

47 Peter Brooks, *Reading for the Plot: Design and Intention in Narrative* (New York: Vintage; Oxford: Clarendon, 1984), pp. 6–7.

48 Alice Meynell, *Prose and Poetry*, introduction by Vita Sackville-West (London: Jonathan Cape, 1947), pp. 219–22.

49 Thomas Carlyle, 'Biography', in *Critical and Miscellaneous Essays*, 3 vols. (London: Chapman and Hall, 1887), vol. II, pp. 245–60 (at p. 249).

50 Meynell, *Prose and Poetry*, pp. 181–2.

51 *Ibid.* p. 182.

52 *Ibid.* pp. 185–9.

53 *Ibid.* pp. 189–90.

54 *Ibid.* pp. 64, 67; George Eliot, 'Margaret Fuller and Mary Wollstonecraft' (*Leader*, 13 October 1855); repr. in *Selected Essays, Poems and Other Writings*, ed. A. S. Byatt and Nicholas Warren (London: Penguin, 1990), pp. 332–3.

55 Julia Cartwright, *Isabella d'Este, Marchioness of Mantua 1474–1539: A Study of the Renaissance*, 2 vols. (London: John Murray, 1903), vol. I, p. ix.

56 Julia Cartwright, *Beatrice d'Este, Duchess of Milan 1475–1497: A Study of the Renaissance* (London: J. M. Dent and Sons; New York: E. P. Dutton and Co., 1926), pp. v–vi.

57 Cartwright, *Isabella d'Este*, p. v.

58 Cartwright, *Beatrice d'Este*.

59 Linda Dowling, *Hellenism and Homosexuality in Victorian Oxford* (Ithaca, NY and London: Cornell University Press, 1994).

60 Foucault, 'Of Other Spaces', p. 22.

7

SALLY LEDGER

Radical writing

Writing to his friend John Hobhouse from Italy in 1820, Byron commented on the term 'radical' that it was entirely new to him: 'Upon reform you have long known my opinion – but *radical* is a new word since my time – it was not in the political vocabulary of 1816 – when I left England – and I don't know what it means – is it uprooting?'[1] Byron's etymological understanding of the term is spot on, and in an abstract way tells us a great deal about the political force of nineteenth-century radicalism. The political temperature was running high in England in 1820: the 'Peterloo Massacre' of the previous year in which eleven peaceful demonstrators were killed was still fresh in the memory, and William Cobbett led a vanguard of popular protests in support of the exiled Queen Caroline. In this fevered political climate the journalist Thomas Wooler gave a characteristically witty account of the meaning of the term 'radical' in his trial parody, 'TRIAL EXTRAORDINARY: MR CANNING VERSUS THE RADICAL REFORMERS':

> JUDGE: What complaint have you to make, Mr Canning, against the men, whom I see there, behind you, looking so thin and pale, clothed in rags, and having pad-locks on their mouths and thumb-screws on their hands.
> MR CANNING: Oh! Don't you know them? I thought all the world knew them! They are the Radicals.
> JUDGE: The Radicals, Sir! What does that name mean?
> MR CANNING: Mean! (What a fool the man must be – *aside*) Mean! Why, it means everything that is bad.[2]

Here the 'Radicals' are characterized simultaneously as an oppressed and as a transgressive body of people in opposition to the legal and political establishment.[3]

Dickens's 'Young Barnacle', in *Little Dorrit*, thinks the mild-mannered middle-aged Arthur Clennam a 'most ferocious Radical'[4] for daring to make some enquiries of his government department. Clearly in the 1850s Dickens was alert to the visceral response of some elements within the upper classes to anyone who seemed to challenge them, and the 'Radical' tag is humorously used to indicate this in his novel from 1857. In the political culture of mid-Victorian England the title of 'Radical' tended to be attached to those politicians who wanted root-and-branch reform of Parliament, and in this particular sense Dickens was of their number.

In this chapter I will focus my attention on three radical cultural 'moments' in the period 1830–1914 and will assess the political complexion of the literatures that grew out of them. Beginning with the literature and visual culture of the anti-Poor Law movement in the 1830s and early 1840s I identify melodrama and satire as the aesthetic modes of choice for radical writers in this period. The middle part of the chapter addresses some of the literature that grew out of the Chartist movement and the 'Condition of England Question' in the 1840s and 1850s, assessing the political force of melodramatic aesthetics in Chartist fiction and in the middle-class novel. In a postscript I will attend to the utopian framing of William Morris's vision of a socialist future in 1890, by which time the melodramatic mode of radical expression in the early and mid-Victorian period had by and large ceded to fantasies of futurism as the new century approached.

The centrality of melodrama in Victorian culture in general has until recently been generally underestimated; its significance to Victorian radical writing and visual culture in particular is indisputable. Forged as an aesthetic of protest in the French Revolution, typical of the revolutionary drama of the period is Sylvain Maréchal's *Le jugement dernier des rois*, first performed, to great acclaim, in Paris in October 1793, two days after the execution of Marie Antoinette. The play's melodramatic denouement involves the swallowing up of a whole crowd of European monarchs by a volcano, which 'consumes their very bodies'.[5] Peter Brooks has influentially characterized melodrama as an 'intense emotional and ethical' genre, 'based on the manichaeistic struggle of good and evil'. The purpose of melodrama is to 'recognize and confront evil, to combat and expel it, to purge the social order'.[6] It is also very much a bodily genre dependent on a theatrical semiotics of gesture rather than dialogue; and it is frequently marked by physical violence. As domestic melodrama developed across the first half of the nineteenth century it acquired a number of readily identifiable additional characteristics: working-class solidarity in response to external threats to working-class domesticity; the suffering of mothers and their children; trial scenes and last-minute reprieves; a preoccupation with the law; criminal aspects; sudden reversals of fortune; secret wills and inheritances; a paternalistic politics.

The literature of the anti-Poor Law movement

The literature and visual culture of the anti-Poor Law movement is readily identifiable as melodramatic: Kenny Meadows's *Punch* illustration from 1843 (see figure 7.1) depicts a Manichean opposition between good and evil fundamental to popular melodrama. The pauper mother and her infant are seated below a weeping angel who cannot bear to look on as the workhouse harridan, overseen by a grinning devil, rips the baby from its mother's breast, the workhouse railings clearly visible in the background. The presence of the angel suggests the iconography of Madonna and child, implying a critique of contemporary Christianity that Douglas Jerrold, to whose polemical essay 'The "Milk" of Poor Law "Kindness"' is an accompaniment, was also quick to exploit. Robert Seymour's illustration for *Figaro in London* from 1836 (see figure 7.2) shows a large-girthed beadle violently refusing financial assistance to three generations of one family; the ragged, emaciated family group, which is here shown protectively huddled together, would be torn asunder were they to enter the workhouse in the background, in which husbands were separated from their wives, and children from their parents. The moral ordering of the illustration is clear, with the skeletal, under-nourished, oppressed family group starkly contrasted with the rotundity not only of the beadle but also of the parish officers in the background who enjoy a drink in the 'New Poor Laws Tavern', heedless of the suffering of the poor.

Meadows's and Seymour's illustrations are typical of scores of others published in the popular and radical press in the service of the anti-Poor Law movement in the 1830s and 1840s. The movement also had at its disposal a diverse print culture, ranging from the Chartist *Northern Star*, the radical weekly *Cleave's Gazette of Variety* and Gilbert À Beckett's comic penny weekly *Figaro in London*, to the Tory *Times* and *Blackwood's Edinburgh Magazine*. This meant that it was truly a cross-class movement that had huge popular as well as radical power. Street literature too was used as a vehicle for anti-Poor Law argument. A broadside from *c.* 1836, *The New Poor Law Bill in Force*, draws on the cruder generic conventions of both satire and melodrama – such infinitely malleable modes in class terms – to articulate its own particular form of protest. The text of the broadside has a repeated chorus that is interspersed in the text, lending it the performative apparel of the melodrama proper. Appealing to a non-elite audience, the broadside focuses hyperbolically on the contrast between

PUNCH'S PENCILLINGS.——N°. LXII.

THE "MILK" OF POOR-LAW "KINDNESS."

Figure 7.1 Kenny Meadows, 'The "Milk" of Poor Law "Kindness"', *Punch, or, The London Charivari* (4 January 1843), p. 46.

bloated parish officials and starving paupers, and also on the lewd potential of the Bastardy clauses. The text proper (with the original lexical errors uncorrected) begins:

Figure 7.2 Robert Seymour, 'The New Poor Laws', *Figaro in London* (20 February 1836), p. 29.

SPOKEN. – Now, Mr. *Blubberhead* the Beadle, fetch in the Overseers' and Churchwardens' 12 bottles of the best Port Wine, yes Sir, and Blubberhead, is there any Vagrants outside wants examining? why, Sir, there is a wonderful lot of people outside, and I think they are all Bones, for there is very little flesh upon them. – Now, Mr. Blubberhead, the Beadle, let in one of those Rascals – Who are you pray, Why Sir, my name is John Pineway, who is been ill Seventeen long months, I have a Wife Confined, and eight Children Starving. –[7]

There is a preoccupation with the bodily effects of consumption of various kinds: the parish officials are rendered full of 'blubber' because of their over-consumption of port wine, whilst the bodies of the starving poor are reduced to (unappealing and, it is implied, barely edible) mere bones. In relation to the paupers brought before the overseer, concerns about consumption are closely linked to concerns about lower-class sexuality and reproduction. The pauper family, with its pregnant wife and eight children, presents a contrast between sexual plenty and economic insuf-ficiency. Malthusian economic theory, which exerted so powerful an influence on nineteenth-century political economy and the legislation that it produced, held that 'a proportion of the population exceeds economic purpose, and thereby turns what had been the source of wealth – labour – into its parasite'.[8] Contemporary fears of working-class sexuality were closely linked, in Malthusian terms, to a fear that the offspring of the poor would consume too much food. Both food consumption and reproduction needed, then, to be firmly regulated, hence the preoccupation with the workhouse dietary and with the separation of husbands and wives in the workhouse so as to prevent further pregnancies. The perceived moral injustice of this was leapt upon by anti-poor law protestors: the broadside here referred to not only satirically attacks an overfed parish hierarchy but goes on provocatively to suggest that major beneficiaries of the Bastardy clauses were parish officials who could themselves impregnate pauper women without sanction.

The satirical vein that runs through *The New Poor Law Bill in Force* is more fully mined in an article written for the Tory *Blackwood's Edinburgh Magazine*. In a savage satirical flourish modelled on Swift's *A Modest Proposal for Preventing the Children of Poor People in Ireland from Being a Burden to their Country* (1729), the author of 'New Scheme for Maintaining the Poor' (1838) proposes a critique of Malthusianism by mischievously suggesting that to keep costs down at the same time as keeping bellies full, the poor should eat one another. The writer argues that given that most workhouse inmates are elderly or infirm, rather than waste time and expense in burying them when they die, the surviving paupers could make a meal of their corpses:

> Three-fourths of the inmates in a union poor-house may be put down as aged and infirm – the other fourth as children and idiots – so that the large majority being composed of the aged and infirm, it follows that there must be a rapid succession – that in the course of Nature they must die faster than any other portion of the population ... I would have, then, those that drop off support those that live on; and I think, after the scheme had been in operation a little while, the supply would be regular and certain. There are but two prejudices to get over – the foolish and unphilosophical repugnance to any kind of flesh, and the very useless and wasteful one of burying the dead.[9]

At the very moment that the 'New Scheme for Maintaining the Poor' was being published in *Blackwood's Edinburgh Magazine*, a young Charles Dickens was halfway through the writing of *Oliver Twist*, a novel that would share with the literature of the anti-Poor Law movement not only the aesthetic modes of popular protest – satire and melodrama – but also a preoccupation with consumption of all kinds.

'I want some more': *Oliver Twist* and political economy

The 'popular front' of the anti-Poor Law movement, with its literature circulated across establishment newspapers, high-brow quarterlies, middle-brow monthlies, penny weeklies and even street literature, was a textual field ripe for intervention from an up-and-coming young novelist who wished to write a commercially viable literature both about and for 'the People'. *Oliver Twist*, published in the monthly *Bentley's Miscellany*, was not cheap; but it made itself available to an audience beyond the middle classes through its stage adaptations, pirated fictional pastiches and, later, Dickens's own electrifying performances.

Much the most memorable melodramatic tableau in *Oliver Twist* – immortalized by George Cruikshank's illustration and by Dickens's pen – is the scene when young Oliver, 'desperate with hunger and reckless with misery', twice asks the master of the workhouse, 'a fat, healthy man', for more: '"Please, sir, I want some more."'[10] It is a moment of high drama in the novel; but it is more than simply that. For it crystallizes one of the central debates in nineteenth-century political economy that exercised both supporters of and protestors against the New Poor Law Act of 1834. The poor's status as consumers, and the amounts that the poor should be permitted to consume, are just as central to Dickens's novel from 1837–9 as they were to the wider body of anti-Poor Law literature. Oliver's demand that he be given a second bowl of gruel provokes a dramatic reaction from the workhouse functionaries: the small boy is caned by the Beadle as he washes outside in the stone yard, and is flogged every night in the dining hall 'as a public warning and example' (*Oliver Twist*, 18). The bodiliness of the melodrama is violently enacted in Dickens's novel. Mr Limbkins, one of the Board of Guardians, predicts, when he hears of Oliver's misdemeanour, that 'That boy will be hung' (15). The exaggerated response to Oliver's desire to consume more gruel than allowed by the workhouse dietary derives from political economy's determination that the poor should not consume the nation's wealth. James Mill, a follower of Jeremy Bentham and one of the leading political economists of the early nineteenth century, argued that political economy was centrally concerned with 'two grand objects, the Consumption of the Community, and that supply upon which the consumption depends'.[11] Adherents of political economy had an ambivalent relationship with consumption in that the desire to consume is what drives the free market; but, conversely, in a world of limited resources consumption it is also a threat, because it cannot continue indefinitely without taking into account, in Mill's words, 'the supply upon which [it] depends'. According to this model, then, the pauper is greedier than the rich man because the rich man *contributes* as well as consumes wealth, whereas the pauper claiming relief *only* consumes.

Levels of consumption are everywhere the object of Dickens's scrutiny in *Oliver Twist*: at Mrs Mann's Baby Farm Oliver and the other infants are 'without the inconvenience of too much food' (6) and are locked into the coal cellar 'for atrociously presuming to be hungry' (7). The Board of Guardians is comprised of 'fat gentlemen' (11) who impose a starvation diet upon the workhouse inmates. Each pauper is permitted 'Three meals of thin gruel a day, with an onion twice a week, and half a roll on Sundays' (13).

Mrs Sowerberry, the wife of the undertaker to whom Oliver is apprenticed, weighs up the costs and benefits of taking Oliver into the family business using the crudest vocabulary of political economy. In response to her complaint that Oliver is 'very small', Bumble assures her that he will grow bigger. Her sharp reply is 'Ah, I daresay he will … on our victuals, and our drink. I see no saving in parish children, not I; for they always cost more to keep, than they're worth' (32). Although the undertaker's wife hardly needs further condemnation, Dickens makes his attack on political economy explicit at this early stage in the novel. Oliver's first meal at the Sowerberrys' consists of scraps that had been set aside for the dog. Dickens reflects:

> I wish some well-fed philosopher, whose meat and drink turn to gall within him, whose blood is ice, and whose heart is iron, could have seen Oliver Twist clutching at the dainty viands that the dog had neglected, and witnessed the horrible avidity with which he tore the bits asunder with all the ferocity of famine; there is only one thing I should like better; and that would be to see him making the same sort of meal himself, with the same relish.   (33)

Consumption in all its forms is thematically linked in *Oliver Twist* to transgression and to criminality. The squalling hungry babies at Mrs Mann's Baby Farm are referred to as 'culprits' and as 'juvenile offenders against the poor laws' (6); and Oliver's demand for more gruel in the workhouse leads to the reflection that 'That boy will be hung' (15). In asking for more food, Oliver is behaving as a consumer: his punishment (the attempt to apprentice him to a chimney sweep) firmly puts him in his place as an object in the market-place rather than the consuming subject he would like to be.

There is an implicit invitation to the reader to compare the meals that the Artful Dodger and Fagin offer to Oliver – sizzling sausages cooking on the fire – with the repast proposed by Mrs Sowerberry (the dog's leftovers – and her very name is suggestive of the kind of bitter sustenance that Oliver will receive at the undertaker's house). All three, though – the Artful Dodger, Fagin and Mrs Sowerberry – are, in the language of political economy, investing in Oliver with an eye to the kind of return they might get.

Mrs Sowerberry has no faith in her investment of food, but the Artful Dodger and Fagin both see a potential return from Oliver in the context of London's criminal underworld.

Despite the haphazard plotting of *Oliver Twist* compared to Dickens's later novels, there is a striking continuity between the 'workhouse' and the 'criminal-London' sections of the novel inasmuch as they are both presented as operating according to the tenets of political economy. Fagin is described by Bill Sikes as a 'covetous, avaricious, in-sa-ti-a-ble old fence' (98), and he is driven by a desire to protect and enlarge his own wealth every bit as fierce as the boldest of the political economists. Fagin may work in a criminal economy rather than a government-sanctioned one, but his desires and motivations are, the novel suggests, the same.

Oliver Twist is packed full of melodramatic devices and is arguably the most full-bloodedly melodramatic novel that Dickens wrote: its narratives of dispersal and reunion and of domestic suffering; its representation of bodily violence and physical affliction; the criminal elements; the providential plotting and wild coincidences; the Manichean structure of good and evil; the lost will; the deathbed confession; Oliver's unexpected inheritance; and the narrative's paternalistic politics; all would, in the 1830s, have immediately aligned the novel with this hugely popular and potentially radical genre. Melodrama as an aesthetic of protest was not, though, confined to the anti-Poor Law movement at the mid-century: some of the writers who responded to Chartism and more broadly to the 'Condition of England Question' in the 1840s and early 1850s would also embrace and interrogate this politically malleable mode of writing.

Chartism and the Condition of England

In 1838 the first Chartist Petition was presented to Parliament. Its demands were constitutional: the so-called 'Six Points' of the Charter called for universal male adult suffrage, secret ballots, the abolition of property qualifications for MPs, payment of MPs, equal electoral districts and annual parliaments. Circling around issues of democracy and political representation, the Chartist movement, as it became, was also firmly allied with protests against working-class poverty and distress, and thus in certain respects shared some of the concerns of the antecedent anti-Poor Law movement. But whilst the anti-Poor Law movement had cross-class support, not least from Tory Radicals such as Benjamin Disraeli, the Chartist movement was feared by many among the middle and upper classes as an incendiary and potentially insurrectionary political force. Such fears quickly surfaced in Thomas Carlyle's pamphlet from 1839 in which Chartists are characterized at best as 'wild inarticulate souls, struggling there, with inarticulate uproar, like dumb creatures in pain, unable to speak what is in them!', and at worst as violent conspirators armed with 'rusty pistols, vitriol bottle and match box'.[12] Middle-class fears were fuelled by the so-called Newport Uprising in November 1839, when 3,000 Chartists marched into the South Wales town. The authorities, fearful of civil disturbance and insurrection, had already made a number of arrests and were holding several Chartists in the Westgate Hotel. Demonstrators, who had congregated outside the hotel to demand the prisoners' release, were shot at by soldiers: more than twenty men were killed and another fifty were wounded. The political temperature rose even higher when several of the Chartists were found guilty of high treason and sentenced to be hanged, drawn and quartered (their sentences were later commuted to transportation to the colonies). Chartism peaked in 1848, a year that witnessed multiple revolutions on the Continent and the publication of Marx and Engels's *Communist Manifesto*. A demonstration on Kennington Common in London in support of the third Charter (the second had been presented to Parliament in 1842), and a subsequent procession to the House of Commons, were both banned: the meeting on the Common went ahead nonetheless, attended by 15,000 demonstrators. The summer of 1848 was marked by multiple Chartist disturbances and large-scale arrests, not least of Ernest Jones, Chartism's leader.

It was the fevered political climate of the late 1830s and 1840s that produced a rash of novels that addressed themselves to the 'Condition of England Question' as well as a rich vein of Chartist literature written by supporters of that cause. 'Seth Thompson, the Stockinger', a short story from 1845 written by the shoemaker (and later journalist) Thomas Cooper, is characteristic of the more moderate literary output of the Chartist movement.[13] Cooper, who had been converted to Chartism after having reported on starving stockingers for the *Leicestershire Mercury*, presents the desperate plight of the industrial poor at the same time as insisting on the essential respectability of working-class domestic arrangements and the Christianity of many Chartists. Emphasizing the 'moral force' dimension of Chartism in the story, the eponymous Seth is saved from poverty by the melodramatic device of the return of a long-lost relative from overseas who has 'made good' in West Indian plantations; the sudden reversal of his fortunes is characteristic of the melodramatic mode.

Altogether more discomfiting is Ernest Jones's *De Brassier: A Democratic Romance* (1851), written after the leader of the Chartist movement had spent two years in Mill Bank jail as a political prisoner. Conscious as he was of the necessity to retain a popular readership for the radical press, Jones insisted, in his Preface to the novel that was first published in his Chartist periodical *Notes to the People*, on the efficacy of popular fictional conventions in advancing social revolution:

> Rowland Hill said, when setting his psalms to opera melodies, 'he did not see why the devil should have all the good tunes to himself.' Rowland Hill was right, (always supposing that the others did belong to the devil).
>
>   In like manner I do not see why Truth should always be dressed in stern and repulsive garb. The more attractive you make her, the more easily she will progress. Let the same moral be conveyed in a tale, and preached in a sermon, the former will make ten proselytes, when the latter will secure but one.[14]

Melodrama was a heterogeneous form, variously drawing on popular crime narratives, Gothicism, tragedy, romance and even satire. Alert to this heterogeneity, Jones mixes his own melodramas with political analysis and quasi-historical reportage. The initial title of *De Brassier: A Democratic Romance* was *The History of a Democratic Movement, compiled from The Journal of a Democrat, the Confessions of a Demagogue, and the Minutes of a Spy*, manifestly drawing attention to itself as a heteroglot form. It has, though, all the hallmarks of radical melodrama. Its opening focuses on a seamstress and a young child, her niece, who are helplessly starving in a garret. The mode of excess characteristic of melodrama has the seamstress 'bur[ying] her face sobbing in her hands' as 'the tears course down [her] cheeks'(35). The arrival home of her brother, the unemployed Charles Dalton, heralds another 'whirlwind of passion' as 'he shook before the faint cries of that starving child like an oak beneath a whirlwind; a wild expression danced within his eyes' (40). Dalton's wife has died in a workhouse, and he, like Dickens's Betty Higden in *Our Mutual Friend* some fourteen years later, regards a return to the 'Poor Law Bastile' as a fate quite literally worse than death: '"… we won't go to the workhouse! We'll die first!"' (39). The exclamatory syntax and heightened emotion of melodrama are equally present in Jones's narratorial interventions as he urges the rich to have pity on the poor: 'one moment stolen from pride and vanity, one small dole from all those riches, would save lives, oh! How precious and how dear!' (47). The physical violence characteristic of many melodramas manifests itself in the brutality of the police as they arrest the protesting Charles Dalton: 'he was stricken down … – at the blow of the baton the blood streamed from the deep cleft in his head' (48).

But Jones was too subtle a writer, and too politically alert, simply to reproduce melodramatic conventions. In *De Brassier* he borrows heavily from melodrama at the same time as he manipulates and interrogates the crime narrative at the heart of the melodramatic plot. Such an interrogation enables a politicizing of his analysis of social and economic oppression beyond the confines of an orthodox melodramatic rhetoric. Melodrama readily incorporated elements of popular crime fiction; crime is in many ways the perfect ingredient of melodrama, as it has an immediate dramatic impact, creates dramatic conflict and thereby implies resolution. It also often makes a *physical* impact, readily melding with melodrama's aesthetic of the body. Typical ingredients of melodramatic crime narratives of the nineteenth century included the seduction of a working-class girl by an aristocratic villain, and a near-obligatory trial scene, in which unjust accusations are made, so that a revelation of the truth is needed to save the hero or heroine from punishment. An acted-out confrontation between the guilty and the innocent parties was also a common trope. All of these – and more – can be promptly identified in *De Brassier*. The seamstress victim is sexually threatened, first by the overseer of the workhouse, and thereafter by a corrupt aristocratic second son, Simon de Brassier. A heroic artisan Chartist plots to save her. Charles Dalton collapses – apparently dead – in a set-piece trial scene, and returns to exact his revenge on his oppressors.

Beginning with these staple ingredients, Jones manipulates them so as to maximize their radical political effects. He reinterprets the criminal elements characteristic of popular melodrama so as to interrogate its politics and to produce a more complex, more nuanced political fiction than would be possible if the moral and dramatic structures of classic melodrama were reproduced wholesale.

Central to the plot of *De Brassier* are two criminal acts of vengeance. The first of these contains all the ingredients of classic melodrama, consisting as it does of a melodramatic confrontation between an aristocratic seducer – the debauched, decadent Walter de Brassier – and his victim, Lucy, also known as 'Maline', who is presented as a fallen woman turned femme fatale. Lucy sets Stanville Hall, Walter de Brassier's ancestral home, on fire, and the crippled old aristocrat becomes engulfed in the flames and dies shrieking: this is classic melodrama, with an admixture of Gothic thrown in for good measure; its political impact is limited by its conventionality.

The second, related act of vengeance in the novel forces the reader to reappraise the somewhat hackneyed scenario, and to see it anew as having a political significance. This second act of vengeance consists of an attack by an ostensibly politically motivated mob on a mansion housing the wicked bourgeois industrialist – Henry Dorville – who has robbed the hapless Charles Dalton of his means of earning a living. The mysterious leader of the mob sets Dorville's mansion on fire and the factory owner dies of his burns. Jones deliberately duplicates the plot here – both acts of vengeance circle around arson attacks on rich men's mansions – so as to invite the reader to compare the two scenarios. The mysterious stranger who leads the attack on Dorville's mansion turns out to be Charles Dalton, returned from the dead to avenge himself on the employer who starved and incriminated him. The fictional device of one returning from the dead, or from overseas, is, as I remarked in relation to 'Seth Thompson, the Stockinger', a highly conventional melodramatic trope: similar devices are used in Gaskell's novels *North and South* (1854–5) and *Sylvia's Lovers* (1863–4). But what is important here is that Jones's juxtaposition of these two acts of vengeance draws attention to the fact that they both result from the exploitation of one class by another.

Hackneyed as the fallen-woman story may be, it has a political resonance that Jones brings out by juxtaposing it with a more obviously political act of class vengeance. The personal tragedies of melodrama are shown to be profoundly political. In this way Jones draws attention anew to the *political* dimensions of the personal dramas at the core of so many melodramatic plots. Through repetition – they were very widely circulated in mid-nineteenth-century English culture – such plots could tend to lose their radical effects, audiences becoming so accustomed to melodrama's rhetoric as to be unable to retain a sense of its political motivation. Jones, though, recovers the initial political impetus of melodrama.

The middle-class 'Condition of England' novels that appeared between the mid-forties and the mid-fifties embraced melodramatic aesthetics to varying degrees as part of a process of the absorption of melodrama into middle-class culture. Benjamin Disraeli's novel, *Sybil: Or The Two Nations* (1845), is the earliest example of the genre, and in general owes more to parliamentary Blue Books than to melodrama.[15] Disraeli would become better known as a Reformist prime minister. An opponent of the New Poor Law of 1834 and a supporter of Lord Ashley's factory reforms, Disraeli was preoccupied in the late 1830s and 1840s with the rise of Chartism. Often described as a Radical Tory, Disraeli would, as prime minister, go on to steer a bill through Parliament in 1867 that would enfranchise a proportion of working-class men. In the early 1840s, preoccupied with the class antagonism that had produced Chartism, he headed a reform group within the Tory party that was at odds with the Tory leader, Robert Peel, and antagonistic to the Utilitarian idea that society was no more than a loose conglomerate of individuals. Disraeli's novel *Sybil* in many ways reads as a piece of propaganda on behalf of Young England, giving expression to Disraeli's essentially reactionary ideal of a feudalized society in which Church and Aristocracy would combine to protect the People's rights.

Catherine Gallagher has noted that *Sybil* is the only one of the 'Condition of England' novels to address the political issue of Representation directly, and so the only one to engage directly with Chartist concerns.[16] But whilst it does at least contemplate the representation of the common people in Parliament, its riposte is not one with which many or even any Chartists would have felt sympathy: the novel suggests that the working classes would best be represented by noble-born aristocrats of old Norman or, better still, Saxon ancestry, whom Disraeli felt had been usurped by a fake Whig aristocracy represented in the novel by the factory-owning Marney family whose workers barely survive on starvation wages: 'the higher the wages the worse the workmen', as Lord Marney puts it.[17]

If the novel sidesteps the issue of the political representation of the people, it does engage at some length with the plight of working-class families under industrial capitalism: it examines the hated truck system of payment; the plight of women and child labourers in mines; the suffering of handloom weavers; and the impoverishment of agricultural workers. But whilst Disraeli borrows from melodrama a concern with the impact of industrialism on working-class domesticity, the sympathetic, even tender representation of lower-class domesticity that would be the hallmark of Elizabeth Gaskell's novelistic responses to the 'Condition of England Question' is altogether absent: Disraeli's descriptions of poverty are almost wholly depersonalized. The following description of a tenement building in a factory town is entirely typical:

> These wretched tenements seldom consisted of more than two rooms, in one of which the whole family, however numerous, were obliged to sleep, without distinction of age, or sex, or suffering. With the water streaming down the walls, the light distinguished through the roof, with no hearth even in winter, the virtuous mother in the sacred pangs of childbirth, gives forth another victim to our thoughtless civilization … while the father of her coming child, in another corner of the sordid chamber, lies stricken by that typhus which his contaminating dwelling has breathed into his veins, and for whose next prey is perhaps destined, his new-born child … These hovels were in many instances not provided with the commonest conveniences.[18]

Symptomatic of Disraeli's dependence on parliamentary Blue Books and reports rather than on the lived experience of the working classes, *Sybil* entirely lacks the structure of feeling of melodrama, even whilst it shares some of its concerns. It does, though, embrace the political paternalism that is characteristic of early Victorian melodrama, and to that extent the category remains useful for an understanding of the novel.

Elizabeth Gaskell's *Mary Barton* (1848), like *Sybil*, is addressed to the middle classes of society rather than to the novel's working-class subjects; but it is altogether a more sympathetic, more powerfully felt response to the sufferings of the poor. In contrast to Disraeli's political manifesto of a novel, Elizabeth Gaskell's purports to be non-political, adopting the pose of a woman ignorant 'of Political Economy, or the theories of trade'.[19] Holding back from a concretely reformist stance, the novel instead makes a heartfelt plea for greater personal understanding and reconciliation between factory owners and their workers.

Importantly eschewing both Carlyle's representation of Chartists as dumb, inarticulate creatures and Disraeli's anonymous Blue Book representation of the poor, Gaskell takes the reader into the homes of factory workers and humanizes them, and in this way her approach is akin to – although much more fully realized than – that of the Chartist Thomas Cooper's. The Bartons' Manchester family home in a time of prosperity is affectionately described and promotes an ideal of working-class domesticity:

> Mrs. Barton produced the key of the door from her pocket; and on entering the house-place it seemed as if they were in total darkness, except one bright spot, which might be a cat's eye, or might be, what it was, a red-hot fire, smouldering under a large piece of coal, which John Barton immediately applied himself to break up, and the effect instantly produced was warm and glowing light in every corner of the room. To add to this … Mrs. Barton lighted a dip by sticking it in the fire, and having placed it satisfactorily in a tin candlestick, began to look further about her, on hospitable thoughts intent. The room was tolerably large, and possessed many conveniences. On the right of the door, as you entered, was a longish window, with a broad ledge. On each side of this, hung blue-and-white check curtains … In the corner between the window and the fireside was a cupboard, apparently full of plates and dishes, cups and saucers, and some more nondescript articles, for which one would have fancied their possessors could find no use – such as triangular pieces of glass to save carving knives and forks from dirtying table-cloths. However, it was evident Mrs. Barton was proud of her crockery and glass, for she left her cupboard door open, with a glance round of satisfaction and pleasure … Opposite the fire-place was a table, which I should call a Pembroke, only that it was made of deal, and I cannot tell how far such a name may be applied to such humble material. On it, resting against the wall, was a bright green japanned tea-tray, having a couple of scarlet lovers embracing in the middle. The fire-light danced merrily on this, and really (setting all taste but that of a child's aside) it gave a richness of colouring to that side of the room. It was in some measure propped up by a crimson tea-caddy, also of japan ware … and, if you can picture all this, with a washy, but clean stencilled pattern on the walls, you can form some idea of John Barton's home. (14–15)

As the novel proceeds, Gaskell contrasts the dignity of working-class domesticity in times of plenty to the devastation of factory families in times of economic depression. The descriptions of John Barton's anguish at the death of the infant boy whom he could barely afford to feed ('"If my child lies dying (as poor Tom lay, with his white wan lips quivering, for want of better food than I could give him), does the rich man bring the wine or broth that might save his life?"' (10)); Jane Wilson's grief at the death of her six-year-old twins ('the mother lifted up her voice and wept. Her cries brought her husband down to try with his aching heart to comfort hers' (75)); and the description of John Barton's helplessness as he visits the desperately situated Davenports in their squalid cellar ('So Barton was now left alone with a little child, crying (when it had done eating) for mammy; with a fainting, dead-like woman; and with a sick man, whose mutterings were rising up to screams and shrieks of agonized anxiety' (60)) – all are heart-rending in their insistent presentation of working-class men and women as feeling subjects.

Generously embracing the structure of feeling of melodrama and adapting it to the middle-class novel, Elizabeth Gaskell also adopted many of the plot devices of this popular genre. Mary Barton's aunt, Esther, is a 'fallen woman' seduced by a social superior; and the threat lurks in the novel that young Mary Barton could go the same way, pursued as she is by Harry Carson, the factory owner's son. The wrongful accusation of the upright workman Jem Wilson; the physical violence of the assassination; the trial scene and last-minute reprieve; the emigration trope; the happy ending and reinstatement of domesticity – all would have been immediately recognizable in a mid-Victorian culture steeped in melodrama. Some commentators have criticized the novel for an apparent disjunction between the sentimental plotline that focuses on Mary Barton and her lovers and the overtly political plotline concerning the Chartist petition of 1839 and economic distress. But if one reads the novel (as contemporary readers would have done) according to the conventions of melodrama, the disjuncture disappears: early and mid-century political melodrama had always insisted on a relationship between socio-political analysis and domestic affect, and in her embrace of this Gaskell shows herself finely tuned to the genre. She is, though, resistant to the by now rather old-fashioned paternalistic politics that so often seeped into early Victorian melodrama (not least in *Oliver Twist*): the reconciliation between John Barton and old Carson is a coming together of fellow men rather than of master and man. Gone too are the moral absolutes of early nineteenth-century melodrama: whilst the novel is never in any doubt as to John Barton's guilt, it insists on demonstrating sympathy for the men who were driven sometimes even to violence by suffering and deprivation.

Postscript: 'Bloody Sunday' and utopia

If the New Poor Law and Chartism produced a rich vein of radical writing in the early and mid-Victorian periods, then later in the century it was the gradual development of socialism in England that gave rise to a body of utopian socialist literature, the best-known example of which is William Morris's fantasy, *News from Nowhere* (1890).[20] Although melodramatic aesthetics persisted in fictional writing throughout the nineteenth century, as Peter Brooks's work on Henry James and Honoré de Balzac has amply demonstrated,[21] its force as a radical aesthetic was by this time more or less spent. Socialist writers such as Morris turned instead to the utopia, a long-established literary and political form whose antecedents include Plato's classical utopia, *The Republic* (360 BC), Thomas More's *Utopia* (1516), Robert Owen's *A New View of Society* (1817) and the American Edward Bellamy's immensely popular *Looking Backward* (1888), to which *News from Nowhere* was a riposte.

Socialism was one of the new, regenerative cultural and political forces of the British *fin de siècle*, with the Social Democratic Federation forming in 1881, William Morris's breakaway Socialist League as well as the Fabian Society coming into being in 1884, and the Independent Labour Party in 1893. Morris's – and the Socialist League's – belief that the existing political and economic system in Britain should be overthrown by force is articulated in *News from Nowhere* in the chapter called 'How the Change Came'. It is here, in chapter 17 of the utopia, that Morris pulls his readers sharply back from an idealized future to the tense political climate of the late 1880s which had culminated in the so-called 'Bloody Sunday' massacre in London's Trafalgar Square in November 1887. It is in this way that Morris's utopia importantly intersects with contemporary political events.

Throughout October 1887, amidst scenes of poverty and unemployment in London brought about by a terrible trade depression, a number of gatherings of trade unionists, workers and socialists had taken place in Trafalgar Square. The government decided to ban any further meetings, and it was the defiance of such radicals as Annie Besant, George Bernard Shaw and Morris himself in leading 5,000 marchers into the Square that led to an attack by mounted police and soldiers that resulted in 200 injuries, seventy-five arrests and three deaths. It did not, though, prevent the development of socialism in England: the Labour Representation Committee, which would become the modern Labour Party, finally formed in 1900. In *News from Nowhere* the 'change' that is modelled on 'Bloody Sunday' is resituated in 1952 rather than 1887, and this is because after the November massacre Morris became convinced that he would not see socialism in his lifetime, but could only imagine it as a possibility for the future; hence his use of the utopian form.

When compared to the series of conflicts and acts of physical violence that propelled melodramatic engagements with social and political questions earlier in the Victorian period, the contours of Morris's utopia are relatively static, as is indicated by its subtitle, 'An Epoch of Rest'. The violence of 'the change' is wholly contained (and historicized) by chapter 17. It could be argued that Morris's epoch of rest, with its childlike, anti-intellectual citizens, could all too easily transmute into H. G. Wells's nightmarish account of the languorous, simple-minded Eloi who fall prey to the energetic and industrious Morlocks in *The Time Machine* (1895); utopia's contingent relationship with dystopia is thoroughly uncomfortable in this instance.

The 'Epoch of Rest' is further characterized by the disappearance of the rural/urban divide, a division which in a general way had greatly preoccupied writers across the nineteenth century. With its debt to Greek arcadias, *News from Nowhere* could be apprehended as a late Victorian pastoral idyll. There is no poverty in Morris's vision of the future, in stark contrast to the content of those naturalistic novels of the late Victorian period that centrally concerned themselves with urban poverty.[22] Morris presents instead an aesthetically pleasing environment that combines beauty with utility. Like Ruskin before him, Morris celebrated the medieval period as a time when art and labour were unified, the two men both importantly contributing to the rise of the Arts and Crafts movement in the late Victorian period. If Morris's vision of the future is in part at least Ruskinian, in his celebration of labour he owes a debt to Thomas Carlyle. Morris's concern with alienated labour, and his insistence on the need for revolution violently to overthrow the established social and political order, also suggest a debt to Karl Marx. So that, as well as envisioning in his utopia a new future, Morris was also very much a man of his time.

If William Morris's medievalism suggests social and political reaction, a closer inspection of *News from Nowhere* reminds us of its radicalism: the Houses of Parliament have been replaced by a compost heap; State Socialism has been tried, has failed, and has been replaced by community power; patriotism and imperialism have been dismissed as 'foolish and envious prejudices'; there are no legal institutions; and there are no prisons. This is 'uprooting' indeed.

News from Nowhere was part of a constellation of utopian fictions at the *fin de siècle* that engaged with socialisms of various kinds. Notable among these was a series of New Woman novels that brought a feminist politics to bear on radical writing, including Jane Hume Clapperton's *Margaret*

Dunmore, or A Socialist Home (1888), Isabella Ford's *On the Threshold* (1895) and Gertrude Dix's *The Image Breakers* (1900). Almost alone amongst socialistic New Woman writers, Margaret Harkness (most notably in *A City Girl* (1887) and *Out of Work* (1888)) determinedly embraced a literary naturalism that had its roots in the French novelist Émile Zola's *Rougon Macquart* series. *A City Girl*, though, with its seduced seamstress Nelly Ambrose, also owes a debt to the multitude of melodramatic fictions that Harkness almost certainly would have read as a young girl; it was, without doubt, the melodramatic mode that most forcefully shaped radical writing of the nineteenth century.

Notes

1 Lord Byron to John Cam Hobhouse, 22 April 1820, *'Between Two Worlds': Byron's Letters and Journals*, ed. Leslie A. Marchand (London: John Murray, 1977), p. 81.

2 [Thomas Wooler], 'TRIAL EXTRAORDINARY: MR CANNING VERSUS THE RADICAL REFORMERS', *The Black Dwarf, A London Weekly Publication*, 4: 15 (19 April 1820), pp. 537–40, at pp. 537–8. Canning was a Cabinet Minister.

3 I use the lower case when using 'radical' adjectivally and the upper case ('Radical') when using it as a noun.

4 Charles Dickens, *Little Dorrit* (1855–7; ed. Stephen Wall and Helen Small, London and New York: Penguin Books, 2003), p. 224.

5 Peter Brooks, 'Melodrama, Body, Revolution', in J. Bratton, J. Cook and C. Lethal (eds.), *Melodrama: Stage, Picture, Screen* (London: British Film Institute, 1994), pp. 11–24, at p. 17.

6 Peter Brooks, *The Melodramatic Imagination: Balzac, Henry James, and the Mode of Excess* (New Haven: Yale University Press, 1976), pp. 12–13.

7 Bodleian Library, John Johnson Collection, 'Poor Law Box 3' (JJ), 'The New Poor Law Bill in Force' (Kent Street, Borough: Sharp, Printer, n.d.). Emphasis in original.

8 Josephine McDonagh, *Child Murder and British Culture 1720–1900* (Cambridge: Cambridge University Press, 2003), p. 117.

9 'New Scheme for Maintaining the Poor', *Blackwood's Edinburgh Magazine*, 43 (April 1838), pp. 489–93, at p. 490.

10 Charles Dickens, *Oliver Twist* (1837–9; ed. Philip Horne, London and New York: Penguin Books, 2003), p. 15. Subsequent references to this novel will be included in parentheses in the main body of the text.

11 James Mill, *Elements of Political Economy* (London: Baldwin, Craddock, and Joy, 1821), p. 2.

12 Thomas Carlyle, 'Chartism', in *Carlyle: Selected Writings*, ed. Alan Shelston (London and New York: Penguin Books, 1980), pp. 155, 152.

13 Thomas Cooper, 'Seth Thompson, the Stockinger', in *Wise Saws and Modern Instances* (1845); repr. in Ian Haywood (ed.), *The Literature of Struggle* (Aldershot and Brookfield: Ashgate, 1996), pp. 46–52.

14 Ernest Jones, *Notes to the People*, 2 vols. (London: J. Pavey, 1851–2), vol. 1, p. 20.

15 Other examples of the genre include Elizabeth Gaskell, *Mary Barton: A Tale of Manchester Life*, ed. Shirley Foster (1848; repr. London and New York: Oxford University Press, 2006); Charles Kingsley, *Alton Locke, Tailor and Poet: An Autobiography* (London: Chapman and Hall, 1850); and Charles Dickens, *Hard Times*, ed. Kate Flint (1854; repr. London: Penguin Books, 2003).

16 Catherine Gallagher, *The Industrial Reformation of English Fiction: Social Discourse and Narrative Form, 1832–1867* (Chicago and London: University of Chicago Press, 1985), p. 202.

17 Benjamin Disraeli, *Sybil: or The Two Nations* (1845; repr. Oxford: Oxford World's Classics, 1998), book 1, ch. 12.

18 *Ibid.* book 2, ch. 3.

19 Gaskell, *Mary Barton*, ed. Foster, Preface, p. 4. Subsequent references to this novel will be included in parentheses in the main body of the text.

20 William Morris, *News from Nowhere: An Epoch of Rest*, in *Commonweal*, January–October 1890. Other examples of the genre include Edward Bellamy's *Looking Backward* (Boston: Ticknor and Co., 1888), Robert Blatchford's *Merrie England* (1895; repr. London: Clarion Press, 1908), and Jane Hume Clapperton's *Margaret Dunmore, or A Socialist Home* (London: Swan Sonnenschein, Lowry and Co., 1888).

21 Brooks, *The Melodramatic Imagination*.

22 See for example George Gissing, *The Nether World* (1889; repr. Hassocks: Harvester Press, 1974) and Arthur Morrison, *A Child of the Jago* (London: Methuen, 1896).

8

KATHERINE NEWEY

Popular culture

> The drama's laws the drama's patrons give,
> For we that live to please, must please to live.
> Prologue written by Samuel Johnson for Mr Garrick
> on the opening of the Drury Lane theatre

The demands of living to please and pleasing to live – that uneasy compact between art and commerce – was one of the central anxieties of Victorian cultural life. The words spoken by David Garrick, standing on the Drury Lane stage in 1747, were much quoted by novelists, critics, visual artists, playwrights and essayists throughout the nineteenth century. Dr Johnson's 'Prologue' speaks of a capricious eighteenth-century audience, but in 1747 Garrick could stand on the stage of Drury Lane and rely on the certainty of his theatre's monopoly on the 'legitimate' theatre. In the theatre, painting and literature, artists, critics, and audiences had a shared sense of British national culture, its aesthetic qualities and class allegiances. By Victoria's accession to the throne in 1837, under the complex pressures of industrialization and urbanization, and a vigorous democratic impulse, British national culture appeared fractured and contentious. Artists, critics and audiences were often at odds over what was pleasing, and how that which pleased could – or should – provide a living. While eighteenth-century cultural certainties and coherence may have been a façade reliant on the acceptance of an exclusive Whig ascendancy, this sense of a coherent national culture had, by the start of the Victorian period, disappeared. The contending discourses of national culture, perhaps artfully glossed over before the French Revolution, became overt, and the ideological conflicts of class and gender became part of the very content of much of British culture, particularly that which we have come to see as 'popular culture'.

This chapter will trace some of those contending discourses in Victorian culture through three 'flashpoints' of cultural activity, which produced anxiety and stirred public debate about appropriate cultural forms and modes of communication. My starting point is the contested genres, media and spaces of popular culture in the 1820s and 1830s. It was in these post-French Revolutionary decades that the split between popular and high culture became a topic of public debate, and when many of the anxieties about popular culture we see as typically 'Victorian' were first articulated. The debate between popular and high culture was apparently about aesthetic quality, but actually betrayed anxieties about the visibility, articulacy and inhabitation of public space by the Other: children, women and working-class men. The outcry over 'legitimacy' in the theatre in the 1820s and 1830s was mirrored by similar concerns over the decadence of popular fiction in the work of popular writers such as G. W. M. Reynolds, William Harrison Ainsworth, and Catherine Gore and Edward Bulwer-Lytton and their silver fork novels; and this lively fictional milieu was visualized by illustrators such as the Cruickshank brothers.

It was in the 1820s and 1830s that what we think of as Victorian popular culture was forged out of a combination of post-French Revolution radical activity and the more quotidian and less oppositional practices engendered by the extraordinary explosion of print culture in the first decades of the nineteenth century. As recent scholarship has shown, the end of the eighteenth and the beginning of the nineteenth centuries was a rich period for the growth of popular print culture. It was in this period that popular audiences developed self-conscious and articulate reading presences. But those very terms 'popular fiction' and 'popular audiences' were terms loaded – indeed, over-determined – from the beginning of the Victorian period to the present day. At one level, 'popular culture' refers to cheaply available, quickly produced, mass circulation, aesthetically accessible fiction, poetry, drama and graphics. But this simple definition already begins to beg questions of value and cultural authority, and class and gender identities.

Many of the terms used to describe the products of popular culture combine apparently neutral, documentary descriptions of cultural practices and products with moral and aesthetic judgements of cultural products and their consumers. For example, the term I use here – 'aesthetically accessible' – to describe the contents of fictions and dramas we loosely term 'popular' is an attempt to provide a comparatively neutral substitute for terms such as 'trash', 'low brow', 'silly novels' or even 'simple'. Similarly, the double meaning of the word 'cheap' already embeds an aesthetic judgement within an apparently simple description of market cost. That which is cheap might also be worthless, of little value or of no account. 'Popular culture' is a term often used interchangeably with the term 'mass culture', and takes as its audience a population undistinguished by rank or hierarchy; mass or popular are also euphemisms for 'working'- or 'lower'-class audience. There is a slippage from 'popular culture' (or 'mass culture') to 'lower class', which demonstrates how economic advantage is linguistically and conceptually intertwined with moral judgement, particularly when speaking from a bourgeois critical position.

'Culture', as Raymond Williams points out, 'is one of the two or three most complicated words in the English language.'[1] In the early Victorian period, culture became an arena where hegemonic power continually attempted to reassert control. Many cultural historians argue that cultural production – the creation and circulation of texts, images, performances, songs and the like – worked to mediate mass culture through channels and genres which enabled middle-class control of working-class culture. By these means, it is argued, popular culture was situated outside the mainstream of British national life, respectable readerships and audiences, and aesthetic value. Morag Shiach argues that the desire to define popular culture 'far from solving "the problem" of popular culture ... serves to confirm its dimensions'.[2] Popular culture, according to Shiach, is a category 'in which the relationship between "the popular" and discourses of society, gender and value [are] constantly reworked in discussions of popular culture'.[3] Shiach echoes Raymond Williams's statement that 'The history of the idea of culture is a record of our reactions, in thought and feeling, to the changed conditions of our common life',[4] arguing that histories of popular culture direct us 'towards a consideration of cultural hierarchies and of the relation between the social and the cultural'.[5]

One of the features of the Victorian popular culture was the energetic circulation of familiar plots, tropes, characters and images. It is possible to find antecedents and parallels in fiction, drama, poetry, painting and the graphic arts between 'high' and popular cultural products; but that kind of hierarchizing is perhaps less interesting than thinking about how these ideas circulated, and what were the effects of such circulation. Such cultural mobility was enabled by speed of communications, and urbanization, and those processes made their first notable impact on British culture in the pre- and early Victorian periods. The city, and particularly the metropolitan centre of London, has always been a focus of popular culture (as opposed to 'folk' literature), but by the 1830s the city had become representative of a new kind of modernity.[6] While eighteenth-century artists, such as Hogarth, had catalogued the city's vices and entertainments, early Victorian city literature combined the radical political stance of much post-Revolutionary literature with a sense of urgency about the material conditions of everyday life, and a degree of sensationalism about their representation. For their mass audiences, city stories (novels, plays, and their illustrations and stage spectacle) offered an oppositional morality, which made visible the corruptions of wealth, and the harmful and dangerous social divisions of the modern city; in this way, a radical political stance was anchored in a moral position which could easily claim authority from Christian precepts.

G. W. M. Reynolds, a Chartist publisher as well as author, starts *The Mysteries of London* with the portentous observation that:

> Amongst these cities there is one in which contrasts of a strange nature exist. The most unbounded wealth is the neighbour of the most hideous poverty; the most gorgeous pomp is placed in strong relief by the most deplorable squalor; the most seducing luxury is only separated by a narrow wall from the most appalling misery … There are but two words known in the moral alphabet of this great city; for all virtues are summed up in the one, and all vices in the other: and those words are WEALTH / POVERTY.[7]

Together with his illustrator, George Stiff, Reynolds gives a moral geography of London, using the familiar binary of rich and poor. This human geography, incorporating a taxonomy of the inhabitants of the modern city, is a familiar trope of this period, and can be found at the beginning of most popular literature in one form or another.[8] Douglas Jerrold uses the close neighbourhood of rich and poor in London as the structuring principle of his novella *St Giles and St James* (1851), and we are most familiar with this trope in Charles Dickens's fictional conceptualizations of London. Reynolds's version is sharpened by his Chartist background and commitment to social change, drawing particularly on his republican convictions. Like most popular artists, Reynolds draws on familiar structures and genres; his plot begins with the familiar trope of estranged brothers, Robert and Eugene Markham, separated by circumstance, involved in life quests which take them to all the dark corners and splendid rooms of London, and beyond. Robert's progress is dogged by the shadowy figure of the Resurrection Man, whose history is a dark echo of Robert's; and we might note here that the figure of the grave robber in a type of haunting makes its appearance again in Dickens's *A Tale of Two Cities*.

Of course, Reynolds's massive text did not emerge fully fledged from his hands without any predecessors. The genealogies of long, serialized fictions, set in the contemporary city, are lengthy, and include the presence of continental European works by Eugene Sue, whose *Les mystères de Paris* (1842–3) was a formational text for Reynolds. It was adapted into the melodrama *Les bohémiens de Paris* by Adolphe D'Ennery and Eugène Grangé, and found its way to London as a variety of plays, *The Bohemians of Paris*, *The Scamps of London* or *The Mysteries of Crime*, staged in 1843. Equally formative was the 'Newgate novel', particularly the wildly popular novels of William Harrison Ainsworth. Ainsworth's use of the 'true story' drawn from *The Newgate Calendar* offered justification for his focus on crime and the criminal as protagonist and romanticized anti-hero. Ainsworth's most notorious Newgate novel, *Jack Sheppard* (1839), was feared because it was seen to carry the power of historical truth; indeed, in an intertextual confusion of play, illustrations and 'real life', the novel and its stage adaptations gained widespread notoriety when they were cited as a cause of the murder of Lord William Russell by his valet, Courvoisier.[9] Ainsworth was quick to deny that his novel was the cause of this crime, but the ruling class's fundamental fear of the power of imaginative literature and performance to incite crime and cultivate immorality in the mass of 'the uneducated' would seem to have been confirmed.

Part of what was at stake in the Courvoisier case was spectatorship: Courvoisier claimed to have seen *Jack Sheppard*, rather than read it.[10] The novel is powerfully illustrated by George Cruikshank, and it is realizations of his illustrations which form the narrative skeleton for the many stage versions of the novel. The city as a place of contrasted vice and virtue in the nineteenth century has a rich performance history, focused around a cluster of melodramas by Douglas Jerrold, John Baldwin Buckstone (adapter of *Life in London* and *Jack Sheppard*), George Almar and William Thomas Moncrieff, staged in the late 1820s and 1830s. Plays such as Jerrold's domestic melodramas *Sally in Our Alley* (1830) and *Martha Willis* (1831) focus on young innocent heroines, and their battles with the wide world outside their homes and villages. It did not escape the notice of contemporary spectators and commentators that these plays were topical in their connection of politics and morality: 'Mr Jerrold has introduced some shrewd remarks on the oppression of the rich against the poor; on the power which wealth gives to do good and evil; and how much the latter preponderates.'[11]

It was Jerrold's skill as a dramatist and polemicist to use the conventions of melodrama flexibly and tellingly, so as to exploit a conventional framework to discuss politically active ideas and issues, in a shorthand which was easily accessible for both audiences and actors. Jerrold mixes simple tales of injustice, love, villainy and charity, with enough features of recognizable contemporaneity to hold an audience into accepting his situations as both universal and particular. His plays, and the London fictions of Reynolds and Ainsworth, offer their audiences maps for modern life, played out in a heady generic mix of radical politics and romantic, melodramatic feeling, in what Trefor Thomas argues is 'an almost revolutionary conjuncture in English life'.[12] They put the ordinary man or woman at the centre of the drama, and attribute heroic status to him or her.

A different geometry of the city and its inhabitants is offered in the novels of fashionable life, 'the silver fork' novels, popular in the 1820s and 1830s.

Charles Dickens parodies, in his inimitable synthetic way, the style and readership of these novels in *Nicholas Nickleby* when Kate Nickleby's job as a companion requires her to read the three volumes of *The Lady Flabella* to the nouveau riche Mrs Wititterly, languishing on a sofa in Cadogan Place, and William Thackeray converted his early satires as Yellowplush into a novelistic style in its own right. The dominance of Dickens's and Thackeray's critical satires of silver fork novels has led to a general devaluing of their impact and the cultural work that this popular form can be seen to be enacting. Edward Bulwer-Lytton, a prolific writer of novels of fashionable life, as well as Newgate novels such as *Eugene Aram*, argued in his Condition of England work *England and the English* (1833) that 'Few writers ever produced so great an effect on the political spirit of their generation as some of these novelists, who, without any other merit, unconsciously exposed the falsehood, the hypocrisy, the arrogant and vulgar insolence of patrician life.'[13]

As the author of *Pelham; or The Adventures of a Gentleman* (1828), Bulwer-Lytton may be accused of some special pleading here, but his directive to read these novels as political novels is a productive one. Winifred Hughes argues cogently for the 'radical instability of tone' of the silver fork school emerging in the Reform era, and its potential political effect; such a reading is borne out by a close examination of the novels of Catherine Gore, one of the most productive novelists of this genre. Gore's novels (and her plays) demonstrate how we can read across genres, and the 'high' and 'popular' boundaries, to discern the effects of far-reaching political changes on even the most apparently frivolous areas of British life. Gore's novels, focusing on the stereotypically feminine spheres of home, fashion, marriage, offer an inside view of the world of Cabinet politics, government and Reform from an outsider – that is, a woman, who, voteless by definition, has no public or civic identity. In *The Hamiltons* (1834), or *The Diary of a Désennuyée* (1836), or *Mothers and Daughters* (1831), as in her comic plays such as *School for Coquettes* (1831) or *Lords and Commons* (1832), Gore offers a feminine view of power, and of the characters and domestic lives of politicians and men of business.

One of the characteristics of popular culture I am tracing is its introduction of plots and character types which are subsequently taken up by 'canonical' writers. Gore's critique of the self-made man of business in her late novel *The Banker's Wife; or Court and City* (1843) anticipates Trollope's portrait of the capitalist Melmotte in *The Way We Live Now* (1875). Gore has not the bitter edge of satire of the later writer, but she draws a far from comic or light-hearted picture of the consequences of the social impact of the aggressive nature of Victorian capitalism. The banker in question, Mr Hamlyn, not content with running his family bank for a modest profit and comfortable life-style, speculates with his clients' money, in order to purchase and maintain a country estate. While trying to generate the cash he needs to do this, he alienates his wife and daughter, and destroys the emotional, as well as economic, security of his home. The novel graphically illustrates the 'specter of scarcity', always in the background of the Victorian middle classes,[14] and contemplates the irony of ruin caused by trying to outrun scarcity, but its strongest feature is the powerful representation of the alienation between the banker and his wife caused by his seduction by wealth. Gore does not gloss over the effect of financial scandal on the Hamlyn women, an effect amplified because of their relative powerlessness to take action to save themselves. Read in this way, these apparently frivolous novels start to do important cultural work, by making visible the invisible constraints of bourgeois femininity. However, the full impact of this 'feminization' of fiction was not felt until the 1860s, when novel-writing and novel-reading women became the focus of a mid-Victorian moral panic over popular culture.

Something happened in 1863. In the late winter and spring of that year, popular culture became an overtly feminized culture of consumption, with the spectacles of ritualized marriages, and sensational revelations of the dark and dirty secrets of intimate domestic relationships enacted on- and off-stage. Across London, adaptations of Mary Braddon's self-described 'pair of Bigamy novels',[15] *Lady Audley's Secret* and *Aurora Floyd*, dominated the stage, while off-stage the whole country seemed consumed by the preparations for the royal wedding: the marriage of the Prince of Wales to Princess Alexandra of Denmark. Adaptations of Ellen Wood's *East Lynne* were to follow, and would endure even longer on the stage, when the bill needed filling or audiences reviving. The intersection of these events offers a fascinating slice into the popular culture of the mid-Victorian period, and its anxieties and enthusiasms. The focus on the material culture of the age, represented by the lavish illustrations of the royal wedding presents and the bride's trousseau (down to the name of the supplier of the perfume for the bride),[16] together with the documentation of the public celebrations (including fireworks across the country, and the free opening of the theatres for the night) on the eve of the Prince of Wales's wedding, provide an ironic contrast to the sensational stories of bigamy and madness in Braddon's and Wood's novels. However, both events perform extreme versions of Victorian middle-class respectability, celebrating both the veneer and the reality of marriage and family, be it the dynastic continuity of the British royal family, or the fictional dynasties of the Carlyle or Audley families. And both phenomena, we might argue now, bore with them evidence of the darker undertones of Victorian bourgeois family life, for those who cared to look.

Of course, the marriage of the Prince of Wales to Princess Alexandra was greeted with public celebration, and few overt murmurs about the unrespectable aspects of the Prince of Wales's life to date. But it is a serendipitous supplement to any study of stage adaptations of sensation fiction in 1863. Those illustrated papers which might usually have carried illustrations of the theatrical sensation of *Lady Audley's Secret* or *Aurora Floyd* – perhaps in the iconic scenes which had caused so much critical comment – Aurora whipping her groom, or Lady Audley pushing George Talboys down the well – were given over to pages of engravings of Princess Alexandra's trousseau, the wedding dresses, the wedding presents, the wedding coach, the honeymoon coach, the chapel at Windsor Castle, and celebratory illuminations in every major city of Great Britain. In the run up to the royal wedding on 10 March 1863, the *Illustrated London News* published several special supplements and followed in verbal and visual detail the minutiae of Princess Alexandra's departure from Denmark, her mode of travel, her arrival in Britain and her travel across the country. Braddon's and Wood's imagined sensations were supplanted by the real sensation of a royal wedding, which was managed by the court to enhance coverage in the popular press and increase the popularity of the royal family (in a way which has become all too familiar in Britain since the 1960s) and staged as a spectacle of 'popular constitutionalism'[17] which Queen Victoria recorded privately as 'a scene in a play'.[18] Such was the saturation of press coverage in words and pictures that the only illustration of the Lady Audley/Aurora Floyd phenomenon in 1863 which I have been able to locate is a sketch of the St James's Christmas parody, *Eighteen Hundred and Sixty Three; or, The Sensations of the Past Season*, in the *ILN*'s regular round-up of the Christmas pantomimes (26 December 1863). Reading the phenomena side by side, there are suggestive parallels in these real-life and fictional spectacles of romantic love. Whether staged as fiction or reality, here is a moment which crystallizes the increasing fetishization and commodification of the rituals of marriage in the mass marketing of love and family formation in mid-Victorian Britain.

The protests against sensation fiction set within bourgeois and genteel homes and apparently respectable and happy marriages were overt and voluble. The rapid appearance of these popular novels in the early 1860s caused a moral panic around what entertainment was suitable for vulnerable classes of readers. These debates were driven by competing claims to fictional, dramatic and visual representations of the feeling individual. The expression of strong feeling, so challenging in popular entertainments such as melodrama thirty years before, was equally challenging in fiction because of the way that female characters' expression of emotion threatened conventional social hierarchies. For some readers and critics, sensation fiction provoked anxieties about transgressions of the boundaries of class, gender and sexuality. For other readers and critics, sensation fiction offered imaginative freedom, amplified on the stage by actresses' powerful physical expressivity in sensation melodramas.

This double reading is implicit in what we might now call the emotional economies or the 'structures of feeling' in sensation fiction. Margaret Oliphant's perceptive reading of a range of sensation novels protests at the ways in which readerly sympathies are focused on the villains or wrong-doers. 'The charm of the book', she writes of Wilkie Collins's *Woman in White*, 'so far as character counts in its effect, is Fosco'. About *East Lynne* she complains that 'From first to last it is she [Lady Isabel] alone in whom the reader feels any interest. Her virtuous rival we should like to bundle to the door and be rid of, anyhow. The Magdalen herself, who is only moder-ately interesting while she is good, becomes, as soon as she is a Magdalen, doubly a heroine.'[19]

Wood's narrative voice encourages this engagement, taking pains to explain carefully how Lady Isabel is made to feel jealous by her husband's close and secret conferrals with Barbara Hare: '[T]he few meetings that Lady Isabel witnessed between her husband and Barbara would have been quite enough to excite her anger and jealousy, and to trouble her peace; but, in addition, Francis Levison took care to tell her of those she did not see.'[20] After Lady Isabel has left her marital home and 'plunged into an abyss of horror' the narrator famously exhorts her readers *not* to do the very thing they are reading about, as if she anticipates her readers' empathetic engage-ment with Isabel's feelings of neglect and jealousy.

> Oh, reader, believe me! Lady – wife – mother! should you ever be tempted to abandon your home, so will you awaken! Whatever trials may be the lot of your married life, though they may magnify themselves to your crushed spirit as beyond the endurance of woman to bear, *resolve* to bear them; fall down upon your knees and pray to be enabled to bear them: pray for patience; pray for strength to resist the demon that would urge you to escape; bear unto death, rather than forfeit your fair name and your good conscience; for be assured that the alternative, if you rush on to it, will be found to be far worse than death![21]

The narrator assumes that married life is difficult, and indeed has shown us how Isabel has come to find it so, but employs her rhetorical skill to persuade her female readers that the abyss of adultery is a fate worse than death. The events that punish Lady Isabel – her return as Madame Vine, her nursing of her own children unknown to them as their mother, and the death of her young son – are narrated in painful detail. They have become the stuff of popular mythologizing and ridicule: 'Dead, dead, and never called me mother!' is the tagline often used to stand for all that is considered problematic about melodrama: its too easy recourse to sentimentality and its bathos.[22]

Harrowing as these incidents were represented to be, or as ridiculous as they eventually became, they offered readers the vicarious experience of heightened emotion, and the chance to fantasize about breaking out of conventional roles and ordinary lives. As Kate Flint argues, this was what was felt to be so dangerous about sensation novels for their predominantly female audience: they challenged 'the ideological premiss that the middle-class woman should be pure, innocent, and relatively passive'.[23] The combination of domestic settings (whether it be bourgeois West Lynne, or stately Audley Court) and criminality was disturbing. For novelists to create, and readers to enjoy, a murderous heroine who looked like a Pre-Raphaelite painting with 'feathery masses of ringlets with every glimmer of gold' who took 'joy and brightness with her',[24] wherever she went, was to destabilize radically the ideal of the 'angel in the house'. Yet even the act of disapprobation led to sensation, as we find in Henry Mansel's imagined scenarios:

> we are thrilled with horror, even in fiction, by the thought that such things may be going on around us and among us. The man who shook our hand with a hearty English grasp half an hour ago – the woman whose beauty and grace were the charm of last night, and whose gentle words sent us home better pleased with the world and with ourselves – how exciting to think that under these pleasing outsides may be concealed some demon in human shape.[25]

Perhaps knowingly, Mansel's famous condemnation of sensation novels falls into the very dangers of sensation he and other critics caution against. He sees sensation novels as evidence of disease in the 'conditions of the body of society' (51) and his recommendations for curing that disease include cultivating 'a taste for the best class of fictions' in the next generation. Ironically, that next generation would fashion the 'New Woman', in both lived experience and cultural production. But fiction as medicine for a diseased body was to find its place in another arena of popular culture, in the popular social movements and entertainments emerging from late Victorian imperial ideology.

By the end of the nineteenth century, popular culture can be used to map a further epochal shift in Victorian Britain. The democratization of reading and viewing audiences, so threatening to public order and good taste in the 1820s and 1830s, and to female morality and bodily health in the 1860s, was now a given of the cultural landscape. After the 1867 and 1884 Reform Acts – the former characterized by prime minister Benjamin Disraeli as a 'leap in the dark' – working-class men had civic visibility; meanwhile, women of all classes were increasingly visible and independent in public. Indeed, popular entertainments were constructed especially to meet the demands and desires of these various constituencies, and it is popular culture which can tell us much about the state of modernity in the late Victorian period. By 1896, when the first 'moving pictures' were shown as part of music hall programmes in Leicester Square, we might argue that the alignment of modernity with technology in popular culture was practically complete. Certainly, popular culture, modernity and femininity (and feminism) met in a variety of popular entertainments, as metropolitan middle- and young working-class women had discretionary cash and time, and increasing freedom to move about in public independently. The phenomenon of the theatre matinee, for example, was a commercial practice which relied on a female audience, and much of the expansion of theatre audiences in the last decades of the nineteenth century was due to increased numbers of women spectators.

Out of the plethora of literatures, entertainments, novelties and technological wonders in the last decades of the nineteenth century from which we could choose to examine the popular cultures which typify the end of the nineteenth century, I want to focus briefly on fictions of empire as they meld older patterns of sensation fiction and children's adventure stories with modern ideas of science and exploration. John Mackenzie has explored at length the power of the idea of empire as an 'ideological cluster' formed out of the social and political conditions of the last quarter of the nineteenth century, and fed by popular culture and the burgeoning commercial culture of the period.[26] Fictions of empire, and particularly those stories in all sorts of popular media aimed at children and young people, became vehicles for a broader change in sociability, and a method of channelling the dangers felt to be implicit in mass literacy into an ideology of 'improvement, self-help, aggressive individualism'.[27]

These fictions offer us a world of possibilities for the adventurous and resourceful hero (the gender is deliberate), who can travel throughout the empire, feeling ownership of all that he sees. By the beginning of the twentieth century, they also offer reassurance to an increasingly doubting public about the imperial project, and offer a mode of education and citizen formation which claimed to be exciting, and educative.[28] In print, the adventure stories of Rider Haggard's African novels hark back to an earlier period of British imperial ascendancy. Captain [Frederick] Marryat's 1820s and 1830s novels of nautical adventure and triumph, in the period during and after the Napoleonic Wars, reinforced the sense that Britannia ruled the waves, and the conviction that the British Navy's role 'changed from that of warrior to the world's policeman'.[29] On the popular stage, imperial melodramas brought together the stories of derring-do with spectacular visual representations of the far-flung empire for local English audiences.[30] The 1881 Drury Lane staging of Augustus Harris and Paul Meritt's melodrama *Youth* showed troops and battles with documentary detail, including real Gatling firearms, so that critic Dutton Cook commented that the smell and fumes from the blank cartridges 'so filled the house … that … the victory of our arms was strongly felt to be dearly purchased'.[31]

When Allan Quatermain, Rider Haggard's indomitable hero, tells 'the strangest story that I know of', he tells a story of a quest into what Joseph Conrad fifteen years later called the 'heart of darkness'. Conrad's metaphor of Africa standing for the unknown interior of the self is played out through the physical actions and incidents of *King Solomon's Mines* (1885), rather than Conrad's psychologized interior drama. The band of three European adventurers (Bram Stoker takes up this structure in *Dracula*) use ancient knowledges from both Europe and Africa to solve the mystery of identity at the heart of King Solomon's Mines. Patrick Brantlinger has called these kinds of adventure stories the 'imperial Gothic', pointing particularly to the combination of imperial derring-do and investment in the occult which characterizes the work of Haggard and his fellow adventurers, such as John Buchan and Richard Jefferies.[32]

But Quatermain is not untouched or unchanged by his encounter with African knowledge. In telling the climactic events of the story, when he and his fellow adventurers bring a combination of British fair play and tribal democracy to the Kukuana people, Quatermain is cognisant of their great power and local knowledge. His desire to communicate that knowledge – or rather, Haggard's tropes of authenticity and education – frame the novel, as Quatermain writes of his desire to give a fuller account than he is able of the Kukuana language, Kukuanaland indigenous flora and fauna, military organization, and domestic and family customs.[33] This combination of science and the occult typifies much popular fiction of the late nineteenth century (one might think again of *Dracula*), and is also to be found in early science fiction, another significant emergent genre at this time. Indeed, the fictions of Haggard and the science fictions of H. G. Wells are vitally connected via imperialist ideology; in *The Time Machine* (1895) the sense of the modern 'ordinary' man adventuring into the darkness of unknown epochs, using modern knowledge to frame encounters with the unknown, offers many parallels to Haggard's stories of Africa.

The idea of a novel as an encyclopedia for adventure and discovery was a powerful aspect of the survival of other kinds of adventure stories, of the type we find in R. M. Ballantyne's earlier shipwreck novel *The Coral Island*

(1858), with its genealogy from *Robinson Crusoe*. These are all narratives which offer the utopian fantasy of building a new society, away from the constraints of mid-century Britain. As J. S. Bratton comments in her introduction to a modern reprint, these desert-island stories are powerful mythic narratives, taking us back to the fundamentals of 'how we live',[34] and, in the course of that journey, enabling self-knowledge and self-fashioning. The same powerful attraction of adventure and experimentation with the basics of survival is part of what explains the immense popularity of Robert Baden-Powell's *Scouting for Boys* (1908), which reads like an adventure novel; as its most recent editor points out, Baden-Powell's text is encyclopedic, embracing '"true crime" anecdotes, stock adventure tales, campfire hints, potted history natural and imperial, [and] first aid tips'.[35] Boehmer notes that *Scouting for Boys* was published at a moment of doubt in British imperial confidence, after defeat in the Boer War. Like other popular fictions surveyed in this chapter, perhaps part of the mass attraction of Baden-Powell's text was its role in creating consolatory fantasies of adventure for a generation which had (to invoke a cliché) seen the sun set on part of the British Empire.

These imperial texts are part of a broader circulation of plots, ideas, and approaches to the physical world beyond Britain, and attempts at its mapping and control. Although I have eschewed offering a definition of popular culture, there are enduring threads in my survey. Even at its most highly inventive and fictive, popular culture makes important claims to authenticity: the most fantastical tales are phrased in the rhetoric of documentary truth. And truth is always improving and educative. The justification of highly coloured narrative stories and vivid spectacles, by virtue of their claim to education and improvement, is one of the unifying features of otherwise diverse entertainments. Furthermore, the fictions and spectacles of popular culture are intensely intertextual, and mix the fictional (*King Solomon's Mines*) with the factual (*Scouting for Boys*). By the end of the Victorian period, this generic boundary shifting was at its most spectacular in theatrical productions, which, in reporting the Crimean or Boer War, for example, used 'real' soldiers re-enacting 'real' battles within fictional plots. If popular culture is at one level as simple as a range of mass-produced texts which appeal to a wide audience, then at its most complex it is constituted by a set of aesthetic practices which cross generic boundaries, challenging readers and spectators to engage with their cultural knowledge and experience at full stretch.

Notes

1 Raymond Williams, *Keywords* (London: Fontana, 1976), pp. 87 and 90.
2 Morag Shiach, *Discourse on Popular Culture* (Cambridge: Polity Press, 1989), p. 19.

3 *Ibid.* p. 34.

4 Raymond Williams, *Culture and Society, 1780–1950* (London: Chatto and Windus, 1958), p. 295.

5 Shiach, *Discourse on Popular Culture*, p. 14.

6 Matthew Buckley, 'Sensations of Celebrity: Jack Sheppard and the Mass Audience', *Victorian Studies*, 44, 3 (Spring 2002), p. 425.

7 G. W. M. Reynolds, *The Mysteries of London*, 6 vols. with illustrations by G. Stiff (London: George Vickers, 1836), p. 2.

8 Anne Humpherys, 'The Geometry of the Modern City: G. W. M. Reynolds and *The Mysteries of London*,' *Browning Institute Studies*, 11 (1983), pp. 73–4.

9 Keith Hollingsworth, *The Newgate Novel, 1830–1847: Bulwer, Ainsworth, Dickens, & Thackeray* (Detroit: Wayne State University Press, 1963), p. 145.

10 *Ibid.* p. 146.

11 D.–G. [George Daniels], 'Remarks', to *Sally in Our Alley* (London: Cumberland, n.d.); first performed Surrey Theatre, 11 January 1830.

12 Trefor Thomas, 'Rereading G. W. M. Reynolds's *The Mysteries of London*', in Alice Jenkins and Juliet Johns (eds.), *Rereading Victorian Fiction* (Basingstoke: Macmillan, 2000), p. 65.

13 Cited in Winifred Hughes, 'Silver Fork Writers and Readers: Social Contexts of a Best Seller', *Studies in the Novel* (Spring 1992), p. 331.

14 Thad Logan, *The Victorian Parlour* (Cambridge: Cambridge University Press, 2001), p. 207.

15 Robert Lee Wolff, 'Devoted Disciple: The Letters of Mary Elizabeth Braddon to Sir Edward Bulwer-Lytton, 1862–1873', *Harvard Library Bulletin*, 22, 1 (January 1974), p. 12.

16 *The Lady's Newspaper*, 28 March 1863, p. 1.

17 John Plunkett, *Queen Victoria: First Media Monarch* (Oxford: Oxford University Press, 2003), p. 51.

18 Cited in Margaret Homans, *Royal Representations: Queen Victoria and British Culture, 1837–1876* (Chicago: University of Chicago Press, 1998), p. 60.

19 'Sensational Novels', in Andrew Maunder (ed.), *Varieties of Women's Sensation Fiction: 1855–1890*, vol. 1: *Sensationalism and the Sensation Debate* (London: Pickering and Chatto, 2004), pp. 12–13.

20 Ellen Wood, *East Lynne*, ed. Andrew Maunder (Peterborough: Broadview Press, 2000), p. 296.

21 *Ibid.* pp. 334–5. Maunder discusses this passage at length in his Introduction, pp. 33–5.

22 See Laurence Senelick '"Dead! And Never Called Me Mother!" The Legacy of Oral Tradition from the Nineteenth-Century Stage', *Theatre Studies*, 26–7 (1979/80–1980/81), pp. 7–20, for a discussion of the uses and misuses of this phrase.

23 Kate Flint, *The Woman Reader 1837–1914* (Oxford: Clarendon Press, 1993), p. 275.

24 Mary Elizabeth Braddon, *Lady Audley's Secret* (1862; Oxford: Oxford University Press, 1987), pp. 70 and 5.

25 [Henry Mansel], 'Sensation Novels', in Maunder (ed.), *Varieties of Women's Sensation Fiction*, vol. 1, p. 38.

26 John Mackenzie, *Propaganda and Empire: The Manipulation of British Public Opinion, 1880–1960* (Manchester: Manchester University Press, 1985), pp. 2–3.

27 *Ibid.* p. 199.

28 Peter Yeandle, 'Lessons in Empire and Englishness: Further Thoughts on the English/British Conundrum', in Helen Brocklehurst and Robert Phillips (eds.), *History, Nationhood and the Question of Britain* (Basingstoke: Palgrave Macmillan, 2004), p. 274.

29 John Peck, *Maritime Fiction: Sailors and the Sea in British and American Novels, 1719–1917* (Basingstoke: Palgrave Macmillan, 2001), p. 52.

30 See Heidi Holder, 'Melodrama, Realism and Empire on the British Stage', in J. S. Bratton *et al.*, *Acts of Supremacy: The British Empire and the Stage, 1790–1930* (Manchester: Manchester University Press, 1991), pp. 129–49.

31 Michael Booth, *Victorian Spectacular Theatre, 1850–1910* (London: Routledge and Kegan Paul, 1981), pp. 69–70.

32 Patrick Brantlinger, *Rule of Darkness: British Literature and Imperialism, 1830–1914* (Ithaca, NY: Cornell University Press, 1988), p. 227.

33 Henry Rider Haggard, *King Solomon's Mines* (1885, World's Classics; ed. Dennis Butts, Oxford: Oxford University Press, 1989), pp. 5–6.

34 J. S. Bratton, 'Introduction', in R. M. Ballantyne, *The Coral Island* (1858, World's Classics; Oxford: Oxford University Press, 1990), p. vii.

35 Elleke Boehmer, 'Introduction', in Robert Baden-Powell, *Scouting for Boys* (1908; Oxford: Oxford University Press, 2004), p. xi.

PART II

Intersections and incursions

9

GOWAN DAWSON

Science and its popularization

In 1887, on the occasion of the golden jubilee of Queen Victoria's accession to the throne, T. H. Huxley declared proudly of the many changes that had occurred during the monarch's long reign:

> This revolution – for it is nothing less – in the political and social aspects of modern civilisation has been preceded, accompanied, and in great measure caused, by a less obvious, but no less marvellous, increase of natural knowledge, and especially of that part of it which is known as Physical Science, in consequence of the application of scientific method to the investigation of the phenomena of the material world.

Huxley was a pioneering biologist, but he was more familiar to the Victorian public as an outspoken proponent of an empirical and naturalistic worldview, gaining notoriety as Charles Darwin's self-styled 'bulldog' during the evolutionary controversies of the 1860s. In his view, it was the application of various scientific procedures to the practices of industry and transportation that had facilitated the economic dynamism by which nineteenth-century society had been transformed. The 'rapid and vast multiplication of … commodities and conveniences of existence' and removal of the 'natural obstacles, which time and space offer to mutual intercourse' were the direct results of employing scientific methods, which had also entailed a 'strengthening of the forces of the organisation of the commonwealth against those of political or social anarchy'.[1] The very success of the Victorian polity, Huxley proclaimed, could be traced back to the empirical and inductive principles adumbrated in the seventeenth century by Francis Bacon and now brought to fruition two centuries later.

These same methods, with their insistence that every inference must be verified by observable facts, explicitly excluded transcendental forms of knowledge that were independent of experience, and, as a consequence, demoted religion to the realms of private emotion. Huxley, in the same jubilee year, contemptuously dismissed the creeds of both Anglicans and

Dissenters as 'tweedle-dum and tweedle-dee theological idiocies', and earlier in his career had observed, with characteristic vitriol, that 'extinguished theologians lie about the cradle of every science as the strangled snakes beside that of Hercules'.[2] For Huxley, who in 1869 coined the term 'agnosticism' to define his own sceptical position in relation to the divine, the erstwhile cultural and political authority of the Church, as well as that of the gentlemanly amateurs who represented its interests in the scientific world, was being usurped by professional men of science like himself who had infiltrated the traditional centres of culture and education while also establishing strongholds of their own in new academic institutions and specialist societies. Imposing physical spaces such as the laboratories and museums of South Kensington where Huxley worked were the most tangible testimony of this new cultural and political importance which science had acquired during the nineteenth century.

The ascendancy of science inevitably had important consequences for other areas of nineteenth-century culture, not least for literature, which was regularly perceived as the antithesis of, and principal bulwark against, the dispiriting and mechanistic creeds of scientific empiricism. Huxley, at the beginning of the 1880s, had belligerently discarded long-established 'school and university traditions' in asserting that 'for the purpose of attaining real culture, an exclusively scientific education is at least as effectual as an exclusively literary education'. Like religion, literature too, in Huxley's opinion, would have to relinquish its erstwhile control of the 'ark of culture' to the newly empowered 'advocates of scientific education'.[3] The literary critic Matthew Arnold responded sharply that, unlike literature, science could not minister to 'our need for conduct, our need for beauty', and he insisted that the 'student of the natural sciences only ... will probably be unsatisfied, or at any rate incomplete, and even more incomplete than the student of humane letters only'.[4]

This protracted dispute over the appropriate balance of the educational curriculum, provoked by the encroachments of science upon ever more aspects of life, is generally perceived to prefigure the growing separation of scientific and literary outlooks that would culminate, in the mid-twentieth century, with C. P. Snow's famous pronouncement that there were now Two Cultures. Literature and science, however, were often considerably more closely related between 1830 and 1914 than such a dichotomous trajectory would suggest, and Huxley and Arnold were actually close friends who shared much common ground. Nevertheless, even the various modes of literary and scientific interconnection in this period seemed to confirm the growing dominance of science over other forms of knowledge.

At the beginning of the period, in 1833, the philosopher John Stuart Mill echoed attitudes prevalent amongst the Romantics in affirming that imaginative literature such as poetry 'act[s] upon the emotions; and therein is ... distinguished from ... its logical opposite, namely ... science', which 'does its work by convincing or persuading'.[5] Two decades later, the theologian John Henry Newman was still insisting that 'poetry ... is always the antagonist to *science* ... the two cannot stand together; they belong respectively to two modes of viewing things, which are contradictory of each other'.[6] Newman's views on poetry, like religion, were self-consciously antiquated, and while the affective and imaginative values of literature continued to be regularly defined in opposition to scientific methods, as well as vice versa, by mid-century the polymathic philosopher of science William Whewell could concede – if a little condescendingly – that science 'must have a dash of poetry' to temper its austere emphasis on facts and inductive reasoning.[7] At the same time, many poets, including Alfred Tennyson, increasingly adopted modern scientific themes and images in their verse, as with the perturbingly defamiliarizing lines

> O earth, what changes hast thou seen!
> There where the long street roars, hath been
> The stillness of the central sea

from section CXXIII of *In Memoriam* (1850), which drew on Charles Lyell's recent theories of gradual and uniform geological change.[8]

More notably, over the following decades the growing popularity of the realist novel, with its aesthetic ideals of accurate observation of minute particulars and narratorial detachment, made literature increasingly analogous with descriptive branches of science such as natural history, prompting some critics to complain that much of the fiction of the period was 'too often an echo of Messrs. Darwin and Huxley' or just 'too scientific'.[9] Leading novelists were certainly not coy in revealing their indebtedness to the methods of contemporary science, and George Eliot explained that her fiction was 'simply a set of experiments in life' in which scientific generalizations were 'clothed ... in some human figure and individual experience', while Thomas Hardy similarly remarked that in his novels he 'aimed ... to make science, not the mere padding of a romance, but the actual vehicle of romance'.[10] Just as the nascent discipline of sociology subsumed the study of human society within the positivist procedures of natural science and understood it as a further manifestation of the same immutable natural laws that had determined the physical world, so novelists like Eliot and Hardy depicted the inexorable workings of cause and effect in determining the different fates of characters, as well as the complex webs of interdependence between individual organisms and the mediums, both biological and societal, which surrounded and shaped them.

By the last decades of the nineteenth century even the most exclusively literary writers appeared to concur with the judgement of Huxley and realist novelists such as Eliot and Hardy that never before had the influence of science been so pervasive or its impact so tangible. In *Plato and Platonism* (1893) the aesthetic critic Walter Pater observed wryly that the Platonic doctrines of art and beauty he was discussing were 'not precisely the question with which the speculative young man of our own day is likely to puzzle himself'. Rather, the propositions with which a studious youth of the late nineteenth century was most apt 'to exercise the patience of his neighbour in a railway carriage, of his dog, or even of a Chinese' were those of 'organism and environment, or protoplasm perhaps, or evolution'.[11] Recent scientific developments like Darwin's theory of evolution or the essential unity of all living matter heralded by the discovery of the primary substance of protoplasm had, as Pater noted, engendered in such contemplative young men a heady sense of intellectual excitement with which philosophical or literary works simply could not compete.

Revising narratives of progress

Pater's rather mordant observation in *Plato and Platonism*, however, also intimates that such putatively stirring topics might equally exasperate many of the less meditative or excitable occupants of railway carriages, as well as Oriental subalterns – placed after dogs by Pater – presumably unacquainted with Western notions of progress, and it is important to recognize that the impact of science during the period between 1830 and 1914, especially in its relation to literature, consistently defies narrow and simplistic characterizations. During the nineteenth century, science could occasion an extremely broad range of responses from a variety of audiences, encompassing exhilaration, hostility, celebration, fear and existential angst, or even the irreverent laughter provoked by cartoons and skits on scientific subjects that filled the pages of satirical magazines like *Punch*. Nor should these varied reactions be dismissed as merely trivial and inconsequential, for the non-scientific public played an important role in shaping science in this period, and practitioners, even including such luminaries as Darwin and Huxley, had to be constantly responsive to the sensitivities and requirements of their different audiences.

Science could undoubtedly also elicit mere apathy and indifference, such as that of 'our young friend Bob', who, in William Makepeace Thackeray's droll and ironic account in the *Roundabout Papers* (1863), 'made sarcastic signals on his nose' when invited, as a Christmas treat, to see a 'great philosopher ... giving a lecture to young folks at the British [i.e. Royal] Institution'.[12] Those who exhibited the most passionate and resolute interest in scientific matters, meanwhile, were likely to be overlooked entirely, as with the Oldham 'common hand-loom weavers' in Elizabeth Gaskell's *Mary Barton* (1848) 'who throw the shuttle with unceasing sound' while 'Newton's "Principia" lies open on the loom, to be snatched at in work hours, [and] revelled over in meal times, or at night', but 'whose existence will probably be doubted by many'.[13] Literary texts like those of Gaskell, Thackeray and Pater are extremely significant resources for assessing the importance of audiences, and not just practitioners, in the making of nineteenth-century science, and for recognizing that reactions to science were considerably more divergent, as well as more subtly nuanced, than is often assumed, especially amongst groups such as children, colonial others and working men in provincial towns whose opinions are rarely taken into account.

It is equally the case that various forms of religion and spirituality remained an extremely significant factor in Victorian society, as witnessed by the fervency of the nonconformist and Roman Catholic revivals, while the distinction between the secular and the sacred in this period was not nearly as unequivocal as suggested in the partisan accounts of Huxley and others, which generally adhere to a simplistic and self-aggrandizing truth-vanquishing-error credo. Many scientists at the cutting edge of their particular disciplines in the late nineteenth century, including the physicists James Clerk Maxwell and Lord Kelvin, continued to view their experimental work as an attempt to provide objective evidence of the existence of a beneficent divine Creator who works in accordance with natural law. Indeed, Kelvin's devout assertions that we are led 'through nature up to nature's God', and that 'overpoweringly strong proofs of intelligent and benevolent design lie all around us', were no less representative of mainstream scientific opinion than Huxley's extravagantly caustic heresies.[14]

Natural theology, the influential doctrine that God's existence and wisdom not only was disclosed through scriptural Revelation but could also be inferred from the evidence of design in the natural world, which was articulated at the beginning of the nineteenth century by the Anglican priest William Paley and brought to wider attention in the mid-1830s by the eight *Bridgewater Treatises on the Power, Wisdom and Goodness of God as Manifested in the Creation* commissioned from the leading scientific authorities of the day, did not simply wither in the face of more empirical and secular modes of science, as the likes of Huxley implied. Instead it remained a resilient and adaptable component of much scientific thought, and even when the kind of demonstrative natural theology associated with Paley began to decline it was frequently replaced by a theology of nature which perceived divine purpose in the natural world without necessarily grounding an inductive argument for God's existence on the evidence of design in nature. The tenets of Darwinian evolution were easily accommodated within a natural theological framework, as was demonstrated by the novelist and clergyman Charles Kingsley in his popular children's book *Madam How and Lady Why* (1870), which accepted evolution but argued that it was merely a secondary mode – the how – by which divine will – the why – operated in the natural world. Even Huxley's own heretical rhetoric was itself permeated with biblical language and symbols, and his loudly proclaimed unbelief actually belied a profound preoccupation with religion.

The very term science, which seems self-explanatory in the modern Anglophone world as a designation for the systematized study of natural phenomena, was not itself devoid of complexities or ambiguities between 1830 and 1914. It was in fact only at the very beginning of this period, with the formation of the British Association for the Advancement of Science in 1831, that science began to shake off its earlier connotations of, amongst other things, knowledge acquired by study, or trained skill (as with Pierce Egan's famous description of boxing as the 'Sweet Science of Bruising' in the 1820s), and assumed a more restrictive meaning relating to experimental method and the investigation of the physical world. Far from being a merely neutral process, however, the gentlemanly, Oxbridge-educated elite who controlled the British Association, satirized by Charles Dickens as the haughty professors of the 'Mudfog Association for the Advancement of Everything', were often imposing their own highly partisan views about which branches of knowledge were worthy of being considered as science and which were not, with botany, for instance, being held in particularly low esteem in comparison with mathematics or astronomy.[15] The particular demarcations instituted by the British Association, as with the varying responses of the children, colonial others and provincial working men portrayed by Gaskell, Thackeray and Pater, indicate that nineteenth-century science ought not to be considered as simply a thing in itself and instead should be seen as largely what its different practitioners and audiences made of it.

At an early meeting of the British Association, Samuel Taylor Coleridge prohibited its members from calling themselves philosophers, prompting Whewell to coin the term 'scientist' as an alternative, which further emphasized the exclusivity, both epistemologically and socially, of who might practise this new form of narrowly defined science. But Whewell's now ubiquitous coinage was actually regarded as an unnecessary and awkward neologism for many decades to come, and only began to come into widespread usage during the 1870s, while the *OED*'s first example of the use of the modern, restrictive definition of science in print is not until 1867. It is certainly the case that Thackeray, echoing Egan, continued to refer to the 'science of the pugilate' into the 1840s and 1850s, even exhorting ironically that the 'manly and trew English Scients of Boxint . . . be took up for honours by the young gentlemen of Cambridge' alongside 'Algibry and Mathamadix', and, in the passage from the *Roundabout Papers* cited earlier, he was still employing the term philosopher rather than scientist in the 1860s.[16] For much of the nineteenth century, then, science remained a shifting, volatile and much contested category, which was detached from other forms of knowledge only very protractedly and irregularly, and often by means of force. Science, in other words, is neither universal nor intrinsic to the structure of the natural world. It is a human construct that is historically and culturally specific – after all, the terms currently used for empirical knowledge in other cultures, like the German *Wissenschaft*, do not correspond precisely with the modern Anglophone sense of science – and it would be perilous simply to read back our own more clearly defined notion of science onto the considerably more complex circumstances of the nineteenth century.

In any case, even in its eventual, more restrictive definition, science rarely signified a unified body of knowledge, and instead generally represented an array of discrete disciplines like botany, chemistry and physiology that were often riven by bitter internal disputes, such as that over the age of the earth between the mathematical physicist Kelvin, who calculated it was no more than 100 million years old, and the geologists Darwin and Lyell, who reckoned on an immensely longer timeframe. Whether regarded as numerous separate fields of inquiry or a more general way of thinking, science was also subject to various forms of popularization between 1830 and 1914, although, once more, this should be considered not as simply a neutral or universal process, but rather as a contingent cultural formation that, again, began to assume a distinctive new form at the very beginning of this period. In the 1820s and 1830s, with the increasing specialization of science heralded by the formation of the British Association at the same time as the emergence of much broader reading audiences and the advent of new industrialized methods of printing, commercial publishers were quick to capitalize on a demand for books and periodicals that conveyed elite scientific knowledge in a self-consciously popular form. As the readership for such publications grew steadily over the following decades, this specifically diffusionist form of popular science became ever more lucrative, and scientific popularizers, whether entrepreneurial publishers, penny-a-liner journalists or itinerant lecturers, played an extremely significant role – perhaps more than that of any elite scientists – in shaping the perception and understanding of science amongst the majority of the population.

Nor should such popularizations be disregarded as merely insipid or vulgar simplifications of the pure truths authorized by elite science; instead, they were themselves often complex and sophisticated productions of knowledge that frequently developed their own indigenous scientific forms, as well as appropriating and adapting the material they were ostensibly popularizing. Popularizers also regularly endowed their scientific writing with an aesthetic or fictive dimension, and such popular science became an integral part of literary culture in the nineteenth century. Similarly, novels and poems themselves frequently employed scientific images and ideas that would have been recognizable to a general readership, often in metaphors that revitalized overly familiar concepts but also added new and unexpected connotations to the original scientific ideas, or in less subtle ways which, like Dickens's literal portrayal of Mr Krook's spontaneous combustion in *Bleak House* (1852–3), deliberately repudiated current scientific orthodoxy. Dickens in fact used the following instalment of his best-selling serial novel to issue a rejoinder to those scientific authorities, including the positivist George Henry Lewes, the anatomist Richard Owen and the chemist Justus von Liebig, who had questioned the reality of spontaneous combustion, portraying them as the expert 'men of science and philosophy' who regale the inquest into Krook's death with 'more learned talk about inflammable gases and phosphuretted hydrogen than the court has ever imagined', but disregard the actual evidence before them and instead 'hold with indignation that the deceased had no business to die in the alleged manner'.[17]

All these forms of popular science were generally outside of the control of the elite forums of the scientific world such as the British Association and the Royal Society, and thus challenged, both implicitly or, like *Bleak House*, more explicitly, the avowals of Huxley and others that only appropriately trained scientific professionals could interpret the natural world. Treating science popularization, including its more literary manifestations, as a significant discursive form in its own right helps decentre the authority of nineteenth-century science and affords a further means of amending the kind of overly simplistic narratives of scientific progress and dominance with which this chapter began, and literature again is a significant factor in this revisionary process.

In Darwin's shadow

Such narratives of scientific progress are normally predicated upon the heroic endeavours of lone men of genius, who, so the story goes, instigate shattering and decisive transformations of our understanding of the physical world. The particular scientific colossus who bestrides the period between

1830 and 1914 is unarguably Darwin, whose theory of evolution by natural selection, first announced in *On the Origin of Species* in 1859 although mostly formulated some two decades earlier, is widely perceived to have had revolutionary consequences not just for science and religion but for virtually every aspect of nineteenth-century experience. In literary culture, to take only one example, Darwin's conception of both the enormous abundance of a world teeming with organisms and the way in which all these different forms of life were actually linked below the surface in a vast interconnected ecological system had profound creative implications for the multi-plot structure of novels such as *Middlemarch* (1871–2), where the numerous characters are connected in what Darwin termed an 'inextricable web of affinities' structured by likeness and divergence. George Eliot's central organizing metaphor of 'unravelling certain human lots, and seeing how they were woven and interwoven' within the 'particular web' of an English provincial town accords precisely with Darwin's evolutionary insight that 'plants and animals . . . are bound together by a web of complex relations'.[18] At the same time, Darwin's own affective and imaginatively charged prose itself bore the imprint of various elements of Victorian literary culture, and over the last few decades he has proved a hugely enabling figure for understanding the reciprocal relations between science and literature in this period, with the *Origin* even being accorded canonical status.

Attributing such revolutionary power to just a single individual is in itself intensely problematic, but Darwin's undoubted and overwhelming dominance, like that of Shakespeare in studies of early modern drama, has also had the effect of virtually obliterating, or at the very least acutely overshadowing, almost everything else that occurred in nineteenth-century science, from the discovery of Neptune by means of mathematical analysis to the gradual development of the Periodic Table. It has similarly eclipsed the literary response to such developments as those in electromagnetic field theory during the 1840s and 1850s, where Michael Faraday's assertion of the permeability of objects and the incessant interrelations between elements in a system appears to have informed Eliot's radical approach to characterization in *Middlemarch* and especially her depiction of the town as a field in which characters do not represent stable or autonomous units and instead extend, like lines of force, as far as their influence on others does.[19] Dorothea Brooke's character is memorable, after all, because of the 'incalculably diffusive . . . effect of her being on those around her' rather than any individual actions of her own.[20] Despite Eliot's wide-ranging scientific interests, though, *Middlemarch* is rarely read as anything other than a thoroughly Darwinian novel, with every other potential influence, like that of Faraday's field theory, simply cast into the shade by Darwin's unassailable domination.

Significantly, the overwhelming ubiquity attributed to Darwin is in fact largely a retrospective invention, as the mechanism of natural selection, Darwin's most distinctive and significant contribution to the many earlier conceptions of organic transmutation, was actually rejected by most commentators at the time (including Huxley himself), and was only revived and then scientifically validated in the 1930s. From the perspective of the 1850s, transmutationist explanations of life were less scientifically reputable than, say, the attempts of physiognomists and phrenologists to analyse character traits by examining the shape of the skull. At the end of the decade even such an assiduous reader as Eliot, another who doubted the efficacy of natural selection, tempered her praise for Darwin's new book by reflecting that evolution 'produce[d] a feeble impression compared with the mystery that lies under the process', and she thought the *Origin* so 'ill-written and sadly wanting in illustrative facts' that it would 'prevent the work from becoming popular'.[21] It is certainly the case that numerous scientific works, such as the anonymous *Vestiges of the Natural History of Creation* (1844) or Ebenezer Brewer's *A Guide to the Scientific Knowledge of Things Familiar* (1847), continued to outsell the *Origin* throughout the nineteenth century.

Recognizing these historical caveats about the initial response to the *Origin* does not, of course, question the huge and compelling explanatory power of Darwinian evolution for various scientific disciplines in our own day. It does, however, suggest that Darwin's significance, and indeed the very accuracy of his theories, was considerably less assured amongst his Victorian contemporaries, and that rival explanations of the natural world were not simply wiped out at a single stroke, but instead continued to retain substantial intellectual credibility as well as exercising an important influence on literature. In assessing the position of science in past cultures like that of nineteenth-century Britain it makes little sense to impose our own present-day judgements about what is scientifically correct or not, as this knowledge is generally based on information, such as modern genetics in the case of evolution, that was simply not available at the time.

Bones bear witness

In order to counteract the distorting and largely retrospective dominance attributed to Darwin in most accounts of science in the period between 1830 and 1914, and to offer a different periodization from that which takes 1859 as the defining moment for the creative interaction of science and literature in the nineteenth century, this section will outline the interplay between Richard Owen's work in vertebrate palaeontology and wider literary culture from the late 1830s to the 1890s and beyond. Owen is today chiefly remembered, if at all, as one of the *Origin*'s most savage critics, and his often scathing attitude towards Darwinism, and especially to his particular *bête noire* Huxley, has ensured that he has either been entirely written out of those triumphalist narratives of scientific progress predicated on evolution or cast as the malevolent enemy of everything that is enlightened and secular. While his admittedly sometimes rather spiky personality did not help matters, Owen was actually, for much of the nineteenth century, one of the most prominent scientific figures in Britain, with the founding of the Natural History Museum in South Kensington and coining of the word 'dinosaur' amongst his numerous achievements, and he was fêted by royalty and politicians as well as many of the period's leading literary writers. Unlike the more reclusive Darwin, who, at least in later life, claimed to have lost the capacity for aesthetic appreciation, Owen numbered Dickens, Thackeray, Eliot, Tennyson, Thomas Carlyle and R. D. Blackmore amongst his friends and acquaintances, and he read their works with evident enthusiasm and enjoyment. His own voluminous scientific writings are suffused with literary references, particularly to the work of Romantic writers like William Wordsworth and Sir Walter Scott, and his significance for Victorian literature – in *Hard Times* (1854), for instance, Dickens records that as part of their utilitarian education 'each little Gradgrind [had] at five years old dissected the Great Bear like a Professor Owen' – is indubitable.[22] Yet, while modern historians have successively reappraised Owen's reputation and discerned in his work many still innovative contributions to scientific thought, even on evolution, literary critics have only very recently given any sustained consideration to his relations with literature, and for the most part remain preoccupied almost exclusively with his purported nemesis Darwin.

Owen's principal field of expertise, although by no means his only one, was anatomy, and he spent much of his career at the Royal College of Surgeons in London. Significantly, his anatomical proficiency also equipped Owen with the requisite skills to excel in the related and rapidly expanding area of vertebrate palaeontology, especially the identification and reconstruction of extinct creatures from fossilized bones and teeth. Most notably, in 1839 Owen inferred the existence of a hitherto unknown giant prehistoric bird in New Zealand from the evidence of just a small fragment of femur bone, a prediction that was spectacularly confirmed four years later with the arrival of a consignment of bones from which Owen was able to reconstruct the entire skeleton of the wingless moa or, as he named it, dinornis. Owen, according to his own somewhat mythologizing account, accomplished this extraordinary vindication of the power of inductive reasoning through the technique of functional correlation, a method of palaeontological reconstruction in which each element of an animal is presumed to correspond mutually with all the others, so that a carnivorous tooth must be accompanied by a particular kind of jawbone, and so on, that facilitates the consumption of flesh. Thus any part, even the mere fragment of a bone, necessarily indicates the configuration of the integrated whole.

This principle had been developed in the 1810s by the renowned French anatomist Georges Cuvier, but it had become increasingly central to the English tradition of natural theology, and Owen's startling discovery of the dinornis, as well as that of the relation between the anatomy and peculiar feeding habits of the sloth-like megatherium in the mid-1840s, were welcomed as indisputable affirmations that only providential design could have produced such perfectly integrated mechanisms, even if Owen himself remained more concerned with the secondary laws by which the deity worked and later adopted an alternative archetypal understanding of vertebrate design. Owen's seemingly miraculous palaeontological feats also became popular and enduring causes célèbres in Victorian Britain.

Although the majority of Owen's scientific work was highly technical and addressed to what he called 'readers "fit but few" in ... out-of-the-way scientific quarto[s]', the distinct nod to Wordsworth's formulation of his own restricted audience in *The Excursion* (1814), which itself alludes to John Milton's invocation to the muse Urania at the beginning of book VII of *Paradise Lost* (1667), 'fit audience let me find though few!', paradoxically indicates Owen's ability to reach beyond an exclusively specialist readership.[23] Indeed, the language in which Owen announced his celebrated discoveries was regularly infused with imaginative wonder and drew on various literary and scriptural archetypes of the resurrection of the dead, as well as Romantic notions of the suggestive power of the fragmentary. While repeatedly insisting on the legitimate scientific grounds of his prediction, Owen acknowledged that the moa had initially been 'pictured in imagination' and that, 'without giving the rein to a too exuberant fancy', he had been able 'as it were, to present a living portrait of the long-lost Dinornis' from just the small fragment of its osseous remains.[24] Kingsley later told Owen that he had 'long felt that you were a poet as well as a philosopher', and it is unsurprising that his audacious deployment of the creative imagination in palaeontological reconstructions during the 1830s and 1840s struck a reciprocal chord with many literary writers of the day.[25] What is more surprising is just how enduring Owen's impact on literature would be.

Fiction in the mid-nineteenth century was generally first published in instalments, whether in the monthly 'parts' popularized by Dickens in the late 1830s or by the more usual method of magazine serialization, and it has been proposed that this gradual, developmental form of narrative reflected the Darwinian tenor of the times.[26] However, this distinctively Victorian mode of publication, for which the term 'parts' was used by the publisher Edward Chapman from at least 1835, actually came to prominence at precisely the time that Owen was first employing Cuvier's famous principle of the 'correlation of parts', and while modern critics have identified the practices of Victorian seriality exclusively with Darwin, for the leading novelists of the period it was clearly Owen, and his renowned palaeontological feats of the creative imagination, who afforded a model for their serialized fictions.

In the fifteenth of its twenty-four monthly parts, the narrator of Thackeray's novel *The Newcomes* (1853–5), Arthur Pendennis, reflects

> As Professor Owen ... takes a fragment of a bone, and builds an enormous forgotten monster out of it ... so the novelist puts this and that together: from the footprint finds the foot; from the foot, the brute who trod on it; from the brute, the plant he browsed on ... and thus in his humble way a physiologist too, depicts the habits, size, appearance of the beings whereof he has to treat; – traces this slimy reptile through the mud, and describes his habits filthy and rapacious ... points out the singular structure of yonder more important animal, the megatherium of his history.[27]

While several critics have noted how this passage reflects Thackeray's characteristic cynicism about narratorial omniscience, with Pen appearing to suggest that many of the details of the history of the most respectable Newcome family are based on inference and hypothetical reconstructions, it has not previously been recognized that the comparison of the role of the novelist with that of Owen becomes still more pertinent in relation to the process of serialization in which Thackeray was engaged.[28] Like the palaeontologist, the serial novelist, who regularly wrote the next instalment only after the previous one was already published, had painstakingly to relate each individual part to a larger and often still conjectural narrative whole in order to build up both character and plot, leaving the expectant audience, whose practice of reading similarly involved moving from part to whole, to predict how the events of each number would fit in – or correlate – with that overall framework.

In *Our Mutual Friend* (1864–5), another novel published in monthly parts, Thackeray's great rival Dickens also made a connection, at least implicitly, between the synecdochic practices of readers 'pursuing a story in portions from month to month' who attempt to 'perceive the relations of its finer threads to the whole pattern' and the 'bony' activities of Mr Venus, the 'articulator of human bones', who, as with the '"... French gentleman" ... represented ... by his ribs only', can construct skeletal wholes from fragmentary parts.[29] At the very beginning of the novel, Dickens remarks of Mrs Podsnap, 'fine woman for Professor Owen, quantity of bone, neck and nostrils like a rocking-horse', while the malevolent amputee Silas Wegg is described as resembling 'some extinct bird', and, as with Owen's celebrated dinornis, his whole identity is represented synecdochically by the portion of his leg bone purchased from a hospital porter by Venus ('where am I?' and 'what did you give for me?', asks Wegg). Moreover, like Owen, the similarly employed Venus exhibits great skill in 'piecing little things together'. In fact, the 'likelihood of small indications leading him onto the discovery of great concealments' enables Venus, like a particularly perspicacious reader, to comprehend the hidden truths of the various false identities developed over the novel's twenty instalments, once more relating anatomical procedures to the predictive reading practices involved in serialized fiction.[30] Significantly, Owen himself was an extremely enthusiastic reader of serial novels, especially those of Thackeray and Dickens, and partook of precisely the same prognosticatory narrative pleasures that those two novelists had identified with his own palaeontological reconstructions.

Even long after the purportedly transformative moment of the *Origin*'s publication in 1859 several leading literary writers continued to employ narrative techniques that closely resembled Owen's use of the Cuvierian principle of functional correlation. In his collection of short stories *Imaginary Portraits* (1887), Pater typically commences his narratives with, as in the case of 'Denys L'Auxerrois', the discovery of an isolated 'fragment of stained glass' that was once 'clearly part of a series', and the 'story shape[s] itself at last' only when the narrator is able to correlate this shard with some tapestries that 'portray the whole subject of which the figure in the stained glass was a portion'.[31] Tellingly, in another story, 'Duke Carl of Rosenmold', it is the accidental disinterring of the fragmentary 'remains of two persons' who can be identified only by the means of so-called 'bone-science' which ends up 'suggesting … the lively picture' of the life of an eighteenth-century German potentate that the narrative recounts.[32]

Hardy, to take only one more example, regularly used the same trope in his novels for either melodramatic or drolly comic effect. The village sexton in *A Pair of Blue Eyes* (1873) tells Elfride Swancourt of his 'strange experiences in digging up after long years the bodies of persons he had known, and recognising them by some little sign'. The sexton is actually only teasing the naïve Elfride, but the man of letters and 'fair geologist' Henry Knight is really able, while clinging desperately to the edge of a cliff, to picture in his 'inner eye' the 'life-time scenes of the fossil[s] confronting him', imaginatively reconstructing 'huge elephantine forms' such as the 'megatherium' from merely the 'mean … relics' of their fossilized remains.[33]

It has long been recognized that in this famous passage Hardy drew extensively on the sixth edition of *The Wonders of Geology* (1848), a popular exposition of current geological knowledge by the palaeontologist and fossil collector Gideon Mantell.[34] However, it has not previously been noted that the book's discussion of fossils is underwritten by explicitly Cuvierian principles, with Mantell observing that 'it is by a profound knowledge of ... the correlation of the different parts of every organized creature, that the scientific observer is enabled to reconstruct the forms of extinct animals ... [from] a few teeth and bones – sometimes but a single relic of this kind'. Significantly, Mantell, despite his bitter rivalry with Owen, also illustrates these principles with the instance of how 'a portion of a femur ... was brought from New Zealand, and submitted to the examination of Professor Owen, who pronounced it to belong to a giant bird'.[35] In *A Pair of Blue Eyes* Hardy emphasizes the diminutive nature of the fossil remains, with Knight reflecting that he is 'to be with the small in his death', and with Mantell's *The Wonders of Geology* as the scene's principal source it seems likely that Knight, making imaginative inferences from fragmentary osseous remains, is deploying something akin to the Cuvierian reconstructive techniques which Owen had made famous.[36] Ironically, however, it is Knight's inability similarly to piece together the small clues given by Elfride about her past that precipitates the novel's tragic denouement.

The long-celebrated palaeontological reconstructions of Cuvier and Owen, with their alluring combination of scientific rigour with apparently intuitive leaps, also lay behind many of the forensic methods deployed by the protagonists of the popular sub-genre of detective fiction. In 'The Five Orange Pips' (1892), Arthur Conan Doyle's legendary sleuth Sherlock Holmes reasons, 'As Cuvier could correctly describe a whole animal by the contemplation of a single bone, so the observer who has thoroughly understood one link in a series of incidents, should be able accurately to state all the other ones', and many of Holmes's best-known cases are solved by his uncanny ability to extrapolate from fragmentary pieces of evidence, including, in 'The Adventure of Shoscombe Old Place' (1925), a small shard of 'a human femur', the 'anatomical significance' of which he can immediately appreciate.[37] Nor was Holmes, or the similarly famous C. Auguste Dupin who earlier drew on Cuvier's ideas in Edgar Allen Poe's 'The Murders in the Rue Morgue' (1841), the only fictional detective to employ such palaeontological methods, for in Arthur J. Rees's *The Shrieking Pit* (1919) David Colwyn is likewise commended for the 'logical skill and masterly deductive powers with which [he] had reconstructed the hidden events of the night of the murder, like an Owen reconstructing the extinct moa from a single bone'.[38] Paradoxically, the modern forensic expertise of both Holmes and Colwyn is established, even well into the twentieth century, by the resemblance of their methods to the functionalist anatomical principles, with all their natural theological connotations, utilized by Cuvier and Owen almost a century earlier.

The surprising durability of Owen's impact on literature establishes important continuities across the entire period covered by this volume which are generally lost in accounts in thrall to the myth of the instantaneous 'Darwinian Revolution'. As late as the first decades of the twentieth century both Thackeray's and Hardy's novels were being praised for their 'correlation of parts, and general design', a literary critical evaluation that drew directly on Owen's use of Cuvier's famous principle in the 1830s and 1840s and its natural theological implications of providential design, even if this was now attributed to the godlike novelist rather than an actual deity.[39] Owen's lasting influence also allows us to plot a different trajectory for nineteenth-century fiction from that which insists on Darwin's virtually exclusive role in shaping the development of the novel's relationship with science. Such a new trajectory would inevitably have to acknowledge, amongst other things, the continuing resilience of natural theology, or at least of ideas originally imbued with its religious meanings and still retaining vestiges of that providentialism, as well as of several other forms of science that would now be considered either obsolete or irremediably heterodox.

Taking bumpology seriously?

It was noted earlier that, from the perspective of the mid-nineteenth century, evolutionary accounts of life would have appeared considerably less reputable than the so-called 'bumpology' practised by phrenologists and physiognomists, and in understanding the interactions between science and literature between 1830 and 1914 it is important to recognize that the boundaries between scientific orthodoxy and heterodoxy were often far more fluid and permeable in this period than in our own. Indeed, at a time when, as the heated deliberations of the British Association in the 1830s attest, what constituted orthodoxy in science was largely still in the process of being decided, it is perilous unambiguously to assign particular practices to the marginal status of heterodoxy, or to employ evaluative terms like 'pseudoscience'. It is also the case that the increasingly triumphalist and omniscient tone of the proponents of empirical science as exemplified by Huxley at the beginning of this chapter was countered by a widespread mystical revival in the final years of the nineteenth century that, even while exhibiting a profound distaste for materialism and positivism, nevertheless still retained an enthusiasm for scientific methods as a means of establishing the reality of occult phenomena, and the movement attracted many leading scientists such as the chemist William Crookes and the evolutionary biologists Alfred Russel Wallace and George John Romanes. Rather than simply taking what in retrospect appear fixed boundaries for granted, then, attention should instead be focused on the complex debates across the nineteenth century from which the very divisions between science and pseudoscience with which we are now so familiar actually emerged.

Literature engaged fully in these debates and is, once again, an extremely valuable resource for interrogating the often arbitrary boundaries established between orthodoxy and heterodoxy that were intended, at least in part, to ensure that the epistemic authority of certain types of science was not compromised by awkward connections with more mystical phenomena. In Bram Stoker's Gothic novel *Dracula* (1897), the physician Abraham Van Helsing, a leading authority on the evolution of the brain but also a devout Roman Catholic and proponent of such equally unconventional methods as blood transfusion and wearing garlic blossoms, chastises the inflexible empiricism of his protégé John Seward, and insists on the shifting nature of scientific categorizations: 'there are things done today in electrical science which would have been deemed unholy by the very men who discovered electricity, who would themselves not so long before have been burned as wizards'. Later in the novel, as Dracula is pursued back to Transylvania by Van Helsing, Seward and their fellow crusaders, the distinctions between the invisible electrical forces utilized in the modern technology of telegraphy and those similarly unseen psychical powers involved in the recently invented technique of telepathy are gradually elided until the two analogous methods of communication are used virtually interchangeably to track the vampire: 'Daily telegrams to Godalming, but only the same story: "Not yet reported." Mina's morning and evening hypnotic answer is unvaried: lapping waves, rushing water, and creaking masts.'[40] There is, as *Dracula* suggests, an inherent similarity between the telegraphic and telepathic methods of disclosing and utilizing otherwise unseen energies that extends beyond merely their etymological resemblance, with the demarcation of their respective exponents as either trustworthy electrical engineers or self-evidently cranky and deceitful conjurors being largely a matter of historical convention. Intriguingly, some of the pioneers of mid-Victorian telegraphy appear to have agreed, and used the skills they developed while laying the Atlantic telegraph cable during the 1850s to attempt communication with the spirits of the dead.

With its eclectic and ultimately redemptive fusion of the orthodox and the heterodox, *Dracula*, published exactly a decade after Huxley's bombastic eulogy to scientific progress at the Queen's golden jubilee, affords a particularly instructive riposte to simplistic assumptions about the over-riding dominance of science in the nineteenth century or sweeping narratives, usually predicated on Darwinian evolution, of its inevitable advancement. Science, as has been emphasized throughout this chapter, was characterized more by complexity, divergence and disagreement during the years between 1830 and 1914 than any putative and progressive amalgamation under the banner, at least in the life sciences, of natural selection. Darwin's ultimate apotheosis did not come until the evolutionary synthesis of the 1930s and rival conceptions of organic form and modification retained considerable credibility throughout the prior period. It is thus essential to avoid imposing our own modern preconceptions, as well as those of a small cadre of partial and self-interested historical actors, onto the diverse ways that science, and its various relations with literature, were understood and experienced by the Victorians themselves.

Notes

1 T. H. Huxley, 'Science', in *The Reign of Queen Victoria: A Survey of Fifty Years of Progress*, ed. T. H. Ward, 2 vols. (London: Smith, Elder, 1887), vol. II, pp. 322–3.

2 Quoted in Leonard Huxley, *Life and Letters of Thomas Henry Huxley*, 2 vols. (London: Macmillan, 1900), vol. II, p. 156; [T. H. Huxley], 'Darwin on the Origin of Species', *Westminster Review*, n.s. 17 (1860), p. 556.

3 T. H. Huxley, 'Science and Culture', in *Collected Essays*, 12 vols. (London: Macmillan, 1893–4), vol. III, pp. 141 and 137.

4 Matthew Arnold, 'Literature and Science' (1882), in *Complete Prose Works of Matthew Arnold*, ed. R. H. Super, 12 vols. (Ann Arbor: University of Michigan Press, 1960–77), vol. X, pp. 68–9.

5 John Stuart Mill, 'Thoughts on Poetry and Its Varieties' (1833), in *Collected Works of John Stuart Mill*, ed. John M. Robson, 33 vols. (Toronto: University of Toronto Press, 1963–91), vol. I, p. 344.

6 John H. Newman, 'The Mission of the Benedictine Order', *Atlantis*, 1 (1858), pp. 16–17.

7 [William Whewell], 'Works of Bacon', *Edinburgh Review*, 106 (1857), p. 316.

8 Alfred Tennyson, *In Memoriam* (1850), in *The Poems of Tennyson*, ed. Christopher Ricks, 2nd edn, 3 vols. (Harlow: Longman, 1987), vol. II, p. 442.

9 [Henry James], 'Current Literature', *Galaxy*, 15 (1873), p. 428; Henry James, 'Daniel Deronda: A Conversation', *Atlantic Monthly*, 38 (1876), p. 690.

10 *The George Eliot Letters*, ed. Gordon S. Haight, 9 vols. (New Haven: Yale University Press, 1954–78), vol. VI, pp. 216–17; *The Collected Letters of Thomas Hardy*, ed. Richard Little Purdy and Michael Millgate, 7 vols. (Oxford: Clarendon Press, 1978–88), vol. I, p. 110.

11 Walter Pater, *Plato and Platonism* (London: Macmillan, 1893), p. 140.

12 W. M. Thackeray, *Roundabout Papers* (London: Smith, Elder, 1863), pp. 160–1.

13 Elizabeth Gaskell, *Mary Barton* (1848), ed. MacDonald Daly (London: Penguin, 1996), pp. 38–9.

14 Quoted in Silvanus P. Thompson, *The Life of William Thomson, Baron Kelvin of Largs*, 2 vols. (London: Macmillan, 1910), vol. I, p. 251 and vol. II, p. 608.

15 Charles Dickens, *Sketches by Boz and Other Early Papers 1833–39*, ed. Michael Slater (London: Dent, 1994), p. 513.

16 [W. M. Thackeray], 'Crinoline', *Punch*, 13 (1847), p. 72; [W. M. Thackeray], 'Science at Cambridge', *Punch*, 15 (1848), p. 201.

17 Charles Dickens, *Bleak House* (1853), ed. Nicola Bradbury (London: Penguin, 1996), p. 532.

18 Charles Darwin, *On the Origin of Species* (1859), ed. J. W. Burrow (London: Penguin, 1968), pp. 415 and 124–5; George Eliot, *Middlemarch* (1871–2), ed. Rosemary Ashton (London: Penguin, 1994), p. 141.

19 See Alice Jenkins, *Space and the 'March of Mind': Literature and the Physical Sciences in Britain 1815–1850* (Oxford: Oxford University Press, 2007), pp. 204–5.

20 Eliot, *Middlemarch*, p. 838.

21 *Eliot Letters*, vol. III, p. 227.

22 Charles Dickens, *Hard Times* (1854), ed. Kate Flint (London: Penguin, 1995), p. 16.

23 'Professor Owen and the Darwinian Theory', *London Review*, 12 (1866), p. 516; William Wordsworth, *The Excursion* (1814), in *The Poems*, ed. John O. Hayden, 2 vols. (London: Penguin, 1977), vol. II, p. 38.

24 Richard Owen, *Memoirs on the Extinct Wingless Birds of New Zealand*, 2 vols. (London: Van Voorst, 1879), vol. I, pp. vi and 107.

25 Quoted in Nicolaas A. Rupke, *Richard Owen: Victorian Naturalist* (New Haven: Yale University Press, 1994), p. 6.

26 See Linda K. Hughes and Michael Lund, *The Victorian Serial* (Charlottesville: University Press of Virginia, 1991), p. 7.

27 W. M. Thackeray, *The Newcomes* (1854–5), ed. Andrew Sanders (Oxford: Oxford University Press, 1995), p. 616.

28 See George Levine, *The Realistic Imagination: English Fiction from* Frankenstein *to* Lady Chatterley (Chicago: University of Chicago Press, 1981), pp. 163–5.

29 Charles Dickens, *Our Mutual Friend* (1865), ed. Adrian Poole (London: Penguin, 1997), pp. 798 and 85–9.

30 *Ibid.* pp. 21, 211, 88 and 300.

31 Walter Pater, *Imaginary Portraits* (London: Macmillan, 1887), pp. 58–60.

32 *Ibid.* pp. 137–9.

33 Thomas Hardy, *A Pair of Blue Eyes* (1873), ed. Roger Ebbatson (London: Penguin, 1986), pp. 129 and 271–2.

34 See Patricia Ingham, 'Hardy and *The Wonders of Geology*', *Review of English Studies*, n.s. 31 (1980), pp. 59–64.

35 Gideon Mantell, *The Wonders of Geology*, 6th edn, 2 vols. (London: Bohn, 1848), vol. I, pp. 145–7 and 129–30.

36 Hardy, *A Pair of Blue Eyes*, p. 271.

37 Arthur Conan Doyle, *The Penguin Complete Sherlock Holmes* (London: Penguin, 1981), pp. 225 and 1106.

38 Arthur J. Rees, *The Shrieking Pit* (London: Lane, 1919), p. 282.

39 Edward Wright, 'The Novels of Thomas Hardy', *Quarterly Review*, 199 (1904), p. 500.

40 Bram Stoker, *Dracula* (1897), ed. Maurice Hindle (London: Penguin, 2003), pp. 204 and 356.

10

JENNY BOURNE TAYLOR

Body and mind

> There is no example of two agents so closely connected as body and mind . . .
> The entire bodily system, though in varying degrees, is in intimate alliance with
> mental functions.
>
> Alexander Bain, *Mind and Body*, 1873 [1]

A third of the way through Elizabeth Gaskell's story 'A Dark Night's Work', the heroine Ellinor Wilkins is suddenly roused from a pleasurable reverie by 'a mysterious noise – heavy, sudden' coming from her father's study, giving rise to 'a mysterious instinct [which] made her feel sick and faint. No sound – no noise. Only by-and-by she heard, what we have all heard at such times of intense listening, the beating of the pulses of her heart, and then the whirling rush of blood through her head.' Creeping down the staircase, she sees, 'with a strange sick horror', the body of Dunster, her father's unpleasant junior partner, 'his head propped on chair-cushions, his eyes open, staring, distended'. 'Ellinor could not have told whether it was reason or instinct that made her act as she did that fatal night', the narrator continues, describing how, almost in a state of trance, she first attempts to revive the dead man, then helps her father and their servant Dixon to bury Dunster's body in the garden. This is the 'dark night's work' that forms the climax of the tale – a 'haunting memory' that 'would come and overshadow her during many, many years of her life' (ch. 6).

'A Dark Night's Work' was published in *All the Year Round* in 1863. Like Wilkie Collins, her fellow contributor to the journal, Gaskell often used short fiction as a means of generic experimentation, and her story shares many of the features of sensation fiction. It explores the effects of secrecy; it sets an extreme event in a familiar middle-class setting and exploits immediate physiological response to generate emotional intensity; and it traces the physical, emotional and social consequences of Dunster's death on Wilkins, on Dixon and above all on Ellinor, as the mental shock of the murder itself becomes 'the incubus of a dreadful remembrance' (ch. 11).

Gaskell's story is one example of the ways in which the intimate interconnections between mental and physical response had become central to the narrative strategies of prose fiction during the mid and late nineteenth century. The complex techniques that became established through the middle decades: the use of first-person narration and free indirect style to represent the complexity of character and the working of consciousness; the development of multiple narrators and multiple plots to emphasize the subjectivism of experience; the use of mystery and suspense to probe the hidden traces of the past and the conflicted nature of motivation – all these contributed to the fictional exploration of interior mental states. 'A solemn consideration, when I enter a great city by night, . . . that every beating heart in the hundreds of thousands of breasts there, is, to some of its imaginings, a secret to the heart nearest it!', observes the narrator of Dickens's *A Tale of Two Cities* (ch. 3). Yet it was the language of the body that rendered this inner mental and emotional life legible in the dense social world of nineteenth-century narrative: the visible codes of physiognomy or phrenology; the subtle internal processes linking the nerves, the mind and the brain; the power of reflex and instinctive response, the embodiment of memory.

The embodied self and its limits 1830–1870

These resources for exploring and representing the complexity of the self were made possible by developments in mental science during the mid-nineteenth century, and debates about the nature of the self and the power and limits of the will formed a prominent feature of intellectual culture. Derived from the Greek term 'soul discourse', the word 'psychology' itself had unstable meanings which gradually narrowed after 1870 to become by 1900 something that we would recognize as a version of the modern experimental discipline. But for most of the nineteenth century the study of the mind represented a broad and controversial field that could encompass almost every aspect of contemporary opinion, and which assimilated and adapted distinct intellectual traditions within specific institutional spaces.

The older theological notion that the soul and the higher rational qualities of the mind struggled to dominate the passions and the body remained a powerful one through much of the nineteenth century. The question of whether the mind can ever really know itself or can only introspectively describe its operations had also been a long-standing debate in philosophy. This belief in the uniqueness of the human mind above and beyond the material body underpinned turn-of-the-century Scottish 'Common Sense' psychology, and was reinforced by the continuing influence of Kantian idealism in which inborn ideas are manifested in a transcendent consciousness. However, other philosophical traditions challenged this faculty-based model of the self. Locke had argued in the mid-seventeenth century that all consciousness derived from experience – from sensations and impressions built up during childhood which link to form chains of memory. This concept of mental association was given a physiological rationale a century later by David Hartley's proposal that the mind responded to vibrations transmitted through the nervous system, and although Hartley was attacked for his passive notion of consciousness, associationism was adapted by writers as diverse as James Mill and Thomas Brown in the early nineteenth century and was a crucial foundation of mid-century mental science.[2]

Associationism helped establish a shift in emphasis from the soul to the mind as the core of selfhood; but it also encountered the challenge of an emergent materialist physiology which undercut the dualistic separation of mind and body with studies of the relationship of the brain and the nervous system. In Germany, Franz Joseph Gall's lectures in the early years of the century had controversially proposed that it was the brain, and not some higher immaterial faculty, that shaped the mind.[3] Charles Bell in England and François Magendie in France established in the 1820s how distinct sensory and motor functions operated within the nervous system, and with the work of Marshall Hall and the German physiologist Johannes Müller in the 1830s the reflex became accepted as the crucial mechanism which linked the nerves, the spinal cord and the regions within the brain.[4] Although it still involved a distinction between the brain-stem and the 'higher' cerebral hemispheres, this concept of sensory-motor reflex made possible a notion of automatic mental action which would be explored and reworked in mid-nineteenth-century Britain, by Thomas Laycock and William Carpenter, and by Alexander Bain, Herbert Spencer and the wide-ranging intellectual G. H. Lewes. In different ways, these writers all combined associationism and sensory-motor physiology to analyse the connections as well as the gradations between reflex, habit, instinct, emotion and thought. 'The brain is only *one* organ of the Mind, and not by any means the exclusive centre of consciousness', insisted Lewes in 1860. 'The word Mind has a broader and deeper signification; it means all Sensation, all Volition and all Thought; it means the whole psychical Life.'[5]

The changing study of the mind involved sharp intellectual controversy and was developed in specific institutional landscapes. In the treatment of the insane, the reforms based on the therapeutic regime of moral treatment prompted the passing of the Lunacy and County Asylums Acts in 1845, advocating the construction of public asylums, and the setting up of a Lunacy Commission to inspect and regulate both public and private institutions; and by 1850 the treatment of the insane had become a respectable branch of an increasingly powerful medical profession. The medical study of nervous disorders such as hysteria, hypochondria and later neurasthenia was a more lucrative specialism, and though it remained based on an economy of fixed bodily energy – particularly on the 'uterine economy' in the case of women – the inadequacy of these physical, or somatic, interpretations became pressing after 1850, as physicians such as Robert Brudenell Carter stressed the crucial role of social and psychological constraint.[6]

As mental physiology became increasingly professionalized and specialized, these contrasting frameworks – together with the notions of identity they invoked – were widely debated and diffused through the extraordinarily rich intellectual culture of mid-nineteenth-century Britain, both in the weightier quarterly periodicals such as the *Westminster Review* and in more popular monthlies such as *Fraser's Magazine* and *Macmillan's Magazine*. Many novelists, as well as poets such as Tennyson and Robert Browning, were actively interested in these questions, and psychological writers themselves frequently made use of literary allusions, in a two-way traffic of interest and influence.

Elizabeth Gaskell, for example, was the cousin of the eminent society doctor Henry Holland, and knew her fellow Unitarian William Carpenter through his sister, the social reformer Mary Carpenter. Charles Dickens was interested in lunacy reform, actively participated in mesmeric performances, and was fascinated by dreams and 'borderline' states of consciousness; his library contained a wide range of psychological works, including a signed copy of E. S. Dallas's *The Gay Science* (1866).[7] Charlotte Brontë was part of the local intelligentsia of Haworth and familiar with the volumes of phrenology and insanity in the Keighley Mechanics' Institute Library.[8] Wilkie Collins drew on contemporary anxieties about the slippery borderline between sanity and madness, and on concepts of 'unconscious cerebration' as sensational devices, and he intervened in the campaign against vivisection in the late 1870s and early 1880s.[9] George Eliot's own reading and close intellectual and emotional partnership with George Henry Lewes placed her at the forefront of debates in mental and biological science. Her novels play on the intricate connections between the body and the mind, but, in exploring how to bring together reason and emotion in shaping an ethical and social basis for identity, Eliot both probes the limits of physiological psychology and anticipates future developments in the study of the mind.[10]

For while physiological psychology had shed many of its radical political implications, by the 1850s the 'language linking mind and body' was still, as Roger Smith has noted, 'awkward, opaque and unsettled'.[11] Journal discussion attempted to reassure readers that the embodied self did not inevitably undermine human agency; but many mental physiologists themselves also noted the limitations of a purely physicalist model of human subjectivity, resisting the idea that the mind could be completely reduced to matter, and stressing their mutual interconnections. 'We say that we are both Body and Mind', wrote Lewes in *The Study of Psychology*. 'We know that we exist as *objects*, perceptible to our senses, and to the sense of others;

as *subjects*, percipient of objects, and conscious of feelings. We live, feed, and move. We think, feel, and will.'[12] Narrowly materialist analysis might describe a mental process, but it could not explain what it actually *feels like* to experience a specific thought or emotion, he went on; the different ways of perceiving and experiencing mind are aspects of a general organic process, in a 'dual-aspect monism' that many contemporary mental scientists shared, and which for Lewes, could even help to explain the working of apparently intangible phenomena such as the soul.[13]

The self as object: physiognomy, phrenology and the bodily economy

Influential in the early years of the century, physiognomy and phrenology both claimed to offer a science for reading character on the outward features of the body, and were widely circulated in popular treatises and manuals. However, their methods and intellectual foundations were very different. Physiognomy's roots were classical and Aristotelian, but were reworked in John Casper Lavater's *Essays on Physiognomy* which appeared in numerous editions from the late 1780s.[14] Lavater argued that all individuals possessed an essence that linked them to the natural world and to the creator – manifested through the combinations of specific features, each of which had a place in a general system of classification. However, he made an important distinction between the study of fixed features such as the shape of the nose or the forehead and the more ambiguous analysis of expression.[15] 'How often does it happen', he asks, 'that the seat of character is so hidden, so enveloped, so masked, that it can only be caught in certain and perhaps uncommon positions of the countenance ...?'[16]

In contrast, phrenology proposed that specific intellectual and emotional propensities were localized in different parts of the brain and could be discerned on the surface of the skull. This materialist interpretation of the character was initially made available in Britain by Gall's collaborator J. G. Spurzheim, but it was George Combe who made phrenology such an important means of self-analysis and self-help with his massively popular *The Constitution of Man* (1828). While physiognomy posited an essential character that experience sharpens or refines, phrenology suggested a set of predispositions, which played an important role in the study of insanity in the 1830s and 1840s, as well as forming a basis, alongside neurology, for the experimental analysis of cerebral localization later in the century. The argument that propensities might be developed for good or ill could support moral treatment in progressive asylums as well as reflect the wider culture of self-help and self-improvement that flourished during the 1830s and 1840s. Both phrenology and physiognomy thus provided a set of visual tools that allowed the inner self to be at once legible and secret – tools that could be fictionally deployed for a range of different purposes.

Charlotte Brontë visited a well-known London phrenologist in 1851, and was favourably impressed by his reading of her advanced intellectual development, her 'fine organ of language' and 'originality and power'.[17] However, her fictional appropriation of the method is more complex. As Sally Shuttleworth and Nicholas Danes have explored, it is phrenology rather than physiognomy that becomes the arena for the struggle for both self-definition and control and social and sexual mastery in her major novels.[18] In *The Professor* (written in 1846 but published posthumously in 1857) the ambiguous narrator William Crimsworth deploys phrenological language both to effect his own social transformation and to dominate others. He notes that he was 'guarded by three faculties – Caution, Tact and Observation' (ch. 4) and submits his pupils to a textbook phrenological analysis – '[H]er organs of benevolence, veneration, conscientiousness, adhesiveness, were extremely small, those of self-esteem, firmness, destructiveness, combativeness, preposterously large' (ch. 12) – establishing his psychological mastery, while exposing his own anxieties and aggression.

This dramatization of how the struggle for social recognition must be founded on internal surveillance is extended in Brontë's representations of women's struggle for self-legitimation and emotional fulfilment. As Shuttleworth has argued, the self emerges 'not as abstract intellectual powers, but as distinct sources of physiological energy' in *Jane Eyre* (1848), as medical theories of a bodily economy in which 'female mental energy would always be overwhelmed by forces of the reproductive system' sit in tension with phrenology's stress on self-control.[19] While the forces of the female reproductive system are dramatized in the figure of Bertha Mason, it is phrenology that provides the means of enacting the erotic power-play of Jane and Rochester's courtship. Jane shrewdly notes Rochester's 'solid mass of intellectual organs, but an abrupt deficiency where the suave sign of benevolence should have been' (ch. 14), and Rochester's reading of Jane's forehead notes her inner dialogue between passion and reason (ch. 19). In *Villette* (1853), Brontë's most explicit exploration of extreme mental states and the medical theories that frame them, phrenology is again the means for Lucy to define and classify others from a position of relative powerlessness. It also predominates in M. Paul's initial reading of Lucy's head at Mme Beck's school, which, Shuttleworth notes, 'inaugurates the system of surveillance into which Lucy has entered and reinforces its central code: if Lucy is to succeed, it must be by a process of *self*-control'.[20] Yet this control leads to her mental collapse, negotiated through the bodily language of the nerves, which is framed even more comprehensively by Dr John's medical gaze.

Physiognomy offered a flexible set of visual codes that connected facial expression to emotional response. Although popular manuals such as Samuel Wells's *New Physiognomy* (1867) tended to stress the significance of static facial features, the emphasis on expression had been taken up and transformed, in particular by Charles Bell, whose work would be an important influence on Charles Darwin's *The Expression of the Emotions in Man and Animals* in 1871. Bell was a devout Anglican, yet had played a significant role in the development of neurology in the early nineteenth century by analysing the motor and sensory functions of the anterior and posterior spinal cord roots.[21] His major treatise, *The Philosophy and Anatomy of Expression in Connection to the Fine Arts* (1806), reprinted throughout the century, offered a detailed account of the interconnections between facial expression, the movements of the body, and the motor and sensory actions of the nerves and brain, demonstrating the uses of anatomy – 'that structure by which the mind expresses emotion' – that formed a vital resource for mid-century painters, in particular the Pre-Raphaelites Holman Hunt and Millais.[22]

This flexibility is echoed in the fictional uses of physiognomy, where visual clues can be revealing and misleading. Late nineteenth-century detective and Gothic fiction (notably Bram Stoker's *Dracula*) make use of the new discipline of criminology, with its concept of facial 'stigmata', clearly to delineate criminal types. Sensation fiction, however, often uses physiognomic codes as a means of generating deception, secrecy and disguise in ways that suggest a range of possible relationships between outer form and inner meaning. Lucy, the femme fatale of Mary Elizabeth Braddon's *Lady Audley's Secret* (1862), for example, relies on her face to charm those around her, playing on the popular belief that beauty of character is reflected in the countenance, so that the disclosure of her villainy seems to undercut the notion that facial features offer a clue to the soul. But Lucy's sinister character is also revealed in more complex physiognomic terms in the portrait that Robert Audley and George Talboys discover when they penetrate her inner chamber: 'Yes, the painter must have been a Pre-Raphaelite', notes the narrator. 'No-one but a Pre-Raphaelite would have so exaggerated every attribute of that delicate face … it was as if you had burned strange-coloured fires before my lady's face, and by their influence brought out new lines and new expressions never seen in it before' (vol. 1, ch. 8). Here Pre-Raphaelitism invokes Bell's argument that nervous response is mutable and multifaceted and that the face can express complex evanescent feelings that are open to a range of readings.

In contrast Magdalen Vanstone's physiognomy in Wilkie Collins's *No Name* (published the same year as *Lady Audley's Secret*) offers 'one of those strange caprices of Nature that science leaves still unexplained'. 'Thus quaintly self-contradictory in the upper part of her face, she was hardly less at variance with established ideas of harmony in the lower', notes the narrator. 'The whole countenance – so remarkable in its strongly opposed characteristics – was rendered additionally striking by its extraordinary mobility' (The First Scene, ch. 1). It is Magdalen's physical mutability that enables her to masquerade a series of feminine roles in pursuit of her name and identity when she and her sister are declared illegitimate. But as this quest becomes more and more obsessive, Magdalen's vitality increasingly takes the form of compulsion, of nervous energy followed by depletion culminating in complete breakdown, as her body acts out the tensions of her inner psychic struggle. Both the face and the body thus become the means of expressing complex inner tensions, as physiognomy becomes integrated into a wider bodily economy.

The self as subject: consciousness, the emotions and the will

'When one thinks of Micawber, always presenting himself in the same situation, moved with the same springs, and uttering the same sounds ... one is minded of frogs whose brains have been removed for physiological purposes', observed G. H. Lewes in 1872.[23] Many of Dickens's characters do dramatize the process whereby mental associations are set by habit and repetition into automatic, reflex movements, yet his fiction also suggests more complex interconnections between a mental response and its physical expression.[24] Mrs Clennam's hysterical paralysis in *Little Dorrit* (1857) is an embodiment of both social and psychic repression: a literalization of her evangelical, punitive Christianity, and the means of denying and expressing the emotions associated with a terrible past, in a novel haunted by the injunction 'Do Not Forget'.[25] Blending an internalized language of the body with a model of identity founded on interwoven strands of memory, Dickens plays on and reworks the intricate negotiations between faculty-based, associationist and physiological models of the self that were a central feature of mid-century psychology.

Thomas Brown had reworked Hartley's passive notion of mental association into a more creative concept of *suggestion*, in which the mind transforms present and past sensations and impressions to produce new combinations. William Hamilton extended Brown's argument by proposing three forms of 'latent mental modification': 'acquired habits' and knowledge that we can access at will; knowledge which is revealed through dreams or other states of suspended consciousness; and forms of mental activity that remain concealed, and which we perceive only indirectly, through their effects. This emphasis on the dynamic and creative power of the mind had a significant impact on mid-century concepts of unconscious mental processes: Brown, for example, developed a theory of emotion that undercut the older distinction between passion and affection, while Hamilton was a powerful influence on the critic E. S. Dallas, whose extraordinary work of literary and psychological theory, *The Gay Science*, argued for a 'science of the laws of pleasure', based on an understanding of the working of the 'Hidden Soul', a transformative force of creative energy that works secretly and automatically to shape all mental activity.

Hamilton's and Dallas's argument about the constant traffic between conscious and unconscious mental states formed one end of a spectrum of discussions on the automatic action of the mind as revealed in dreams, states of divided consciousness, trance and derangement. 'Modern psychology has taught us to regard the difference between a sensation and an idea, a perception and an imagination, as one of degree, and not of kind', wrote James Sully in 1876, summarizing developments in the analysis of dreams in the *Cornhill Magazine*. The 'sources and originating impulses of our dream-fancies', Sully argued, can take the form of external sensory stimulation (such as the sound of a barking dog or a creaking door); involuntary sensations arising within the body (such as the pulse of blood in the ears); or the effects of specific bodily conditions such as indigestion, and the response to muscular impulses arising from irritation or fatigue. Yet while the combination of these bodily processes and the residual memories of past events provide the raw material of dreams, Sully continued, this cannot explain their internal significance and structure. Summarizing the work of John Abercrombie, J. A. Symonds, Henry Holland and Alfred Maury, he argued that the mind remains partially active during sleep, combining apparently chaotic images through particular laws of mental association. 'In dream-life' external pressures and inhibitions are withdrawn 'so that delicate threads of association, which have no chance, so to speak, in our waking state, now exert their fine potency.'[26]

Dreams thus were a clear example of the interconnectedness of body and mind while illustrating the limitations of purely somaticist explanations. Mental states such as 'double consciousness' were more contentious, as concepts of cerebral localization encountered associationist, memory-based models of identity, and they formed a strand in the analysis of physical and emotional shock that would develop in the 1860s. In a discussion of 'The Brain as a Double Organ' in 1852, for example, the society doctor Henry Holland described 'the great disorder of mind from this sort of double dealing with itself', and while he conceded that mental duality may have some connection with the physical doubleness of the cerebrum, he stressed that all consciousness takes the form of a continuous, rapidly changing flow which, in states of double consciousness, 'passes by alteration from one state to the other, each having the perception of external impressions and appropriate chains of thought, but not linked together by mutual gradations, or by mutual memory'.[27]

Although in *Hard Times* (1854) Dickens satirized the more rigid and utilitarian aspects of early nineteenth-century associationism and retained the faculty-based idea of the immaterial soul, he stressed the centrality of memory in shaping an integrated self by drawing on its more fluid and creative aspects. David Copperfield becomes 'the hero of his own life' through recalling his past and bringing together his mature and childhood self in writing, even though in doing so he carefully selects and edits his memories in a way that tallies with the more regulatory aspects of the associationist tradition.[28] Redlaw, the chemist in the Christmas Book *The Haunted Man* (1848) makes a Faustian pact with his ghostly double to be released from the 'sorrow and trouble' of painful memories – to lose 'not knowledge; no result of study; nothing but the intertwisted chain of feelings and associations, each in its turn dependent on, and nourished by, the banished recollection' (ch. 1). But in this state of induced double consciousness he destroys the social and familial bonds of everyone he encounters – with the exception of a 'savage' child outside human sociability. Dickens thus uses the moralized fantasy of the Christmas Book format to emphasize that it is the interwoven strands of memory, including the recollection of pain, that create social bonds through emotional identification.

Yet Dickens also suggests that the more anarchic, unpredictable forces within the mind, closely linked with bodily processes, have their own kind of intelligence. In *A Christmas Carol* he satirizes the simplistic 'heavy supper' theories of dreams: '"You may be an undigested piece of beef, a blob of mustard, a crumb of cheese ... There's more of gravy than of grave about you whoever you are!"', Scrooge tells Marley's ghost (Stave One). Nonetheless Scrooge needs to be taken back physically to the unhappy scenes of his childhood via that embodiment of dream, the shape-shifting First Spirit, so that he may undergo his emotional re-education. In Dickens's most radical Christmas Book, *The Chimes* (1844), the poverty-stricken porter Toby Veck can only be liberated from his 'mechanical' trot and trance-like acceptance of the tenets of Political Economy by a terrible vision of the possible future it will create; this radical break with dominant assumptions is triggered by the Bells as extensions of his own unconscious mental processes. 'As the functions of Toby's body, his digestive organs for example, did of their own cunning, and by a great many operations of which he was altogether ignorant ... arrive at a certain end', notes the narrator, 'so his mental faculties, without his privity or concurrence, set all these wheels and springs in motion, with a thousand others, when they worked to bring about his liking for the Bells' (First Quarter). This automatic process is the necessary precondition for the wilder extravagances of dream, in which 'Monsters uncouth and wild, arise in premature, imperfect resurrection', as Toby experiences his situation 'not as a reflection but a bodily sensation' (Third Quarter).

The freedom of fantasy in the Christmas Books highlights this interweaving of physical, mental and emotional processes in which mechanical or automatic behaviour is the starting point of a more subtle exploration of the mind. This exploration recurs through Dickens's fiction – in the trance-like states of Oliver Twist; or in the way that the will-lessness of Arthur Clennam and of Pip reflects their unconscious ignorance of their own histories. The physical response to psychic shock triggered by an association with an unbearable memory is clearest perhaps in *A Tale of Two Cities* (1859), where the repetitive act of making shoes is both Doctor Manette's means of maintaining a form of self-hood through his years of incarceration, and the alternative self to which he briefly reverts on Lucy's marriage. Manette is both doctor and patient, and his analysis of his own condition of double consciousness at once extends and inverts contemporary accounts of the psychic effect of physical trauma. Indeed in 1865 Dickens was himself involved in a train crash of the kind that stimulated a widespread discussion of the delayed mental effects of accidents that would contribute to the concept of trauma as the meeting place of body and mind in the work of Pierre Janet and Sigmund Freud in the 1890s.[29]

Dickens's fascination with liminal states of consciousness is reflected, too, in his active involvement with mesmerism, in which individuals were placed in artificially induced trance states, tapping into sources of vital energy and revealing hidden memories and at times extraordinary feats. Peaking in the 1840s and 1850s, mesmerism probed the mind's latent capacities, and its stimulated trances contributed to James Braid's definition of hypnotism as a means of diagnosing and treating nervous complaints that would become central to the analysis of hysteria and traumatic neurosis in the 1880s and 1890s. Mesmerism itself, though, was regarded with increasing suspicion by the medical profession: William Carpenter, for example, argued that its induced trances made individuals particularly vulnerable to the wills of others. During the 1840s Carpenter and Thomas Laycock had revised the reflex theory I have outlined above to emphasize the connections between the sensory-motor reflex and the 'higher' capacities of the cerebral hemispheres. In the 1855 edition of his compendious *Human Physiology*, Carpenter proposed that in states of suspended consciousness the 'higher' seat of the intellect could also be subject to automatic impulses, in an *ideo-motor* action in which thoughts themselves could trigger a reflexive response, creating 'mere thinking automata – their whole course of thought and of action being determined by suggestion conveyed from without'.[30] This made it all the more important, he argued, that the will be developed and exercised from early childhood onward to avoid these dangerous states of 'unconscious cerebration'.

Carpenter's insistence on the need to exercise the will contrasts with the 'dual aspect monism' of Bain, Spencer and Lewes, who all proposed a more dynamic analysis of the emotions as the crucial, interactive link between mind and body. Alexander Bain combined sensory-motor physiology and association psychology into a relational concept of identity, in which the self is motivated by spontaneous waves of internal energy.[31] While he recognized a distinction between emotional states and 'intellectual consciousness', emphasizing the importance of habits of *attention* to control emotional impulses, he also stressed that 'while we can check or diminish an outburst of feeling by an effort of voluntary restraint ... the whole brain, with all its connexions in the general framework of the body, is concurrent and participant in a state of mental emotion'.[32] Feelings can unpredictably revive others, while motives are rarely simple: 'in the conflict of opposite motives it is extremely common to have one feeling in the actual opposed to the other in idea'.[33]

Herbert Spencer also rejected the opposition between 'the cognitive and emotive faculties' in his transformation of associationism into a totalizing theory of evolution in which all structures progress from simple to complex forms.[34] Although he made an important distinction between gradations of feeling in line with this overarching paradigm – from feelings arising within the body, to those derived from external sensations, to complex emotional responses to the external environment – he stresses that consciousness depends on emotional awareness as much as rational thought. Both are equally involved in the formation of organic memory, rooted in the body, in which experience is assimilated, and passed between generations. Lewes too argued in *The Physiology of Common Life* that habits constitute a learned reflex, formed through repetition into automatic actions; but his account of the relationship between mind, body and external world is subtler than Bain's or Spencer's. As we have seen, Lewes includes within 'Mind' all forms of psychic life, and the environment means a range of complex social and cultural processes to which the mind responds as 'an active co-operant ... a variable mechanism which has a *history*'.[35]

George Eliot's representations of the embodied self and her insistence on the importance of an ethical realm beyond its immediate demands highlights the paradox pinpointed by Lewes – that 'Mind' includes the body as a whole, yet that physical explanations cannot explain the complexities of consciousness – and realizes its social implications. In *Silas Marner* (1865), Silas's repetitive, mechanical weaving is, like Dr Manette's shoe-making, a way of holding a kind of 'self' together; however, Marner's solitary confinement springs from social isolation rather than literal imprisonment. Eliot places far greater stress than Dickens does on physical transformation as the correlative of the mental thought: 'Strangely Marner's face and figure shrank and bent themselves into a constant mechanical relation to the objects of his life, so that he produced the same sort of impression as a handle or a crooked tube, which has no meaning standing apart' (ch. 2). Yet in both texts a part of another's body – golden hair – becomes a memory object that brings the subject back to himself. Lucy's hair forms the 'golden thread' that metonymically links Manette's past and present; Eppie's golden curls metaphorically stand for, then displace, Marner's lost gold by forming a link with the wider community.

In his discussion of 'thinking and feeling' in 1860 Lewes describes how 'general Consciousness is composed of the sum of sensations excited by the incessant simultaneous action of internal and external stimuli', taking as example the background noise of a mill wheel – a sound so familiar that it is only actively observed when it ceases.[36] In the same year *The Mill on the Floss* also opens with the 'rush of the water and the booming of the mill', creating a 'dreamy deafness' which underpins the phantasmagoric fusing of past and present. Significantly, the novel appeared a year after the publication of Darwin's *Origin of Species* (discussed elsewhere in this *Companion*), and it sets Maggie Tulliver's consciousness within wider processes of organic inheritance and social change (the town, St Oggs, has 'inherited a long past without thinking of it' (book 1, ch. 12)). *The Mill on the Floss* is itself a conceptual palimpsest, which sets Spencer's account of evolution alongside Darwin's stress on change, beside Bain's analysis of emotion and Lewes's description of consciousness. Maggie's 'conflict between the inward impulse and the outward fact, which is the lot of every passionate and impulsive nature', is achieved through evoking these at times dissonant models of individual and collective identity (book 4, ch. 2).[37]

As children, Maggie and Tom emphasize the unpredictability, even perversity of inheritance. Tom's stubborn determination represents an advance on his parents' incapacity in the face of financial ruin; but his struggle is for return and self-identity rather than change: he undermines Spencer's claim that progress involves greater heterogeneity and complexity. Maggie's inheritance of the dark hair and quick wit of her father is described ironically in Darwinian terms as a 'small mistake of nature' – the result of the '"crossing o' breeds"' (book 1, ch. 2); but her 'misfitting' is above all the result of the rigid gender codes. Described as 'young animals', both children embody a process of recapitulation that would be elaborated later in the century, where individual development reproduces that of the species, and both are ultimately unable to survive. But while Tom's stubborn will fixes his mind and body into increasingly rigid forms, Maggie's 'primitive' passion (expressed in her beating of her 'fetish') can be read as fundamentally continuous with her 'higher' feelings of affection and sympathy and elaborates Spencer's insistence on the cognitive role of emotion. Although the climax of the novel hinges on the tension between Maggie's overwhelming sexual passion for Stephen Guest (echoing Bain's and Lewes's sense of the physical roots of emotional waves or drives) and the higher claims of memory, Eliot also breaks down the boundary between the 'inward impulse and the outward fact': Maggie's socially disastrous return – her question that 'if the past is not to bind us, where does duty lie?' – is rooted in the self's internalized adaptation to the 'subtle inextricable associations' of memory, which, as Michael Davis notes, 'enables the organism to "infer" attributes of the external world beyond those which it directly perceives'.[38]

After 1870: degeneration and beyond

'It seems almost as if during sleep we returned to the undeveloped mental condition of infancy, with the single difference that our emotions are more various and our images are furnished by a larger field of experience', noted James Sully in 1876. He came back to this point in an article on 'The Dream as a Revelation' in the *Fortnightly Review* in 1893, where he extended the notion that the dream reveals traces of former selves. Dreams, he argued, bring together the individual past of childhood; the 'remote past' of our evolutionary ancestors – 'the organic substrate of our conscious personality which links us to the animal series'; and 'a recurrent reinstatement of our "dead selves," an overlapping of the successive personalities, the series of whose doings and transformations constitutes our history'.[39]

These overlapping meanings point to the ways in which the relationship between mind and body shifted after 1870, and Sully himself provides an important link between mid-century physiological psychology and later developments. As a student in the early 1860s he had read Hamilton, Bain, Spencer and Lewes; but had also gone on to study in Germany under the physicist Hermann von Helmholtz. He began his career as a journalist, writing on psychology and aesthetics (including a piece on 'George Eliot's Art') as well as on Helmholtz's theory of sound waves and evolutionary theory. Sully thus participated in the wider mid-century intellectual culture, but he also played a key role in establishing psychology as an academic discipline in later decades, with textbooks such as *The Outlines of Psychology* (1884) and *The Human Mind* (1892). A good friend of Robert Louis Stevenson, whose *A Child's Garden of Verses* he particularly admired, Sully was a leading figure in the establishment of child psychology: *Studies of Childhood* (1895) draws on the 'recapitulation' model of childhood made up of stages of development, but it also studies children's play and regards childhood, like dreaming, as a multi-layered psychic structure shaping adult identity.

Although links with earlier work persisted, psychology, psychiatry and neurology diverged into specialized fields after 1870, though they all shared a growing emphasis on empirical observation and experiment, and participated in the adaptation of evolutionary theory into the widespread concepts of degeneration. Some aspects of psychiatry, alongside the developing field of criminology, became increasingly deterministic. Henry Maudsley, for example, combined sensory-motor physiology and the theory of mental degeneration into a gloomy model of heredity in which 'no-one can escape the tyranny of his organisation; no-one can escape the destiny that is innate in him and unconsciously and irresistibly shapes his ends'.[40] Charles Darwin's cousin Francis Galton argued for the selective breeding of humans as well as animals to prevent the spread of hereditary criminality in which 'vicious instincts ... may become the normal characteristics of a healthy race'.[41] In 1890 H. Havelock Ellis drew on the work of Cesare Lombroso, Gregor Mendel and George Savage to argue that the criminal represents a form of atavism, in which older forms persist into the present in the right environment. He 'remains a child all his life long – a child of larger growth and with greater capacity for evil', he noted, in an observation echoed by Van Helsing on the Count in Bram Stoker's *Dracula*, which appeared in 1897.[42]

Much of the fiction of the 1890s hinges on the burdens of both heredity and modernity on the individual self – in Hardy's *Tess of the d'Urbervilles* (1891) and *Jude the Obscure* (1895); in George Gissing's representations of urban degeneration in *The Nether World* (1889) and in the anxious, neurasthenic response to modernity in *In the Year of Jubilee* (1894) and *The Whirlpool* (1897). But 'degeneration' formed only one strand in a range of debates about the relationship of the body and the mind, and it is too limiting to read these writers purely within its framework. George Gissing's *Born in Exile* (1897) explores the social as well as the psychological meanings of the idea of 'double consciousness', and Hardy's short story 'The Withered Arm' (1888) is a compelling account of a long-buried secret taking the form of a bodily symptom. Indeed psychology, psychiatry and neurology all encountered the limits of biological determinism as the nineteenth century drew to a close, and in different ways they probed the meaning and the limit of the 'material' itself as an explanatory category, recognizing that the relationship between mind and body was far more complicated than had previously been imagined. The use of hypnotism to study and treat hysteria in the 'laboratory' conditions of the clinic was developed by J.-M. Charcot in Paris in the 1870s and 1880s within a firmly degenerationist framework; but his emphasis on the condition as a purely functional disorder was challenged by Hippolyte Bernheim, whose work emphasized the curative power of the hypnotic trance, in which subjects performed acts of which they had no memory and which, Bernheim argued, illustrated a process of *ideodynamism*, or the ability of a mental process to be enacted in the body.[43]

The failure of Charcot to explain both hysteria and hypnosis in solely functional terms as against Bernstein's concept of hysteria as a psycho-somatic condition contributed to the emergence of psychodynamic psycho-therapy in the work of Pierre Janet and Sigmund Freud in the 1890s, both of whom, albeit in different ways, analysed hysterical symptoms and forms of traumatic neurosis as bodily representations of psychic conditions whose roots must be sought in the past. In his 1893 article Sully had related the 'successive personalities' displayed in dreams to 'the phenomena of double or alternating personality', and the mid-century notion (suggested by Henry Holland) that 'double consciousness' can be explained through viewing the localized functions of the brain through an associative, memory-based model of the mind was extended and transformed in a clinical context in French studies of cases of double and multiple personality, by Eugene Azam and by Janet himself.[44]

The key figures to make this work available in Britain, Edward Gurney and F. W. H. Myers, were interested in how studies of multiple selfhood might help explain psychological states that moved beyond purely physio-logical explanations, and with the philosopher Henry Sidgwick they set up the Society for Psychical Research in 1882. The SPR aimed to study cases of spirit manifestations, automatic writing and telepathy (a term Myers coined) within a rigorously scientific framework, and Myers and Gurney drew on French studies of double or multiple personality to explore how the 'self' might exist beyond the boundaries of the body. 'Just as the old orthodoxy was too narrow to contain men's knowledge, so the new orthodoxy of materialistic science is too narrow to contain their feelings and aspirations', Myers noted in 1886, and his posthumously published *Human Personality and the Survival of Bodily Death* (1903) argued that the 'supraliminal consciousness', hinted at in cases of multiple personality, offers a glimpse of a transcendent identity, beyond both the body and the boundaries of death itself.

Myers was also an acquaintance of Robert Louis Stevenson, and praised the manuscript of *The Strange Case of Dr Jekyll and Mr Hyde* (1886), though he raised 'certain points which I think you might expand or alter with advantage', particularly about the credibility of Hyde.[45] Stevenson was fascinated by the phenomenon of double personality, and there are similarities between his fictional case and that of Myers's account of 'Louis V', a 'quiet, well behaved, obedient child' who developed a second personality – 'violent greedy and quarrelsome' – following a 'sudden shock', which 'has effected in this boy a profounder severance between the functions of the right and left hemispheres of the brain than has perhaps ever been observed before'.[46] The atavistic, ape-like Hyde echoes Charcot's degenerationist account of double consciousness in which the 'civilized' left is set against the 'primitive' right hemisphere; and the story, as many critics have noted, can be read in the light of contemporary theories of both degeneration and sexual inversion. But while Stevenson's story, with other Gothic *fin de siècle* stories of transformation such as Wilde's *The Picture of Dorian Gray* (1891) and H. G. Wells's *The Invisible Man* (1897), literalizes a process of physical mutation, all raise a wider set of questions about the workings of consciousness in relation to the body. Jekyll's laboratory used to be a dissecting room, but his own interests are 'rather chemical than anatomical', and his 'mystical and transcendental' scientific methods are seen as profoundly subversive by his more conventional friend Dr Lanyon because they push the methods of experimental science to blur the boundaries of the material and spiritual, mind and body. Hyde is uncanny precisely because he is a physical presence yet cannot be pinned down in physiognomic terms, while Jekyll, in his final 'Full Statement of the Case', describes his body as simultaneously material and ethereal: an 'incongruous compound', a 'mist-like transience'.[47]

For while physicalist explanations of the mind had become established by the 1870s, the question raised by Lewes – that the inductive method cannot explain the subjective experience of consciousness – returned with force in the late nineteenth century. It was emphasized by critics of associationism such as James Ward in the *Encyclopaedia Britannica* in 1886; but also stressed by psychologists growing out of the physiological tradition such as James Sully and William James, whose detailed analysis of consciousness as a stream extended Henry Holland's and G. H. Lewes's accounts of mental flow. Indeed, in his early 1879 essay 'Are We Automata?' James refuted T. H. Huxley's argument 'that feelings are merely juxtaposed without mutual cohesion, because the nerve-processes to which they severally correspond awaken each other in that order' by citing Lewes. Far from returning to a kind of dualism, James (who was a President of the Society for Physical Research in the 1890s) returned to the work of Darwin, Lewes, Spencer and Helmholtz to suggest that 'the mind is at every stage a theatre of simultaneous possibilities. Consciousness consists in the comparison of these with each other', so that 'The highest distillate thus *represents* in the last analysis nothing but sensational elements. But this is far from meaning that it implies nothing but the passive faculty of sensation.'[48]

Conclusion

> He began to wonder whether we could ever make psychology so absolute a science that each little spring of life could be revealed to us.
> (Oscar Wilde, *The Picture of Dorian Gray*, ch. 4)

In the Conclusion to his *Studies in the History of the Renaissance* (1873) Walter Pater argued that 'our physical life' is made up of the 'perpetual motion' of elements: 'the passage of the blood ... the modification of the tissues of the brain under every ray of light and sound'. His description of the intensification of these physiological processes into 'impressions ... in perpetual flight ... constantly forming and reforming itself on the stream, to a single sharp impression ... that strange, perpetual weaving and unweaving of ourselves' chimes closely with James Sully's account in his study of *Illusions* (1881), of consciousness as 'a closely woven texture in which the mental eye often fails to trace the several threads or strands' and which 'change continually, just as the contents of the kaleidoscope vary with every shake of the instrument'.[49]

Pater's injunction to push this expanded, complex notion of sensation as the basis of consciousness to its fullest extent is one of the starting points of Wilde's *The Picture of Dorian Gray*, and in exploring the limits of sensation itself the story offers a telling example of the paradoxical relationship between the body and the mind at the close of the century. Dorian's fatal wish that the portrait should absorb the effects of experience gives a materialist tweak to the Faustian pact that Redlaw made in *The Haunted Man*: as his body evades the traces of time, so the portrait becomes the embodiment of embodied memory. The splitting of Dorian's timeless beauty and the portrait's traces of experience, too, extends the distinction within the physiognomic tradition between the stress on dynamic expression and on static features that Braddon had played on in *Lady Audley's Secret*. Yet while this further undermines physiognomy's stress on essential identity it also paradoxically reinscribes the fundamental truth of the picture itself. Dorian speculates that his transformation is a mysterious chemical process, at once material and immaterial: 'Was there some subtle affinity between the chemical atoms, that shaped themselves into form and colour on the canvas and the soul that was within him? Could it be that what that soul thought, they realised?' (ch. 7). And while he is set up as the subject of Lord Henry's psychological 'vivisection', Henry's quest to understand the self breaks down the boundary between observer and object, and with it psyche and soma, completely: 'as one watched life in its curious crucible of pain and pleasure, one could not wear over one's face a mask of glass, nor keep the sulphurous fumes from troubling the brain and making the imagination turbid with monstrous fancies and misshapen dreams … Who could say where the fleshly impulse ceased, or the psychical impulse began?' (ch. 4).

Notes

1 Alexander Bain, *Mind and Body: The Theories of Their Relation*, 2nd edn (London: Henry S. King, 1873), pp. 2–4.

2 Rick Rylance, *Victorian Psychology and British Culture 1830–1880* (Oxford: Oxford University Press, 2000), pp. 22–69; Edward S. Reed, *From Soul to Mind: The Emergence of Psychology from Erasmus Darwin to William James* (New Haven: Yale University Press, 1997).

3 Edwin Clarke and J. S. Jakyna, *The Nineteenth-Century Origins of Neuroscientific Concepts* (Berkeley: University of California Press, 1987), p. 33.

4 Roger Smith, *The Norton History of the Human Sciences* (New York: Norton, 1997), p. 412.

5 George Henry Lewes, *The Physiology of Common Life*, 2 vols. (Edinburgh and London: William Blackwood and Sons, 1860), vol. II, pp. 4–5.

6 See Janet Oppenheim, *'Shattered Nerves': Doctors, Patients and Depression in Victorian England* (New York and Oxford: Oxford University Press, 1991), pp. 13–15.

7 Fred Kaplan, *Dickens and Mesmerism: The Hidden Springs of Fiction* (Princeton: Princeton University Press, 1975).

8 Sally Shuttleworth, *Charlotte Brontë and Victorian Psychology* (Cambridge: Cambridge University Press, 1996), ch. 1.

9 Jenny Bourne Taylor, *In the Secret Theatre of Home: Wilkie Collins, Sensation Narrative and Nineteenth-Century Psychology* (London: Routledge, 1988).

10 Sally Shuttleworth, *George Eliot and Nineteenth-Century Science: The Make-Believe of a Beginning* (Cambridge: Cambridge University Press, 1983); Rylance, *Victorian Psychology*; Michael Davis, *George Eliot and Nineteenth-Century Psychology: Exploring the Unmapped Country* (Aldershot: Ashgate, 2006).

11 Roger Smith, 'The Physiology of the Will: Mind, Body, and Psychology in the Periodical Literature, 1855–1875', in Geoffrey Cantor and Sally Shuttleworth (eds.), *Science Serialized: Representations of the Sciences in Nineteenth-Century Periodicals* (Cambridge, Mass.: MIT Press, 2004), p. 81.

12 George Henry Lewes, *Problems of Life and Mind*, third series, vol. I: *The Study of Psychology* (London: Trübner and Co., 1879), p. 10.

13 On 'dual aspect monism' see Thomas Dixon, *From Passions to Emotions: The Development of a Secular Psychological Category* (Cambridge: Cambridge University Press, 2003), pp. 142–4.

14 See Jenny Bourne Taylor and Sally Shuttleworth (eds.), *Embodied Selves: An Anthology of Psychological Texts 1830–1890* (Oxford: Oxford University Press, 1998), pp. 3–4.

15 See Lucy Hartley, *Physiognomy and the Meaning of Expression in Nineteenth-Century Culture* (Cambridge: Cambridge University Press, 2001), pp. 32–42.

16 J. C. Lavater, *Essays in Physiognomy*, trans. T. Holcroft (1789; repr. in Taylor and Shuttleworth (eds.), *Embodied Selves*, p. 9.

17 See Shuttleworth, *Charlotte Brontë and Victorian Psychology*, p. 259 n. 2.

18 Nicholas Danes, *Amnesiac Selves: Nostalgia, Forgetting and British Fiction 1810–1870* (Oxford: Oxford University Press, 2001), ch. 2.

19 Shuttleworth, *Charlotte Brontë and Victorian Psychology*, p. 154.

20 *Ibid.* p. 223.

21 Clarke and Jakyna, *The Nineteenth-Century Origins*, pp. 110–12; Hartley, *Physiognomy and the Meaning of Expression*, ch. 2.

22 Julie F. Codell, 'Expression over Beauty: Facial Expression, Body Language, and Circumstantiality in the Painting of the Pre-Raphaelite Brotherhood', *Victorian Studies*, 29 (1985), pp. 255–90.

23 G. H. Lewes, 'Dickens in Relation to Criticism', *Fortnightly Review*, 17 (February 1872), pp. 141–54.

24 See Athena Vrettos, 'Defining Habits: Dickens and the Psychology of Repetition', *Victorian Studies*, 42, 3 (1999–2000), pp. 399–436.

25 See Jane Wood, *Passion and Pathology in Victorian Fiction* (Oxford: Oxford University Press, 2001), pp. 43–58.

26 James Sully, 'The Laws of Dream-Fancy', *Cornhill Magazine* (November 1876), pp. 537–55, at pp. 538, 537.

27 Henry Holland, *Chapters on Mental Physiology* (1852; repr. in Taylor and Shuttleworth (eds.), *Embodied Selves*, p. 129.

28 Danes, *Amnesiac Selves*, ch. 3, at p. 148.

29 See Jill L. Matus, 'Trains, Trauma and the Railway Disaster – the Dickensian Connection', *Victorian Studies*, 43, 3 (2000–1), pp. 413–36.

30 William B. Carpenter, *Principles of Human Physiology*, 5th edn (London: John Churchill, 1855), p. 548.

31 See Rylance, *Victorian Psychology*, ch. 5.

32 Alexander Bain, *The Emotions and the Will* (London: John W. Parker and Son, 1859), p. 8.

33 *Ibid.* p. 41.

34 Herbert Spencer, *The Principles of Psychology* (London: Longman, Brown, Green and Longman, 1855), p. 584.

35 G. H. Lewes, *Problems of Life and Mind*, first series, *The Foundations of a Creed* (London: Trübner, 1874), vol. II, p. 162. On Lewes's work see Rylance, *Victorian Psychology*, ch. 7.

36 Lewes, *The Physiology of Common Life*, p. 65.

37 For a full exploration of this process, see Shuttleworth, *George Eliot and Nineteenth-Century Science*, ch. 3.

38 See Michael Davis, *George Eliot and Nineteenth-Century Psychology*, p. 76.

39 James Sully, 'The Dream as a Revelation', *Fortnightly Review*, 59 (March 1893), pp. 354–65, at pp. 359, 355–6.

40 Henry Maudsley, *Body and Mind* (London: Macmillan & Co., 1873), p. 76.

41 Francis Galton, *Inquiries into Human Faculty and Its Development* (London: Macmillan, 1883), p. 62.

42 H. Havelock Ellis, *The Criminal* (London: Walter Scott, 1890), p. 214.

43 See Roger Luckhurst, *The Invention of Telepathy 1870–1900* (Oxford: Oxford University Press, 2002), p. 101.

44 See Ian Hacking, *Rewriting the Soul: Multiple Personality and the Sciences of Memory* (Princeton: Princeton University Press, 1995), ch. 11.

45 Letter from Myers to Stevenson (21 February 1886); cited in Paul Maixner (ed.), *Robert Louis Stevenson: The Critical Heritage* (London: Routledge and Kegan Paul, 1981), p. 213.

46 F. W. H. Myers, 'Multiplex Personality', *Nineteenth Century*, 20 (November 1886), pp. 648–66, at pp. 649–50.

47 Michael Davis, 'Incongruous Compounds: Re-reading *Jekyll and Hyde* and Late-Victorian Psychology', *Journal of Victorian Culture*, 11, 2 (2006), pp. 207–225, at p. 211. See also Luckhurst, *The Invention of Telepathy*, pp. 190–6.

48 William James, 'Are We Automata?' *Mind*, 13 (January 1879), pp. 1, 13.

49 James Sully, *Illusions: A Psychological Study* (London: C. Kegan Paul & Co., 1881), p. 197.

11

ANDREW SANDERS

Writing and religion

In the summer of 1867 the Reverend Charles Lutwidge Dodgson, now better known to the world as 'Lewis Carroll', set off on his only trip beyond the shores of England. He travelled with his friend and fellow Oxford don Canon Henry Liddon, to Russia. This was an unusual destination for cultured and curious Englishmen at the time. Italy, France or even Germany would have seemed more obvious choices, but Liddon, with Dodgson's evident acquiescence, had a pilgrimage in mind. Their spiritual goal lay beyond what Western Europe had to offer. Liddon was seeking both to extend his knowledge of the Orthodox Church and to foster the spiritual links between the state churches of England and Russia in the hope of some ultimate alliance between those European Christians who rejected not simply the authority of the pope but also current movements within Roman Catholicism to declare the Holy Father infallible. Dodgson was less assiduous in his sense of mission than Liddon, but, as the journal he kept during the trip across Europe reveals, he was full of intellectual curiosity.

Both men were determined to encounter religious customs which appeared, at a distance, to be both rich and strange. They travelled by train via Brussels and Cologne (where Dodgson experienced elaborate Catholic ceremonial for the first time) and then on to Berlin, where they visited the new Synagogue in the Oranienburgstrasse (Jewish worship striking Dodgson as 'perfectly novel to me & most interesting'). After extended sight-seeing stop-overs in Lutheran Danzig and Königsberg they finally arrived at St Petersburg on 27 July. On their first Sunday in Russia they went to the morning liturgy celebrated at St Isaac's Cathedral. Notwithstanding the splendour of Orthodox worship, Dodgson's assured sense of Anglican decorum remained unassailed ('the more one sees of these gorgeous services, with their many appeals to the senses, the more, I think, one learns to love the plain, simple ... service of the English church'). In early August they went south to Moscow and then east to Nizhni Novgorod, where they heard an Islamic call to prayer for the first time, a sound which seemed to Dodgson to possess 'an indescribably sad & ghostlike effect' and which, had it been heard at night, 'would have thrilled one like the cry of a Banshee'.

The main object of their journey was, however, realized on their return to Moscow. On 12 August, accompanied by an amenable Russian bishop who could speak broken English, they travelled out to the much-venerated Troitsa-Sergeevskaya Lavra for an extended interview with the Metropolitan of Moscow (which was conducted in an exotic mixture of Russian, French and English). Although he was evidently more intrigued than rapt by the experience, Dodgson nevertheless found the day 'memorable'. At the monastery and later in Moscow both men indulged in the then novel experience for Englishmen of purchasing icons. On Sunday 18 August an Orthodox bishop secured them favoured places in the Assumption Cathedral for the morning liturgy. Liddon remained for the whole of the long service, but Dodgson slipped away to the English church and to a chaster form of worship which was evidently more to his taste. He was not, however, impervious to the aesthetic appeal of Russian Orthodox architecture, for he returned to the Kremlin that same night in 'a flood of cold, clear moonlight' which, he noted, brought out 'the pure white of the walls & towers, & the glittering points of light on the gilded domes, in a way that sunlight could never do'.[1]

Lewis Carroll's Russian adventure typifies something of the genuine curiosity that marked responses to religious experience and worship in nineteenth-century Britain. If relatively few middle-class travellers ventured as far as Moscow, many others, fired by a new romantic fascination with both the Catholic south and the Gothic north, travelled to the Mediterranean and through Germany and Switzerland. Their goals were no longer those sought out by the eighteenth-century aristocratic Grand Tourists. In common with many other educated Victorians, travellers like Dodgson were drawn not simply by safe and long-established parallels between English and German Protestantism or by the stark contrasts between Protestant and Catholic devotion, but also, if tentatively, by the exotic splendours of Orthodoxy, by the new self-confidence of emancipated European Jewry and even by the eeriness of brief encounters with Islam and Buddhism. Despite the determination of reforming Henrician and Elizabethan divines to create a distinctively 'English' church, religious and cultural insularity was no longer a clear option to the nineteenth-century heirs of those Reformation divines. Britain was a power both in divided Christian Europe and in a wider world. Its expanding Empire was first to encounter and then rule nations who did not share its Anglican, let alone its Christian inheritance. Other churches, other sects and other religions, once seen merely as political threats or as challenges to missionary enterprise, now had to be understood before they could be withstood. In some cases an encounter with the 'other' sowed deep seeds of doubt about conventional Anglicanism and opened up into a full embrace of a new religion.

It would be wildly inaccurate to describe Victorian Britain as 'multicultural'. It was, however, as a result of a gradual evolutionary process, a 'plural' society. That plurality had first been affirmed by the repeal in May 1828 of the late seventeenth-century Test and Corporation Acts, acts which had rigorously excluded religious nonconformists from civil and military office. In March 1829 English Roman Catholics were granted similar civil rights. Thus Parliament, the army and the navy, the legal profession, the magistracy and the administration of local government, formerly the exclusive preserve of members of the Church of England, were opened up to those once classed as Dissenters and Recusants. In 1860 the first two Jews elected to the House of Commons were permitted to omit from the obligatory Parliamentary oath the words 'on the faith of a Christian'. Eleven years later the two ancient English universities finally abolished religious tests, allowing non-Anglicans to matriculate and to graduate (no such religious tests had applied to Scottish universities). In 1885, five years after first being elected member for Northampton, the free-thinking Charles Bradlaugh won the right to affirm, rather than take an oath on the Bible, thus becoming the first overtly non-confessional MP. The influence of religious nonconformity was pervasive in the life of Victorian England. The 'Dissidence of Dissent' and the often narrow moral heritage of English Puritanism were to become major themes in Matthew Arnold's provocative critique of modern society, *Culture and Anarchy* (1869). English Unitarians, by far the most liberal, best-educated and richest element in the dissenting body, were to dominate local government in the burgeoning industrial cities of Liverpool, Birmingham and Manchester. The Revd William Gaskell, the minister of Cross Street Unitarian Chapel in Manchester and the husband of the novelist Elizabeth Gaskell, preached to a congregation made up of some of the most influential middle-class families in the city (the first mayor of Manchester after the 1838 charter of incorporation was a member, as were six subsequent mayors and fifteen Members of Parliament).[2]

Nevertheless, as even Elizabeth Gaskell's novels serve to suggest, high-minded Dissenters, whether Unitarian, Presbyterian or Quaker, were rarely either elegant or romantic enough to figure as major characters in fiction. Dissenters themselves, however liberal their political culture, still tended to be puritanically suspicious of imaginative literature and of novels in particular. The title character in Gaskell's *Ruth* (1853) may be rescued from suicide by the virtuous minister, Thurstan Benson, but the novel seems to have caused sufficient moral offence amongst members of the Cross Street congregation for some to threaten to burn it.[3] Significantly, when Mr Hale abandons his Anglican orders in *North and South* (1855) his critical doubts about religious formularies lead him not to Unitarianism but to the genteel poverty and independence of a free-lance tutor in Milton Northern (a city which is very obviously Manchester). His pupil, the manufacturer Mr Thornton, is given no specific creed, while his daughter, Margaret, clings resolutely to Church of England doctrine. Elsewhere in Gaskell's work Anglican clergy, Anglican worship and Anglican manners seem to maintain their easy-going traditional sway.

Quakers, many of whom, like Unitarians, had risen to positions of wealth, respectability and influence by the beginning of Queen Victoria's reign, generally received a good press from Victorian novelists (one thinks of the philanthropic bankers-cum-shopkeepers, the Foster brothers, in Gaskell's *Sylvia's Lovers* (1863)). Representatives of the far more numerous and far less socially established members of Wesleyan sects seem, however, to have attracted far more prejudiced comment. Some of that prejudice was undoubtedly socially snobbish in origin but other elements may be rooted in a well-established literary antipathy to puritan kill-joys. Poorly educated and avowedly teetotal, Methodists were generally intolerant of secular literature and of the novel in particular.[4] The sympathetic portraits of Seth Bede and of the heroic woman preacher, Dinah Morris, in George Eliot's *Adam Bede* (1859) can be countered by Charlotte Brontë's picture of the congregation at Briar Chapel in *Shirley* (1849) and by the perceived hypocrisy of Alec d'Urberville's appearance as an 'extremest antinomian' preacher in Hardy's *Tess of the d'Urbervilles* (1891). Other Calvinist nonconformists generally fare even worse. The tightly knit sect that meets in Lantern Yard in Eliot's *Silas Marner* (1861) is notable for its judgemental narrow-mindedness. Despite the occasional thoughtfully provocative representation of a dissenting minister, such as the Revd Arthur Vincent in Margaret Oliphant's *Salem Chapel* (1863), and subtle fictional analyses of the declining radicalism of English dissent in William Hale White's *The Revolution in Tanner's Lane* (1887), the mode of comic disapproval seems to have been firmly established for contemporary readers by the line of Dickens's antipathetic caricatures of extremist, intolerant, ill-educated, millenarianist, hypocritical ranters. The red-nosed Mr Stiggins in *Pickwick Papers* (1837) arrives drunk at a meeting of the Brick Lane Branch of the United Grand Junction Temperance Association. The preacher at the Little Bethel Chapel, attended by Mrs Nubbles in *The Old Curiosity Shop* (1841), is 'by trade a Shoemaker, and by calling a Divine' who tells his congregation 'what he meant to convince them of before he had done it, and it was clear that if he only kept to one-half of his promises, and forgot the other, he was good for that time at least'. In *Dombey and Son* (1847–8) the Revd Melchisedek Howler, having initially announced 'the destruction of the world for that day, two years at ten in the morning', finally declares, 'on very urgent solicitation', that it has two further years 'but had informed his followers that, then, it must positively go'. In *Bleak House* (1852) the odiously sanctimonious Mr Chadband twists the word 'truth' into the revelatory distortion 'terewth'. If each may owe as much to Ben Jonson's Zeal-of-the-Land Busy as to a Victorian reality, the traditional literary link between artisan puritanism and hypocrisy still evidently held sway for many nineteenth-century readers.

In the opening years of the century the Church of England remained heavily influenced by the late eighteenth-century earnestness of the Evangelical movement. Under the guidance of William Wilberforce, Evangelicals had spearheaded the great popular campaign against the slave trade and in 1833 had finally succeeded in persuading a recalcitrant Parliament to abolish slavery within the British Empire. These campaigns remain the most distinguished historical examples of the galvanization of a variety of extra-parliamentary pressure groups, and they were profoundly to mark the social consciences and the social attitudes of the Victorian generations.[5] Although the strict moral ethos fostered by Anglican Evangelicalism was often regarded as a middle-class norm, to their contemporaries and their descendants alike Evangelical ministers and their families were seen as the most austere and extreme embodiments of 'Victorian' values. As Owen Chadwick notes:

> The children of evangelical pastors lived austere lives without novels or cards or dancing. Waltz and polka reeked of vice, but all dances were odious. They were kept from entering worldly society. But they were given the run of good libraries, were encouraged to varied interests of natural history or music or good literature, and were early used to help in Sunday school or visit poor parishioners or copy important letters. Shakespeare was bowdlerised and idle words excised from the songs of the music room. At Christmas their festivities were rather devout than gluttonous, and they were not allowed Christmas trees. They were expected to have straight hair and not curls nor ringlets, eschewed gauze bonnets, preferred green and grey colours to red or lilac. Evangelicals disapproved of fox-hunting parsons, shooting parsons, cricketing parsons, ballroom parsons. They did not disapprove of wine.[6]

Despite a grudging admiration of their uprightness their habitual inclination to moralization won them relatively few friends amongst creative writers. They were often associated with smugness and with a hypocrisy, a kill-joyism and an oppression of children which exceeded that of the most pharasaical of Dissenters. Dickens's Miss Murdstone in *David Copperfield* and the censorious Miss Barbary in *Bleak House* spring readily to mind. The restrictive evangelical parent was caricatured in Samuel Butler's *The Way of All Flesh* (1903); the self-centredly proselytizing clergyman was satirized in Anthony Trollope's Obadiah Slope in *Barchester Towers* (1857); the narrow-minded child-hater was demonized in Charlotte Brontë's Mr Brocklehurst in *Jane Eyre* (1847). Yet it is to *Jane Eyre* that we also have to turn in order to glimpse something of the spiritual power and the missionary zeal of Victorian Evangelicalism. Brocklehurst may stand for the kind of religious definition with which Charlotte Brontë had no truck but the Revd St John Rivers is the representative of an altogether more sturdy, admirable and selfless faith. Rigid, repressed and unbending he might appear at times, and he is no natural partner for Jane, but, in the closing pages of *Jane Eyre*, he is presented as an example of a vibrantly loving missionary faith which complements, rather than contradicts, Jane's achievement of temporal content:

> A more resolute, indefatigable pioneer never wrought amidst rocks and dangers. Firm, faithful, and devoted; full of energy and zeal, and truth, he labours for his race: he clears their painful way to improvement: he hews down like a giant the prejudices of creed and caste that encumber it. He may be stern, he may be exacting, he may be ambitious yet: but his is the sternness of the warrior Greatheart who guards his pilgrim-convoy from the onslaught of Apollyon. His is the exaction of the apostle, who speaks but for Christ, when he says – 'Whosoever will come after me, let him deny himself and take up his cross and follow me.' (vol. III, ch. 12)

There is nothing mealy-mouthed about St John Rivers. Some Evangelical readers of *Jane Eyre* might have supposed, on a first reading of the novel, that Jane would properly have atoned for the sin of falling in love with a singularly fleshly married man by taking up St John's offer to share in his missionary life in India. This was never part of Brontë's scheme, but she clearly recognized the moral force of reminding us at the very end of the novel of St John's sacrifice in the midst of Jane's celebration of her worldly happiness.

Most historians of Victorian religion tend to comment on juxtaposed oppositions rather than on complements and compromises. They have often dwelt extensively on Evangelical earnestness and Evangelical hypocrisy, on Tractarian piety and Tractarian absurdity, on the crisis of faith and the loss of faith. They have described comfortable rural rectories and stinking churchless slums and they have considered intellectual turmoil in the Universities and religious complacency in the suburbs. Relatively few have accounted for the vast Anglican middle ground where a modest faith, whether tested or not, managed to flourish amongst rich and poor alike. Trollope's Barchester novels may comment wryly on church politics and church fashion but they seek neither to justify nor to undermine the basic tenets of the Christian faith. Trollope and Thackeray, in common with many other Victorian writers, assumed that Anglicanism was the faith of a gentleman and that that gentleman was better for having such a faith. Dickens, often impervious to the niceties of religious argument, consistently affirmed his belief that a non-sectarian Christianity was essential to social cement, social morality, social action and social hope. Even the agnostic George Eliot never mocks the well-meaning, if ineffectual, clerics of the Established Church who people her novels. Amongst the mid-century's most principled and liberal Anglicans was the small but influential group of would-be radical 'Christian Socialists' centred on the Revd F. D. Maurice. While many Victorian Evangelicals espoused a social conservatism, Maurice and his followers wore their social consciences on their sleeves. It was Maurice's most avid disciple, the Revd Charles Kingsley, who declared to the working men of England on the day after the great Chartist demonstration in April 1848: 'There will be no true freedom without virtue, no true science without religion, no true industry without the fear of God and love to your fellow citizens. Workers of England, be wise, and then you *must* be free, for you will be fit to be free.'[7] Kingsley, who had once stutteringly announced to a group of sceptical artisans that he was a 'Ch-Ch-Ch-Church of England parson and a Ch-Ch-Ch-Chartist', was to prove a more effective propagandist in fiction than he was an orator or a social reformer. His *Alton Locke: Tailor and Poet* (1850) is one of the most vivid and eloquent of the so-called 'Condition of England' novels of the 1840s and 1850s. Written in the form of an autobiography, it traces Alton's development from Baptist roots, through a radical Chartism and an exposure to Carlylean philosophy to a Christianized social gradualism. Though deeply prejudiced against contemporary Catholicism and profoundly critical of all aspects of the Oxford Movement, Kingsley remains, with his colleague Thomas Hughes (the author of *Tom Brown's Schooldays* of 1857), an energetic apologist for the down-to-earth, anti-intellectual social mission of Victorian Christianity, a mission often characterized by the epithet 'Muscular Christianity'.

Though far from 'muscular' in its theology, the greatest single religious poem of the Victorian age, Tennyson's *In Memoriam A.H.H.* (1850), equally declines to proclaim a narrow or sectarian faith. Tennyson, the son of a Lincolnshire clergyman, wrote his great elegy in memory of Arthur Henry Hallam, a Cambridge contemporary who had been at once an intimate friend and the shrewdest early critic of his poetry. Hallam, who died prematurely in 1833, emerges in the poem as the ideal young Victorian, a thinker and a believer, and as the potential reformist politician cut off before his prime. After his death a friend had described Hallam as a man 'subject to occasional fits of mental depression' which at length 'merged in a peaceful Christian faith'. His own father had commented on Hallam's 'habitual benevolence' which had ripened into 'that exalted principle of love towards God and man, which animated and almost absorbed his soul during the latter period of his life'.[8] These characteristics, coupled with a sense that Hallam could exert a benign posthumous influence, shine through Tennyson's own confession of a faith in *In Memoriam*. It is a faith which has been tested by phases of unconsolable desolation, gloom, self-doubt and acute religious questioning. Tennyson's optimistic resolution of these doubts lies in the notion that just as the living Hallam had reflected the humanity of Christ so the dead Hallam shares in Christ's divine transfiguration. The poem's argument embraces both the pre-Darwinian concept of a benign evolutionary process and a Romantic confidence in the steady perfectability of humanity. It sees history and prehistory, geological time and the patterns of human experience, as integral to a grand divine plan. The final vision is of a God who is all in all, determining the 'one far-off-divine event / To which the whole creation moves'. This is a Last Judgement from which Hell and Damnation are effectively excluded.[9] Tennyson's enduringly popular poem almost certainly sustained the faith of many of those who were to be shaken by the implications of Darwin's *On the Origin of Species* (1859). It was, however, unlikely to have pleased those contemporary Evangelicals who were so exercised by the Calvinistic obsession with predestination. Tennyson sees the survival of the morally fit as a crucial part of a divine plan in which the whole of humanity is predestined to salvation. It is small wonder that comforting lines from his poem were so often carved on the graves of the millions of Britons who fell in the First World War.

During the nineteenth century no single volume of Tennyson's verse outsold John Keble's *The Christian Year*, which first appeared in print in 1827. By 1868 the volume had sold some 265,000 copies and, despite its anonymous publication, had earned its author election to the Oxford professorship of poetry in 1831. After his death Keble was to be honoured by the foundation of a new college at Oxford. His contribution to Victorian religious history lay less in his talent as a poet than in his inspiration of the religious revival known as the 'Oxford Movement'. *The Christian Year* had provided meditative poems for each Sunday and for each major feast day in the Anglican calendar, and had thus served as a companion to the Book of Common Prayer, reminding its users of the spiritual importance of a pattern of festival and ritual observance. It was, however, John Keble the preacher who came to be seen by his disciples as the prophetic voice who had alerted England to the rising tide of secular reformism in the early 1830s. His Oxford Assize Sermon, delivered on 14 July 1833, was ostensibly a criticism of the Whig Government's suppression of certain Anglican sees in Ireland and the redistribution of their resources.

Its theme was quickly taken up by a group of like-minded clerical dons as a call to action against the interference of the British state in the supposedly historically sacrosanct concerns of the Church of England (the fact that the sermon had been preached on Bastille Day was not lost on Keble's friends). The Oxford Movement, as it came to be called, first articulated its case in a series of 'Tracts for the Times'. The very title of the Tracts was indicative of how distinctive and threatening the 'times' were for those drawn by historical patterns and established traditions. Keble's closest associates at Oxford, E. B. Pusey, the Professor of Hebrew, and John Henry Newman, the vicar of the University Church of St Mary, were to form a radical vanguard determined to defend and propagate what they saw as the essential 'catholicity' of the Church of England, a church set aside from other European Protestant churches by its liturgy and by its claims to have retained the 'Apostolic Succession' in its threefold orders of bishops, priests and deacons. It was Newman who pushed these claims to an extreme in 1842 in the ninetieth of the Tracts by arguing for an essentially 'catholic' interpretation of the Thirty-Nine Articles (which had defined Anglican doctrine since Elizabethan times).

Newman's ideas caused outrage not only amongst Evangelicals who rejoiced in the name of 'Protestant', but also among moderate and liberal churchmen and those bishops who felt called to condemn such a dangerous challenge to the religious status quo. Newman resigned his living and, after a period of profound self-examination, was received into the Roman Catholic Church in October 1845, to be followed by a slow but steady trickle of like-minded Anglicans throughout the nineteenth century. What ostensibly seemed liked the rout of the Oxford Tractarians was in fact to prove a defining moment: Pusey and Keble remained steadfast and through their influence a new kind of High Church Anglicanism began to emerge (at the time referred to as 'Puseyism'). It was an approach to faith which placed an emphasis on the sacramental life, on ritual worship and on 'the beauty of holiness'. In a world which often saw itself as increasingly cut off from its historic roots, starved of aesthetic definition and deprived of spirituality the part of the church shaped by the Oxford Movement sought both to restore the physical beauty of churches and to refine the worship that took place in them. The sensibilities, sympathies and susceptibilities of those religious-minded Victorians which had been moulded by Romantic medievalism were to give substance to their convictions by transforming parishes and parish life through the length and breadth of England. Dickens may have caricatured the early Tractarians in *Bleak House* as 'ecclesiastical dandies' intent on putting the clock back, but these were earnest men and women determined to change the future of society by nurturing their roots in the past. The heirs of the Oxford Movement were eventually to style themselves 'Anglo-Catholics': Catholic in their theology and religious practice, but profoundly Anglican in their awareness of a distinctive Anglican tradition and in their resistance to papal pretensions and to Roman authority.

Leading principles of the Oxford Movement were to be put into practice not only in Henry Liddon's mission to establish a working relationship with the Orthodox Church but also in the profound influence they had over a good deal of the art and literature of the mid-century. If and when the allure of Rome had been resisted, Tractarian ideals began to permeate the life of the entire Church of England. The contentious appointment of the undemonstrative Francis Arabin to the Cathedral Deanery in Trollope's *Barchester Towers* serves to demonstrate the advance of these often modest ideals. Trollope carefully delineates Arabin's religious evolution:

> As a young boy Arabin took up cudgels on the side of the Tractarians, and at Oxford he sat for a while at the feet of the great Newman. To this cause he lent all his faculties. For it he concocted verses, for it he made speeches, for it he scintillated the brightest sparks of his quiet wit. For it he ate, drank and dressed, and had his being ... Mr Arabin was ordained, and became a fellow soon after taking his degree, and shortly after that was chosen professor of poetry. And now came the moment of his great danger. After many mental struggles, and an agony of doubt which may well be surmised, the great prophet of the Tractarians confessed himself a Roman Catholic. Mr Newman left the Church of England and with him carried many a waverer. He did not carry off Mr Arabin, but the escape which that gentleman had was a very narrow one ... Every thing was against him: all his worldly interests required him to remain a Protestant; and he looked on worldly interests as a legion of foes, to get the better of whom was a point of extremest honour.   (ch. 20)

Arabin is saved for the Church of England by the influence of 'a poor curate of a small Cornish parish' who teaches him that 'the safety which he was about to seek within the gates of Rome was no other than the selfish freedom from personal danger'. He is then taken in hand by the Master of his Oxford college, 'a High Churchman ... within moderate limits' who regards 'the enthusiasm of such as Newman as a state of mind more nearly allied to madness than to religion'. In Trollope's novel Arabin emerges more as a natural ally of the old high-and-dry tradition of the close at Barchester than as an encourager of Anglo-Catholic innovation but he is nonetheless a typical enough representative of the new order. His opposition to the Evangelical Proudies, and their protégé Slope, is sufficient testimony to his churchmanship.

A similar moderate Tractarian sensibility is evident in the high moral tone, the sacramentalism and the deep respect for conscientious clergymen evinced in the novels of Charlotte Mary Yonge (who was directly influenced by John Keble). The early Tractarians' fascination with the sacramental piety and ritualism associated with Archbishop Laud, Lancelot Andrewes and Nicholas Ferrar in the seventeenth century is recalled in John Mason Neale's *Shepperton Manor: A Tale of the Times of Bishop Andrewes* of 1845 and J. H. Shorthouse's *John Inglesant* of 1880. Neale, a gifted translator of hymns from the Greek and Latin, was to influence the development of English hymnody and to enhance its role in congregational worship. Victorian choral celebration was also to be marked by publication of *Hymns Ancient and Modern* in 1861, an innovative collection which, as its title suggests, brought together the inherited tradition of Christian song with newer examples from hymn writers working in the Romantic mode (such as Henry Francis Lyte, the author of *Poems Chiefly Religious* of 1833 and best remembered for his 'Abide with Me').

The Tractarian spirit is more directly evident in the work of the two Rossetti sisters, Maria and Christina. Maria, who was professed as an Anglican nun in 1873, proved to be a particularly alert Christian commentator on Dante (her *The Shadow of Dante* was published in 1871). A restrained devotionalism marks Christina Rossetti's striking religious verse and is also evident in her overtly pious, but now relatively neglected, prose works such as *Called to be Saints: The Minor Festivals Devotionally Studied* of 1881 and *The Face of the Deep: A Devotional Commentary on the Apocalypse* of 1892.

The Rossetti sisters' Italian ancestry (their father was a political refugee) played its part in their resistance to the allure of Roman Catholicism. Other English converts, notably the future cardinals Newman and Henry Edward Manning, saw an inevitability in the process of their change of religious allegiance. Newman's experience in particular helped him to shape a theology of 'development' in which his own complex grasp of the inherited Christian doctrinal tradition was opened up to embrace that of the entire Western church. He was to describe his own conversion in a slightly laboured work of fiction, *Loss and Gain: The Story of a Convert* of 1848 and more persuasively in his autobiographical confession *Apologia Pro Vita Sua* of 1864 (itself provoked by the antipathy of Charles Kingsley to the Catholic understanding of 'truth'). Newman had returned to the writing of fiction in 1856 with his novel *Callista: A Sketch of the Third Century*, an often persuasive account of faith, heresy and persecution in Roman North Africa. It is a far more impressive achievement than the once internationally popular historical novel by Nicholas Wiseman, Cardinal Archbishop of Westminster, *Fabiola: A Tale of the Catacombs* of 1854. The uses of fiction as Catholic propaganda were also recognized by Lady Georgiana Fullerton, who had been received into the Roman Church in 1846 'after an interval of devout Puseyism'. Her melodramatic modern novel *Grantley Manor* (1847) is concerned with the marriage of an English Catholic woman to the son of a Catholic-hating Anglo-Irishman. *Constance Sherwood* (1865), by contrast, describes the sufferings of Catholics and divided loyalties in the England of Elizabeth I. Prominent conversions, like those of Newman, Manning and Fullerton, coupled with the increase in the Catholic population of England owing to mass immigration from famine-wracked Ireland, helped transform the position of the Roman Catholic Church from that of a despised, semi-secretive sect to a confident and highly influential element in English religious culture.

To twenty-first-century readers, however, the most prominent literary Catholic of the Victorian period is one of whom most of his contemporaries would scarcely have heard. Gerard Manley Hopkins, having come under the influence of the Oxford Movement at Oxford, converted to Roman Catholicism in 1866 soon after his graduation. In 1868 he joined the noviciate of the Society of Jesus and he spent the remainder of his short life as a devout Jesuit teacher and academic. His highly innovative poetry, most of which was published posthumously in 1918, was never much appreciated by his Jesuit superiors, though it charts a rapt and a joyous fascination with Divine Creation and the struggles of a man attempting to articulate his faith in times of spiritual darkness. Hopkins's poetry often explores delicate doctrinal issues and rejoices in theological niceties, but it is also rooted deeply in a Ruskinian awe at the wonder of the natural world.

The natural world consistently awed and delighted Hopkins. Conversely, a new scientific interpretation of the nature of Nature was to serve to disturb and even confound the faith of other Victorians. As Tennyson's *In Memoriam* suggests, the geological theories propounded by Buckland, Chambers and Lyell could be assimilated into a new religious understanding of a creative evolutionary process. The same could not be said of the ideas of Charles Darwin, first set before the public in *On the Origin of Species by Means of Natural Selection* in 1859. As these theories were propagated by Darwin and developed by his disciples they came to represent a profound threat to the basic doctrines of the Christian religion, whether those doctrines were defined by the authority of the Roman Church or were derived by literalist Protestants from the Bible. Catholics may have been offered anathemas but the contortions of faith and interpretation of the gifted geologist and devoutly fundamentalist Plymouth Brother Philip Gosse were described by his son, Edmund, in his *Father and Son* of 1907.

Some religious apologists found themselves able to equate Darwinian ideas with the principle of Divine design while others seem to have been serenely unmoved by any intellectual challenge to a spiritual understanding. A great swathe of British Christians were profoundly shaken by what has since been described as the Victorian 'Crisis of Faith'. This 'crisis' was evident enough in the pre-Darwinian years as a result of the propagation of the so-called 'Higher Criticism', a close examination of the historical basis of Scripture which had been initiated by German scholars in the first third of the nineteenth century. These scholarly doubts wrecked the Evangelical faith of the young George Eliot (whose first published work in 1846 was a translation of a key work of the Higher Criticism, David Friedrich Strauss's *The Life of Jesus, Critically Examined*). They also seem to occasion a turning point in the life of Elizabeth Gaskell's Mr Hale in *North and South* (though the Unitarian Gaskell is somewhat imprecise about quite what aspect of his faith Mr Hale has lost). It has been properly argued that the religious crisis that so affected Victorian Christians was more rooted in temperament and a wider culture than it was in Darwinism. Matthew Arnold's poem 'Dover Beach' (written *c.* 1851, but not published until 1867) speaks, for example, of a 'Sea of Faith' which has retreated with a 'melancholy, long, withdrawing roar'.

It is, however, undoubtedly true that the implications of *The Origin of Species* presented an intellectual excuse to abandon or at the very least to question the fundamentals of their faith.[10] The term 'agnostic', coined by Darwin's chief apologist T. H. Huxley, was readily taken up by Leslie Stephen (author of *An Agnostic's Apology* of 1893), who having renounced his Holy Orders in 1861 wrote: 'I now believe in nothing, to put it shortly; but I do not the less believe in morality etc. etc. I mean to live and die like a gentleman if possible.'[11] Thomas Hardy, despite claiming to have remained 'churchy' by inclination, also recognized the role of Darwin's theories in undermining his Christian faith. It was with reference to Tess Durbeyfield's instinctive Godlessness that Hardy was to describe the late century's cultural, moral, religious and intellectual dilemmas as 'the ache of modernism'. That ache is nowhere better described than in one of the late century's notable best-sellers, Mary Ward's *Robert Elsmere* of 1888. Ward's moving account of the battles of faith and rational doubt were the occasion of the long review article '*Robert Elsmere* and the Battle of Belief' published in the journal the *Nineteenth Century* by no less a figure than W. E. Gladstone.

Gladstone, who as a young man had been deeply touched by the teaching and practice of the Oxford Tractarians, retained his Anglican faith until his dying day. His great rival, Benjamin Disraeli, though a practising member of the Church of England, tended, at least in his published fiction, to discuss the Christian faith from a distinctly Jewish perspective. Disraeli's father, Isaac, a once celebrated man of letters, had left the London Jewish congregation to which he belonged in 1817 and had his sons, including the twelve-year-old Benjamin, baptized. The younger Disraeli was thus freed from the civil disabilities which still limited the educational and political activities of British Jews; he also became the vanguard of a new Jewish generation willing and increasingly able to contribute fully to national life. During Disraeli's lifetime the social profile and the civil aspirations of Britain's small but growing Jewish community changed radically. Although London's Jews still lacked the kind of prominent architectural splendour witnessed in Berlin by Lewis Carroll, their respectability and quiet influence gradually helped diminish the old social prejudices evident in the characterization of the arch-criminal Fagin in Dickens's *Oliver Twist* of 1837–8. By 1864 Dickens was prepared, after due representation had been made to him, to offer an *amende honorable* in describing a worthy, upright and wrongly calumniated Jew in Mr Riah in *Our Mutual Friend*. Disraeli had introduced the dazzlingly sophisticated Sidonia in the middle of a thunderstorm in his novel *Coningsby* of 1844. He is, we are told, of an Aragonese noble family which had 'secretly adhered to the ancient faith and ceremonies of their fathers: a belief in the unity of the God of Sinai, and the rights and observances of the laws of Moses'. Sidonia, who has 'exhausted all the sources of human knowledge', is a kind of Jewish *Übermensch* shot through with elements of that quintessential romantic outsider the Count of Monte Cristo, but in both *Coningsby* and its sequel *Tancred, Or the New Crusade* of 1847, he is also a supremely perceptive critic of contemporary culture. The 'New Crusade' of *Tancred* is no matter of conquering armies or enforced conversion, but the vehicle for the resolution of the philosophical and religious dilemmas of the nineteenth century. Tancred, who finds the church of his birth conflicting in its opinions, 'its decrees contradictory, its conduct inconsistent', is advised by Sidonia to seek his destiny in Jerusalem. The Land of the Book still retains its mystery, and in the mystery lies the answer which seems to elude the Protestant English. In a key moment Sidonia declares a faith which speaks of a confident pride in the centrality of Jewish experience to gentile Christianity:

> I believe that God spoke to Moses on Mount Horeb, and you believe that he was crucified, in the person of Jesus, on Mount Calvary. Both were, at least carnally, children of Israel: they spoke Hebrew to the Hebrews. The prophets were only Hebrews; the apostles were only Hebrews. The churches of Asia,

which have vanished, were founded by a native Hebrew; and the church of Rome, which says it shall last for ever, and which converted this island to the faith of Moses and of Christ, vanquishing the Druids, Jupiter Olympus, and Woden, who had successively invaded it, was also founded by a native Hebrew.

Tancred's mission, or 'crusade', does indeed lead to a moment of revelation in the Holy Land and the novel ends with even his aristocratic parents, the Duke and Duchess of Bellamont, arriving in Jerusalem in pursuit of their own enlightenment.

Tancred may have struck readers of 1847 as high flown and fantastic. Readers of George Eliot's *Daniel Deronda* of 1876 almost certainly reacted very differently to the parallel, but equally earnest, urge expressed in the novel to seek ultimate answers in the Middle East. Deronda, who discovers not only his Jewish race but also his Jewish identity during the course of the novel, is, however, setting out for Jerusalem with more concrete aims and aspirations:

> I am going to the East to become better acquainted with the condition of my race in various countries there ... The idea that I am possessed with is that of restoring a political existence to my people, making them a nation again, giving them a national centre, such as the English have, though they too are scattered over the face of the globe. That is a task that presents itself to me as a duty: I am resolved to begin it, however feebly. I am resolved to devote my life to it. At the least, I may awaken a movement in other minds, such as has been awakened in my own.

Daniel, brought up as an English gentleman, is ostensibly rejecting both his 'Englishness' and his gentlemanly status. Throughout *Daniel Deronda* the agnostic Eliot had meticulously described Jewish life and religious practice amongst poor Jews in Germany and London. Her hero has no desire to develop into another Sidonia, nor does he seek to lead a 'new crusade', but he does seem to embody Eliot's own yearning after answers which lie beyond European sophistication, European rationalism and European scepticism. At times *Daniel Deronda* seems to be stating an early case for Zionism; at others it seems simply to be exploring alternatives to the culture of an island increasingly left high and dry by a receding sea of faith.

As Eliot recognized, for the Jewish poor who settled in the slums of Whitechapel, Jerusalem remained a distant dream, both physically and ideologically. These were the poor so vividly described in the novels of Israel Zangwill, whose three most successful works of fiction, *Children of the Ghetto* (1892), *Ghetto Tragedies* (1893) and *Dreamers of the Ghetto* (1898), capture the dilemmas of life in a complex and singularly secular city where the 'ghetto' fosters few ideals and America seems more golden than Jerusalem. Zangwill's London Jews are both sojourners and exiles, both wanderers and explorers. Their journeys are not necessarily pilgrimages, but despite their being exclusively 'Studies of a Peculiar People' (to quote the subtitle of *Children of the Ghetto*), his books represent Jews who are in a sense paradigms of those nineteenth-century English gentiles who had found themselves alienated from old certainties and severed from their religious and cultural roots. These gentiles, doubters, agnostics and the residually faithful alike, were all exploring different perspectives and seeking new and challenging horizons.

Notes

1 For Dodgson's 'Journal of a Tour of Russia' see *The Works of Lewis Carroll*, ed. Roger Lancelyn Green (London: Hamlyn, 1965), pp. 965–1006.

2 See Valentine Cunningham, *Everywhere Spoken Against: Dissent in the Victorian Novel* (Oxford: Clarendon Press, 1975), pp. 131–2. Jenny Uglow, *Elizabeth Gaskell: A Habit of Stories* (London: Faber and Faber, 1993), p. 87. See also Barbara Brill, *William Gaskell 1805–84: A Portrait* (Manchester: Manchester Literary and Philosophical Publications, 1984), p. 26–34.

3 Cunningham, *Everywhere Spoken Against*, p. 48. See also *The Letters of Mrs Gaskell*, ed. J. A. V. Chapple and Arthur Pollard (Manchester: Manchester University Press, 1966), p. 223.

4 For this see Cunningham, *Everywhere Spoken Against*, pp. 57ff.

5 For the social and spiritual impact of the Evangelical movement see Ford K. Brown, *Fathers of the Victorians: The Age of Wilberforce* (Cambridge: Cambridge University Press, 1961).

6 Owen Chadwick, *The Victorian Church: Part 1*, 3rd edn (London: Adam and Charles Black, 1971), pp. 444–5.

7 For a useful account of the early Christian Socialists see Edward C. Mack and W. H. G. Armitage, *Thomas Hughes: The Life of the Author of Tom Brown's Schooldays* (London: Ernest Benn, 1952). See also R. B. Martin, *The Dust of Combat: The Life of Charles Kingsley* (London: Faber and Faber, 1959).

8 Arthur Henry Hallam, *Remains in Verse and Prose … with a Preface and Memoir* (London: John Murray, 1862), Preface, pp. xxxi, xliii.

9 For Victorian arguments about damnation see Geoffrey Rowell, *Hell and the Victorians: A Study of the Nineteenth Century Theological Controversies concerning Eternal Punishment and the Future Life* (Oxford: Clarendon Press, 1974).

10 See for example the opening chapter of Owen Chadwick's *The Victorian Church: Part 2* (London: Adam and Charles Black, 1970) and Robert M. Young, 'The Impact of Darwin on Conventional Thought', in Anthony Symondson (ed.), *The Victorian Crisis of Faith* (London: SPCK, 1970). See also Gillian Beer, *Darwin's Plots: Evolutionary Narrative in Darwin, George Eliot and Nineteenth-Century Fiction* (London: Routledge and Kegan Paul, 1983). For a recent survey of the ambiguous relationship of religion and science in the nineteenth century see Nicolas

A. Rupke, 'Christianity and the Sciences', in Sheridan Gilley and Brian Stanley (eds.), *The Cambridge History of Christianity*, vol. VIII: *World Christianities c.1815–c.1914* (Cambridge: Cambridge University Press, 2006), pp. 164–80.

11 Quoted by Noel Annan in *Leslie Stephen: The Godless Victorian* (London: Weidenfeld and Nicolson, 1984), p. 2.

12

JOHN PLUNKETT

Visual culture

'Seeing,' says the proverb, 'is believing,' but seeing also is feeling. And this
is George Eliot's great gift that she sees and makes her readers see the
personages of her tale.
[E. S. Dallas], *The Times* (1866)[1]

E. S. Dallas's review of George Eliot's *Felix Holt the Radical* (1866) exemplifies the way nineteenth-century literature, and realism in particular, often
defined its practice through visual tropes. The period had an almost com-
pulsive fascination with visuality because it was the crucible for working
through broader tensions between the material and the ideal, imagination
and reality, the seen and the unseen. Dallas's praise is typically double-edged
in that seeing is simultaneously knowing and feeling, an epistemology and a
phenomenology. His praise equates the truth-value of Eliot's work with the
vividness of her pictorial style, defined as the capability of imagining a scene
as if it was a painting. Nonetheless, for all Eliot's corresponding realism,
Dallas's invocation of the proverb actually emphasizes that seeing is a
perceptual, subjective process. The concrete 'seeing' of Eliot and her readers
is lauded precisely because it is an ideal and imaginative, yet embodied, act.
Seeing might be believing, but the Victorians' fascination with processes of
perception and illusion, often explored through optical devices, meant they
were all too aware of how such belief could be misplaced.

The multivalent discourses of nineteenth-century visuality are evident
in the conflicting function of the large number of pictorial and optical tropes
in literary texts. Taken as a whole, their prevalence reflects the intimate
relationship between literature and the burgeoning variety of visual media.
Many studies have demonstrated their creative interaction, whether
through tracing the influence of different visual arts and technologies upon
individual writers or through more general explorations, such as the impact
of photography and painting upon conceptions of realism. One notable
study by Martin Meisel has gone so far as to argue that a common aesthetic
style, combining narrative with pictorialism, runs through much nineteenth-
century literature, painting and drama.[2] However, the nature of visuality is,
as Kate Flint has argued, concerned with much more than 'the question of
how the world summoned up through language relates to artistic practices

of the time'.[3] Rather, its importance stems from the way it addresses a 'whole range of issues of representation and perception'; and the fuzziness of the relationship between the perceiving self and the external world was the underlying concern of many optical motifs.[4] This chapter thus traces the impact of new modes of visuality in two principal ways: the prevalence of optical and pictorial tropes in the literature of the period, and the way that the growth of illustrated publications created a reading experience that was a combination of visual and verbal.

The expanding field of nineteenth-century visuality was fostered by a proliferation of new technologies for capturing, recording, projecting, enlarging and disseminating images, and the widespread popular interest in them. To take one example – an exhibition of optical devices from the early 1850s that is remarkable only for its typicality – visitors to Short's Observatory in Edinburgh could experience the infinity of space via two telescopes; see a magnified image of small insects and animaculae projected onto a screen courtesy of a solar microscope; enjoy a movable view over Calton Hill using a camera obscura, and reproduce it if desired through a camera lucida (figure 12.1).[5] If these attractions were not enough, they could be enveloped by large painted panoramas of London, Edinburgh and Paris, in a format ideal for encompassing the sweep of these modern cities, and where the breadth of the scene always far exceeded the natural field of vision, so that the eye was unable to take it in from a single viewpoint.

The exhibition at Short's Observatory typifies the nineteenth-century fascination with the scope and limits of visuality. Traditionally, natural theology had valorized the eye as the ideal optical instrument, designed by God, for appreciating the divinely created beauties of the world. However, the multiple attractions at Short's present a series of technological devices that, in different ways, augment and supersede the ability of the eye. They signified a vastly enlarged visual field, created by the desire to be able to picture, and consequently observe, every detail of the physical environment. The seeming dominance of the material world, and thus of a version of realism based on exteriority, was established by the expansion of what could be visualized.

Short's Observatory did not include photography, the new imaging technology that was the culmination of the desire to record objectively every minute and fleeting detail. Its public advent was marked by Louis Daguerre's and Henry Fox Talbot's announcements of their respective daguerreotype and calotype processes in 1839 (the calotype was a negative/positive process, whereas in the daguerreotype the image was captured directly on a chemically prepared surface of polished metal). Ongoing

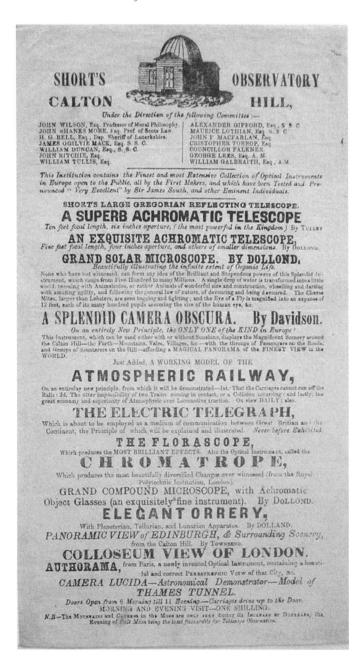

Figure 12.1 Handbill for Short's Observatory, Calton Hill, Edinburgh, c. 1850.

improvements in photography meant that more and more aspects of the world were pictured, whether it was hitherto unseen geographical locations or the smallest inhabitants of the natural environment. Writing in 1857, Elizabeth Eastlake declared that the camera 'literally does no more than wink his eye, tracing in that moment, with a detail and precision beyond all human power, the glory of the heavens, the wonders of the deep, the fall, not of the avalanche, but of the apple, the most fleeting smile of the babe, and the most vehement action of the man'.[6] By the late 1870s, when Eadward Muybridge managed to take a series of instantaneous photographs showing the movement of a galloping horse, even the smallest moments in time could be captured and visualized. X-rays, perfected by Wilhelm Conrad Röntgen in 1895, emerged out of a similar desire in that they penetrated the seemingly solid boundary of the skin to make even previously unseen phenomena visible, and consequently knowable.

When the Lumière brothers gave their first commercial cinematograph show in December 1895, it was only the latest technological embodiment of the desire to reproduce visually every aspect of the external world. Revealingly, when the future film-maker Georges Méliès saw the Lumières' film, *Le repas de bébé* (1895), what struck him was not so much the movement of the Lumière family at dinner, but instead the incidental detail of the rustling leaves of the trees in the background.[7] This fascination with the objective recording of the physical world, and correspondingly with the contingent, everyday particularity of detail, characterized the impact of new visual technologies, and was fundamental to their pervasive influence upon the dominant conception of literary realism. Critics of the period were themselves highly sensitive to the convergence between this modern visuality and literary realism, as is exemplified by one response to the advent of the cinematograph:

> Literature, too, has ever hankered unconsciously after the Cinématograph. Is not Zola the M. Lumière of his art? And might not the sight of a Cinématograph have saved the realist from a wilderness of lost endeavour? As the toy registers every movement without any expressed relation to its fellow, so the old and fearless realist believed in the equal value of all facts. He collected information in the spirit of the swiftly moving camera, or of the statistician. Nothing came amiss to him, because he considered nothing of supreme importance.[8]

The commentary is more pessimistic than most in its teleological presumption that literature had been slavishly seeking to achieve the totalized looking and recording that had been realized by the cinematograph; and that its omniscient gaze made redundant the previous efforts of realist writers. Nonetheless, it exemplifies the way new visual media provided models for literary realism, albeit that realism is here represented by the uncompromising naturalism pioneered by Émile Zola, which only emerged as a literary movement in the 1880s, and which was both an extension and a break from mid-century versions of realism.

An unintended consequence of the technological visualization of the physical world was, paradoxically, to foreground subjective aspects of perception. The greater the seeming precision and objectivity of photography, for example, the more it called attention to the limits of human physiology. Significantly, the popularity of photography was almost matched by the enormous success of optical devices like the kaleidoscope and the stereoscope. The appeal of these philosophical toys owed much to the way they demonstrated to the user that the self actively produced its own sense of being-in-the-world. Several critics, most notably Jonathan Crary, have argued that the growth of interest in physiological optics in the 1820s and 1830s, and concomitant devices such as the stereoscope and the phenakistoscope, challenged the positivism of enlightenment conceptions of a stable, transparently perceived, external, physical world.[9]

The phenakistoscope, for example, was an early moving-image device announced in 1832 by Belgian scientist Joseph Plateau. It was the product of a number of experiments on persistence-of-vision and retinal after-images, which were undertaken by Plateau and other scientific luminaries such as Michael Faraday and Peter Mark Roget. The phenakistoscope created the illusion of a moving image that, through its deceptive quality, demonstrated the contingency of human perception. The device's effect was produced through a series of drawn images that were experienced as animated when viewed through slits in a revolving disc. The stereoscope, which was also developed in the early 1830s, similarly called attention to the limits of perception. The device was initially designed by Charles Wheatstone to demonstrate that the perception of objects in three-dimensional space was caused by the uniting of dissimilar pictures seen by left and right eyes. In so doing, it demonstrated the subjective role of the mind in depth perception, and helped to explain why humans could often be deceived by optical illusions. As a device, the stereoscope created an immersive 3-D image that was wholly virtual in that it had no physical referent, yet its phenomenal realism was nonetheless deeply effective. The motto of the London Stereoscopic Company was 'Seems Madam, NAY IT IS!'; while the *Leisure Hour* rapturously declared that the stereoscope 'transports you to the spot. You are not sensible of a picture – do not think of it as a picture; the illusion is complete, and the mind as well as the eye, dwells on the actual scene.'[10] It is notable though that, while the stereoscope was pioneered in the 1830s, it only achieved commercial popularity in the 1850s, when photography was used to produce large numbers of stereographs for the device. The device's

Figure 12.2 Foldout stereoscope, *c.* 1860.

realism was thus an amalgamation of objective and subjective modes of visuality, indicative of the way that these two paradigms intermingled as much as they opposed each other (figure 12.2).

New forms of attention that emphasized the phenomenology of perception were also created by the excess of visual stimuli, from railways to department stores, felt to characterize modern living. In *Human, All Too Human* (1878), Friederick Nietzsche wrote that 'With the tremendous acceleration of life mind and eye have become accustomed to seeing and judging partially or inaccurately, and everyone is like the traveller who gets to know a land and its people from a railway carriage.'[11] The way of life dominated by industrialization, steam and perpetual motion produced two parallel effects, the adaptation of the human eye to the transient *and* the transformation of the observer into a transient figure, unable ever to achieve a fixed perspective. Nietzsche's comment exemplifies the way that new modes of visuality frequently acted as metonyms for the more fragmented nature of modern perception itself.

Given the proliferation of visual technologies and the stress on the subjectivity of perception, the problem of observing and perceiving correctly became not only a concern in itself, but a trope for expressing a range of political and social anxieties. In *Past and Present* (1839), Thomas Carlyle made the breakdown of a stable visual field both cause and symptom of the 'Condition of England' question. In so doing, he prefigures Marx and Engels, who, in *The German Ideology* (1845), famously described the work of ideology as akin to that of a camera obscura, in which everything appeared upside-down.[12] *Past and Present* uses the example of Midas, whose touch turned everything to gold, to critique the dominance of materialism, in both a commercial and a philosophical sense, because it privileged matter over the ideal, visible surface over depth:

> The secret of gold Midas, which he with his long ears never could discover, was, That he had offended the Supreme Powers; – that he has parted company with the eternal inner Facts of the Universe, and followed the transient outer Appearances thereof; and so was arrived *here*. Properly it is the secret of all unhappy men and unhappy nations ... Foolish men mistake transitory semblance for eternal fact, and go astray more and more.[13]

Carlyle resists the drive towards a visuality based wholly on external appearance by arguing that the unseen – the realm of the transcendental 'inner Facts of the Universe' – is more powerful than the seen. It is matter itself that is transient and spectral. His belief that the symbolic is always immanent within the material, and that realism involves more than visible surface, is part of an important alternative strand of visuality in Victorian literature and culture. It is evident, for example, in Pre-Raphaelite painting as well as in the symbolism found in some of Dickens's major novels: the fog in *Bleak House* (1853), the prison in *Little Dorrit* (1857).

Writers and critics freely used optical and pictorial tropes to refer to *both* the objective recording of concrete detail and the more subjective, internal realism of the imagination. George Eliot, for example, neatly encapsulates this duality in the famous chapter 17 of *Adam Bede* (1859), 'In which the Story Pauses a Little', in which she defends her realism against those critics who would prefer more idealized characters:

> Certainly I could, my fair critic, if I were a clever novelist, not obliged to creep servilely after nature and fact, but able to represent things as they never have been and never will be. Then, of course, my characters would be entirely my own choosing, and I could select the most unexceptionable type of clergyman, and put my own admirable opinions into his mouth on all occasions. But you must have perceived long ago that I have no such lofty vocation, and that I aspire to give no more than a faithful account of men and things as they have mirrored themselves in my mind. The mirror is doubtless defective; the outlines will sometimes be disturbed; the reflection faint or confused; but

I feel as much bound to tell you, as precisely as I can, what reflection is, as if I were in the witness-box narrating my experience on oath.[14]

Eliot's invocation of her realist practice as a form of mirroring suggests a transparent reflection of the external world, in all its flaws. Conversely, she fully acknowledges that the mirror can never be a wholly faithful reflection in that it is mediated through her imagination. For all Eliot's striving for her fiction to be a visualization of reality, the very exposition of her artistic methods within the narrative serves to break the illusion of mimesis. Literary appropriations from the visual arts were double-edged in that while they were often used to promote different versions of realism, the very act of borrowing called attention to its constructed nature.

Eliot's work as both novelist and reviewer also typifies the creative crossover between literature and painting. Her articles for the periodical press, carried out before she undertook a career as a novelist, demonstrate that her conception of realism was heavily indebted to her interest in the visual arts. In Eliot's review of the third volume of John Ruskin's *Modern Painters* for the *Westminster Review* she claimed, 'The truth of infinite value that he teaches is *realism* – the doctrine that all truth and beauty are to be attained by a humble and faithful study of nature.'[15] Her own literary criticism, like that of so many of her contemporaries, was saturated with pictorial rhetoric. Thus, in an 1857 review of Holme Lee [Harriet Parr]'s popular novel *Kathie Brand* (1856), Lee was accused of failing to realize her scenes vividly: 'the author writes about them, does not paint them … An artist would have suffered his imagination to dwell on such scenes until, aided by his knowledge, direct or indirect, would describe as if he saw them and we should read as if we saw them too.'[16] Eliot's judgement reflects the way pictorialism functioned as a dominant critical standard, but also the fact that, because there was no specialized language of literary criticism, critics often used terms borrowed from painting.

Eliot carried the privileging of pictorial effect into her fiction, most notably in chapter 17 of *Adam Bede*, wherein she analogized her fictional practice with the realism of Dutch painting: 'It is for this rare, precious quality of truthfulness that I delight in many Dutch paintings, which lofty minded people despise.' In so doing, she turned away from the idealism of Italian Renaissance and German Romantic painting, 'from cloud-born angels, from prophets, sybils, and heroic warriors'.[17] The comparison between genre painting and the novel was an oft-made one, seeking to emphasize not only its pictorialism but, as Eliot noted of Dutch painting, its attention to the seemingly unimportant forms of material and physical detail, 'those homes with their tin pans, their brown pitchers, their rough curs, and their clusters of onions'.[18]

Eliot's interest in making meaning out of the most contingent visual detail is part of a broader nineteenth-century epistemology. In keeping with the new technologies of image-making, the drive for realism was motivated by a belief that visuality was key to making the world observable, and thus controllable. Peter Brooks is one of many critics who have noted that nineteenth-century realism treats seeing as equivalent to knowing:

> The dominant nineteenth-century tradition, realism, insistently makes the visual the master relation of the world, for the very premise of realism is that one cannot understand human beings outside the context of the things that surround them, and knowing these things is a matter of viewing them, detailing them, and describing the concrete milieux in which men and women enact their destinies. To know, in realism, is to see, and to represent is to describe.[19]

This epistemology underpins the popularity of nineteenth-century pseudo-sciences such as physiognomy and phrenology, which were based on the assumption that an individual's character could be classified by reading the surface of the body. Soon after its advent, photography was also used by psychologists to try and identify certain 'types', particularly criminals and the insane. In the 1870s, the polymath scientist Francis Galton went so far as to develop a method of classifying criminal 'types' through the production of a composite photograph made up of eight super-imposed images of the sitter, which supposedly sloughed away individualistic features to reveal their essential character.

The correlation between visuality and knowledge is probably most fully embodied in literature by detective fiction, and Sherlock Holmes in particular. Holmes's mastery of the visible world also brings him control over it. Watson refers to Holmes as 'the most perfect reasoning and observing machine that the world has ever seen'.[20] Holmes's attention to the most inconsequential detail through close observation makes the world comprehensible. As Holmes solves even the most inscrutable cases put before him, Watson, as well as the reader, is taught to understand the world through its visual signs. Holmes's famous exposition of his method is that 'By a man's finger nails, by his coat-sleeve, by his boots, by the callosities of his forefinger and thumb, by his expression, by his shirt-cuffs – by each of these thing a man's calling is revealed.'[21] Ronald Thomas has succinctly noted that Holmes, like the camera and other nineteenth-century observing machines, makes visible what is invisible to all those around him.[22]

It was not only novelists who drew inspiration from the visual arts. In addition to a large body of ekphrastic poems, poets also engaged with the way that devotion to the material world often seemed to accentuate the antipathy between realism and the ideal. Robert Browning's dramatic monologue 'Fra Lippo Lippi' (1855) uses the career of a Florentine painter, Lippo Lippi (1406–69) to work through the tension between idealism and realism, which, as with Carlyle, was translated in terms of the relationship between the seen and unseen. (The speakers of Browning's dramatic monologues include several painters and sculptors.) Browning's Lippi is an earthly Florentine monk, a street urchin who was taken in by the Carmelite monastery as a child and trained as a painter. Lippi's method derives from the observational skills learnt while begging in the streets; he consequently offends the Prior by his realistic painting on the wall of his church. Accurately capturing the less than righteous motivations of those who come to worship, Lippi is condemned by the church hierarchy because they view such realism as merely documenting visual surfaces. As with Eliot's praise of Dutch genre painting, they also associate it with the lowness of everyday life:

> Face, arms, legs and bodies like the true,
> As much as pea and pea! it's devil's game!
> Your business is not to catch men with show,
> With homage to the perishable clay,
> But lift them over it, ignore it all,
> Make them forget there's such a thing as flesh.
> Your business is to paint the souls of men–
> Man's soul, and it's a fire, smoke … no, it's not.
> It's vapour done up like a new born babe –
> (In that shape when you die it leaves your mouth)
> Its … well, what matters talking, it's the soul![23]

Lippi's painting fascinates worshippers and monks alike; however, he is told that his realism pays too much attention to the materiality of men's bodies. Yet, for Lippi, there is no way to the ideal except through the material: how can he paint a soul he asks ironically? It is through the sensuous visual surfaces of his painting – the 'wonder at lines, colours, and what not' – that he encourages appreciation of God's work. Lippi thus attempts to deconstruct the dominant antithesis between idealism and materialism.

In keeping with the dominant characterization of literary realism, pictorial and optical tropes were frequently used as figures for imaginatively positioning the reader as either a spectator or an observer. Pierce Egan's enormously successful *Life in London* (1821) claimed to provide a camera obscura view of the fast haunts of London. Reading the text was made analogous to viewing a camera obscura, primarily because it offered a detached, yet intimately voyeuristic, glimpse of the London underworld:

> The author, in consequence, has chosen for his readers a *Camera Obscura* view of London, not only from its safety, but because it is so *snug*, and also possesses the invaluable advantage of SEEING and not being *seen*. The author of the *Devil upon two Sticks*, it appears, preferred taking a *flight* over the houses for his remarks and views of society; but if I had adopted that mode of travelling, and perchance had fallen to the ground, an hospital might have been the reward of my presumption.[24]

Life in London uses the camera obscura to signify a close-up realism which yet keeps the reader at a safe distance. Egan proposes his method as an advance upon the realism of Alain René Le Sage's *Le Diable boiteux* (1707), translated as *The Devil upon Two Sticks* (1708). In Le Sage's novel, the devil Asmodeus reveals the life of Madrid by lifting the roofs off all the houses. In contrast to this lofty approach, Egan's narrative goes down to street level in order to reveal the secrets of London life.

Whereas Egan uses an optical device to materialize the position of his readers, Dickens uses one to stand for the way his novels functioned as popular entertainments. Nowhere is this more evident than at the end of *The Old Curiosity Shop* (1841), where Dickens uses the moving panorama as a figure for both the imaginative journey of his readers and the novel's status as a visual show. At the beginning of the final chapter, the narrator declares that 'The magic reel, which, rolling on before, has led the chronicler thus far, now slackens in its pace, and stops. It lies before the goal; the pursuit is at an end.'[25] The reader's passage through the novel, the 'magic reel', is equated with viewing a moving panorama, the dominant exhibition practice for panoramas from the 1820s. Dickens's use of the moving panorama clearly positions him as lecturer-cum-showman, whose role is to explain the moving scene passing before his readers. The pun on the magic real/reel also stresses that the pictorial scenes experienced by his readers took place as much within their imagination as on the pages of the text.

In contrast to most literary pictorialism, references to optical devices in Victorian literature usually serve to emphasize the active role of the mind's eye. Optical devices often figured the working of imagination and memory. In *Middlemarch* (1872) and *Adam Bede*, for example, Eliot uses the diorama as a figure to suggest the way individuals could be captivated by the shifting scenes of memory. When a sunny evening sets off involuntary memories in Bulstrode of his happy youth, in contrast to his present fallen status, Eliot declares that 'The mind has as many moods as the temper, and shifts its scenery like a diorama.'[26] A similar preoccupation with mental vision breaking into the external world is evident at the beginning of Thomas Hardy's *Jude the Obscure* (1895), in the moment prior to Jude's first fateful encounter with Arabella. Such are Jude's dreams of a glittering academic future at Christminster that Hardy notes 'he was now standing quite still, looking at the ground as though the future were thrown thereon by a magic lantern'.[27] This reverie is immediately interrupted by the 'soft cold substance' of the pig's penis thrown by Arabella.

Unsurprisingly, given that they questioned the boundary between the seen and the unseen, inner vision and physical reality, optical tropes were particularly prominent in Gothic literature. Gothic promoted a visuality – populated by ghosts, spirits, dreams and the unconscious – which was much more unstable than that of the stolidly material. In Edgar Allan Poe's 'The Fall of the House of Usher' (1839), the narrator learns that his friend Roderick Usher is suffering from 'phantasmagoric conceptions'.[28] The Gothic tales of Sheridan Le Fanu are similarly littered with optical tropes that stand for an excessive reverie of thought. In one story, two medical students take lodgings at an old, gloomy, untenanted house. One of them is visited at night by a recurring vision of a portrait of an old man that seemed 'mysteriously glued to the window frame'.[29] The narrator describes the 'exquisite anguish and profound impressions of unearthly horror, with which this strange phantasmagoria was associated'.[30] The phantasmagoria was an extremely popular magic lantern ghost show in which the projected image appeared as if from nowhere among the audience. Le Fanu's allusion emphasizes the way that the student's experience falls between dream and reality.

The convergence between literature and visual media was, however, as deeply embedded in its material presentation as it was in textual description. Illustration in particular played a key role in the appeal of a significant proportion of nineteenth-century novels, periodicals and, in a few notable examples, collections of poetry. Writing of W. H. Ainsworth's *Jack Sheppard* (1839), Thackeray asked, what does the reader remember? 'George Cruikshank's pictures – always George Cruikshank's pictures.'[31] Artists did much more than slavishly 'illustrate' scenes from a text: the translation from verbal to visual was a creative process whereby, at its best, each provided a standpoint on the other. When Aubrey Beardsley's publishers sent him page proofs of his 1896 edition of Alexander Pope's *The Rape of the Lock* (1712), he stressed the supplemental meaning provided by his drawings by crossing out the word 'illustrated' on the title page and replacing it with 'embroidered with nine drawings by Aubrey Beardsley'.[32]

Robert Patten has argued that a more sophisticated notion of what illustration does can be recovered through its etymological derivation from the Latin *illustrare*, which suggests a different function from the Greek *mimesis*: '*Illustrare* performs three kinds of verbal work: it can illuminate, enlighten, light up; it can expound, elucidate (bring light out), even embellish; it can set off, render famous or illustrious (luminous, shining).'[33] Illustration could expand on the meaning of a particular scene; it could emphasize its importance; and, crucially, it could add meaning through picturing elements that were not in the text. The prevalence of illustration in Victorian literature replicates the intra-textual fascination with visuality in that it created an overall reading experience that was a combination of visual and verbal.

A proliferation of popular illustrated publications first came to the fore during the 1830s and 1840s, facilitated by a revival in wood-engraving and a tremendous overall expansion in the market for print media. Nowhere is the harnessing of graphic media to the burgeoning market for fiction at the beginning of the Victorian period better exemplified than in the launching of Dickens's career. Famously, his initial commission for what would become his first novel, *The Pickwick Papers* (1836–7), was to write the letterpress to accompany etchings by the more established sporting and comic artist Robert Seymour. Dickens was far from content with being a junior partner, desiring that Seymour illustrate his text rather than vice-versa. In circumstances not helped by Dickens's peremptory treatment, Seymour committed suicide after the second monthly issue. The amount of text was thence doubled, from sixteen pages to thirty-two, while the number of etchings was reduced from four to two.

The production of illustrated fiction was stimulated by, and indeed was part of, a more general growth of illustrated periodicals and newspapers. The 1820s saw the commencement of twopenny illustrated miscellanies such as the *Portfolio* (1823–5) and the *Mirror of Literature, Amusement and Instruction* (1822–47). These were the precursors to two illustrated 'improving' journals, the *Penny Magazine* (1832–45) and the *Saturday Magazine* (1832–45), whose advent was a landmark in the production of cheap periodicals for a newly literate working-class readership. The high-quality illustrations of these inexpensive journals were an important element of their remarkable success.

At the genteel end of the literary market were the annuals, keepsakes and books of beauty. These were gorgeously ornate illustrated publications produced in great numbers for the Christmas season between the mid-1820s and the mid-1840s. They combined elegantly finished steel-plate engravings with verse from luminaries such as Sir Walter Scott, Robert

Southey and, on one occasion, an aged William Wordsworth. Although often derided for their vapid excess of commodified sentimentality, they provided an important publishing outlet for women poets such as Laetitia Landon and Felicia Hemans. In *Middlemarch*, Rosamund is given the latest *Keepsake*, 'the gorgeous watered-silk publication which marked modern progress at the time', by an admirer, Ned Plymdale, so that they could be looking together over 'the ladies and gentleman with shiny copper-plate cheeks and copper-plate smiles, and pointing to comic verses and sentimental stories as interesting'.[34] Elsewhere, the fashion for all things 'pictorial' during the 1830s and 1840s is exemplified by the efforts of Charles Knight, publisher of the *Penny Magazine*, in his multi-volume works, the *Pictorial Shakespeare* (1838–41), *Pictorial History of England* (1837–44) and *Pictorial Bible* (1836–8). Contemporary life also received its own weekly visual chronicle with the advent of the *Illustrated London News* in May 1842, the first newspaper to be explicitly devoted to pictorial journalism. Its opening address celebrated the marriage of visual and verbal created by its engravings: 'Art – as now fostered, and redundant in the peculiar and facile department of wood engraving – has, in fact, become the bride of literature.'[35]

The large number of illustrated publications was very much part of the new mode of nineteenth-century visuality; they seemed to presage a world of instant and immediate images. Writing in the unillustrated *Blackwood's Magazine* in 1844, the silver fork novelist Catherine Gore described the excitement caused by the rapid growth of illustrated novels and newspapers:

> The pictorial printing-press is now your only wear! Everything is communicated by delineation. We are not *told*, but *shown* how the world is wagging. The magazines sketch us a lively article, the newspapers vignette us, step by step, a royal tour. The beauties of Shakespeare are imprinted on the minds of a rising generation, in woodcuts; and the poetry of Byron engraven in their hearts, by means of the graver. Not a boy in his teens has read a line of Don Quixote or Gil Blas, though all have their adventures by heart.[36]

Gore argued that the new world of images was compelled by the speed of modern life; there was no longer enough time to read a newspaper or a novel, only to take in latest narratives – whether fact or fiction – in graphic form. She went so far as to predict that the world of letters would be replaced by the world of emblems.

The most prominent journal format to take advantage of the new potential of illustration was the penny miscellany that emerged in the 1840s: most of them used an eye-catching engraving to head up their weekly serial fiction. As Wilkie Collins noted in an 1858 article on the spread of mass-market journals, 'Wherever the speculative daring of one man could open a shop ... the unbound picture quarto instantly entered, set itself up obtrusively in the window, and insisted on being looked at by everybody' (figure 12.3).[37] Examples of best-selling penny fiction magazines include the *Family Herald* (1842–1940), the *London Journal* (1845–1928), *Reynolds's Miscellany* (1847–69) and *Cassell's Illustrated Family Paper* (1853–67). The circulation of these periodicals was enormous; in 1852–3, the weekly circulation of the *London Journal* was over 500,000; in comparison, Dickens's *Bleak House*, issued as a monthly serial from March 1852 to September 1853, only averaged sales of around 34,000 per issue.

Illustration was believed to play a particularly important role in the appeal of cheap journals and serial fiction because it attracted semi-literate readers. One costermonger interviewed by Henry Mayhew about his reading habits for *London Labour and the London Poor* (1861) declared that his fellow street-folk were 'very fond of illustrations. I have known a man, who couldn't read, buy a periodical what had an illustration, a little out of the common way perhaps, just that he might learn from someone, who *could* read, what it was all about.'[38] However, the same immediacy of appeal that encouraged engravings to be used by improving journals like the *Penny Magazine* also led to anxieties over the corrupting influence of sensationalist illustrations in penny-issue serial fiction and journals. An illustration from G. W. M. Reynolds's long-running serial *The Mysteries of London* (1844–8) exemplifies the type of engraving that aroused concern. Portraying the strangulation of her maid by Lady Ravensworth and the Resurrection Man, a grave-robber by the name of Anthony Tidkins, it vividly captures the violence of the murder and the horror of the victim in her last moments (figure 12.4).

The association of visuality with commodification and graphic spectacle was accentuated when advances in printing meant that colourful illustrations began to appear on the front of cheap books. The famous 'yellowback' books emerged in the mid-1850s; they were so-called because they were bound using glazed yellow paper laid over boards, with a striking picture on the front 'calculated to ensnare the eye of the passing traveler' (figure 12.5).[39] However, while the yellowback is another example of a cheap illustrated format, it was precisely such industrialization of art that motivated John Ruskin to launch a stinging critique of popular illustration in *Ariadne Florentina* (1876). Denouncing engravings from the *Cornhill Magazine* and *Barnaby Rudge*, he argued that they typified the way the entire illustrative art industry was 'enslaved to the ghastly service of catching the last gleams in the glued eyes of the daily more bestial English mob, – railroad born and bred, which drags itself about the black world under its

THE

LONDON JOURNAL:

And Weekly Record of Literature, Science, and Art.

No. 412.—Vol. XVI. FOR THE WEEK ENDING JANUARY 15, 1853. [Price One Penny.

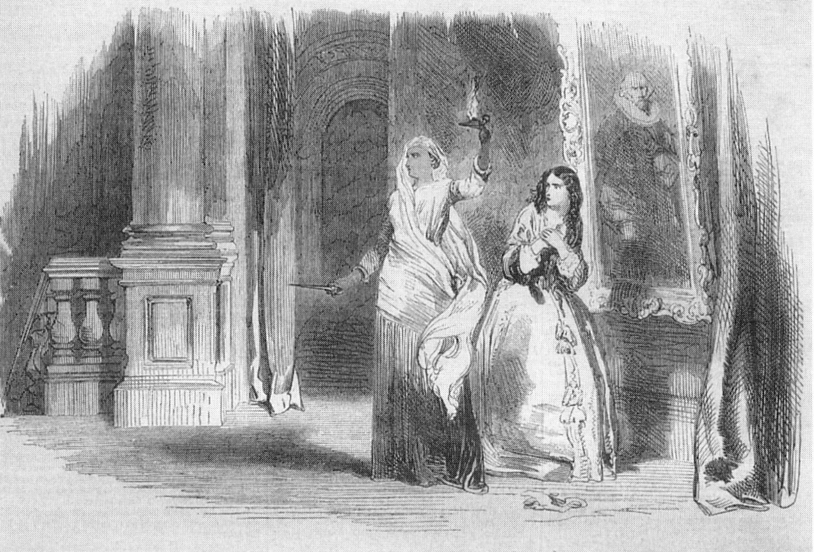

[ELLEN DE VERE AND THE AYAH IN THE PICTURE GALLERY.]

THE WILL AND THE WAY.

BY THE AUTHOR OF

THE JESUIT," "THE PRELATE," "MINNIGREY," ETC.

CHAPTER XL.

The strongest resolutions oft are wrung
From the heart's weakness; passion's voice
Drowning weak conscience's whisperings.

Old Play.

Although still weak, and suffering from his wound, Meeran Hafaz no longer kept his couch—despite the remonstrances of his medical attendants and the entreaties of the Khan, he persisted in leaving it: the physical pain he endured was nothing weighed in the scale against the mental torture to which his forced inactivity had condemned him. With the young Indian, life was action; he was a being of impulse—a creature to whom excitement and emotion were as necessary as the fulcrum to the lever, or the main-spring to the watch; his mental enjoyments proceeded rather from that quick sensibility which admires the beautiful in art and nature, than the intellectual analysis and appreciation of it. Thus, without being a sensualist in taste, he was a materialist: fine as the line of demarcation is, it is perfectly possible to draw it.

The first feeling of consolation he experienced since the morning of the duel, was from the visit of the ayah, who came to inform him that his rival had actually departed on his journey to Italy. The intelligence appeared to afford him mingled satisfaction and regret: satisfaction, that he was no longer basking in the light of Ellen's beauty, breathing his heart's young hope, impassioned vows, into her willing ear—rivating yet closer the delicious bonds which knit them like one soul together; regret, that he had escaped him—for on his couch of agony—compared to which Ixion's wheel must have been a bed of roses—he had sworn a fearful oath to have the life of Henry Ashton.

"'Tis well!" he said, a faint smile illuminating his pale features, like a fading sunbeam resting on a corse. "I can breathe more freely now I know that seas divide them! Never, never, must they meet again!"

Zara—who, as usual, had seated herself upon the ground—gazed for an instant upon her foster-son with a cold, mocking expression of contempt.

"Seas divide them!" she repeated; "resolution, long ere this, would have placed a grave between your rival and yourself! This land of gloom and shadows has broken the temper of your soul, Meeran, or you would never prate of seas—they may be crossed! The grave," she continued, lowering her voice, "is narrower than the sea—its depths are less profound—*but they are impassable!* When before did one of your race receive an insult, and let the insulter live?"

The countenance of Meeran became darkly shadowed: the words of the temptress had roused all that was evil in his nature, and recalled the scene of his humiliation so vividly before him, that again he saw the flashing eye of his insulting rival, the curl of his scornful lip, as, in the presence of Ellen and her friends, he crushed his pride and trampled on his pretensions, by reminding him of the charity extended by the Ashtons to his father.

"He *shall* die!" he muttered between his clenched teeth; "but not yet—not yet! It would be envy, not revenge, to slay him in his dream of happiness, his trusting confidence in the bright future; for what is death?—a momentary pang—oblivion—rest! No," he added, "he must *awaken* first—when, one by one, I have stripped life of its illusions—when I have wrung his heart till the strained nerves are dead to every sense of agony—when hope and feeling are alike extinct—then, and not till then, will I place my heel upon his neck, and crush the reptile! I can no longer torture—I must humble ere I destroy!"

"Words!" replied the ayah, "words! Long ere this I had mixed for him the draught, which in our own land rids love and ambition of their rival—hate, of its victim—but for the fear that Ellen's lips might taste it!"

It had frequently been in the power of the speaker to perpetrate the crime she meditated; for since her arrival at the abbey she had daily made coffee for the drawing-room: her foster-child preferred it after the manner of the East, and Zara had prepared it for her from childhood.

"Thank heaven," exclaimed Meeran, whose very heart trembled at the thought of risk to Ellen, "you did not attempt it!"

Their further conversation was interrupted by the Khan, who came to announce the visit of the warrener to his young charge: there was a degree of sadness in the tone in which the old man spoke to him—for he felt that confidence no longer existed between them, and that the estrangement was becoming wider every hour.

"Admit him!" exclaimed Meeran, impatiently; and the next moment, Will Sideler, who had followed closely on the steps of his conductor, entered the apartment, which the renegade quitted: he did not wish to be directed a second time to wait in the ante-chamber, under the insulting pretext of preventing intrusion.

"Well," demanded his employer, impatiently, "have you succeeded?"

"I had succeeded," replied the ruffian, "and the packet was safe in my possession, when ——"

"Pshaw!" interrupted Meeran—who, in his contempt for the sordidness of the instrument he descended to employ, imagined that the warrener was merely trying to extort more gold from him, by some well fabricated tale—"I am no niggard, to drive a huckster's bargain with a thing like thee! Name thy price, man, and give me the packet!"

Figure 12.3 'Ellen De Vere and the Ayah in the Picture Gallery', *The London Journal: A Weekly Record of Literature, Science and Art*, 16 (15 January 1853), p. 289.

Figure 12.4 [Murder of her Maid, Lydia, by Lady Ravensworth and the Resurrection Man], in
G. W. M. Reynolds, *The Mysteries of London*, vol. II (London: John Dicks, 1867), p. 273.

breadth ... incapable of reading, of hearing, of thinking, of looking'.[40]
Revealingly, Ruskin links the predominance of grotesque and lurid scenes
in popular illustration with the transient mode of modern looking fashioned
by the railway.

For those novelists whose work sought to utilize the potential of illustration, the synthesis between visual and verbal was achieved in several different ways. Dickens, for example, paid intense supervisory attention to the
design of the illustrations for his works, often providing – whether the artist
desired it or not – detailed instructions on the subject and composition, as
well as suggestions for improvement. Whereas Dickens had to rely on

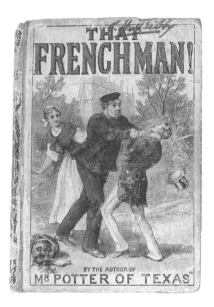

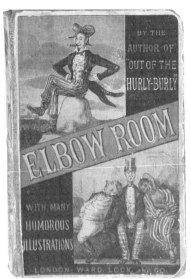
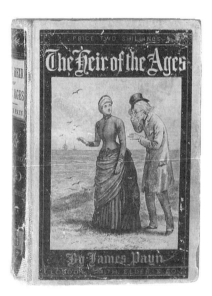

Figure 12.5 A selection of 'Yellowback' railway novels. Archibald Clavering Gunter, *That Frenchman!* (London: George Routledge and Sons, 1889); Mary Elizabeth Braddon, *One Life – One Love* (London: Simpkin, Marshall, Hamilton, Kent & Co., 1891); Max Adeler, *Elbow-Room: A Novel without A Plot* (London: Ward, Lock and Co., 1876); James Payn, *The Heir of the Ages* (London: Smith, Elder, 1887).

Figure 12.6 Illuminated letter, William Makepeace Thackeray, *Vanity Fair*
(London: Smith Elder, 1879), p. 121.

constant monitoring to achieve the marriage of text and illustration he
desired, Thackeray did not face such difficulties in that he, uniquely, produced his own illustrations for *Vanity Fair* (1847–8), *Pendennis* (1849–50)
and *The Virginians* (1857–9). Previously, he had been taught etching by
Cruikshank and had lived as a bohemian art student in Paris in the years
1833–5. Thackeray's role as both writer and artist means that his novels are
notable for their integration of word and image. The subtitle of *Vanity Fair*
is 'Pen and Pencil Sketches of English Society', and he uses the illustrations
to elaborate the textual narrative. In one well-known illustration, 'Becky's
Second Appearance in the Character of Clytemnestra', he suggests Becky's
status as a murderess, a detail only hinted at in the text. Thackeray's artistic
work includes not only full-page illustrations but illuminated capitals at the
opening of chapters, which satirically elucidate themes in the narrative.
Chapter 13, for example, begins with a vignette of the self-obsessed George
Osborne admiring himself in a mirror, with the illuminated capital – a large
egotistical 'I' – cleverly constituting the reflected image (figure 12.6).

   In contrast to Thackeray and Dickens, George Eliot was more sceptical of
the creative potential of illustrations, believing that they formed a kind of
subservient preface to the text. The only text of Eliot's initially published
with illustrations was *Romola* (1862–3), and it is possible to see her reluctance as stemming from a belief that they would compromise the way her

pictorialism was created by linguistic means alone. In a letter to Frederic Leighton in September 1862, who was being paid handsomely to illustrate the serial publication of *Romola* in the newly launched *Cornhill Magazine*, Eliot set out her concern that the literary text necessarily played only a small role in the artist's visual interpretation:

> I am quite convinced that the illustrations can only form a sort of overture to the text. The artist who uses the pencil must otherwise be tormented to misery by the deficiencies or requirements of the one who uses the pen, and the writer, on the other, must die of impossible expectations.[41]

For Eliot, the relationship between illustrator and writer was inevitably one of mutual disappointment in that the artist was always bound by the demands of the novelist, while the novelist was invariably disappointed because the engravings would never reproduce their own mental picture of the text.

The translation from verbal to visual that worried Eliot was precisely the feature that fascinated the Pre-Raphaelites. The relationship between painting and poetry was integral to this movement, the most obvious example being the number of Pre-Raphaelite paintings based on literary sources, such as Holman Hunt's *The Eve of St Agnes* (1847–57) and *The Lady of Shalott* (1886–1905), and John Everett Millais's *Ophelia* (1851) and *Mariana* (1851). The Pre-Raphaelite fascination with the creative dynamic between visual and verbal is equally evident in the illustrative work they carried out, mostly for collections of poetry and for the popular periodicals *Once a Week* (1859–80), *Good Words* (1860–96) and the *Cornhill Magazine* (1860–1939). Holman Hunt and Edward Burne-Jones executed designs for *Once a Week*, while Millais's work included illustrating Trollope's *Framley Parsonage* for the *Cornhill Magazine*.

The Moxon Tennyson (1857), an edition illustrated by Millais, Holman Hunt and Dante Gabriel Rossetti among others, typifies the Pre-Raphaelite interest in integrating text and image in a creative partnership. In a letter to William Allingham in January 1855, Dante Gabriel Rossetti declared that, out of the corpus of Tennyson's work, he would attempt designs for the 'Vision of Sin' and 'Palace of Art' because they were 'those where one can allegorize on one's own hook on the subject of the poem, without killing, for oneself and everyone, a distinct idea of the poet's. This, I fancy, is *always* the upshot of illustrated editions.'[42] For Rossetti, a too literal rendering of the text would deny both artist and reader the counterpoint created by the translation from visual and verbal.

Hunt's design to accompany 'The Lady of Shalott' in the Moxon Tennyson portrays an extended moment when Lancelot flashes into the mirror and

Figure 12.7 Holman Hunt, 'The Lady of Shalott', *Poems* (1857; London: Edward Moxon, 1860), p. 67.

the Lady surrenders herself to the curse that she believes will come upon her when she looks directly at the world (figure 12.7). The threads of her weaving fly up wildly, snake-like, seeming to imprison her. The unravelling web is paralleled by the sensuous unloosing of her hair, which flows unchecked across, and frames, the top of the scene. Art seemingly has to be given up for sexual desire, which in turn leads to death, in a poem which embodies the way that the power of looking, and by extension access to visuality itself, was highly gendered (the Lady, whose view of the outside world is mediated through the mirror, is 'half sick of shadows'). Tennyson's poem states that, immediately prior to the cracking of the mirror:

> She left the web, she left the loom,
> She made three paces thro' the room,
> She saw the water-lily bloom:
> She saw the helmet and the plume,
> She looked down to Camelot.

Yet Hunt's design inevitably digresses in that his static illustration cannot encompass the temporal narrative of the poem. In his illustration, the Lady stares down into space rather than towards Camelot, her eyes seemingly white and pupil-less, while Lancelot rides away with his back towards the tower. The lack of any exchange of gaze emphasizes the one-sided nature of their encounter.

The Pre-Raphaelite interest in the synthesis between painting and poetry is nevertheless most fully explored by the 'double' works of art of Dante Gabriel Rossetti, in which painting and poems were produced together as an interlinked whole. The initials 'PRB' appeared for the first time at the Hyde Park Corner Free Exhibition on 24 March 1849, when Rossetti exhibited his first major painting *The Girlhood of Mary Virgin*, with an accompanying sequence of two sonnets attached to the picture frame on a piece of gold-leaf paper. Rossetti's usual method was to execute the painting first and to compose the poem subsequently; the most significant exception to this is 'The Blessed Damozel', the painting for which was executed over twenty years after the poem. In Rossetti's 'double' works, the poems and paintings are free-standing works, yet simultaneously part of an overall artwork that is a composite entity of the textual and visual materials.

Of the two sonnets accompanying Rossetti's *The Girlhood of Mary Virgin* the first describes the virtue exhibited in her youth, while the second explicates the Christian iconography of the painting, calling attention to the act of interpretation itself. We learn that Mary's unfinished embroidery symbolizes that the Annunciation is not yet come, while each one of a large pile of books in the centre of the painting is emblematic of a particular virtue, with Charity at the top. Rossetti's interest in ekphrastic poetry is also evident in his series of 'Sonnets for Pictures', which were published in the Pre-Raphaelite journal, the *Germ* (1850). These sonnets took their inspiration from paintings such as Giorgione's *A Venetian Pastoral* and Ingres's *Angelica Rescued from the Sea-Monster*. According to Sophia Andres, they reflect 'his early attempts to translate painting into poetry and thus achieve not only destabilization of hitherto established boundaries between visual and verbal texts but also a new synthesis of the spatial and temporal arts'.[43]

The Pre-Raphaelite interest in the book as total work of art, produced by a creative partnership of artist, writer and printer, was taken further by William Morris and the Arts and Crafts movement. In January 1891, Morris founded the Kelmscott Press to produce books after the fashion of fifteenth-century pre-capitalist printed works. Between 1891 and 1898, the Kelmscott Press produced fifty-three books, which foreground the visual and material features of the book, from the typeface and lineation to the binding and type of paper. As Morris declared, 'it was the essence of my undertaking to produce books which it would be a pleasure to look upon as pieces of printing and arrangement of type'.[44] Kelmscott publications are characterized by their elaborate Gothic type, sumptuous ornamentation, hand-made paper and illuminated devices. They were published in limited editions of a few hundred (there were only 425 copies of the Chaucer folio for example), and were a rejoinder to the commercial mass-production of books.

Kelmscott books provide a sensuous rather than utilitarian reading experience: they arrest the eye with their wealth of visual detail. Books produced by the press include the Edward Burne-Jones illustrated *The Works of Geoffrey Chaucer* (1896), and editions of Ruskin's *The Nature of Gothic* (1892) and Dante Gabriel Rossetti's *Ballads and Narrative Poems* (1893). The visuality of Morris's designs is exemplified by the Kelmscott *News from Nowhere* (1892) (figure 12.8). The frontispiece and first page form a visual whole because, as Morris realized, 'the unit of the book is not one page, but a pair of pages'.[45] The frontispiece is an illustration of the house on the Thames that marks the gateway to the dream-world discovered by William Guest. On the first page there is also the decorative Gothic border with heavy illuminated capitals, reducing the text to two or three words a line. Unlike the usually sparse combination of white page and black type, the Gothic type and illuminated capitals foreground the reading experience by filling the field of vision.

The translation from verbal to visual in the case of illustration, and vice-versa with regard to the use of pictorial and optical tropes, suggests that Victorian culture was characterized by a pervasive intermediality between print and visual media. This crossover, however, did not go unchallenged. In *The Renaissance* (1873), Walter Pater attacked the way that popular criticism regarded poetry, music and painting as 'but translations into different language of one and the same fixed quantity of imaginative thought, supplemented by certain technical qualities of colour, in painting; of sound, in music; of rhythmical words, in poetry'.[46] His critique typifies the way that the Aesthetic movement challenged the pictorialism of much literary

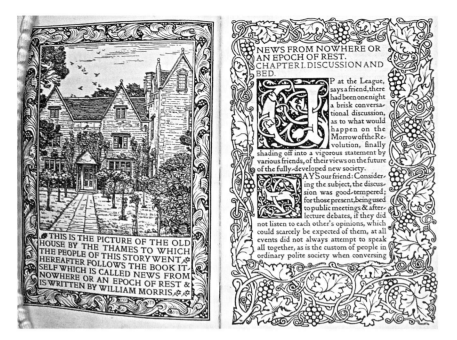

Figure 12.8 William Morris, *News from Nowhere: Or an Epoch of Rest, Being Some Chapters from a Utopian Romance* (Hammersmith: Kelmscott Press, 1892), frontispiece.

realism. However, even though Aestheticism rejected the material solidities of the mid-Victorian period in favour of the more evanescent world of perception, visuality remained a dominant critical and experiential concern. Whereas Matthew Arnold had claimed that the aim of the critic was to see the object as it really is, Pater extended this by declaring that 'the first step towards seeing one's object as it really is, is to know one's impression as it really is'.[47] This ongoing friction between divergent models of visuality reflects its functioning as a key motif for competing aesthetic concerns. It also typifies the way that the literary fascination with visuality was part of a broader phenomenon whereby the impact of new visual media stemmed not so much from their technology in itself, but from their constant appropriation by a competing range of scientific and cultural purposes.

Notes

1 [E. S. Dallas], 'Reviews', *The Times*, 26 June 1866, p. 6. Kate Flint uses the same phrase, albeit from G. H. Lewes, for her piece, '"Seeing Is Believing": Visuality and Victorian Fiction', in Francis O'Gorman (ed.), *A Concise Companion to the Victorian Novel* (Oxford: Basil Blackwell, 2005), pp. 4–24.

2 Martin Meisel, *Realizations: Narrative, Pictorial, and Theatrical Arts in Nineteenth-Century England* (Princeton: Princeton University Press, 1983).

3 Flint, 'Seeing Is Believing', p. 26.

4 *Ibid.*

5 The camera obscura is an optical device in which an external landscape is reproduced in a darkened box or chamber by light passing through a miniature hole in its side. The camera lucida was a device used as a drawing aid by artists; it allowed artists to see a reflected image of their chosen subject superimposed upon their paper or canvas.

6 Elizabeth Eastlake, 'Photography', *Quarterly Review*, 101 (April 1857), p. 453.

7 See Dai Vaughn, 'Let There Be Lumière', in Thomas Elsaesser and Adam Barker (eds.), *Early Cinema: Space Frame Narrative*, 2nd edn (London: BFI, 1994), p. 64.

8 O. Winter, 'Review', *New Review* (February 1896) repr. in Colin Harding and Simon Popple (eds.), *In the Kingdom of Shadows* (London: Cygnus Arts, 1996), p. 15.

9 Jonathan Crary, *Techniques of the Observer: On Vision and Modernity in the Nineteenth Century* (Cambridge, Mass.: MIT Press, 1992).

10 'A Word on the Stereoscope', *Leisure Hour*, 3 (1858), p. 346.

11 Friedrich Nietzsche, *Human, All Too Human: A Book for Free Spirits*, trans. R. J. Hollingdale (Cambridge: Cambridge University Press, 1986), p. 132.

12 Karl Marx and Friedrich Engels, *The German Ideology*, trans. S. Ryazanskaya (Moscow: Professional Publishers, 1964), pp. 11–12.

13 Thomas Carlyle, *Past and Present and Heroes and Hero Worship* (London: Chapman and Hall, 1893), p. 7.

14 George Eliot, *Adam Bede* (London: Penguin Popular Classics, 1994), pp. 176–7.

15 [George Eliot], 'John Ruskin's *Modern Painters, Vol. III*', in *Selected Essays, Poems and Other Writings*, ed. A. S. Byatt (Harmondsworth: Penguin, 1991), p. 368.

16 [George Eliot], 'Belles Lettres,' *Westminster Review*, 66 (1857), p. 321.

17 Eliot, *Adam Bede*, p. 176.

18 *Ibid.*, p. 177.

19 Peter Brooks, *Body Work: Objects of Desire in Modern Narrative* (Cambridge, Mass.: Harvard University Press, 1993), p. 88.

20 Sir Arthur Conan Doyle, 'A Scandal in Bohemia', in *The Penguin Complete Sherlock Holmes* (Harmondsworth: Penguin, 1981), p. 9.

21 Sir Arthur Conan Doyle, 'A Study in Scarlet', in *The Penguin Complete Sherlock Holmes*, p. 23.

22 Ronald Thomas, 'Making Darkness Visible: Capturing the Criminal and Observing the Law in Victorian Photography and Detective Fiction', in Carol T. Christ and John O. Jordan (eds.), *Victorian Literature and the Visual Imagination* (Berkeley: University of California Press, 1995), p. 135.

23 Robert Browning, 'Fra Lippo Lippi', *Norton Anthology of English Literature*, ed. Stephen Greenblatt (New York: Norton, 2000), p. 1377.

24 Pierce Egan, *Life in London, Or, The Day and Night Scenes of Jerry Hawthorn, ESQ, and his elegant friend Corinthian Tom, accompanied by Bob Logic, the Oxonian, in their Rambles and Sprees through the Metropolis* (London: Sherwood, Neely, and Jones, 1821), p. 19.

25 Charles Dickens, *The Old Curiosity Shop* (London: Chapman and Hall, 1913), p. 504.

26 George Eliot, *Middlemarch*, ed. Rosemary Ashton (Harmondsworth: Penguin, 1994), p. 521.

27 Thomas Hardy, *Jude the Obscure*, ed. C. H. Sisson (Harmondsworth: Penguin, 1985), p. 80.

28 Edgar Allan Poe, *Tales of Mystery and the Imagination* (London: Ward, Lock and Co., 1891), p. 218.

29 Sheridan Le Fanu, 'An Account of Some Strange Disturbances in Aungier Street', in *Best Ghost Stories of J. S. Le Fanu* (New York: Dover Publications, 1964), p. 364.

30 *Ibid.*

31 Quoted in Meisel, *Realizations*, p. 274.

32 See Nikolas Frankel, 'Aubrey Beardsley "Embroiders" the Text', in Richard Maxwell (ed.), *The Victorian Illustrated Book* (Charlottesville: University Press of Virginia, 2002), p. 262.

33 Robert Patten, 'Serial Illustration and Storytelling in *David Copperfield*', in Maxwell (ed.), *The Victorian Illustrated Book*, p. 91.

34 Eliot, *Middlemarch*, p. 269.

35 'Our Address', *Illustrated London News*, 1 (14 May 1842), p. 1.

36 [Catherine Gore], 'The New Art of Printing', *Blackwood's Edinburgh Magazine*, 55 (January 1844), p. 47.

37 Wilkie Collins, 'The Unknown Public', *Household Words*, 18 (21 August 1858), p. 217.

38 Henry Mayhew, 'The Literature of Costermongers', in *London Labour and the London Poor*, 4 vols. (London: Griffin, Bohn, and Co., 1861), vol. I, p. 25.

39 [Andrew Wynter], 'Our Modern Mercury', *Once a Week*, 4 (2 February 1861), p. 162.

40 John Ruskin, 'Notes on the Present State of Engraving in England', in *Ariadne Florentina* (London and Orpington: George Allen, 1876), p. 236.

41 George Eliot, *The George Eliot Letters*, ed. Gordon Haight, 9 vols. (London: Oxford University Press, 1954–78), vol. IV, pp. 55–6.

42 Quoted in Sophia Andres, *The Pre-Raphaelite Art of the Victorian Novel: Narrative Challenges to Visual Gendered Boundaries* (Columbus: Ohio State University Press, 2005), p. 40.

43 *Ibid.* p. xx.

44 William Morris, *A Note by William Morris on His Aims in Founding the Kelmscott Press, Together with a Short Description of the Press by S. C. Cockerel, & An Annotated List of the Books Printed Thereat* (London: Kelmscott Press, 1898), p. 1.

45 *Ibid.* p. 5.

46 Walter Pater, *The Renaissance*, ed. Adam Phillips (Oxford: Oxford University Press, 1986), p. 83.

47 *Ibid.* p. xxix.

PART III

The centre and the periphery

13

PATRICK BRANTLINGER

Empire and nationalism

Romantic and Victorian writers made both nation and empire central to 'English literature', a phrase that can mean either writing by anyone using the English language or writing exclusively by English authors. The second meaning implies that literatures are nation-based: English literature is the expression or the possession of England. But what about writers from Scotland or Ireland? 'British literature' is equally problematic; thus, even before the Irish Republic gained independence in 1922, 'Irish literature' had its own national and often nationalist resonance. From the Act of Union of 1707, which joined England and Scotland in a single polity, 'Great Britain' or the 'United Kingdom' developed simultaneously as a modern nation-state and as an expanding empire. Because Britain consisted of England plus the 'internal colonies' of Wales, Scotland and Ireland, and also of an overseas empire including both India and territories of 'white settlement' in Canada, Australia, New Zealand and South Africa, the interplay of nation and empire in literature is extraordinarily complex. Like Irish literature, formerly colonial literatures, often written in English, are now postcolonial – obviously no longer British.

Throughout the nineteenth century, literary works not overtly focused on themes of nation and empire nevertheless played a role in the imaginative forging of English and British identities.[1] Domestic novels – Jane Austen's *Pride and Prejudice* (1813), for example, or Charles Dickens's *David Copperfield* (1850) – can be read as microcosmic versions of Whig history, the success stories of their protagonists implicitly mirroring the success stories of nation and empire. As French novelist Honoré de Balzac declared, 'The novel is the private history of nations.'[2] Further, many writers explicitly celebrated or criticized Britain and its Empire, often doing both simultaneously. Thus, Dickens's novels tend to be highly critical of social and political conditions in England. Yet he writes as a reformer who hopes those conditions will be remedied by English honesty and kind-heartedness. When he writes about other countries, moreover – the United States in *American*

Notes (1842) and *Martin Chuzzlewit* (1844), Italy in *Pictures from Italy* (1846) and *Little Dorrit* (1857), France in *A Tale of Two Cities* (1859) – he suggests that conditions are worse in those non-British places.

Writers who celebrated English national identity and the British Empire ranged from Captain Frederick Marryat with his patriotic maritime novels in the 1830s and 1840s, through Alfred, Lord Tennyson, author of the Arthurian epic *Idylls of the King*, to Rudyard Kipling, whose poetry and fiction, starting in the 1880s, made him the unofficial 'laureate of the Empire'. From the time of Queen Victoria's coronation in 1837 to the First World War, a veritable industry of imperialist adventure narratives written mainly for boys extolled English pluck and heroism, outcomes of race or 'blood'. Patriotism and imperialism in literature echoed many other aspects of Victorian culture, from political rituals to supposedly scientific theories of Anglo-Saxon racial supremacy. The English were 'the imperial race', whose destiny was to rule other races for their benefit.

From Romantic to Victorian literature

Romantic writers often portrayed Ireland or Scotland in nostalgic terms, as 'nations' with colourful, legendary pasts that were gradually merging with England into a less colourful modernity. It was the task of Celtic revivalism and also of the 'national tale', writes Katie Trumpener, to evoke 'an organic national society, its history rooted in place' – distinct from but not necessarily antagonistic to modernizing Britain. Maria Edgeworth's *Castle Rackrent* (1800) and Sydney Owenson's (Lady Morgan's) *The Wild Irish Girl* (1806), for example, portrayed 'the contrast, attraction, and union of disparate cultural worlds'. National tales typically end 'with the traveler's marriage to his or her native guide, in a wedding that allegorically unites Britain's "national characters," or, to quote the title of an 1814 national tale by Christian Johnstone, "The Saxon and the Gaël"'.[3]

Most national tales depict Celtic traits and customs as relatively static. With Sir Walter Scott's Waverley novels, however, historical fiction gained a dynamism that influenced later novelists and even historians.[4] Scott's *Waverley* (1814) portrays the forging of modern Britain through the defeat of Jacobitism in 1745 and the gradual, peaceable merger of Celtic with English peoples – of Highlands with Lowlands and both of these with England. So, too, in *Ivanhoe* (1819), Scott interprets the history of England after the Norman Conquest of 1066 as the unification of the modern nation-state of Great Britain through the fusion of the Anglo-Saxons with the Norman 'race'. Scott uses the term 'race' interchangeably with 'nation' and without the invidious biological significance that it came to have in the

Victorian period. But from *Ivanhoe* forward, writing that deals with Britain's Anglo-Saxon heritage makes the racial origin and composition of the modern nation-state and its empire a central theme. In the overtly imperialist literature of the Victorian and Edwardian eras, nationalism and racial chauvinism are indistinguishable, as in Kipling.

Scott also wrote about the British in India in *Guy Mannering* (1815) and *The Surgeon's Daughter* (1827). As Trumpener notes, in Anne Monkland's 1828 novel *Life in India, or the English in Calcutta*, 'the Waverley novels both entertain colonial administrators and educate them for their new duties'.[5] The narrator of *Guy Mannering* imagines the lawyer Pleydell wondering how 'an officer of distinction' such as Colonel Mannering could have come 'from India, believed to be the seat of European violence and military oppression'.[6] The novel appeared in the midst of controversy, following the Warren Hastings trial in the 1790s, about how to reform the East India Company. Scott was aware that British activities in India had often been morally dubious, even criminal; but Mannering's upright, gentlemanly character signals Scott's belief that Britain's role in India was improving. His depiction of Mannering gestures towards later portrayals of self-sacrificing British soldiers and administrators of the Raj, as in many of Kipling's stories.

While several major Romantic poets – Blake, Byron, Shelley – viewed empire in all its forms as 'tyranny', others, including Wordsworth and Coleridge, after initially sympathizing with the French Revolution, grew politically conservative and wrote in positive terms about Britain and its Empire. After aiding Italian nationalists, Byron died in Greece in 1824, where he had sailed to support its nationalist struggle against the Ottoman Empire. Later poets – Swinburne, Clough, George Meredith – also sympathized with Italian nationalists as they fought for independence from the Austro-Hungarian Empire. Robert and Elizabeth Barrett Browning, living in Italy, opposed

> Austria wearing a smooth olive-leaf
> On her brute forehead, while her hoofs outpress
> The life from these Italian souls ...[7]

After the deaths of Shelley and Byron, however, few poets voiced wholesale criticism of the British Empire. Nevertheless, defending British imperial expansion was another matter.

For Romantic writers, two aspects of imperialism were prominent: the often scandalous deeds of the East India Company and the crusade to abolish slavery. These prompted many authors besides Blake, Shelley and Byron to criticize British activities overseas. Also, the start of British colonization in Australia did little to instill pride in the Empire: the First Fleet (1788) established a penal settlement at Botany Bay, and British criminals continued to be transported 'down under' until 1868. But reform of the East India Company coupled with Romantic interest in 'the Orient' caused many writers to look more positively on British involvement in Asia. The abolitionist crusade led to the outlawing of the slave trade in 1807 and of slavery in all British territory in 1833. Both abolition and reform in India encouraged belief in British imperial responsibility, which in turn encouraged patriotism.

The British campaigns against *sāti* and *thāgi* (or 'suttee' and 'thuggee,' Hindu widow-burning and the cult of the Thugs, highway robbers and murderers) were seen as evidence that British rule in India could civilize instead of corrupt. They were also seen as evidence that India itself – far more than the East India Company – needed reforming or civilizing. In missionary discourse, Hinduism was typically portrayed as an evil religion that encouraged crime and licentiousness. In 1839, Philip Meadows Taylor published his best-selling *Confessions of a Thug*, the most influential novel about India before Kipling's *Kim* (1901). Taylor served the Nizam of Hyderabad as a soldier and policeman; based on testimony made to him by a jailed Thug, *Confessions* suggests that India in general is lawless. The young Queen read it avidly, as did many others.[8] If in the 1700s crimes were committed by employees of the East India Company, during the Victorian era, thanks partly to Taylor's novel and then to literary reactions to the 'Sepoy Mutiny' or Rebellion of 1857–8, India itself was portrayed as criminal and in dire need of British rule.

'The Orient' is central as well in John William Kaye's *Peregrine Pultuney; or, Life in India* (1844); John Lang's *The Wetherbys, Father and Son; or, Sundry Chapters of Indian Experience* (1853); and William Arnold's *Oakfield; or, Fellowship in the East* (1853). And India figures, peripherally at least, in Charlotte Brontë's *Jane Eyre* (1847), Elizabeth Gaskell's *Cranford* (1853) and Wilkie Collins's *The Moonstone* (1868). In Collins's mystery novel, an Englishman has stolen a 'fabulous diamond' from a Hindu temple during the battle of Seringapatam in 1799. But the Indians who travel to England to retrieve the jewel murder the second thief, the seemingly virtuous Godfrey Ablewhite. The solution to the mystery proves the innocence of all of the English characters except Ablewhite, while suggesting that India continues to be a place of crime, violence and religious fanaticism.

William Makepeace Thackeray wrote about India in several novels and stories. Although he was sent to live in England in 1817 and never returned to the subcontinent, Thackeray was born in Calcutta in 1811. In *Vanity Fair* (1848), fat, cowardly, lying Jos Sedley, tax collector in the Indian backwater of Boggley Wollah, hardly suggests that the British deserve their Oriental dominion. In *The Newcomes* (1855), however, Colonel Newcome is, like Scott's Guy Mannering, an honest, upright imperial servant. He is duped by an Indian scoundrel, the shady financier Rummun Loll; the Colonel and his son Clive lose their fortune much as Thackeray had lost his through what he viewed as Indian skulduggery. *The Newcomes* thus also stresses Indian lawlessness.

Few Victorian novels seem farther removed from imperial issues, or even for that matter from national ones, than Gaskell's *Cranford*, which depicts the quiet lives of a group of spinsters in an English village. But Gaskell emphasizes the domesticity of her main characters through episodes that inject wider, indeed globe-spanning, events and ideas into Cranford's routines. Above all, the return from India of Miss Matty's long-lost brother Peter ironically foregrounds the connection between the village and the British Raj. Although he talks to the village rector in down-to-earth terms, Peter enjoys stretching the truth for his lady auditors; his tallest tale concerns a hunting expedition in the Himalayas, when he shot a 'flying creature'. To his dismay, he discovered that 'he had shot a cherubim!'[9] Peter's conflicting roles as purveyor of tall tales and as the rescuer of his sister from her financial troubles perhaps express Gaskell's sense of the East India Company as at once morally dubious and a source of economic prosperity even for stay-at-homes like Miss Matty.

Though also domestic in orientation, Gaskell's other novels register her awareness of both nation and empire. *North and South* (1855) examines regional differences between the agrarian southern counties of England and the industrializing, urban midlands. The marriage of Margaret Hale to the factory owner John Thornton symbolizes the sort of national unification Scott portrays through marriages in *Waverley* and *Ivanhoe*. In *Mary Barton, A Tale of Manchester Life* (1848), Gaskell depicts the struggles against poverty and injustice of John Barton, factory worker, and his daughter Mary. Starvation and a strike lead John to murder the son of the factory owner, Mr Carson. After Barton's apprehension and trial, Mary is united with her working-class lover, Jem Wilson, now cleared of the charge of murder, and the two emigrate to Canada.

Emigration narratives and adventure fiction

One of many 'social problem' novels written in the 1840s and 1850s, *Mary Barton* portrays class conflict, poverty and starvation in England, while treating emigration to the colonies as a source of social progress. So, too, in Dickens's novels emigration often signals hope for characters whose lives have been blighted by poverty and class oppression. For many Victorian writers, the solution to what Thomas Carlyle called 'the Condition of England Question' lay in emigration.

The Great Famine in Ireland (1845–50) made leaving that sorry portion of the Empire an urgent necessity for millions. John Stuart Mill declared that the peasants of Ireland have 'learnt to fix their eyes on a terrestrial paradise beyond the ocean, as a sure refuge both from oppression of the Saxon and from the tyranny of nature'.[10] Most works that take the Famine as theme, such as *The Black Prophet* (1847) by Irish novelist William Carleton, are critical of British misrule, and specifically of the failure of government in London to provide adequate relief. An exception is Anthony Trollope's *Castle Richmond* (1860), which treats the Famine as a providential dispensation, making way for the modernization of Ireland. The Famine spurred Irish nationalism, expressed in the writings of Young Ireland and their journal *The Nation*, part of the prelude to Fenianism and ultimately to independence for the Irish Republic. In contrast to Scotland, there would be no peaceful unification of Ireland with England.

Novels about emigration – Marryat's *The Settlers in Canada* (1844), for instance, or Edward Bulwer-Lytton's *The Caxtons* (1849) – are typically also adventure stories, as the immigrants undergo perilous voyages and forge new futures on colonial frontiers. Often echoing Defoe's *Robinson Crusoe*, many of the first writings from the colonies are emigration and settler narratives. Thus, Charles Rowcroft's novel *Tales of the Colonies, or, The Adventures of an Emigrant* (1843) recounts William Thornley's struggles to establish a farm and raise his family in Tasmania. Rowcroft has little to say in favour of social conditions back in England; they have caused Thornley to emigrate in the first place. But Tasmania is no utopia either: Thornley is often 'only just saved from being shot by the bushrangers and burnt by the natives'. Besides the aborigines, Thornley has to deal with 'the convict system', which one of the settlers denounces as 'wilfully scattering abroad the seeds of moral contagion, and inoculating the new country with diseases in their rifest state. That is a bad beginning for a new empire!' The magistrate who explains 'the system', however, calls it 'a balance of evils' and adds that there is less crime in 'Van Diemen's Land' than 'in England and Ireland'.[11]

Canadian literature, too, began with accounts of emigration and frontier life, including Catharine Parr Traill's *The Backwoods of Canada* (1836). In her epistolary narrative, Mrs Traill writes that she 'has endeavoured to afford every possible information to the wives and daughters of emigrants of the higher class who contemplate seeking a home amid our Canadian wilds'. Her desire, she says, is to provide 'utility in preference to artificial personal refinement', for 'the struggle up the hill of Independence is often a severe one'.[12] But 'independence' is what the emigrant can expect if she and her husband persevere. In 1852, Mrs Traill paid homage to Defoe with her children's book *Canadian Crusoes*, while in the same year her sister, Susanna Moodie, contributed *Roughing It in the Bush*. Similarly, fiction in New Zealand begins with Major Henry B. Stoney's *Taranaki: A Tale of the War* (1861) and Mrs J. E. Aylmer's *Distant Homes: or The Graham Family in New Zealand* (1862). Both authors recount establishing frontier homesteads in perilous conditions, including conflict with the Maoris.

Starting in the 1830s, much imperialist adventure fiction was written mainly for boys. Novels about brave, young sailors by Marryat and others flourished in that decade alongside stage melodramas featuring the stock character Jack Tar, as in T. P. Cooke and Douglas Jerrold's play *Black-Ey'd Susan* (1829). Like Marryat's midshipmen, Jack is 'the innocent ruler of the world'.[13] In *Masterman Ready* (1841), his version of Robinson Crusoe, Marryat depicts the shipwreck of the Seagrave family on a desert island. Their survival depends on the practical wisdom and experience of the title character, an older version of Jack Tar. With Ready's help the Seagraves, like Crusoe, are able to transform their island into a model colony. When young William Seagrave asks about 'the nature of a colony', his father responds by describing the rise of the British Empire and its victories over its Spanish, Dutch and French rivals. Today, says Mr Seagrave, 'the sun is said, and very truly, never to set upon ... English possessions; for, as the world turns round to it, the sun shines either upon one portion or another of the globe which is a colony to our country'. Mr Seagrave adds, however, that when a colony becomes 'strong and powerful enough to take care of itself, it throws off the yoke of subjection, and declares itself independent'. He offers the United States as an illustration, and adds that even 'barbarians and savages' may in the future form 'a great nation'. This prompts William to wonder whether, if 'nations rise and fall', England may one day 'fall, and be of no more importance than Portugal is now?' This will be 'the fate of our dear country', says his father, though so far in the future as to cause no present worry.[14]

Among writers of boys' adventure fiction, both Robert Ballantyne and W. H. G. Kingston began publishing in the 1840s. They would soon be emulated by Captain Mayne Reid, Dr Gordon Stables, G. A. Henty and many others. Kingston often imitated Marryat's midshipman novels, as in *Marmaduke Merry the Midshipman* (1862) and *The Three Midshipmen* (1873). He was also a propagandizer for both the Empire and emigration, serving as an official of a colonization society while publishing such tracts as *How To Emigrate; or, The British Colonists* (1850). In one of Kingston's most popular tales, *Peter the Whaler* (1851), the boy-hero's father tells him,

'Wherever you wander, my son, remember you are a Briton, and cease not to love your native land.'[15] That line can be taken as the main theme of everything that Kingston wrote.

Ballantyne's best-selling 'Robinsonade', *The Coral Island* (1858), features a trio of plucky English lads who survive shipwreck, pirates and cannibals, and celebrates the work of evangelical missionaries in the South Pacific. Ralph Rover's sentiment is Ballantyne's: 'God bless and prosper the missionaries till they get a footing in every island of the sea!'[16] Ralph and the other boy-heroes travel to central Africa for an encore in *The Gorilla Hunters* (1861). These and many similar adventure stories inspired Robert Louis Stevenson to pen *Treasure Island* (1882), a novel that in turn prompted H. Rider Haggard to write *King Solomon's Mines* (1885). Haggard was inspired as well by the many accounts of European explorers of sub-Saharan Africa, including David Livingstone's *Missionary Researches and Travels in Southern Africa* (1857) and Henry Morton Stanley's *How I Found Livingstone* (1872).

Haggard's own brief adventures as a colonial official and ostrich farmer in southern Africa were disillusioning. He grew to respect the Zulus, however, who defeated the British at the Battle of Isandhlwana in 1879. Zulus in *King Solomon's Mines*, *Allan Quatermain* (1887) and *Nada the Lily* (1892) are noble savages. In contrast, Haggard's portrayal of the cannibalistic Amahagger in *She* (1887) suggests that he believed other African 'tribes' or 'races' were distinctly inferior to the white race, or at least to the Anglo-Saxon branch of that race. Haggard helped to seize the Transvaal from the Boers, whom he deemed less capable of self-government than the Zulus. As he saw it, Britain's 'mission' was 'to conquer and hold in subjection' the inferior races and peoples of the world, 'not from thirst of conquest but for the sake of law, justice, and order'. Only Britain, Haggard believed, among 'all the nations of the world appear[s] to be able to control coloured races without the exercise of cruelty'.[17]

As in all myths and tales of superheroes, boys' adventure fiction relies on the infantile fantasy of omnipotence – of invulnerability and total control basic to most versions of imperialist and racist ideology. Such fiction entails hero-worship of the juvenile, white adventurers in one direction, and racist denigration of 'the natives' in the other. (Haggard's Zulus are a partial exception to this rule.) In the highly popular Jack Harkaway stories, writes Louis James, 'Those with dark skins are grouped in a miscellaneous category of "savages," embracing Red Indians, South Sea Islanders, African Negroes, [Asian] Indians, and Australian aborigines. Generally they are treacherous and "by nature and instinct, very cruel." They can be killed without compunction.' The destruction of 'the natives' reflects what was happening on many colonial frontiers, 'the violence and brutality of an expanding empire'.[18] When G. A. Henty's boys follow Kitchener, Baden-Powell and other British military heroes into colonial wars, they are invariably on the side of the victors. Even if the authors of imperialist adventure fiction do not state it as a law of nature, the non-white races of the world, no matter how bravely they fight, prove their inferiority by being killed or conquered by the white, British heroes.

The 'imperial race' and character

Most journals and biographies of British explorers, military men and missionaries, such as those by and about Livingstone, read as triumphs of character over the forces – and races – of darkness. Though its orientation is usually towards the future – geographical exploration, the expansion of the Empire, civilizing 'the natives' – adventure fiction sometimes also teaches patriotic history lessons. Thus, Charles Kingsley's *Westward Ho!* (1855) celebrates the brave deeds of English sailors during the Elizabethan era. Its hero, Amyas Leigh, is 'a symbol, though he knows it not, of brave young England longing to wing its way out of its island prison, to discover and to traffic, to colonize and to civilize, until no wind can sweep the earth which does not bear the echoes of an English voice'. Amyas's 'Saxon' blood makes him simultaneously a 'savage' fighting machine and a natural 'gentleman'. 'Saxon' victories over the Spanish villains Kingsley interprets as founding moments of the British Empire. He declares that his novel ought to be 'sung' to 'all true English hearts … as an epic', proclaiming 'the same great message which the songs of Troy, and the Persian wars, and the trophies of Marathon and Salamis, spoke to the hearts of all true Greeks of old'.[19] Like Kingsley's *Hereward the Wake* (1866), *Westward Ho!* expresses his belief in the absolute superiority of the Teutonic or, more specifically, the Anglo-Saxon race.

In much imperialist discourse, hero-worship and racism go hand-in-hand. Though he did not identify any of his contemporaries as full-fledged heroes, 'Hero-Worship' was the secular religion that Carlyle espoused. Faith in great men (Carlyle never discussed great women) entailed an authoritarianism that underpinned the racism he expressed in 'On the Nigger Question' (1849) and in his support for Governor Eyre, after Eyre's brutal termination of the Jamaican Rebellion in 1865. High moral character, including honour, courage and patriotism, was the hallmark of the Victorian 'gentleman', heir of chivalry and natural leader of the 'imperial race'. This is the figure that John Ruskin paints in *A Knight's Faith* (1885), his tribute to Sir Herbert Edwardes and his military exploits in India in the 1840s. Ruskin wishes to demonstrate 'how a decisive soldier' could also be a 'benevolent governor [who could] win the affection of the wildest races, subdue the treachery of the basest, and bind the anarchy of dissolute nations, – not with walls of fort or prison, but with the living roots of Justice and Love'.[20]

In George Otto Trevelyan's 1866 epistolary novel *The Competition Wallah*, the protagonist and narrator, Henry Broughton, has passed the Indian Civil Service exam (he is 'the competition wallah'). Henry goes to India to assume his duties five years after the Rebellion of 1857–8, and is writing home to a friend. He notes that during the Rebellion 'in many an isolated station a dozen or two of the Imperial race stood at bay for months before a hundred times their number of infuriated enemies, disciplined by English skill'. The Rebellion was a 'blaze of Oriental fanaticism, which … at length yielded to the courageous perseverance, and the unconquerable energy of our race'.[21] The term 'race' is here, as in many other Victorian texts, a collective synonym for 'character', understood as an immutable set of traits – for 'the imperial race', these traits are invariably virtues, antithetical to Oriental failings.

Samuel Smiles published his worldwide best-seller *Self-Help* (1859) immediately after the Indian Rebellion. It preaches that individual self-reliance adds up to 'national character'. Smiles begins with an epigraph from Mill: 'The worth of a State, in the long run, is the worth of the individuals composing it.' Great nations – Smiles has Britain in mind – are those with the greatest individual self-reliance and liberty; weak nations have little or no individualism and liberty. The weak ones are uncivilized or barbaric; they deserve to be ruled by nations of superior character. India is an example; Smiles offers the British heroes of the Rebellion as illustrations of 'self-help' at its best:

> The recent terrible struggle in India has served to bring out, perhaps more prominently than any previous event in our history, the determined energy and self-reliance of the national character. Although English officialism may often drift stupidly into gigantic blunders, the men of the nation generally contrive to work their way out of them with a heroism almost approaching the sublime.

Smiles lauds the bravery of the men and women of the 'English race' who knew, because of their race, the outcome in India would be their 'ultimate triumph'.[22]

In the third volume of his 'Young England' trilogy, *Tancred; or, the New Crusade* (1847), future prime minister Benjamin Disraeli has the wise Sidonia tell the protagonist: 'A Saxon race, protected by an insular position, has stamped its diligent and methodic character on the century. And when a superior race, with a superior idea to Work and Order, advances, its state will be progressive … . All is race; there is no other truth.'[23] In the earlier *Sybil; or, The Two Nations* (1845), Disraeli's heroine, daughter of Chartist Walter Gerard, overcomes the class barrier to marriage with the aristocratic hero by discovering that her ancestors were 'Saxon' nobles. Disraeli considered the modern 'Whig aristocracy' a fraud, created during the Reformation; he looked back to Anglo-Saxon times for the roots of a genuine aristocracy. It is ironic that the Jewish Disraeli, though a convert to Anglicanism, should express any version of Anglo-Saxonism or even of historical explanation in terms of race. His tactic, however, is to assert the precedence of Anglo-Saxons in British history, while also claiming the racial superiority of the 'Semites', including both Arabs and Jews, over all other races as the founders of the world's greatest religions and empires. This is the lesson Tancred learns from Sidonia and also, in a visionary moment on Mount Sinai, from the Angel of Arabia. 'The thoughts of all lands come from a higher than man', the Angel tells the Englishman; 'but the intellect of Arabia comes from the Most High'.[24] To foil the anti-semitism he encountered throughout his career, Disraeli asserts a pro-semitism.

The limitations of nineteenth-century racial theories – Disraeli's as well as others' – are evident when Sidonia identifies the Jews as a 'pure race' of 'Caucasian origin': if the Jews are Caucasian, so are all Arabs, and so, too, are all Anglo-Saxons and Celts. The more inclusive a racial category becomes, the less sense it makes. In an early letter, George Eliot declared that Disraeli's 'theory of "races" … has not a leg to stand on … The fellowship of race, to which D'Israeli [*sic*] exultingly refers the munificence of Sidonia, is so evidently an inferior impulse which must ultimately be superseded that I wonder even he, Jew as he is, dares to boast of it.'[25] Partly in response to what she saw as Disraeli's shallow if positive treatment of history in racial terms, Eliot portrayed Jewish characters and Judaism in her final novel, *Daniel Deronda* (1876). Through Mordecai Lapidoth, brother of the beautiful Mirah, Daniel learns the history of the Jews and their religion. He begins to feel an affinity for this nationless nation; after discovering his own Jewish roots through his mother, he marries Mirah and travels with her to Palestine, mirroring Tancred's 'new crusade'. It is with their trip that the novel concludes, gesturing towards a cultural cosmopolitanism or an internationalism transcending nations and races. Eliot thus critiques racism, including both pro- and anti-semitism, as well as narrow-minded versions of nationalism.

By the 1870s, however, the theory that race was the main engine of history had become hegemonic. Three years after Disraeli's Sidonia declared that 'All is race', Dr Robert Knox, in his quasi-scientific *The Races of Men* (1850), proclaimed: 'race is everything: literature, science, art, in a word, civilization, depend on it'.[26] Knox belonged to a growing number of authorities who contributed to what appeared to be a new science of race, an early version of physical anthropology. The race scientists influenced Charles Darwin and other evolutionists, including Alfred Russel Wallace and Thomas Henry Huxley. The Darwinians rejected the view that human races were separate species, insisting instead that the similarities among them were far more significant than differences such as skin colour. Nevertheless, after publication of *The Origin of Species* (1859), evolutionism was used to support new versions of racism – for instance, in the eugenics movement, initiated by Darwin's cousin Francis Galton.

In most taxonomies of races the 'Aryan', 'Germanic', 'Teutonic' or, in Britain and North America, the 'Anglo-Saxon' race led the pack. The 'dark races' of the world were doomed to eternal inferiority and perhaps to extinction. British success in empire-building seemed to prove both points. In *Greater Britain* (1868), Charles Wentworth Dilke viewed the colonies of white settlement as an Anglo-Saxon 'family' whose ultimate interest lay in racial unity. James Anthony Froude's *Oceana* (1886) echoed Dilke's book: the Anglo-Saxon 'family' has carried 'the genius of English freedom' around the globe. Froude's advocacy of a 'commonwealth', binding Britain, Australia, New Zealand, Canada and South Africa together, is based on 'race' and character:

> Amidst the uncertainties which are gathering round us at home … it is something to have seen with our own eyes that there are other Englands besides the old one, where the race is thriving with all its ancient characteristics … let Fate do its worst, the family of Oceana is still growing, and will have a sovereign voice in the coming fortunes of mankind.[27]

The future prosperity and freedom of 'Englands' plural depend on maintaining racial solidarity, an intercolonial patriotism. For Froude, as for Dilke, the indigenous peoples the Anglo-Saxon race encountered on colonial frontiers were expendable and about to disappear.

Gothic endings

During the decades of the 'new imperialism', from 1880 to the start of the First World War, the very existence of the British Empire seemed to prove the superiority of the 'imperial race'. Nevertheless, the emergence of new rivals for empire – the United States, the newly unified Germany, and to some extent Italy, Belgium and Japan – gave pause to the notion that the Anglo-Saxons were the only imperial race. Troubles in the Crimea, the Indian Rebellion, the Jamaican uprising of 1865, defeat by the Zulus in

1879 and the Boers in 1883, and the bloody, costly second Anglo-Boer War of 1899–1902 aroused both jingoism and its shadowy opposite, anxiety about Britain's global supremacy. The influx of immigrants from Ireland, the continent and the Empire into Britain raised the spectre of colonization in reverse. One outcome was the subgenre of 'imperial Gothic' writing.[28] Even the greatest imperial civilization might decline and fall into barbarism, as happens in Richard Jefferies's apocalyptic *After London* (1885). In the lead-up to the First World War, there were also many invasion fantasies, such as Sir George Chesney's *The Battle of Dorking* (1871). The invaders are often supernatural, moreover, involving the notions of atavistic reincarnation or demonic possession, as in Bram Stoker's *Dracula* (1897).

If the Empire was a source of pride, it was also a source of foreign otherness and, perhaps, racial and national degeneration. At the outset of *A Study in Scarlet* (1887), the first of the Sherlock Holmes stories, Dr Watson returns from Afghanistan to London, 'that great cesspool into which all the idlers and loungers of the Empire are irresistibly drained'.[29] The 'idlers and loungers of the Empire' might include Watson himself, but Watson is undoubtedly referring to the 'lascars', Indians and Andaman islanders who crop up in a number of Holmes's cases. However, a theme that often recurs in imperial Gothic fiction is 'going native', in which a British or European character sheds civilization in favour of non-civilized, perhaps even savage customs. In Joseph Conrad's *Heart of Darkness* (1899), its narrator Marlowe takes the trip to King Leopold's Congo that Conrad himself made in 1890. Marlowe captains a steamer up the Congo River to the 'Inner Station', where he encounters the remarkable Mr Kurtz. His main task is to bring Kurtz back to civilization, but the chief obstacle is Kurtz. The supposed exemplar of Europe's civilized virtues, Kurtz has instead gone native, ruling over the Africans around him like a petty tyrant or a god. Using metaphors and conventions drawn from Gothic fiction, Conrad likens Kurtz's transformation to demonic possession and Marlowe's trip to a nightmare journey through the underworld. Kurtz's dying words, 'The horror! The horror!' may be his verdict on Africa – 'the dark continent' – and hence one meaning of the story's title. But they are just as clearly an indictment of Kurtz's behaviour and, beyond that, of European imperialism. Marlowe compares the British Empire favourably to other empires, but he makes no exception when he says: 'The conquest of the earth, which mostly means the taking it away from those who have a different complexion or slightly flatter noses than ourselves, is not a pretty thing when you look into it too much.'[30]

Writers of early science fiction, mirroring imperialist adventure fiction, often deployed Gothic conventions to express anxieties about foreign invasions and racial degeneration. Bordering on science fiction, Haggard's *She* and Stoker's *Dracula* express both concerns. Stevenson's *Dr Jekyll and Mr Hyde* (1886), portraying what can be construed as demonic possession, depicts Hyde as racially degenerate and as an Irish hooligan. In Bulwer-Lytton's 1872 *The Coming Race*, the monstrous but superior Vril-ya threaten to surface from their underground realm and conquer the world, perhaps exterminating mere humans. So, too, in *The War of the Worlds* (1898), H. G. Wells imagines an invasion of Martians who are fortunately destroyed by disease before they can destroy humanity. Between 1880 and the First World War, there were many other 'invasion scare' fantasies, including my favourite, P. G. Wodehouse's 1909 *The Swoop ... A Tale of the Great Invasion*. In Wodehouse's parody, Britain is simultaneously invaded by hordes of Germans, Russians, Chinese, Young Turks, Moroccan brigands and cannibals in war canoes, as well as the Swiss Navy, the Prince of Monaco and the Mad Mullah, until a plucky boyscout named Clarence Chugwater comes to its rescue.

Late Victorian and Edwardian English writers may also have felt anxious about a kind of literary invasion. Authors from Ireland – William Butler Yeats, Lady Jane Gregory, Oscar Wilde, J. M. Synge, George Bernard Shaw, James Joyce – gained prominence simultaneously with other non-English writers, including the Polish-born Conrad. English literature was definitely no longer written just by English authors. Irish writers in particular often expressed nationalist aspirations, as in Yeats's poem 'Easter 1916'. Yeats was, however, critical of what he saw as myopic versions of Irish nationalism; Joyce was even more critical.

Most colonial authors were not advocates of decolonization. They were often, however, acutely aware that colonial writing tended to be imitative of British and European literary conventions and trends, and they strove to achieve literary originality – a version of cultural independence. Ironically, colonial writers frequently did so by ventriloquizing indigenous voices, typically in elegiac form. A common colonial genre was the lament of the dying warrior, as in American poet Henry Wadsworth Longfellow's 'Song of Hiawatha' (1855). Thus, in Thomas Pringle's *African Sketches* (1834), 'the founding artwork of South African English literature',[31] several poems are spoken by 'natives' who are either dying or the last of their tribe. In one poem, the Boers exterminate the tribe of 'the captive of Camalú' and enslave its speaker, who wishes for death instead of bondage:

> Death the frail body only kills –
> But Thraldom brutifies the mind.[32]

Pringle was an ardent abolitionist who, after his return to England in 1826, became secretary to the Anti-Slavery Society.

After slavery was outlawed in British territories in 1833, the abolitionist movement continued its work through the Aborigines Protection Society, founded in 1837. One source of criticism and anxiety about imperialism was awareness of conflict and slaughter on colonial frontiers. The apparently total extinction of the Tasmanian aborigines by 1876 caused a crisis of conscience in both Australia and Britain; James Bonwick's *The Last of the Tasmanians* (1870) offers the best contemporary account. In general, however, British writers either assumed or asserted that Great Britain was the greatest nation the world had ever seen; one proof of that greatness was its Empire, on which 'the sun never set'. For some, another proof was that primitive races like the Tasmanians were rapidly disappearing before the advance of white 'civilization'.

Empire's authors

Also representing national and imperial greatness was the category of 'English literature' as such. Many of its authors – even if they were Irish or Scottish or colonial, and even if they sometimes criticized British politics and society – were canonized as national and often imperial heroes and heroines. Great writers – Shakespeare above all – were viewed as national treasures. In the Victorian period, even contemporary authors sometimes achieved that stature. Sir Walter Scott was immensely popular, but his dual nationalities made his status equivocal. Among women writers, Elizabeth Barrett Browning was sometimes called 'the queen of poetry', and by the time of her death George Eliot was widely venerated as a sage and, in Lord Acton's words, 'the greatest genius among women known to history'.[33]

It was Dickens, however, who emerged as the quintessential English novelist – 'chief in thy generation born of men', as Swinburne put it. In his funeral sermon, Benjamin Jowett declared: 'He whose loss we now mourn occupied a greater space than any other writer in the minds of Englishmen during the last thirty-five years.'[34] Dickens condemned many aspects of British politics and culture, so his canonization as a national icon is perhaps surprising. Among the failings of his compatriots that Dickens mocked was the narrow-minded patriotism that, in *Our Mutual Friend*, is an aspect of 'Podsnappery':

> Mr Podsnap's world was not a very large world ... he considered other countries ... a mistake, and of their manners and customs would conclusively observe, 'Not English!' when, PRESTO! with a flourish of the arm, and a flush of the face, they were swept away.[35]

Nevertheless, Dickens could himself wax patriotic and even bellicose when the security or honour of Britain seemed at stake. The obituaries, moreover, identify Dickens as the conscience of the nation. He 'led us to sympathize with these good, true, sincere, honest English characters of ordinary life', Jowett declared, 'and to laugh at the egotism, the hypocrisy, the false respectability of religious professors and others'.[36]

Still another Victorian author who became a national icon during his lifetime was Tennyson. Reviewing *Poems, Chiefly Lyrical* in 1830, W. J. Fox hailed Tennyson as promising to join the ranks of those poets who 'can blast the laurels of the tyrants, and hallow the memories of the martyrs of patriotism', acting powerfully 'upon national feelings and character, and consequently upon national happiness'.[37] Especially in his role as Poet Laureate from 1850 until his death in 1892, Tennyson often made poetry a medium for the public expression of patriotic and imperialist sentiments, as in 'Ode on the Death of the Duke of Wellington' and 'The Charge of the Light Brigade'. Reviewing the four parts of *The Idylls of the King* that Tennyson published in 1859, future prime minister William Ewart Gladstone called 'the Arthurian Romance' 'highly national', and yet both Christian and 'universal' in its appeal.[38] Begun in the 1830s and completed in 1885, *The Idylls*, despite the pastoral title, constitutes an epic, the genre that narrates the founding of an empire or a nation. Acting as exemplary imperialists, King Arthur and the knights of his Round Table carve a civilization – the original version of England – out of the wilderness. In 'To the Queen' (1873), Tennyson writes:

> The loyal to their crown
> Are loyal to their own far sons, who love
> Our ocean-empire with her boundless homes
> For ever-broadening England, and her throne
> In our vast Orient, and one isle, one isle,
> That knows not her own greatness.[39]

Like Dilke and Froude, Tennyson hoped the Empire would one day form a commonwealth united by race. The Queen conferred a peerage on him in 1883, the ultimate sign that he had become a national icon.

'English literature' – that is, writing in the English language – is now a global phenomenon, the result of British imperial expansion over four centuries. Much contemporary writing in English comes from 'postcolonies' and is frequently critical of the imperialist past. The Nobel Prize list reveals just how international, and postcolonial, English literature has become. Rudyard Kipling was the first English winner of the Prize, in 1907. Later winners include Rabindranath Tagore from India (1913); William Butler Yeats (1923), George Bernard Shaw (1925), Samuel Beckett (1969) and Seamus Heaney (1995) from Ireland; Patrick White (1973) from Australia;

Wole Soyinka (1986) from Nigeria; Nadine Gordimer (1991) and J. M. Coetzee (2003) from South Africa; and Derek Walcott (1992) and V. S. Naipaul (2001) from the Caribbean. The sun may have set on the British Empire, but it is still rising on postcolonial literature in English.

Notes

1 In *Imagined Communities: Reflections on the Origin and Spread of Nationalism* (rev. edn, London: Verso, 1991), Benedict Anderson stresses the role that novels have played in forging national identities in the modern era. In *Culture and Imperialism* (New York: Knopf, 1993), Edward Said contends: 'Without empire ... there is no European novel as we know it' (69). Elaborating on this proposition in *The Colonial Rise of the Novel* (New York: Routledge, 1993), Firdous Azim argues that 'the novel is an imperialist project, based on the forceful eradication and obliteration of the Other' (37). But while empires may be exclusive, racist and even genocidal, they are also inclusive – and so are novels. Postcolonial novels concern the inclusion through representation of 'the Other', though they are often also about empire and its effects.

2 Honoré de Balzac, *Physiology of Marriage*, vol. II: *Petty Worries of Conjugal Life*, trans. George B. Ives (Philadelphia: George Barrie and Son, 1895), p. 231.

3 Katie Trumpener, *Bardic Nationalism: The Romantic Novel and the British Empire* (Princeton: Princeton University Press, 1997), pp. xii, 141.

4 Thomas Babington Macaulay declared that Scott combined 'the history of government' with 'the history of the people' in exemplary fashion. Macaulay, 'History and Literature', in *The Varieties of History from Voltaire to the Present*, ed. Fritz Stern (Cleveland: Meridian Books, 1956), p. 87. Thomas Carlyle also learned from Scott to treat history as peopled by individual characters rather than generalities or abstractions.

5 Trumpener, *Bardic Nationalism*, p. 258.

6 Sir Walter Scott, *Guy Mannering* (London: Penguin Books, 1995), p. 210.

7 The quotation is from *Casa Guidi Windows*, Part II, lines 418–20, in *The Poetical Works of Elizabeth Barrett Browning*, ed. Ruth M. Adams (Boston: Houghton Mifflin, 1974), p. 248. Robert Browning's most notable poem about Italian nationalism is 'The Italian in England', whose speaker is either Giuseppe Mazzini or someone like him.

8 According to Balanchandra Rajan, 'Queen Victoria [sat] up at night reading the galleys of *Confessions of a Thug* because she could not wait for publication.' *Under Western Eyes: India from Milton to Macaulay* (Durham, NC: Duke University Press, 1999), p. 182.

9 Elizabeth Gaskell, *Cranford* (1853), ed. Elizabeth Porger Watson (London: Oxford University Press, 1972), p. 159.

10 Mill quoted in Sean Cronin, *Irish Nationalism: A History of Its Roots and Ideology* (Dublin: Academy Press, 1980), p. 88.

11 Charles Rowcroft, *Tales of the Colonies, or, The Adventures of an Emigrant*, 3 vols. (London: Saunders and Otley, 1843), vol. II, pp. 207, 234. Rowcroft also authored *The Bushrangers of Van Diemen's Land* (1846).

12 Catherine Parr Traill, *Canada and the Oregon: The Backwoods of Canada: Being Letters from the Wife of an Emigrant Officer...* (London: M. A. Nattali, 1846), pp. 1–5.

13 J. S. Bratton, 'British Heroism and the Structure of Melodrama', *Acts of Supremacy: The British Empire and the Stage, 1790–1930* (Manchester: Manchester University Press, 1991), p. 58. See also Jeffrey Richards (ed.), *Imperialism and Juvenile Literature* (Manchester: Manchester University Press, 1989).

14 Frederick Marryat, *Masterman Ready* (1841; London: Thomas Nelson, n.d.), pp. 140–1.

15 W. G. H. Kingston, *Peter the Whaler* (1851; London: J. M. Dent, 1906), p. 21.

16 Robert Ballantyne, *The Coral Island: A Tale of the Pacific Ocean* (1858; Oxford: Oxford University Press, 1990), p. 231.

17 H. Rider Haggard, 'The Transvaal', *Macmillan's Magazine*, 36 (May 1877), p. 78.

18 Louis James, 'Tom Brown's Imperialist Sons', *Victorian Studies*, 17, 1 (September 1973), pp. 97, 99.

19 Charles Kingsley, *Westward Ho!* (1855; New York: Dodd, Mead, 1941), pp. 21, 12.

20 John Ruskin, *A Knight's Faith: The Works of John Ruskin*, ed. E. T. Cook and Alexander Wedderburn, 39 vols. (London: George Allen, 1902–12), vol. XXXI, p. 384.

21 George Otto Trevelyan, *The Competition Wallah* (1866; New York: AMS Press, 1977), pp. 38, 45.

22 Samuel Smiles, *Self-Help* (1859; Boston: Ticknor and Fields, 1864), pp. 214, 215.

23 Benjamin Disraeli, *Tancred; or, the New Crusade* (1847; The Bradenham Edition, vol. X, New York: Knopf, n.d.), p. 149.

24 *Ibid.* p. 299.

25 George Eliot, *Selections from George Eliot's Letters*, ed. Gordon Haight (New Haven: Yale University Press, 1985), p. 45.

26 Robert Knox, *The Races of Men: A Fragment* (1850; Miami: Mnemosyne, 1969), p. 90.

27 James Anthony Froude, *Oceana, or England and Her Colonies*, 2 vols. (London: Longmans, Green, 1886), vol. II, p. 17.

28 Patrick Brantlinger, *Rule of Darkness: British Literature and Imperialism, 1830–1914* (Ithaca, NY: Cornell University Press, 1988), pp. 227–53.

29 Sir Arthur Conan Doyle, *The Annotated Sherlock Holmes*, ed. William S. Baring-Gould, 2 vols. (New York: Clarkson N. Potter, 1957), vol. I, p. 145.

30 Joseph Conrad, *Heart of Darkness* (1899; New York: W. W. Norton, 1963), p. 7.

31 Stephen Gray, *South African Literature: An Introduction* (New York: Harper and Row, 1979), p. 196.

32 Thomas Pringle, *African Poems of Thomas Pringle*, ed. Ernest Pereira and Michael Chapman (Durban: University of Natal Press, 1989), p. 48.

33 Gail Turley Houston, *Royalties: The Queen and Victorian Writers* (Charlottesville: University Press of Virginia, 1999), p. 117; Lord Acton, 'George Eliot's Life', *Nineteenth Century*, 17 (March 1885), p. 485.

34 Charles Algernon Swinburne, *The Best of Swinburne*, ed. Clyde Kenneth Hyder and Lewis Chase (New York: Thomas Nelson, 1937), p. 300; Jowett quoted in George H. Ford, *Dickens and His Readers: Aspects of Novel-Criticism since 1836* (New York: W. W. Norton, 1966), p. 109.

35 Charles Dickens, *Our Mutual Friend* (1865; Oxford: Oxford University Press, 1989), p. 128.
36 Quoted in Ford, *Dickens and His Readers*, p. 109.
37 W. J. Fox, '*Poems, Chiefly Lyrical [1830]*,' in John D. Jump (ed.) *Tennyson: The Critical Heritage* (London: Routledge and Kegan Paul, 1967), p. 33.
38 William Ewart Gladstone, 'W. E. Gladstone on the *Idylls of the King* [1859] and Earlier Works', in Jump (ed.), *Tennyson: The Critical Heritage*, p. 250.
39 Alfred Tennyson, *The Poems of Tennyson*, ed. Christopher Ricks (London: Longman, 1969), p. 1755.

14

BRIDGET BENNETT

Transatlantic relations

What difference does it make to understandings of the English literature of the period 1830–1914 to consider literary texts in transatlantic terms? What in any case might constitute a transatlantic approach or a transatlantic methodology when critically reading English literature of this period? This chapter addresses these questions first by giving a brief account of the current critical paradigms governing the ways in which transatlantic relations have been theorized and debated. Next it will move on to a series of exemplary readings that will demonstrate the ways in which so-called 'transatlantic' approaches to literary texts can provide ways of challenging more nation-based definitions of writers and texts, allowing for a shift in focus and of emphasis and, ultimately, new readings.

Defining transatlantic literary relations

Transatlantic literary relations have not yet been as fully theorized as other models of transatlantic relations, though this is certainly changing.[1] Earlier interpretations of these literary relations were frequently comparativist and Anglophone. They often stressed an anxiety of influence model, showing the ways in which American authors modelled themselves on British authors while also, gradually, trying to produce a literature that reflected the particular conditions of life in the United States. This posited a somewhat one-way version of influence, elevating British writers and English literature (narrowly defined) over the work of American writers, who were shown as always trying to escape from English literature's dominating presence. Furthermore, this became a way of reading American literature as a form (or extension) of English literature. In this reading American literature was interpreted as somehow changed by being produced from a new national experience, rather than in its own right.[2]

As a model for understanding the relationships between the literature being produced in Britain and in the United States, then, its limits are clear.

This may be one reason why, as a way of thinking about the literary, it has had a currency for those working on American literature for a longer period than for those whose focus is English literature, more narrowly defined. It also tended to concentrate on the works of white, mainly male, authors on both sides of the Atlantic and exclude the contributions being made to United States literature by slave narratives, captivity narratives and other forms of writing that did not easily fit such an explanation. As the literary canon expanded to include the writings of more diverse ethnic groups as well as women writers, increasingly complex ideas about literary, social and cultural interaction emerged. The theoretical models offered by New Historicism and postcolonialism, by feminism and cultural studies, all allowed networks and relationships that had previously had little investigation to be apprehended and explored.

At the same time, within the discipline of American Studies, models of American exceptionalism, the belief that the United States was a special case unlike other nations, were also being challenged and overturned, dynamizing the discipline and opening it up to new debates. Within British literary studies, scholars were starting to focus on new readings of canonical texts, as well as on the impact of newly assessed non-canonical texts. The impact of postcolonial studies was especially significant. So, for instance, the ways in which Emily Brontë's *Wuthering Heights* or Charlotte Brontë's *Jane Eyre* (both published in 1847) might be productively read within the contexts of debates about the abolition of transatlantic slavery were added to readings of Jane Austen's *Mansfield Park* (1814) which had already shown that novel's profound engagement with plantation slavery in the West Indies. It is within this cultural and critical milieu that the possibilities of reading literary texts within a transatlantic context have been seen as a way of leading to a deeper understanding of literary culture on both sides of the Atlantic.

Thinking geographically about what might constitute the transatlantic leads logically to a model that includes all those places that border the Atlantic. The consequence of this is to pose a challenge to nation-based definitions and writing in English. So, for instance, a focus on the United States gives way to one of a hemispheric idea of America. One result of this is that the largely monolingual model of the transatlantic which has focused on the relationship between two nation-states, Britain and the United States, gives way to a very different cultural, linguistic and political model, one which is more pluralistic and polyglot. Yet the way in which the transatlantic has been theorized has often been more conservative than this, sometimes for good reasons of manageability, shared languages and obvious cultural overlaps. It has often focused upon English speakers and writers, frequently white men, from Britain and the United States, for instance the mutually supportive intellectual relationship between Thomas Carlyle and Ralph Waldo Emerson, who first met in Scotland in 1833 when Emerson visited Carlyle at his home. It has celebrated or denigrated what has been called the 'special relationship' between the colonizer and its former colony. It has suggested, in fact, albeit somewhat elliptically at times, that what the transatlantic pertains to is two nations in particular. While that cultural relationship has been the subject of very significant critical investigations for understandable reasons, the model of transatlanticism need not be one that concentrates on that relationship. The massive influence of Paul Gilroy's seminal *The Black Atlantic* (1992), which posited a diasporic reading of black experience over a national one, and took the Atlantic as a key site of exchange, cannot be overestimated.

Transatlantic approaches to literary texts and authors have become increasingly common in recent years. This is illustrated by the following examples. *Symbiosis* (subtitled *The Journal of Anglo-American Literary Relations*) is a British-based twice-yearly journal that hosts a biennial conference. Its subtitle suggests a particularly Anglophone understanding of what constitutes the transatlantic. The *Journal of Transatlantic Studies* has emerged from the British-based Transatlantic Studies Association, which also hosts an annual conference. The journal's remit moves away from an Anglophone focus. Several academic centres or seminar series have also emerged, for instance the Maastricht Centre for Transatlantic Studies. Bernard Bailyn's International Seminar on the History of the Atlantic World, based at Harvard University, is widely considered as a seminal intervention in the theorization of transatlanticism from the discipline of history. Edinburgh University Press has a book series which has emerged from the STAR (Scotland's Transatlantic Relations) project. A recent work, *Transatlantic Literary Studies: A Reader* (2007) is aimed both at students and at academics and is designed, as its blurb states, 'to provide accessible, annotated examples of theoretical frameworks that might provoke further work in the field, as well as important pieces of literary criticism that demonstrate different possibilities of comparative analysis'.[3] A good deal of critical work is being produced within the Academy, then, that uses the rubric of the transatlantic to describe itself and furthers the range and quantity of work produced within that rubric.

The focus of this chapter needs to be conceived of within the context of this theorization but also within the parameters of periodization that govern this volume and the changing material conditions that affected the lives of British and Americans in particular. Technological advances transformed the nature, speed, cost and efficacy of transatlantic travel between 1830 and

1914, allowing for faster and safer travel. The most famous transatlantic ship was also the most fated: the loss of the *Titanic* in 1912 has become a marker of the beginning of the end of that mode of transatlantic travel. Five years after this, in 1919, the first non-stop transatlantic flight took place. Within decades commercial airlines became the preferred mode of travel for journeys across the Atlantic. Transatlantic telegraphy was firmly established as a reliable and cheap method of communication by the mid-century. William Cooke and Charles Wheatstone had patented the electrical telegraph in 1837. The first successful transatlantic cable was laid in 1858, but it was not until 1866 that a reliable cable connection was established that could transmit words rapidly across the Atlantic. The possibilities offered by such rapid communications of news across the ocean were speedily recognized and taken up. The absence of adequate copyright legislation until the passing of the 1891 International Copyright Act was a matter of great contestation. British books were frequently published in pirated copies in the United States. In reading tours of the United States in 1842 and again in 1867–8, Charles Dickens repeatedly attacked the injustices of copyright legislation and argued not only that they were unfair to British authors, but that they hindered the development of American literary culture. While pirated British texts were so cheap within the United States, how would texts by American writers ever be able to compete? Some British writers took steps to make sure they were resident in the United States when their books came out, therefore securing copyright protection as a result of residency. But the prolific novelist Frederick (Captain) Marryat was furious when he took this step in 1837 only to be told that he would have to renounce his British citizenship and become a US citizen if he wanted to protect his work. His frustration at this cast a shadow over his experiences in the United States which would emerge in his *Diary in America* (1839).

Frances Trollope and Charles Dickens: transatlantic travellers

Two key pieces of travel writing that introduced the United States to a British audience were Frances (Fanny) Trollope's *Domestic Manners of the Americans* (1832) and Charles Dickens's *American Notes* (1842). British writers had been fascinated by the new nation and what it offered since the period of the American Revolution (1776). For some it seemed to promise radical alternatives to British life. The poets Samuel Taylor Coleridge and Robert Southey, for instance, planned to establish a utopian community known as the Pantisocracy in Pennsylvania, though they abandoned the idea after Coleridge's marriage and the birth of his son. When Trollope – the mother of the prolific novelist Anthony – went to the United States in 1827 she hoped to become involved with the utopian plans of Frances (Fanny) Wright, who had founded the Nashoba Commune in Tennessee, constructed on the principles of Robert Owen's New Harmony settlement in Indiana. Wright was a Scottish-born radical who had taken United States citizenship in 1825. Nashoba was envisaged as providing educational opportunities for slaves who would eventually be relocated to Haiti as free, and educated, men and women. Like New Harmony, the Nashoba experiment represented an enthusiasm for the possibilities offered within a new republic as well as a recognition of the political and ethical problems caused by the existence of slavery. Both projects failed, however. Trollope's finances were extremely unstable: she had arrived in the United States with three of her children and two servants and, along with her more high-minded ideals, a more prosaic fantasy of a capitalist venture. She hoped to boost the flagging family finances by opening an emporium in Cincinnati in which goods might be sold to the newly emerging American markets. This, too, was to prove a failure. But Trollope had realized that a travel book of her experiences and her reflections on American life might prove popular. A number of travel books had been written by British authors before hers appeared. One in particular had made a mark. That was Basil Hall's *Travels in the United States* (1829), which described Americans in terms that were frequently profoundly unflattering to them. Trollope would go on to invoke the model of Hall and even quote him quite substantially in her own work, devoting chapter 31 to an account of American reactions to Hall's book. She appropriated his critical depiction of American manners in a patronizing way that also infuriated Americans. Many of the British writers who produced accounts of their American travels followed very similar templates. Outrage about the continued existence of slavery augmented by expressions of abolitionist sentiment formed a central part of the critique of the United States that these writings often engaged in. Alongside this a strong strain of crude anti-Americanism also recurs, taking the form of accusations of provincialism, uncouthness and a lack of polish. Both Trollope and Dickens frequently write of their horror at the amount of spitting both in public and in private. Dickens could be caustically funny about the resemblances between the United States and England. At one point he notes:

> Pittsburg [*sic*] is like Birmingham in England; at least its townspeople say so. Setting aside the streets, the shops, the houses, waggons, factories, public buildings, and population, perhaps it may be. It certainly has a great deal of smoke hanging about it, and is famous for its iron-works.[4]

Yet this rather easy attack on both Pittsburgh and Birmingham is tempered by his praise of its beautiful location and the high quality of the hotel he stayed in. This was a characteristic of Dickens's response to the United States: he repeatedly admired the country and its ideals and aspirations but attacked what he saw as its more sordid realities. Dickens would go on to satirize Americans in the same manner in his novel *Martin Chuzzlewit* (1843–4), which represented them as being caught in an irreconcilable mismatch between lofty political aspirations and bathetic realities.

Harriet Beecher Stowe: transatlantic citizen?

One example of an exemplary transatlanticist whose work had a huge impact on both sides of the Atlantic is the American novelist Harriet Beecher Stowe, whose 1852 novel *Uncle Tom's Cabin* rapidly became an international best-seller, making her a celebrity. It has recently been claimed that 'In the nineteenth century . . . it would have been odd *not* to consider Stowe in relation to Europe . . . she viewed herself as a transatlantic citizen.'[5] She was an enthusiastic reader of Charles Dickens, George Eliot, Charles Kingsley, Charlotte Elizabeth Tonna and Walter Scott, to name a few of the British writers who were literary influences, and became friends with Elizabeth Barrett Browning, among others.[6] In return, many British writers were readers of Stowe, like the general British reading public and the wider European reading world: Tolstoy was an admirer of *Uncle Tom's Cabin*. The remarkable American sales figures for the novel were added to by extraordinary British sales which were boosted by her visit to Britain in 1853, during which she experienced huge popular acclaim. She travelled extensively in Europe after that triumphant tour, and was met by great excitement wherever she went. In addition to the many meetings she had with British writers, and the correspondence she had with others (such as George Eliot) whom she never met but still considered personal friends, she wrote an account of her European experience which she published as *Sunny Memories of Foreign Lands* (1854).

British readers and non-readers alike flocked to see stage adaptations of her most famous novel, as well as parodies. Thomas Hailes Lacy's *Uncle Tom's Cabin: A Drama of Real Life* was first performed on 1 February 1853.[7] In 1864 his parodic version, mischievously titled *The Tyrant! The Slave!! The Victim!!! & The Tar!!!!*, was subtitled a 'Transatlantic Sensation Drama'.[8] What did the word 'transatlantic' mean in this context? Was the description intended to dilute, in some way, the Americanness of Stowe's novel? *Uncle Tom's Cabin* was frequently applauded in Britain as a strikingly American piece of writing. When Stowe arrived in Britain for a tour during which she was feted enthusiastically, she heard her work being discussed in terms of the way it had transformed British ideas about American writing. A speaker in Scotland remarked:

> We have long been accustomed to despise American literature – I mean, as compared with our own. I have heard eminent *litterateurs* say, 'Pshaw! The Americans have no national literature.' It was thought that they lived entirely on plunder – the plunder of poor slaves, and of poor British authors. [Loud cheers.] Their own works, when they came among us, were treated either with contempt or with patronizing wonder... Let us hear no more of the poverty of American brains, or the barrenness of American literature. Had it produced only Uncle Tom's Cabin [*sic*], it had evaded contempt just as certainly as Don Quixote, had there been no other product of the Spanish mind, would have rendered it forever illustrious.[9]

Stowe was cast here as both visiting American celebrity writer who demonstrated that American writing was more than a weak imitation of British writing, and as abolitionist activist who was able to access an already existing transatlantic network of anti-slavery activism. Was it within this context that the advertisers of Lacy's parody used the word 'transatlantic'? Thinking of what meanings that word might have had for a contemporary British audience who were likely to have encountered this advertisement necessitates an understanding of the transatlantic aspect of abolition in addition to a consideration of Stowe's reputation as a literary celebrity on both sides of the Atlantic. Stowe's tour of Britain followed to some degree the pattern, albeit on the other side of the ocean, of the American tour earlier undertaken by Dickens. Both were celebrated writers; both were recognized wherever they went; both had a political agenda in their travels, though that of Stowe was more central to her intention than that of Dickens. While Dickens agitated about international copyright while he toured the United States, one of Stowe's motives for visiting Britain in 1853 was to secure copyright for her *Key to Uncle Tom's Cabin*. When she returned to Britain in 1856 it was to establish copyright for her novel of that year (completed while she was travelling across the Atlantic), *Dred*. Her final visit was to establish copyright for *The Minister's Wooing* (1859). Whatever these private opportunities offered by her travels, it was as a celebrity author and abolitionist that she travelled across the Atlantic in 1853. She participated in debates on abolition that were more urgent and organized and engaged more people than a subject that was of pressing concern chiefly to authors and publishers. Lacy's drama, published during the US Civil War, was cast in transatlantic terms with a hyperbolic title that undermined the seriousness of Stowe's moral mission.

Oscar Wilde's American adventures

One of the most celebrated literary travellers to the United States was Oscar Wilde. He arrived in New York on 2 January 1882 at the invitation of the producer Richard D'Oyly Carte, who was putting on a production of Gilbert and Sullivan's *Patience*, which satirized the aesthetic movement. The production had enjoyed massive success in London and it was hugely popular in New York. Yet the New York audience did not have the same degree of recognition of both the figure of the aesethete and the movement that produced him as did a London audience. D'Oyly Carte recognized that bringing the arch exponent of aestheticism to the United States to lecture and to be seen as a public celebrity would greatly benefit the production, and the profits. Wilde set the tone of his tour immediately when he was reputed to have announced knowingly 'I have nothing to declare except my genius.'[10] While this may be apocryphal, the fact that it immediately gained credence as an account of his actual words does show that he was recognized as having a genius for understanding how to develop and respond to his celebrity status and to make sure that he was noticed on both sides of the Atlantic as well as on both sides of the Irish Sea. And noticed he was, both approvingly and disapprovingly. Dressed in knee-length breeches and black silk stockings, a purple coat with lilac lining and a lacy shirt, and with his hair flowing, he delivered his first lecture in New York to a sold-out Chickering Hall. Richard Ellmann quotes him as saying retrospectively 'Strange ... that a pair of silk stockings should so upset a nation.'[11]

He was invited to a series of social events at which he was lionized by many of the most prominent social and literary figures of the day. On one occasion he attended a reception for Louisa May Alcott, author of the best-selling *Little Women* (1868), and on another he met the American novelist Henry James, visiting Washington from home in Britain for a few weeks, who called on him at his hotel after he heard that Wilde had argued that no English novelists could match their Americans counterparts W. D. Howells and James. Their meeting was disastrous, and the chief difficulty was a competitiveness about which man was the more transatlantic (in James's case) and transnational (in Wilde's, though that is not a word he would have used). Again, it is Ellmann who puts this pithily:

> James remarked, 'I am very nostalgic for London.' Wilde could not resist putting him down. 'Really?' he said, no doubt in his most cultivated Oxford accent. 'You care for places? The world is my home.' He felt himself to be a citizen of the world ... To James, master of the international theme, this was offensive. He had his own view, as an American living abroad, of floating citizens of the world.[12]

However badly these two transplanted writers got on, Wilde had one encounter with a writer that was a great success, and that he recounted fondly. When he visited Philadelphia on 17 January he was asked his opinion of American poets and named Ralph Waldo Emerson and Edgar Allen Poe but most particularly Walt Whitman as significant and admirable examples. Whitman had famously celebrated himself in *Song of Myself* (1855) as 'Walt Whitman, an American, one of the roughs, a Kosmos'. Whitman invited Wilde to visit him in Camden after he had heard that Wilde had praised him. Wilde's greeting to the poet who had relentlessly celebrated US democracy and had expressly taken the United States as his subject took the form of transcending the national and instead focusing on the aesthetic. He said, 'I come as a poet to call upon a poet.'[13] He went on to explain his long acquaintance with *Leaves of Grass*: he had apparently read his mother's copy of William Michael Rossetti's edition of Whitman's poetry and had carried *Leaves of Grass* with him to read on walks while an undergraduate.[14] The pair then discussed English poetry and poets, including Alfred Tennyson and particularly Algernon Charles Swinburne who had published the celebratory poem 'To Walt Whitman in America' in the collection *Songs before Sunrise* (1871). This early and public enthusiasm greatly helped Whitman gain a British following. Indeed, in 1887 Whitman would receive a letter from an ardent group of followers in Bolton, Lancashire, who called themselves the Bolton Whitman Fellowship, met for weekly readings of his work, and even (in the case of two of them) travelled to Camden to meet him in 1890 and 1891, later publishing accounts of their meeting in *Visits to Walt Whitman in 1890–91 by Two Lancashire Friends* (1917).[15] Whitman knew about and was grateful for Swinburne's support, even saying that if he were to visit Britain he would like to meet his fellow poet. But Swinburne's appreciation was tempered in the following years, resulting in the 1887 *Fortnightly Review* attack, 'Whitmania'.[16] Still, when Wilde visited Whitman on 18 January 1882 relations were cordial, and the American poet passed his greetings through the younger man and gave him a photograph to send on to Swinburne. Wilde wrote to him and received a reply on 2 February in which Swinburne reiterated his praise of Whitman, though he also stated, ominously, that:

> This of course does not imply that I do – rather it implies that I do not – agree with all his theories or admire all his work in anything like equal measure – a form of admiration which I should by no means desire for myself and am as little prepared to bestow on another: considering it a form of scarcely indirect insult.[17]

In his article written five years later he would opt for more direct forms of insult, but at present all parties were content and Wilde acted as a go-between once more, copying some parts of the letter on to Whitman. He had a further meeting with him in May in which Whitman kissed Wilde on the lips in what seems to have been an acknowledgement of his own, and Wilde's, homosexuality. Whitman was also visited in 1877 and again in 1884 by the British socialist and activist Edward Carpenter, who was one of his most devoted readers. Carpenter identified with Whitman as a gay writer and as one who had a particular interest in democracy. He would later publish an account of his experience as *Days with Walt Whitman* (1906).

Ellmann notes that very soon these three poets found reasons to recant or at least revise their earlier opinions of each other. Though Whitman celebrated Wilde's aestheticism in his first meeting with him, he later critiqued it. Wilde's enthusiasm for Whitman waned in the light of his more critical comments. Nonetheless in their initial enthusiastic personal responses to each other in which letters, photographs and meetings brought them together, the three showed that the Atlantic was no divide to their admiration for each other, nor did it inhibit their reading of each other's works or desire to communicate in a manner that transcended their differences and celebrated their poetic achievements.

Wilde's heavy lecture schedule while he was on his 1882 tour took him across vast areas of the United States and Canada. He was the subject of popular songs; his work was pirated and sold in cheap copies (and publicly he argued that this just advertised his lectures still further); he talked of Ruskin, Morris and aestheticism; he visited the silver miners of Leadville, Colorado and described his experiences in brilliant and generous terms. He met American writers such as Oliver Wendell Holmes, Julia Ward Howe and Henry Wadsworth Longfellow. The last of these told Wilde about his visit to Queen Victoria, who had invited him to visit her at Windsor Castle and who assured him that he was, as he had found, very widely known in England, saying 'All my servants read you.' Longfellow was unable to decide whether this was a 'deliberate slight'.[18] Wilde's tour was, above all, that of a celebrity in terms that are still recognizable: a literary celebrity for sure, but chiefly a public figure whose fame built upon itself and who was famous, in part, for being famous. After all, Wilde's most significant writing was produced in the years after his visit to the United States. Unlike Charles Dickens or Harriet Beecher Stowe whose work preceded them and established their writing reputations before their transatlantic tours, Wilde visited the United States as a young man at the start of his career with all his future before him. Little did anyone realize how far he was to fall, and how fast. In 1895, days before Wilde was sentenced to two years' hard labour, the American novelist Willa Cather, still a student, wrote an article that described Wilde's situation in national terms, saying 'It is the beginning of a national expiation for national art that is artificial and insincere, for the school which claims that nature imitates art.'[19] For this American writer whose chief focus was the Prairies and the ways in which immigrants were transformed into Midwesterners – Americans – by their experience of living on the land, Wilde's focus on English society, like Wilde himself, had always been suspect and unhealthily precious, even sybaritic. Cather's sturdy and pioneering Bohemians, Russians and Swedes did not swap aphorisms in drawing rooms. As a writer she had set herself the challenge of answering Whitman's call in his poem 'O Pioneers!' of establishing herself as a bard of the prairies who would write an explicitly national drama of migration, settlement and integration. Her protagonists were often Europeans who were in the very process of becoming American: they carried their languages and cultures with them, creating a cultural and ethnic patchwork on the Midwestern landscape in which Indians, for Cather, largely existed only as relics. Her attack on Wilde was also an antagonistic response to what he represented in aesthetic terms, as well as acknowledgement that Wilde's public, sexual downfall which was the result of flouting convention was markedly different from that of her own discreet lesbianism.

Henry James's transatlantic life and death

The many Americans living in England in the last decades of the nineteenth century included the wealthy heiresses who were marrying into the aristocracy such as Jennie Jerome, who would become the mother of Winston Churchill; journalists such as Harold Frederic who was the London correspondent of the *New York Times* from 1884 to 1898 and was also a prolific novelist; Henry Harland the novelist and founding editor, in 1894, of *The Yellow Book*; and artists like James McNeill Whistler, a long-time resident. The presence and visibility of such figures had a profound effect on the cultural and social world of London in particular. An American woman, Nancy Astor, would become the first woman MP to take up her seat in the House of Commons in 1919, though she had settled in England in 1904. The most significant American novelist (arguably the most celebrated American) to make England his permanent home around this period was undoubtedly Henry James, who gave up his US citizenship in 1915, having lived in England for years prior to this. T. S. Eliot would follow his example some years later, in 1927. To many, James was the epitome of the cosmopolitan expatriate, a significant precursor of the American writers who spent formative periods in Europe, especially London and Paris, in the early decades of the twentieth century. These included, to name just a few, Djuna Barnes, Gwendolyn Bennett, Countee Cullen, H. D., T. S. Eliot, Ernest Hemingway, Langston Hughes, James Weldon Johnson, Nella Larsen, Alain Locke, Jean Toomer, Ezra Pound and Gertrude Stein. James spent three years of his childhood travelling throughout Europe with his parents and siblings, who included his eminent brother William and sister Alice. He learned French, German and Italian and had a thorough grounding in European culture and history, which had a profound impact on his life and writing. His sophisticated engagement with European culture is evident throughout his work. He was widely and deeply read in American, English, French, German, Italian and Russian literature. Important novelistic influences included Charles Dickens and Honoré de Balzac. Critics concur that one of his most significant and lasting influences was the American novelist Nathaniel Hawthorne, who had himself lived in England for a number of years while he was the US Consul to Liverpool from 1853 to 1857. Hawthorne went on to live in Rome and Florence from 1857 to 1859, providing one model for a transatlantic literary life. James himself moved to England in 1876, and although he visited the United States periodically after this, notably in a tour in 1904–5, he never again made it his home.

One of James's earliest works, written after he had left the United States, was a widely read book titled *Hawthorne* (1879). It combined literary criticism with biography. While parts of the book were welcomed by American critics, especially because it treated a renowned American author with great seriousness, other elements were met with far less favourably. Chief of those was a much-quoted passage in which James, by this time living in England, appeared to lament the inadequacies of life in the United States. He wrote:

> If Hawthorne had been a young Englishman, or a young Frenchman of the same degree of genius, the same cast of mind, the same habits, his consciousness of the world around him would have been a very different affair; however obscure, however reserved, his own personal life, his sense of the life of his fellow-mortals would have been almost infinitely more various. The negative side of the spectacle on which Hawthorne looked out, in his contemplative saunterings and reveries, might, indeed, with a little ingenuity, be made almost ludicrous; one might enumerate the items of high civilization, as it exists in other countries, which are absent from the texture of American life, until it should become a wonder to know what was left. No State, in the European sense of the word, and indeed barely a specific national name. No sovereign, no court, no personal loyalty, no aristocracy, no church, no clergy, no army, no diplomatic service, no country gentlemen, no palaces, no castles, nor manors,

nor old country-houses, nor parsonages, nor thatched cottages nor ivied ruins; no cathedrals, nor abbeys, nor little Norman churches; no great Universities nor public schools – no Oxford, nor Eton, nor Harrow; no literature, no novels, no museums, no pictures, no political society, no sporting class – no Epsom nor Ascot![20]

This lengthy list seemed to suggest a thoroughgoing criticism of the United States by an American who had chosen to leave the country. It appeared to cast the US and its inhabitants once more as the provincial counterparts to a more dominant and sophisticated European culture and history, in the manner of the critical works of travel that Americans had resented, discussed earlier. James was encountering one of the critical issues associated with being a transplanted figure. When he wrote about the United States, and especially in later years when his absence had been for a much longer period, what kind of authority or knowledge was associated with that writing? The impact of expatriation is very hard to measure, but an expatriated writer can become the easy victim of charges of snobbery or even simple ignorance of the real conditions of the country he has left behind. James certainly came in for criticism over what he wrote about American life in this book, and he was sensitive to what was said about him by his compatriots. His biographer Leon Edel, in his account of the affair, writes that 'America . . . had suddenly made him feel cast aside.'[21] Yet it was James who would make Americans feel that he had cast them aside in 1915, at the end of his life, when he renounced his US citizenship and became a British subject. His motivations for this were complex. Long residence in Britain and absence from the United States, and the fact that in a period of war he was classified as an alien and this restricted his ability to travel to his home Lamb House in Rye, were the main ones. He wrote to his nephew that:

> I have spent here the best years of my life – they practically *have* been my life: about a twelvemonth hence I shall have been domiciled uninterruptedly in England for forty years, and there is not the least possibility, at my age, and in my state of health, of my ever returning to the U.S. or taking up relation with it as a country.[22]

The prime minister Herbert Asquith acted as one of his four witnesses, which no doubt was immeasurably symbolic in an already watertight case. As James lay dying, the following year, he was awarded the Order of Merit, and a plaque has been erected to his honour in Poets' Corner in Westminster Abbey. Both details suggest honours usually associated with British writers. But the ashes of this important transatlanticist were taken back to the United States by his sister-in-law to the cemetery in Cambridge in which his sister Alice, brother William and parents had found their own final resting places.

What does it add to readings of James's work if they are done through a transatlantic lens? Or, at least, in what ways does it change views of him and of his writings? Should he be thought of as British as he was, at least in political terms, when he died, or as American? Does it really matter? Thinking of him as a writer who exemplifies the transatlantic within a broader context of reading transatlantically may be helpful here. James becomes less of an anomalous figure and more one who fits a pattern of cultural exchange of which he is only one (albeit a particularly clearcut) example. Perhaps it would be possible to say that a transatlantic focus more broadly would not make James himself look very different, but would reveal that many other writers might start to look more like him. The *New York Times*, in its response to news of James's renunciation of his citizenship, made a similar point succinctly when it argued,

> It is easy enough to be severe or sarcastic at this defection and to insist that an American should remain an American. But, after all, the United States wants no citizens by compulsion. And as a literary absentee Mr James has a long line of predecessors, Byron and Landor, Turgenieff, Heine, Wagner, Nietzsche rise at once in the memory. To the literary man choice of his scene is to be granted.[23]

What a transatlantic focus seems to offer is a method of moving beyond readings that prioritize national origins or locations over other features of a work or writer. It can allow the complexities of engagement, influence, hybridity and impact to be felt. It can, particularly when focused on the historical period 1830–1914, reveal the construction during the nineteenth century of cultural models on both sides of the Atlantic that interacted with each other significantly. It can offer alternative interpretations of literary texts and a literary and cultural milieu that may once have looked very familiar.

Notes

1 Susan Manning and Andrew Taylor (eds.), *Transatlantic Literary Studies: A Reader* (Edinburgh: Edinburgh University Press, 2007), pp. 1–13.
2 More recently some critics have challenged this. Paul Giles, for instance, has suggested that the traditions should be read as 'heretical alternatives to each other' which mutually modify and affect each other. Paul Giles, *Transatlantic Insurrections: British Culture and the Formation of American Literature, 1730–1860* (Philadelphia: University of Pennsylvania Press, 2001), p. 2.
3 Manning and Taylor (eds.), *Transatlantic Literary Studies*.
4 Charles Dickens, *American Notes for General Circulation* (1842), ed. John S. Whitley (London: Penguin Books, 1985), p. 200.

5 Denise Kohn, Sarah Meer and Emily B. Todd (eds.), *Transatlantic Stowe: Harriet Beecher Stowe and European Culture* (Iowa City: University of Iowa Press, 2006), p. xv.

6 *Ibid.*

7 See the University of Worcester's AHRC-funded Victorian Plays project, http://victorian.worc.ac.uk/modx/.

8 Kohn *et al.* (eds.), *Transatlantic Stowe*, p. xi. In fact the full subtitle was 'An Entirely and Supernaturally Original Nautico-Domestic Transatlantic Sensation Drama'.

9 Cited in Joan D. Hedrick, *Harriet Beecher Stowe: A Life* (Oxford: Oxford University Press, 1994), p. 234.

10 Richard Ellmann, *Oscar Wilde* (London: Hamish Hamilton, 1987), p. 152.

11 *Ibid.* p. 157.

12 *Ibid.* p. 170.

13 *Ibid.* p. 160.

14 *Ibid.*

15 See Carolyn Masel, 'Whitman and the Bolton Whitman Fellowship', in Janet Beer and Bridget Bennett (eds.), *Special Relationships: Anglo-American Affinities and Antagonisms, 1854–1936* (Manchester and New York: Manchester University Press, 2002), pp. 110–38.

16 Algernon Charles Swinburne, 'Whitmania', *Fortnightly Review*, 42 (August 1887), pp. 170–6.

17 Cited in *ibid.* p. 163.

18 Ellmann, *Oscar Wilde*, p. 172.

19 *Nebraska State Journal*, 19 May 1895, p. 12. Cited in William M. Curtin (ed.), *The World and the Parish: Willa Cather's Articles and Reviews*, 2 vols. (Lincoln: University of Nebraska Press, 1970), vol. I, p. 154.

20 Henry James, *Hawthorne* (London: Macmillan and Co., 1883), p. 43.

21 Leon Edel, *Henry James: A Life* (London: Flamingo, 1996), p. 248.

22 Cited in *ibid.* p. 703.

23 Cited in Fred Kaplan, *Henry James: The Imagination of Genius* (London: Hodder and Stoughton, 1992), p. 560.

15

ALISON CHAPMAN

European exchanges

Written around 1851, Matthew Arnold's 'Dover Beach' describes the 'tremulous cadence slow' (line 13) of pebbles on the shore.[1] The melancholy lyrical impression produced by this 'eternal note of sadness' (line 14) underlines the over-determined border with the European continent, figuring contemporary anxieties about political insecurity. There was reason to fear for what Tennyson terms in 1852 England's 'sacred coasts': in December 1851, Louis Napoleon Bonaparte's *coup d'état* raised invasion fears in Britain.[2] A civilian rifle club movement was established to protect the vulnerable south coast, which Tennyson himself joined. Meanwhile, Pre-Raphaelite artist William Holman Hunt was working on a painting on the south coast of England originally entitled *Strayed Sheep, Our English Coasts* (1852), depicting sheep perilously close to the cliff edge, suggesting an acute sense of national defencelessness.[3] For Arnold, the monumental 'Glimmering and vast' (line 5) cliffs of Dover morph into 'a darkling plain/Swept with confused alarms of struggle and flight/Where ignorant armies clash by night' (lines 35–7). Arnold's poem (like Thomas Hardy's pre-World War 1 poem 'Channel Firing') offers an acute epistemological anxiety about invasion and the disintegration of identity. It is, indeed, impossible to imagine Britishness without reference to a fraught relationship with Europe. Although British collective national identity was often seen in the nineteenth century to be challenged by the continent, the collective invention of Britishness was contingent upon the nation's relationship with other countries. Furthermore, in this period of the emergent nation-state, Britain saw itself as the prototype of other nations' emerging and struggling identity. Liberals, in particular, projected British social order and constitutional history onto their European neighbours, especially in the cause of Italian independence (the Risorgimento).[4] Ironically, then, at the very period in which British boundaries and borders seemed so permeable and vulnerable, British identity was shoring up its 'glimmering and vast' self against the fragility and struggle of other nations.

The concept of Europe for the Victorians embraced both a definable geographical space (however subject to frequent internal border changes) and an epistemological sense of otherness. The British, whose contact with Europe suddenly opened up again with the end of the Napoleonic Wars in 1815 and the beginnings of mass tourism on the continent, had a sense of Europe as both relational and oppositional. To be European implied a shared identity based on classical and Christian culture and religion, and this common heritage underlay their colonizing projects; but it also, at the start of the nineteenth century, encoded some painful asymmetrical distinctions in culture, religion and politics.[5]

To complicate further this map of Europe, Britain was invested politically, culturally and aesthetically in some European countries over others. Such distinctions were grounded in the Grand Tour route, taking aristocratic young men to that ancient centre of European history and culture, Rome, by way of the delights of Paris. This legacy of prioritizing France and Italy survived, exemplified by the diverse French and Italian literary translations that dominated the Victorian book market. Translations from French favoured a wide range of writers, from the early modern chivalric *Aucassin et Nicolette* (praised in Pater's *The Renaissance* (1873)), to the daringly modern George Sand (whose *Works* were edited and partially translated by Matilda Hays in 1847). In Italian, Dante Alighieri was especially popular and, as a figure for patriotism and exile, translations and studies of Dante took on contemporary political meanings. As Ralph Pite notes, there was a 'growing connection between translation and Risorgimento feeling', and the many essays on Italian literature published in the periodicals suggest that a recovery of the Italian tradition was linked to British liberal sympathy with Italian nation building.[6] For example, pro-Italy campaigner Theodosia Trollope published translations from Italian (such as Niccolini's *Arnold of Brescia* in 1846) and essays on Italian literature for a British audience (such as her review of Guerrazzi's *The Ass* in the *Athenaeum* (13 March 1858, pp. 329–30)).

Anglo-German relations were also significant for the Victorian engagement with Europe: Queen Victoria's Hanoverian roots exemplified the close cultural and political bonds with Germany, although the Franco-Prussian War (1870–1) raised fears about continental trade. Many British writers had Germanic influences and ties, such as George Eliot, Matthew Arnold and the poet Mathilde Blind, but German unification did not inspire the patriotic fervour of the Italian Risorgimento. Towards the century's end, with growing political tensions between Germany and Britain, *Punch* enjoyed satirizing Germany and novels such as George Chesney's *The Battle of Dorking* (1871) and Captain W. F. Butler's *The Invasion of England*

(1888–9) capitalized on renewed invasion fears in Britain.[7] Although David Constantine argues that the nineteenth century witnessed 'an increasing interest in the other literatures of Europe, from modern literature to the writings of the Middle Ages and the folk literature of countries from Portugal to Serbia', and that German literary culture was on the ascendancy by the end of the century, the history of Britain's literary exchange with Europe has largely been related as the history of engagement with France and Italy.[8]

But *literary* invasions were not always seen to be a bad thing. The point famously made by De Quincey in 1821, that British literature needs foreign influence to save it from 'superannuation', was widely shared throughout the century, and generic innovation in Britain was fuelled by European influences.[9] For example, the rise of Victorian narrative realism, with its debt to such writers as Victor Hugo and Gustave Flaubert, was the offspring of the cross-Channel invention of the novel that forged transnational communities of writers and readers during precisely the pre-Victorian period when British political relations with France were particularly hostile.[10] The Francophile Swinburne's *Poems and Ballads* (1866) earned notoriety partly for the influence of Baudelaire; Robert Buchanan's famous attack on Swinburne and his followers, as the 'fleshly school', was prompted by his sense of their debt to 'immoral' French literature. Such European influences are apparent in the many periodicals that carried frequent essays on and translations from European literature, and some periodicals – such as the *Foreign Quarterly Review* (1827–46) and the *British and Foreign Review; or, European Quarterly Journal* (1835–44) – were explicitly committed to a European scope; and the literature market was, to a large extent, European.[11] Such networks represent an 'archaeology of transnational culture'[12] that uncovers fascinating and complex European interchanges in the long nineteenth century, and challenges Anglocentric disciplinary formations of Victorian literature.[13] This chapter traces examples of such an 'archaeology' through Victorian encounters with France and Italy, mapping the uneasy doubleness of the conception of the continent in terms of tensions between aesthetic impressions and politics, especially in response to revolutions.

France

During Victoria's reign, the British evinced a paranoid political fear of post-Revolutionary France, often representing it as an imploded and immoral society (as exemplified by the frankness of French avant-garde poetry and the naturalist novel). And yet France was Britain's nearest counterpart in

Europe in terms of its modernity, imperialism and economic strength, and the traffic between the two countries was extensive. Reactions to Louis Napoleon Bonaparte, nephew of Napoleon Bonaparte, exemplify the ambiguous British attitude to France. Democratically elected as President (in December 1848) and self-proclaimed Emperor Napoleon III (after the *coup d'état* in December 1852), Louis Napoleon was lambasted, ridiculed and celebrated by the British (who were not above aligning with him when it suited, as with the Crimean War in 1854–6). Elizabeth Barrett Browning, for example, repeatedly states in letters her approval of his self-anointed title as Emperor precisely *because* he is a popularly endorsed democrat. This neat sidestepping of the thorny issues of despotism and democracy attempts to resolve contrasts (or what she terms in *Aurora Leigh* 'A serious riddle')[14] by attesting their compatibility. Other writers, such as Robert Browning in *Prince Hohenstiel-Schwangau, Saviour of Society* (1871), were not so convinced.

While Paris – a city transformed by the Emperor's commission of the 'Haussmann Renovations' – was a favourite destination, especially for the social season, it was also where British outcasts relocated, such as Thackeray's Becky Sharpe (from *Vanity Fair* (1847–8)), Robert Browning's father (after being sued for breach of promise and defamation of character in 1852) and Oscar Wilde (after his release from prison in 1897). As a city of enchantment, a nexus of the European intellectual elite and a political theatre, the complex foreignness of Paris is often understood in dialectic with its neighbour across the channel, London. Paris is frequently represented in the nineteenth century as a supremely urban space, the representative city of modernity: Walter Benjamin's 'capital of the nineteenth century', Paris became associated with spectacle and public display, both a written text and, as Vanessa Schwartz suggests, a visual field. Until the defeat of the Commune in 1871, Paris represented 'the seemingly limitless powers of the collective action of the urban masses that resulted in numerous revolutions punctuating French history until the suppression of the Commune [in 1871]'.[15] Schwartz argues that, during the Third Republic, the revolutions were cultural and not political, and increasingly based on popular visual spectacle (most forcefully represented by the figure of the *flâneur*), but earlier depictions of Paris also inscribe the city as a transformative textual as well as visual space.

For Frances Trollope, Paris is a contradictory, puzzling and over-stimulating visual field which she interprets (and sometimes makes safe) for her British readers, negotiating the literary and political cityscape, comparing the city with its English counterpart, and offering a passport to social networks available in the city. Trollope's *Paris and the Parisians in 1835* was part of the explosion of travelogues that gave first-person impressions rather than catalogues of sites and appropriate literary responses as offered by John Murray's popular *Handbooks*. This innovative narrative, borrowing heavily from novelistic devices, desired to wander 'off the unbeaten track', motivating a new generation of tourists intent on discovering fresh contact with other cultures, as parodied in E. M. Forster's *A Room with a View* (1908). The urge to represent unmediated engagements with another European culture underwrote the travelogue. For example, Charles Dickens's *Pictures from Italy* (1846) explains his subjective impressionistic 'sketches' of this most overdetermined of countries by proclaiming that 'There is, probably, not a famous Picture or Statue in all Italy, but could be easily buried under a mountain of printed paper devoted to dissertations on it.'[16]

The success of *Paris and the Parisians* established the travelogue as a significant sub-genre, positioning Trollope as an important conduit between the continent and Britain. For Trollope, Paris is a cityscape of enchanting architecture and glittering society, with a dark underside of urban poverty. Carnival and reality punctuate her narrative, licensed in the preface and first letter as a series of impressionistic accounts: 'I will then discourse to you, as well as I may, of such things as leave the deepest impression among the thousand sights and sounds in the midst of which I am now placed.'[17] As a guide to a city that is at first 'startling', then overstimulating and intense (I, 33), Trollope recommends the charms of Parisian society to improve British manners, despite baseless popular allegations of French immorality. Trollope is at pains to point out that French indelicacy is often a result of circumstance attributable to household arrangements, and especially to the lack of sewers and drainage ('the smell of the continent' (I, 230)). While Trollope, a conservative monarchist, disapproves of French revolutionary politics, she nevertheless praises many aspects of Paris and its inhabitants, especially the freedom given to women in comparison with Britain. Trollope's Paris is a heterogeneous city, represented in the diversity of her letters' subjects on the theatre, gardens, street police and cleaning beds, clergy and sermons, fashion, popular fêtes, balls, visits of politicians, conversations with Frenchmen on literature, and improvements to the city. Such eclecticism is a feature of Paris's inherent doubleness, where the incompatible exists in juxtaposition. In a flamboyant conceit, she compares Paris to a theatre whose scenes she glimpses behind to witness the jumbled performances of crown and liberty, Catholics and Jews, military spectacle and protestations of eternal peace (II, 280–1).

Trollope's sense of her own position in Paris is supremely self-conscious. Although such an individualistic account of travel is a feature of the developing travelogue genre, it also marks Trollope as the self-aware mediator between the British reader and Paris as the foreign other. This mediation, however, falters at key moments in the text, when the contradictions inherent in the city threaten to overwhelm the narrator. Letter 37, which recounts a visit to the Paris Morgue after a young woman's murdered and 'mangled' body is found in the Seine, is one such moment: the visit is one of profound horror and irresistible sensationalism, despair at the evidence of urban poverty and exhilaration at the spectacle of corpses on open display to the crowds of visitors. For Trollope, this crime signifies an incomprehensible barbarity and savagery (1, 358) although, later in the chapter, she tries to explain the recurrent suicides exhibited in the Morgue (ostensibly for identification purposes) as a result of 'light litera-ture' popular with the French. Despite the moralizing, Trollope also admits to a dreadful fascination, to the 'power' of the 'shuddering sensa-tion' (1, 360) captured in the very word *La Morgue*, that identifies her with the crowds of curious Parisians who visit for entertainment (indeed, a similar popular entertainment as the 'light literature' on whose influ-ence she blames the suicides). Although terming the Morgue a 'gathering place of sin and death' that 'most foully violates the sanctity of life' (1, 361), her protestation that she had to steel herself to visit is under-mined by the repeated assertion that it is irresistible in its attraction to the viewer, including herself, as she is led by and becomes part of the crowd of Parisians that flow through its doors (1, 362). Trollope removes herself from yet identifies with 'the thousands who flocked to the Morgue' (1, 386). The Morgue signifies the ambiguity of Paris and challenges the separateness of the foreign viewer: a compelling 'citadel of death ... placed in the very centre of moving, living, laughing Paris' (1, 361). The absolute otherness of unclaimed corpses on display aligns Trollope, the otherwise careful mediator between British culture and foreignness, with the theatrical spectacle that is Paris.

The unsettling nature of the Morgue is partly ascribed by Trollope to its public display of the private: the grief of those searching for the missing, the corpses displayed behind glass with their clothes hanging next to them, and the publication of suicide notes in French newspapers. In fact, the cityscape of Paris is often, for British writers, the space of the private sphere turned inside out, the chiasmus of revolution where violent public politics displays and displaces the domestic and homely. As Richard Maxwell suggests, this is the dynamic of the Paris of Dickens's *A Tale of Two Cities* (1859), where revolutionary Paris operates on a powerful public civic space and where private life and its secrets are not exempt from the gaze of the masses. In contrast, London is depicted as a city of stable private space, in direct contrast to the Paris residence of the Manettes that is all too vulnerable to 'A Knock at the Door' of accusing citizens (book 3, ch. 7).[18]

A Tale of Two Cities announces this dialectic between Paris and London in its very title, but it is also important to note that, while the historical novel's emphasis is on the corrupt eighteenth-century social causes and their violent consequences, influenced by Carlyle's cautionary tale of cause and effect in *The French Revolution* (1837), Dickens also indirectly alludes to contemporary European politics. The repeated phrase 'recalled to life' is one of the code words, in Maxwell's terms, of the echo-chamber that is the novel (xi), which also refers to the Risorgimento – the struggle for Italian independence that derives from the Italian for 'resurgence' or 'resurrection'. *A Tale* repeatedly draws on resurrectionist motifs: the grave robbery of Mr Cruncher, the fragile return to life of Dr Manette, Sydney Carton's sacrificial death and symbolic resurrection in Lucy Manette's son. The issues of *All the Year Round* where Dickens first published his novel contain several essays on the subject of Italy and the Risorgimento, suggesting a symbolic patterning of contents. The issue for 2 July 1859, for example, includes an essay describing the revolution in Florence, where a popular uprising peacefully ousted the Austrian Duke.[19] The emphasis in this article on the orderliness of the Florentine patriotic crowd in the streets, the tranquil steps towards the revolution that even allowed for a reasonable bedtime each night, and the moderation of anti-Austrian popular nationalist politics, is also a feature of other accounts.[20] Florence's sedate attempt to overthrow an unpopular regime represents a stark contrast with the murderous masses in *A Tale of Two Cities*, where the actions of the crowds are anything but controlled and moderate. Reading the historical novel, with its detailed account of the violence of the French Revolution, alongside essays on the contemporary Risorgimento, offers two sharply different models of popular political agency. The contrast between Parisian and Florentine revolutions suggests a liberal historiography, where the lesson of the past is heeded in a natural progression to justice. Sydney Carton's imagined prophecy at the end of the novel, where he willingly offers himself to be executed in the guillotine in place of the aristocrat Darnay, suggests such a reading:

> I see a beautiful city and a brilliant people rising from this abyss and, in their struggles to be truly free, in their triumphs and defeats, through long years to come, I see the evil of this time and of the previous time of which this is the natural birth, gradually making expiation for itself and wearing out. (389)

Carton's imagined posthumous prophecy is 'recalled to life' by the Risorgimento, implicitly making good the lesson of the French Revolution in Dickens's novel. Indeed, the Victorian novel might be said to be innately European: populated by European characters and places, consumed by a European audience, and also participating in a complex network of

European literature, culture and politics. The continent, furthermore, offers an ambitious scope, and novelists such as George Eliot, who wrote with an increased sense of the international as her career progressed (exemplified by *Daniel Deronda* (1876)), looked to the continent as a wider, progressive and ambitious panorama.

One of the period's major generic innovations, the novel-poem, was inaugurated by Elizabeth Barrett Browning's own version of the European novel: *Aurora Leigh* (1856). The heroine is an Anglo-Italian poet who appreciates the French sense of civic freedom as sharply different from the British: 'poet's heart/Can swell to a pair of nationalities,/However ill-lodged in a woman's breast' (6, 50–2). Aurora, in her walk through the city, muses on the importance of 'a completer poetry' (6, 207) of a prophet-poet over the material emphasis of socialist thinkers such as Charles Fourier. '[F]air fantastic Paris', 'This poet of the nations' (6, 81, 53), is the embodiment of this poetic ideal. Aurora is ironically interrupted in her abstract contemplation by a pressing material reality: she suddenly glimpses Marian, the former working-class betrothed of Aurora's cousin Romney, who has fallen pregnant after a rape. Such an abrupt collision between Paris's sensory attractions and social reality is reminiscent of Frances Trollope's early travelogue (however sharply Barrett Browning differed from Trollope's conservative politics). Furthermore, in *Aurora Leigh*, the abrupt collision points to the necessity of incorporating social reality into 'a completer poetry', which is only resolved at the end of the novel-poem with Aurora's romantic and philosophical reconciliation with Romney and his ambition for a renewed society. In fact, the apocalyptic and ecstatic ending of *Aurora Leigh*, with Romney's and Aurora's shared vision of a New Jerusalem as a material and spiritual resurrection, anticipates the imagined prophecy of Carton at the end of *A Tale of Two Cities*, published two years after the novel-poem, echoing Barrett Browning's progressive liberal historiography that links together the revitalized futures of newly liberated European nations as well as individual citizens.

Paris's double characterization as a place of ugly social reality and sensory beauty is also evident in the many French villains and seducers in Victorian novels that represent the (often erotic) allure as well as the danger of 'Gallomania' (Trollope 1, 228), such as Rochester's lover, the French opera singer Celine, in Charlotte Brontë's *Jane Eyre* (1847). In the bohemian Paris that emerged later in the century, such contrasts are less oppositional. In George du Maurier's *Trilby* (1894) – a tissue of allusions to nineteenth-century European politics, popular culture and fashion radiating from Paris – the city slips almost seamlessly between its compelling spectacle (the Paris of which Little Billee, looking out from the Louvre windows, 'could never have enough') and a darker underworld represented by the Morgue (which haunts the text, as Paul Vita argues, and is identified with the villain Svengali).[21]

While some key Anglo-French texts emphasize provincial France beyond its capital – such as Robert Browning's narrative poem *Red Cotton Night-Cap Country* (1873), set in Normandy, and A. Mary F. Robinson's lavishly illustrated *The Fields of France* (1905), a homage to the attractions of France beyond its capital – Britain's Victorian literary exchanges with France overall suggest the allure of Paris. Towards the end of the century, the Aesthetic movement made Paris its cultural centre, under the influence of the 'decadent' movement (after J. K. Huysmans's *À Rebours* (1884)) and the French Symbolists (such as Flaubert and Baudelaire), and epitomized by Benjamin's reconception of Baudelaire's Parisian *flâneur*. British writers influenced by French aesthetic modernity at the end of the century reasserted urban Paris as the centre of European modernity and the heart of Anglo-French literary relations. *Fin de siècle* France was dangerously, thrillingly revolutionary, but this time the revolution was moral, cultural and aesthetic.

Italy

Although the fraught conceptual zone between Britain and France was ironically one of the few stable geographical borders in this period, other national territorial boundaries within Europe shifted dramatically. For some writers, the sense of the permeability of national borders and boundaries is liberating, offering intellectual exchange and cultural cross-fertilization, represented most forcefully in accounts of travel into northern Italy over the Alps. Christina Rossetti's response to her 1865 journey into Italy internalizes the transition between north and south as a creative force, inspiring sonnet 22 of her 'Later Life' sequence. However, in a revision of the Romantic celebration of the 'overwhelming' (line 1) masculine sublimity of the Alps, the journey is remembered for the specific feminine beauty of the garden of forget-me-nots:

> All Switzerland behind us on the ascent,
> All Italy before us we plunged down
> St. Gothard, garden of forget-me-not:
> Yet why should such a flower choose such a spot?[22]

The zenith of this tradition is Alice Meynell's 'The Watershed' (1923), which describes travelling over the Alps in exhilaratingly aqueous terms. The journey from the 'Black mountains', 'melancholy sky' and 'sterile fields' of the north seems like a pressure, as if travelling against northward rivers;

and yet moving against that pressure produces a sense of release and liberation.[23] Such internalization of transgression is depicted in euphorically sexual terms in the final stanza, once into Italy, where summer bursts, the south unfolds, strife ends, and the speaker 'flowed to Italy' (line 21). The landscape of Italy connotes expansiveness, expressiveness, possibility, even eroticized pleasure or *jouissance*.

Italy inspired such rhapsodic description in many writers, although with a sting. Italy, as a country that did not exist as a geographical or political entity until unification in 1861, was renowned for a beauty that was conventionally signified as feminine ('la bella Italia'). There is a long Western rhetorical tradition of Italy as a tragic fallen woman: in the words of the sonnet by Italian poet Vincenzo da Filicaia, 'Se tu men bella fossi', or 'Less wretched if less fair'. This translation (one of many in the nineteenth century) is offered by Barrett Browning's *Casa Guidi Windows* (1851), which rails against Italy's feminized representations as politically enervating and ineffective.[24] Thus, although many Victorian writers and artists represent Italy as a creative space of possibility, 'Italia' has a double bind for the female writer who identifies with the oppressed country. This feminized legacy of Italy was popularized by Germaine de Staël's *Corinne, or Italy* (1807). The eponymous heroine, an Anglo-Italian *improvisatrice*, represents poetic power and fame as well as personal tragedy. As the novel's sub-title suggests, Corinne is synonymous with the struggle for Italian nationhood, and her romantic unhappiness and death at the end of the novel figure the impasse of the rhetorical association of Italy with the feminine for both political and professional ends. Such doubleness is echoed through the genealogy of women's poetry haunted by *Corinne*, including Letitia Elizabeth Landon's metrical translations of Corinne's improvisations from the French, as well as Felicia Hemans's 'Corinne at the Capitol' (1830), which celebrates Corinne's coronation as public affirmation of her 'thrilling power' (line 28), and yet concludes with asserting that a woman by the 'humblest hearth' is happier (line 47).[25]

Throughout the period women writers negotiated the challenge represented by *Corinne* through representations of Italy. Sandra M. Gilbert asserts that women 'revitalize the dead metaphor of gender to transform Italy from a political state to a female state of mind', by seeking liberty from the patriarchal north.[26] But this process was problematic and gave women a limited model of writing and political agency. Through the association of gender and nationhood, women writers had a licence to campaign for political as well as professional and personal liberty, and women writers were vocal in their pro-Risorgimento politics, including Barrett Browning, whose *Aurora Leigh* confronts and revises the legacy of Corinne by giving her heroine requited love and a successful poetic career. Such lesser-known figures, however, as Theodosia Trollope (née Garrow, daughter-in-law of Frances Trollope), Isa Blagden, Eliza Ogilvy and Harriet Hamilton King demonstrate the range of responses to the problem and opportunity of the fictive precursor Corinne. Trollope campaigned for Italy's liberty through her translations and reviews of patriotic Italian poets, her own poetry published in British gift books and the *Tuscan Athenaeum* (edited by her husband Thomas Adolphus Trollope), and journalism for the *Athenaeum* as the Florence correspondent during the Tuscan Revolution. Trollope's poetry mobilizes the sensibility and lyrical modality inherent within the construction of the English Poetess for political ends, something recognized by Landor's poem 'To Theodosia Garrow', which describes her as 'wakening Italy with song/Deeper than Filicaia's'.[27] 'Deeper' is also to be understood as more intense; indeed, W. S. Landor extravagantly describes Trollope's 1847 contribution to *Heath's Book of Beauty*, 'The Cry of Romagna', in superlative terms: 'Sappho is far less intense, Pindar is far less animated.'[28] Trollope, known as the 'new Corinne' in Florence,[29] carefully negotiated her public status after her move to Florence in 1844 as a poetess and political campaigner whose authority came from her personal impressions and eye-witness accounts, as well as her 'natural' feminine identity with the struggle of oppressed Italians. Her very first letter as correspondent for the *Athenaeum* underscores her authority for speaking about Italian politics by the collective pronoun: 'We have made at Florence a revolution with rose-water' (Trollope 1). Although her writing career was tragically curtailed by tuberculosis, Trollope's revised version of *Corinne* gained success and acclaim through her advocacy for Italian freedom in a wide variety of genres and print media, as well as the Trollope salon in Florence (run by Theodosia, Thomas Adolphus Trollope and Fanny Trollope). The political agency, in other words, of Trollope's writing did not just rest on the intensity and animation of her poetry which, as Landon's praise reminds us, sound dangerously close to the superlatively feminine and apolitical lyric modality of the poetess.

Barrett Browning also bases her political, public authority on 'personal impressions' in the Preface to her narrative poem on the first unsuccessful Tuscan Revolution, *Casa Guidi Windows* (1851), which attempts to license an intervention in politics through personal impressions of expatriate Florentine residence. But, unlike Trollope, Barrett Browning's poetry seeks a new model for women's political poetics that attempts to do away with the pathological and enervating identification of poet and Italy altogether. *Casa Guidi Windows* explicitly rejects the feminized representations of Italy's dead patriotic poets, and instead her muse is the voice of a child under her apartment window, who sings 'O bella libertà', and who inspires her to urge heroic action for Italy, rather than passive appreciation and longing. Barrett Browning's most strident pro-Risorgimento stance in *Poems before Congress* (1860) pushes even further at the limits of the female lyric voice (the title refers to a congress of European nations on the Italy question which ultimately failed to meet). Like the Preface of *Casa Guidi Windows*, this 1860 volume begins by resting poetic authority on direct experience of Italian politics and people. The Preface also argues for an expanded notion of patriotism to include investment in countries beyond the interests of one's homeland: 'So, if patriotism be a virtue indeed, it cannot mean an exclusive devotion to one's country's interests, – for that is only another form of devotion to personal interests, all of which, if not driven past themselves, are vulgar and immoral objects.'[30] The provocative opening poem, 'Napoleon III in Italy', daringly tests such a formula in its rhapsodic celebration of the French Emperor's controversial investment in the Risorgimento, a foreign policy of intervention that left Britain suspicious of the Emperor's imperial ambitions:

> We, poets of the people, who take part
> With elemental justice, natural right,
> Join in our echoes also, nor refrain.
> We meet thee, O Napoleon, at this height
> At last, and find thee great enough to praise.
> Receive the poet's chrism, which smells beyond
> The priests, and pass thy ways; –
> An English poet warns thee to maintain
> God's word, not England's.   (stanza 5)

Barrett Browning as a self-named 'English poet' explicitly repudiates her 'natural' allegiance to English interests, and crowns Napoleon emperor with the sacramental oil of 'the poet's chrism'. Poetry is thus reformulated as an active public political agency, proclaiming that, through Napoleon III's military intervention, Italy 'rises up' and 'lives anew'. The poem's insistent refrain, 'Emperor/Evermore', underlines the text's double purpose as a performative praise poem. Although Barrett Browning's daring experimentalism, her self-conscious and radical reformulation of women/lyric/nation, was celebrated in Italy, where she became an important pro-Risorgimento voice, her volume was poorly received in Britain. In the most scathing review, William Edmonstone Aytoun condemns her for 'Poetic Aberrations', declaring: 'We are strongly of the opinion that, for the peace and welfare of society, it is a good and wholesome rule that women should not interfere with politics', and objecting particularly to 'Napoleon III in Italy' as 'a fit of insanity'.[31] If British women were seen to be 'mothers of the nation', licensed to address nation-building through their feminine empathy and sensibility, there were ideological limits to the scope of their patriotism. Significantly, after the reception of *Poems before Congress*, Barrett Browning makes a lucrative turn to an American audience for her periodical publications, advocating unification to a sympathetic readership invested in the connections between European nation-building and the looming American civil war.[32]

Although women writers faced a double bind in writing on behalf of, and identifying with, 'la bella Italia', possibilities were also offered to women through the experience of travelling to and living in Italy. For the middle- and upper-class writer, Italy in the Victorian period provided a social, literary and cultural network mapped for the newcomer by the popular Murray's Handbooks (which list important cultural sites and expatriate contacts, such as English pharmacies, bankers and booksellers), and focused around expatriate salons (such as the 'Villino Trollope') and reading rooms (such as the famous Vieusseux in Florence, which functioned as a meeting-place where expatriates accessed European print culture, received correspondence, and met other expatriates, travellers and Italians). Some networks nurtured an Anglo-American lesbian sub-culture of literary and artistic women, exemplified by the American actress Charlotte Cushman's international circle in Rome, which included American sculptress Harriet Hosmer, American journalist Kate Field, and British writers Isa Blagden and Matilda Hays (Cushman's partner). As Martha Vicinus argues, 'Within the highly gendered world of the expatriate bourgeoisie, women found that they could have a range of emotional relationships with women, as well as asexual friendships with men. Romantic friendships far from home presented emotional and erotic opportunities for women free from the strict boundaries of marriage and heterosexual virginity.'[33] While Aurora Leigh's matriarchal unit with Marian Erle and her baby son is an idyllic Florentine interlude before her reconcilation with Romney, other women writers explored passionate female friendships as a viable alternative to heterosexuality (what Barrett Browning terms 'female marriage').[34] Isa Blagden, for example, a close friend of the Brownings in Florence and a salon hostess, regularly shared her lodgings with other women writers (such as Frances Power Cobbe and Kate Field), balancing propriety with intimacy.

In the feminized 'bella Italia', despite its own Catholic version of patriarchy, British expatriates were afforded room to test the limits of British sexual conventions. For Isa Blagden, residence in Italy launched her career as a poet and novelist. While Blagden's reputation rests on her correspondence with Robert Browning, her poetry is remarkable for its articulation of an Italian expatriate identity. 'My Monogram', for example, plays with Blagden's initials (and that of her pseudonym Ivory Beryl) to suggest that she conflates the pagan and Christian in 'Circles of love and of pleasure,/ Barred by a cross of flame'.[35] Blagden's poems, novels (especially *Agnes Tremorne* (1861)) and periodical writing are underpinned and also undermined by an unstable doubled national identification as a mediatrix of Italian politics and culture. As the first stanza of 'My Monogram' suggests, the doubled positions precariously 'Unite, and divide, and measure' (line 3). As with Nathaniel Hawthorne's exploration of pagan and Christian collisions in his Italian romance *The Marble Faun* (1860), the pagan, for all its sensual pleasure and expansiveness, cannot exist safely within modern Italy, suggested by the relationship between Miriam (possibly modelled on Blagden herself) and the faun-like Donatello, with disastrous effects in the murder of the monk who stalks and persecutes Miriam.

While women poets exhibit an intense personal and professional identification with Italy, however, writing by men in this period suggests a more uneasy relationship. Although a staunch supporter of Italian independence, Robert Browning's opinion of Napoleon III was not so enthusiastic as his wife's; their project to produce a volume together on Italian politics quickly came to nothing. Although Browning declared later in his life that 'Italy was *my* university', his complex relationship with Italy is often one of displacement and loss; indeed, one of his courtship letters to Barrett complains that 'Italy is stuff for the use of the North.'[36] In 'Home Thoughts, from Abroad' (1845), the speaker's intense and vivid description of the pastoral delights of an English April is ironically contingent on his foreign perspective (implicitly in the South), and the urgency of his homesickness ('the chaffinch sings on the orchard bough/In England – now!') is underlined by an acute sense of displacement, which makes common English buttercups 'Far brighter than this gaudy melon-flower!'[37] Such a painful dialectic is replayed elsewhere, associating Italy, its culture and its landscape with desire and longing. 'Love among the Ruins' (1855) juxtaposes the speaker's eager romantic reunion in a landscape, presumably Italian, full of fragments of a fallen glorious empire. The immediacy of the moment in which the lovers 'extinguish sight and speech/Each on each' (*Poems*, p. 529, lines 71–2) is juxtaposed with the folly of the imperial and militaristic past, leaving the speaker to conclude 'Love is best' (line 84). And yet the association of love with the Italianate landscape of fallen glory makes this simple and abrupt ending problematic, offering an illusory sense of closure, and implying the fragility and contingency of emotion. Italy's monumental past, exhibited in fragments throughout its cities and landscapes, the poem suggests, makes the immediate consolation of romantic love urgent yet also transient. In 'A Toccata of Galuppi's' (1855), music may imaginatively and even fantastically reproduce the pleasurable allure of Venice in its glory to an armchair travelling speaker who has never left England, but the speaker also realizes that the composer, 'like a ghostly cricket', reminds him of mortality: '"Dust and ashes, dead and done with"' (lines 34, 35). Francis O'Gorman notes Browning's investment in resurrectionist rhetoric,[38] and indeed the historical past for Browning can be recalled and mediated through art, but this is a temporary resurrection that leaves the speaker, and implicitly also the reader, desolate. While Browning relishes mining Italy's history for his dramatic monologues – such as 'Andrea del Sarto', 'Fra Lippo Lippi', and the dazzling achievement of *The Ring and the Book* – the re-creation of historicized voices is conditional and contingent in its performativity, self-consciously underlining the displacement between past and present. The immediacy of the dramatic monologue is ironically overlaid with the temporality of its textuality, creating a disjunctive hybrid form. Furthermore, while *The Ring and the Book* repeatedly returns to resurrectionist motifs to assert the vitality of poetic language, such assertions are often conditional: 'something dead *may* get to live again' and mankind 'resuscitates, *perhaps*'.[39] Unlike Barrett Browning's performative patriotic poetics, which attempt to reanimate the overly aestheticized 'bella Italia', Robert Browning's Italian poetic resurrections are far more liminal, insistently questioning the performative power of the poet and the relation between past and present.

Barrett Browning's intense and informed poetic engagement with Italian politics is deeply embedded in Europe of the 1850s, but nevertheless casts a long shadow over the second half of the century. Her bold experiments with poetic form and her challenge to the English Poetess revolutionized women's literary traditions. Particularly after the success of the epic *Aurora Leigh*, perhaps the most European of Victorian texts, women writers had a renewed passport to international themes and forms. Not only did Barrett Browning develop 'the origins of a new poetry', to adopt Dorothy Mermin's phrase, that revise the hyper-feminized lyric modality of the poetess, but *Aurora Leigh* was also talismanic of a new ambition, epic range and daring formal experimentation that influenced such bold achievements as George Eliot's historical novel set in Renaissance Italy, *Romola*, serialized in 1862–3. Eliot celebrates *Aurora Leigh* in the *Westminster Review*: 'no poem embraces so wide a range of thought and emotion, or takes such complete possession of our nature'.[40] Eliot specifically praises the novel-poem's 'yearning sympathy with multiform human sorrow', and the scrupulously researched *Romola* similarly develops a politicized doctrine of sympathy through its heroine – a sympathy that correlates the personal and public body, and enfranchises women in nation-building through their 'natural' propensity for sympathetic identification with the other.[41] *Romola* warmly responds to Barrett Browning's poetical and personal identifications with the struggle for Italian unity, and participates in European historiography by forging implicit parallels between the republican government of Savonarola in the 1490s and the forging of a united Italy under King Victor Emmanuel in 1861. But other responses to Barrett Browning's Italian identifications in the later nineteenth century remained negative. Henry James's study of the Italian expatriate world in *William Wetmore Story and His Friends* (1903) dismisses Barrett Browning for her lack of disinterestedness in Italian affairs. James implies that her 'case' is pathological, and complains that Italian politics was 'a possession, by the subject, riding her to death, that almost prompts us at times to ask wherein it so greatly concerned her'.[42] As Frederick Wegener argues, James, although a supporter of united Italy, prefers the writer to address disinterested impressions rather than a passionate involvement in revolutionary politics.[43] Italy becomes a place of aesthetic experiences, of impressions devoid of overt political pressure.

But if, for James, Italy is a palimpsest of memory, an atmosphere, it is also the place of terrible, strange resurrections, suggesting the symbolic weight of the Risorgimento, that resurrection of Italian nationality, had an afterlife. In 'The Aspern Papers' (1887), for example, a literary editor arrives in Venice to pursue the remains of the dead poet Jeffrey Aspern (a fictive American Shelley) by ingratiating himself into the palazzo inhabited by Aspern's former mistress, the now aged Miss Juliana Bordereau, and her elderly niece. The atmosphere of Venice, that 'city of exhibition' (4), offers 'a palpable imaginable *visible* past' (Preface, xxxi). The editor finds Aspern's former mistress an ancient 'relic', a link to a lost era of the literary remains he so longs to possess, but also uncanny: 'most dead of all did poor Miss Bordereau appear, and yet she alone had survived' (4). In the narrator's first encounter with Juliana she is represented as 'some ghastly death's head', a 'miracle of resurrection': 'She was too strange, too literally resurgent' (14–15). This resurgence of the past he so worships is a grotesque risorgimento, and the irony of the denouement is that the resurrected past fails to offer itself up to the narrator, who is invited to marry Juliana's niece in return for the papers. His appalled rejection of her suit leads her to burn Aspern's remains, pointing to the irony of the poet's name, the transience of the past, and the dark failure of the literary editor to seize Aspern through his papers. For James, history is 'art-romance', in Jonah Siegel's words, and all the more so for being just out of reach.[44] This is the 'working convention' of Italy, which the Aspern papers themselves signify: the 'inexhaustible charm' of a place that so visibly offers and refuses its secrets (xxviii).

James's resurrections are aesthetic yet painful pleasures of an Italy that refuses to yield itself up to the foreigner. Towards the end of the century, as post-unification Italy modernized and industrialized, British writers valued the emerging nation less for its politics and more for its sensory impressions. In particular, there is a renewed investment in the literary and cultural rebirths of the Renaissance, inspired by Jacob Burckhardt's *Civilization of the Renaissance in Italy* (1860), Pater's *Renaissance* (1873) and J. A. Symond's *Renaissance in Italy* (1877). In *Aurora Leigh*, which emphatically asserts the literary value of the contemporary 'full-veined, heaving, double-breasted Age' (5, 216), the active political poetics of the experiential impression allows future readers to:

> touch the impress with reverent hand, and say
> 'Behold, – behold the paps we all have sucked!
> This bosom seems to beat still, or at least
> It sets ours beating: this is living art,
> Which thus presents and thus records true life.' (5, 218–22)

The 'living art', predicated in *Aurora Leigh* on transnational sympathies, is transformed into something quite different. The continuity of the past, implied by Ruskin's well-known assertion that 'on the Continent, the links are unbroken between past and present', becomes more problematic by the end of the century.[45] While the aestheticist attraction to France is grounded in its cultural modernity, Italy's allure becomes its very inaccessibility, its ghostliness, and the urgent politicized Anglo-Italian identifications give way to a sense of the uncanniness of Italy's layered past, its alluring otherness, and the impossibility of artistic possession. As Vernon Lee, that superlative writer of the transient Italian impression, declares in 'Out of Venice at Last': 'Venice is always too much and too much so. I cannot cope with it, it submerges me.'[46]

Notes

1 *The Poems of Matthew Arnold*, ed. Kenneth Allott and Miriam Allott (London: Longman, 1979), p. 255.
2 'Ode on the Death of the Duke of Wellington' (line 172), in *The Poems of Tennyson*, ed. Christopher Ricks, 3 vols. (Harlow: Longman, 1969), vol. II, p. 488.

3 See Jonathan P. Ribner, 'Our English Coasts: William Holman Hunt and Invasion Fear at Midcentury', *Art Journal*, 55 (1996), pp. 45–55.

4 See Maura O'Connor, *The Romance of Italy and the English Political Imagination* (Basingstoke: Macmillan, 1998). Sometimes, indeed, the relation works the other way, such as in volume III of Ruskin's *Stones of Venice* (1853), which makes implicit prophetic connections between the fall of Venetian power in the Renaissance and contemporary Britain.

5 Joseph A. Buttigieg, 'Introduction' to 'Forum – Europe's Southern Question: The Other Within', *Nineteenth-Century Contexts*, 26 (2004), p. 312.

6 Ralph Pite, 'Italian', in Peter France (ed.), *The Oxford History of Literary Translation in English*, vol. IV: *1790–1900* (Oxford: Oxford University Press, 2006), p. 252.

7 See Todd E. A. Larson, 'Anglo-German Relations', in James Eli Adams (ed.), *Encyclopedia of the Victorian Era*, 4 vols. (Danbury, Conn.: Grolier, 2004), vol. I, p. 49.

8 France (ed.), *Oxford History of Literary Translation*, vol. IV, p. 211.

9 Thomas De Quincey, *Works*, ed. Grevel Lindop, 21 vols. (London: Pickering and Chatto, 2000–3), vol. III, p. 18.

10 See 'Introduction' to Margaret Cohen and Carolyn Denver (eds.), *The Literary Channel: The Inter-National Invention of the Novel* (Princeton: Princeton University Press, 2002), p. 12.

11 This is powerfully demonstrated in Patrick H. Vincent, *The Romantic Poetess: European Culture, Politics and Gender 1820–1840* (Durham, NH: University of New Hampshire Press, 2004).

12 Cohen and Denver, *The Literary Channel*, p. 14.

13 Sharon Marcus, 'Same Difference? Transnationalism, Comparative Literature, and Victorian Studies', *Victorian Studies*, 45 (2003), pp. 677–86.

14 Elizabeth Barrett Browning, *Aurora Leigh*, ed. Margaret Reynolds (New York: W. W. Norton, 1996), book 6, line 76.

15 Vanessa R. Schwartz, *Spectacular Realities: Early Mass Culture in Fin-de-Siècle Paris* (Berkeley: University of California Press, 1998), pp. 3, 5.

16 Charles Dickens, *Pictures from Italy*, ed. Kate Flint (London: Penguin, 1998), p. 5.

17 Frances Trollope, *Paris and the Parisians in 1835*, 2 vols. (London: Bentley, 1835), vol. I, p. 2.

18 See Richard Maxwell, 'Introduction' to *A Tale of Two Cities* (London: Penguin, 2000), pp. xiii–xiv.

19 'Revolution at Florence, Exactly Described', *All the Year Round*, 2 July 1859, pp. 221–8.

20 See, for example, Theodosia Trollope, *Social Aspects of the Italian Revolution* (London: Chapman and Hall, 1861), p. 1.

21 Paul Vita, 'Returning the Look: Victorian Writers and the Paris Morgue', *Nineteenth-Century Contexts*, 25 (2003), pp. 241–56, at p. 254.

22 Christina Rossetti, *The Complete Poems*, ed. R. W. Crump (Harmondsworth: Penguin, 2001), pp. 355–6, lines 9–12.

23 Angela Leighton and Margaret Reynolds (eds.), *Victorian Women Poets: An Anthology* (Oxford, Blackwell, 1995), p. 522.

24 *Casa Guidi Windows*, ed. Julia Markus (New York: Browning Institute, 1977), p. 6, line 169.

25 Leighton and Reynolds, *Victorian Women Poets*, pp. 5–6.

26 Sandra M. Gilbert, 'From Matria to Patria: Elizabeth Barrett Browning's Risorgimento', in Angela Leighton (ed.), *Victorian Women Poets: A Critical Reader* (Oxford: Blackwell, 1996), p. 28.

27 The poem is cited in Kate Field, 'English Authors in Florence', *Atlantic Monthly* (December 1864), pp. 660–71, at p. 663.

28 Philip Kelley and Ronald Hudson (eds.), *The Brownings' Correspondence*, 16 vols. (Winfield, Tex.: Wedgestone Press, 1984), vol. XI, p. 163.

29 Thomas A. Trollope, *What I Remember*, 2 vols. (New York: Harper, 1888), vol. II, p. 159.

30 Elizabeth Barrett Browning, *Poems before Congress* (London: Chapman and Hall, 1860), p. vii.

31 W. E. Aytoun, 'Poetic Aberrations', *Blackwood's Edinburgh Magazine*, 87 (April 1860), pp. 490–4, at p. 492.

32 See Alison Chapman, '"Vulgar Needs": Elizabeth Barrett Browning, Profit and Literary Value', in Francis O'Gorman (ed.), *Victorian Literature and Finance* (Oxford: Oxford University Press, 2007).

33 Martha Vicinus, 'Laocoöning in Rome: Harriet Hosmer and Romantic Friendship', *Women's Writing*, 10 (2003), pp. 353–66, at p. 353.

34 Scott Lewis (ed.), *The Letters of Elizabeth Barrett Browning to her Sister Arabella*, 2 vols. (Waco, Tex.: Wedgestone Press, 2002), vol. I, p. 506.

35 Isa Blagden, *Poems* (Edinburgh: Blackwood, 1873), pp. 126–7 (lines 1–2).

36 Lilian Whiting, *The Brownings: Their Life and Art* (London: Hodder and Stoughton, 1911), p. 246; Elvan Kinter (ed.), *The Letters of Robert Browning and Elizabeth Barrett, 1845–1846*, 2 vols. (Cambridge, Mass.: Harvard University Press, 1969), vol. I, p. 50.

37 *Robert Browning: The Poems*, ed. John Pettigrew and Thomas J. Collins, 2 vols. (New Haven: Yale University Press, 1981), vol. I, p. 412, lines 7–8, 20.

38 Francis O'Gorman, 'Browning, Grief, and the Strangeness of Dramatic Verse', *Cambridge Quarterly*, 36 (2007), pp. 155–73.

39 Robert Browning, *The Ring and the Book*, ed. Richard D. Altick (New Haven: Yale University Press, 1971), book I, pp. 722, 712.

40 George Eliot, 'Contemporary Literature', *Westminster Review* (January 1857), pp. 246–326, at p. 306.

41 See Elizabeth Barnes, *States of Sympathy: Seduction and Democracy in the American Novel* (New York: Columbia University Press, 1997).

42 Henry James, *William Wetmore Story and His Friends*, 2 vols. (Edinburgh: Blackwood, 1903), vol. II, p. 54.

43 Frederick Wegener, 'Elizabeth Barrett Browning, Italian Independence, and the "Critical Reaction" of Henry James', *Studies in English Literature*, 37 (1997), pp. 741–61.

44 Jonah Siegel, *Haunted Museum: Longing, Travel and the Art-Romance Tradition* (Princeton: Princeton University Press, 2005).

45 E. T. Cook and Alexander Wedderburn (eds.), *Works of John Ruskin*, 39 vols. (London: G. Allen, 1903–12), vol. VI, p. 12.

46 'Out of Venice at Last', in Catherine Maxwell and Patricia Pulham (eds.), *Vernon Lee: Hauntings and Other Fantastic Tales* (Peterborough, Ontario: Broadview, 2006), p. 340.

GUIDE TO FURTHER READING

1 Authors and authorship

Carey, John, *The Intellectuals and the Masses* (London: Faber and Faber, 1992).

Dooley, Allan C., *Author and Printer in Victorian England* (Charlottesville and London: University Press of Virginia, 1992).

Eliot, Simon, *Some Patterns and Trends in British Publishing 1800–1919*, Occasional Papers of the Bibliographical Society 8 (London: The Bibliographical Society, 1994).

Erickson, Lee, *The Economy of Literary Form: English Literature and the Industrialization of Publishing: 1800–1850* (Baltimore: Johns Hopkins University Press, 1996).

Feather, John, *A History of British Publishing*, 2nd edn (London and New York: Routledge, 2006).

Feltes, Norman, *Literary Capital and the Late Victorian Novel* (London: University of Wisconsin Press, 1993).

Modes of Production of Victorian Novels (London: University of Chicago Press, 1986).

Freedman, Jonathan, *Professions of Taste: Henry James, British Aestheticism and Commodity Culture* (Stanford: Stanford University Press, 1986).

Gagnier, Regenia, *Idylls of the Market Place* (Stanford: Stanford University Press, 1986).

Hammond, Mary, *Reading, Publishing and the Formation of Literary Taste in England: 1880–1914* (Aldershot: Ashgate, 2006).

Jordan, John O. and Robert Patten (eds.), *Literature and the Marketplace: Nineteenth-Century British Publishing and Reading Practices* (Charlottesville and London: University Press of Virginia, 1991).

Weedon, Alexis, *Victorian Publishing: The Economics of Book Production for a Mass Market, 1836–1916* (Aldershot: Ashgate, 2003).

White, Allon, *The Uses of Obscurity* (London: Routledge and Kegan Paul, 1981).

2 Readers and readerships

Brantlinger, Patrick, *The Reading Lesson: The Threat of Mass Literacy in Nineteenth-Century British Fiction* (Bloomington: Indiana University Press, 1998).

Collins, Philip, *Reading Aloud: A Victorian Métier* (Lincoln: Tennyson Research Centre, 1972).

Cunningham, B. and M. Kennedy (eds.), *The Experience of Reading: Irish Historical Perspectives* (Dublin: Social History Society of Ireland, 1999).

Flint, Kate, *The Woman Reader 1837–1914* (Oxford: Clarendon Press, 1993; repr. 1995).

Hayward, J., *Consuming Pleasures: Active Audiences and Serial Fictions from Dickens to Soap Opera* (Lexington: University Press of Kentucky, 1997).

Klancher, Jon, *The Making of English Reading Audiences, 1790–1832* (Madison: University of Wisconsin Press, 1987).

Leedham-Green, E., T. Webber, G. Mandelbrote, K. Hanley, A. Black and P. Hoare (eds.), *The Cambridge History of Libraries in Britain and Ireland*, 3 vols. (Cambridge: Cambridge University Press, 2006).

Raven, J., H. Small and N. Tadmor (eds.), *The Practice and Representation of Reading in England* (Cambridge: Cambridge University Press, 1996).

Sutherland, John, *Victorian Fiction: Writers, Publishers, Readers* (Basingstoke: Macmillan, 1995).

Vincent, David, *The Rise of Mass Literacy: Reading and Writing in Modern Europe* (Cambridge: Polity Press, 2000).

Waller, Philip, *Writers, Readers and Reputations: Literary Life in Britain, 1870–1918* (Oxford: Oxford University Press, 2006).

3 Life writing

Adams, James Eli, *Dandies and Desert Saints: Styles of Victorian Manhood* (Ithaca, NY: Cornell University Press, 1995).

Altick, Richard D., *Lives and Letters: A History of Literary Biography in England and America* (New York: Knopf, 1966).

Booth, Alison, *How To Make It as a Woman: Collective Biographical History from Victoria to the Present* (Chicago: University of Chicago Press, 2004).

Cockshut, A. O. J., *Truth to Life: The Art of Biography in the Nineteenth Century* (New York: Harcourt Brace Jovanovich, 1974).

Eakin, Paul John (ed.), *The Ethics of Life Writing* (Ithaca, NY: Cornell University Press, 2004).

Epstein, William H. (ed.), *Contesting the Subject: Essays in the Postmodern Theory and Practice of Biography and Biographical Criticism* (West Lafayette, Ind.: Purdue University Press, 1991).

France, Peter and William St Clair (eds.), *Mapping Lives: The Uses of Biography* (Oxford: Oxford University Press, 2002).

Fuchs, Miriam and Craig Howes (eds.), *Teaching Life Writing Texts* (New York: Modern Language Association, 2008).

Gilmore, Leigh, *Autobiographics: A Feminist Theory of Women's Self-Representation* (Ithaca, NY: Cornell University Press, 1994).

Jolly, Margareta (ed.), *Encyclopedia of Life Writing* (London: Fitzroy Dearborn, 2001).

Joyce, Simon. 'On or About 1901: The Bloomsbury Group Looks Back at the Victorians', *Victorian Studies* (Summer 2004), pp. 631–54.

Law, Joe and Linda K. Hughes (eds.), *Biographical Passages: Essays in Victorian and Modernist Biography* (Columbia: University of Missouri Press, 2000).

Machann, Clinton, *The Genre of Autobiography in Victorian Literature* (Ann Arbor: University of Michigan Press, 1994).

Peterson, Linda, *Traditions of Victorian Women's Autobiography* (Charlottesville: University of Virginia Press, 1999).

Sanders, Valerie, 'Victorian Life Writing', *Literature Compass*, 1 (2004), VI, 113, pp. 1–17.

Whittemore, Reed, *Whole Lives: Shapers of Modern Biography* (Baltimore: Johns Hopkins University Press, 1989).

4 The culture of criticism

Armstrong, Isobel, *Victorian Scrutinies: Reviews of Poetry 1830–1870* (London: Athlone Press, 1972).

Ashton, Rosemary, *G. H. Lewes: A Life* (Oxford: Clarendon Press, 1991).

Brake, Laurel, *Subjugated Knowledges: Journalism, Gender and Literature in the Nineteenth Century* (London: Macmillan, 1994).

Camlot, Jason, *Style and the Nineteenth-Century British Critic: Sincere Mannerisms* (Aldershot: Ashgate, 2008).

Erickson, Lee, *The Economy of Literary Form: English Literature and the Industrialization of Publishing, 1800–1850* (Baltimore: Johns Hopkins University Press, 1996).

Gross, John, *The Rise and Fall of the Man of Letters: English Literary Life since 1800* (London: Weidenfeld and Nicolson, 1969; rev. edn, London: Penguin Books, 1991).

Mullan, John, *Anonymity: A Secret History of English Literature* (London: Faber and Faber, 2007).

Orel, Harold, *Victorian Literary Critics* (London: Macmillan, 1984).

Parrinder, Patrick, *Authors and Authority: English and American Criticism 1750–1990* (London: Macmillan, 1991).

Small, Ian, *Conditions of Criticism* (Oxford: Clarendon Press, 1990).

Treglown, Jeremy and Bridget Bennett (eds.), *Grub Street and the Ivory Tower: Literary Journalism and Literary Scholarship from Fielding to the Internet* (Oxford: Clarendon Press, 1998).

5 Women's voices and public debate

Brake, Laurel, *Subjugated Knowledges: Journalism, Gender and Literature in the Nineteenth Century* (London: Macmillan, 1994).

Broomfield, Andrea L., 'Much More Than an Antifeminist: Eliza Lynn Linton's Contribution to the Rise of Victorian Popular Journalism', *Victorian Literature and Culture*, 29, 2 (2001), pp. 267–83.

D'Albertis, Deirdre, 'The Domestic Drone: Margaret Oliphant and a Political History of the Novel', *Studies in English Literature, 1500–1900*, 37, 4 (1997), pp. 805–29.

Frankel, Oz, *States of Inquiry: Social Investigations and Print Culture in Nineteenth-Century Britain and the United States* (Baltimore: Johns Hopkins University Press, 2006).

Fraser, Hilary, Judith Johnston and Stephanie Green, *Gender and the Victorian Periodical* (Cambridge: Cambridge University Press, 2003).

Hamilton, Susan (ed.), *Criminals, Idiots, Women and Minors: Nineteenth Century Writing by Women on Women*, 2nd edn (Peterborough, ON: Broadview, 1995).

Heilmann, Ann, *New Woman Strategies: Sarah Grand, Olive Schreiner, Mona Caird* (Manchester: Manchester University Press, 2004).

Holcomb, Adele M., 'Anna Jameson: The First Professional English Art Historian', *Art History*, 6, 2 (1983), pp. 171–87.

Johnston, Judith, *Anna Jameson: Victorian, Feminist, Woman of Letters* (Aldershot: Scolar, 1997).

Onslow, Barbara, *Women of the Press in Nineteenth-Century Britain* (New York: Palgrave Macmillan, 2000).

Thomas, Clara, *Love and Work Enough: The Life of Anna Jameson* (Toronto: University of Toronto Press, 1967).

6 Writing the past

Bann, S., *The Clothing of Clio: A Study of the Representation of History in Nineteenth-Century Britain and France* (Cambridge: Cambridge University Press, 1984).

Bowler, P. J., *The Invention of Progress: The Victorians and the Past* (Oxford: Blackwell, 1989).

Buckley, J. H., *The Triumph of Time: A Study of the Victorian Concepts of Time, History, Progress and Decadence* (Cambridge, Mass.: Harvard University Press; London: Oxford University Press, 1967).

Burrow, J. W., *A Liberal Descent: Victorian Historians and the English Past* (Cambridge: Cambridge University Press, 1982).

Chandler, A., *A Dream of Order: The Medieval Ideal in Nineteenth-Century English Literature* (London: Routledge and Kegan Paul, 1971).

Chapman, R., *The Sense of the Past in Victorian Literature* (London: Croom Helm, 1986).

Culler, A. D. *The Victorian Mirror of History* (New Haven: Yale University Press, 1985).

Dale, P. A., *The Victorian Critic and the Idea of History: Carlyle, Arnold, Pater* (Cambridge, Mass.: Harvard University Press, 1977).

Dellheim, C., *The Face of the Past: The Preservation of the Medieval Inheritance in Victorian England* (Cambridge: Cambridge University Press, 1982).

Fraser, H., *The Victorians and Renaissance Italy* (Oxford: Blackwell, 1992).

Glen, H., *Charlotte Brontë: The Imagination of History* (Oxford: Oxford University Press, 2002).

Jann, R., *The Art and Science of Victorian History* (Columbus: Ohio State University Press, 1985).

Jenkyns, R., *The Victorians and Ancient Greece* (Oxford: Blackwell, 1980).

Lowenthal, D., *The Past Is a Foreign Country* (Cambridge: Cambridge University Press, 1985).

McCaw, N., *George Eliot and Victorian Historiography: Imagining the National Past* (Basingstoke: Macmillan, 2000).

Morris, K. L., *The Image of the Middle Ages in Romantic and Victorian Literature* (London: Croom Helm, 1984).

Onega, S. (ed.), *Telling Histories: Narrativizing History, Historicizing Literature* (Amsterdam: Rodopi, 1995).

Reilly, J., *Shadowtime: History and Representation in Hardy, Conrad and George Eliot* (London: Routledge, 1993).

Rosenberg, J. D., *Carlyle and the Burden of History* (Cambridge, Mass.: Harvard University Press, 1985).

Sanders, A., *The Victorian Historical Novel, 1840–1880* (London: Macmillan, 1979).

Shaw, H. E., *The Forms of Historical Fiction: Sir Walter Scott and His Successors* (Ithaca, NY: Cornell University Press, 1983).

Turner, F. M., *The Greek Heritage in Victorian Britain* (New Haven: Yale University Press, 1981).

Vance, N., *The Victorians and Ancient Rome* (Oxford: Blackwell, 1997).

White, H. V., *Metahistory: The Historical Imagination in Nineteenth-Century Europe* (Baltimore and London: Johns Hopkins University Press, 1974).

7 Radical writing

Gallagher, Catherine, *The Industrial Reformation of English Fiction 1832–1867* (Chicago and London: University of Chicago Press, 1985).

Guy, Josephine M., *The Victorian Social-Problem Novel* (Basingstoke: Macmillan, 1996).

Hadley, Elaine, *Melodramatic Tactics: Theatricalized Dissent in the English Marketplace, 1800–1885* (Stanford: Stanford University Press, 1995).

Ledger, Sally, *Dickens and the Popular Radical Imagination* (Cambridge and New York: Cambridge University Press, 2007).

Livesey, Ruth, *Socialism, Sex, and the Culture of Aestheticism in Britain, 1880–1914* (Oxford and New York: Oxford University Press, 2007).

Thompson, E. P., *William Morris: Romantic to Revolutionary* (London: Lawrence and Wishart, 1955).

8 Popular culture

Bailey, Peter, *Popular Culture and Performance in the Victorian City* (Cambridge: Cambridge University Press, 1998).

Brantlinger, Patrick, *Rule of Darkness: British Literature and Imperialism, 1830–1914* (Ithaca, NY: Cornell University Press, 1988).

Cantor, Paul A. and Peter Hufnagel, 'The Empire of the Future: Imperialism and Modernism in H. G. Wells', *Studies in the Novel*, 38, 1 (Spring 2006), pp. 36–56.

Cvetkovich, Anne, *Mixed Feelings: Feminism, Mass Culture, and Victorian Sensationalism* (New Brunswick, NJ: Rutgers University Press, 1992).

Gilmartin, Kevin, *Print Politics: The Press and Radical Opposition in Early Nineteenth-Century England* (Cambridge: Cambridge University Press, 1996).

Klancher, Jon, *The Making of English Reading Audiences, 1790–1832* (Madison: University of Wisconsin Press, 1987).

Maidment, Brian, *Reading Popular Prints, 1790–1870* (Manchester: Manchester University Press, 1996).

Meisel, Martin, *Realizations* (Princeton: Princeton University Press, 1983).

Mullin, Donald, *Victorian Plays: A Record of Significant Productions on the London Stage, 1837–1901* (New York: Greenwood, 1987).

Plunkett, John, *Queen Victoria: First Media Monarch* (Oxford: Oxford University Press, 2003).

Vlock, Deborah, *Dickens, Novel Reading, and the Victorian Popular Theatre* (Cambridge: Cambridge University Press, 1998).

9 Science and its popularization

Beer, G., *Darwin's Plots: Evolutionary Narrative in Darwin, George Eliot and Nineteenth-Century Fiction*, 2nd edn (Cambridge: Cambridge University Press, 2000).

Bowler, P. J., *The Non-Darwinian Revolution: Reinterpreting a Historical Myth* (Baltimore: Johns Hopkins University Press, 1989).

Cantor, G., G. Dawson *et al.*, *Science in the Nineteenth-Century Periodical: Reading the Magazine of Nature* (Cambridge: Cambridge University Press, 2004).

Dawson, G., *Darwin, Literature and Victorian Respectability* (Cambridge: Cambridge University Press, 2007).

England, R. (ed.), *Design after Darwin, 1860–1900*, 4 vols. (Bristol: Thoemmes, 2003).

Frank, L., *Victorian Detective Fiction and the Nature of Evidence: The Scientific Investigations of Poe, Dickens, and Doyle* (Basingstoke: Palgrave, 2003).

Jenkins, A., *Space and the 'March of Mind': Literature and the Physical Sciences in Britain 1815–1850* (Oxford: Oxford University Press, 2007).

Levine, G., *Darwin Loves You: Natural Selection and the Re-enchantment of the World* (Princeton: Princeton University Press, 2006).

Lightman, B., *Victorian Popularizers of Science: Designing Nature for New Audiences* (Chicago: University of Chicago Press, 2007).

Luckhurst, R., *The Invention of Telepathy 1870–1901* (Oxford: Oxford University Press, 2002).

Rupke, N. A., *Richard Owen: Victorian Naturalist* (New Haven: Yale University Press, 1994).

Secord, J. A., *Victorian Sensation: The Extraordinary Publication, Reception, and Secret Authorship of Vestiges of the Natural History of Creation* (Chicago: University of Chicago Press, 2000).

Turner, F. M., *Contesting Cultural Authority: Essays in Victorian Intellectual Life* (Cambridge: Cambridge University Press, 1993).

White, P., *Thomas Huxley: Making the 'Man of Science'* (Cambridge: Cambridge University Press, 2003).

10 Body and mind

Caudwell, Janis McLaren, *Literature and Medicine in Nineteenth-Century Britain* (Cambridge: Cambridge University Press, 2004).

Cooter, Roger, *The Cultural Meaning of Popular Science: Phrenology and the Organization of Consent in Nineteenth-Century Britain* (Cambridge: Cambridge University Press, 1984).

Danes, Nicholas, *Amnesiac Selves: Nostalgia, Forgetting and British Fiction 1810–1870* (Oxford: Oxford University Press, 2001).

Davis, Michael, *George Eliot and Nineteenth-Century Psychology: Exploring the Unmapped Country* (London: Palgrave Macmillan, 2006).

Dixon, Thomas, *From Passions to Emotions: The Invention of a Secular Psychological Category* (Cambridge: Cambridge University Press, 2003).

Fass, Ekbert, *Retreat into the Mind: Victorian Poetry and Mental Science* (Princeton: Princeton University Press, 1988).

Greenslade, William, *Culture, Degeneration and the Novel* (Cambridge: Cambridge University Press, 1994).

Luckhurst, Roger, *The Invention of Telepathy* (Oxford: Oxford University Press, 2002).

Oppenheim, Janet, *The Other World: Spiritualism and Psychical Research in England 1850–1914* (Cambridge: Cambridge University Press, 1985).

Rylance, Rick, *Victorian Psychology and British Culture 1850–1880* (Oxford: Oxford University Press, 2000).

Scull, Andrew, *The Most Solitary of Afflictions: Madness and Society in Britain 1700–1900* (New Haven: Yale University Press, 1993).

Scull, Andrew (ed.), *The Insanity of Place/The Place of Insanity: Essays on the History of Psychiatry* (London and New York: Routledge, 2006).

Shuttleworth, Sally, *Charlotte Brontë and Victorian Psychology* (Cambridge: Cambridge University Press, 1996).

Smith, Roger, 'The Physiology of the Will: Mind, Body, and Psychology in the Periodical Literature, 1855–1875', in Geoffrey Cantor and Sally Shuttleworth (eds.), *Science Serialized: Representations of the Sciences in Nineteenth-Century Periodicals* (Cambridge, Mass.: MIT Press, 2004), pp. 81–110.

Taylor, Jenny Bourne and Sally Shuttleworth (eds.), *Embodied Selves: An Anthology of Psychological Texts 1830–1890* (Oxford: Oxford University Press, 1998).

Winter, Alison, *Mesmerised: Power of Mind in Victorian Britain* (Chicago: University of Chicago Press, 1998).

Wood, Jane, *Passion and Pathology in Victorian Fiction* (Oxford: Oxford University Press, 2001).

11 Writing and religion

Brown, Ford K., *Fathers of the Victorians: The Age of Wilberforce* (Cambridge: Cambridge University Press, 1961).

Chadwick, Owen, *The Victorian Church*: Part 1 (London: Adam and Charles Black, 1966).

The Victorian Church: Part 2 (London: Adam and Charles Black, 1970).

Church, R. W., *The Oxford Movement: Twelve Years 1833–1845* (London: Macmillan, 1932).

Cunningham, Valentine, *Everywhere Spoken Against: Dissent in the Victorian Novel* (Oxford: Clarendon Press, 1975).

Gilley, Sheridan and Brian Stanley (eds.), *The Cambridge History of Christianity*, vol. VIII: *World Christianities c.1815–c.1914* (Cambridge: Cambridge University Press, 2006).

Knoepflmacher, U. C., *Religious Humanism and the Victorian Novel: George Eliot, Walter Pater, and Samuel Butler* (Princeton: Princeton University Press, 1965).

McLeod, Hugh, *Religion and Society in England 1850–1914* (Basingstoke: Macmillan, 1996).

Rowell, Geoffrey, *Hell and the Victorians: A Study of the Nineteenth Century Theological Controversies concerning Eternal Punishment and the Future Life* (Oxford: Oxford University Press, 1974).

Royle, Edward, *Victorian Infidels: The Origins of the British Secularist Movement 1790–1866* (Manchester: Manchester University Press, 1974).

Symondson, Anthony (ed.), *The Victorian Crisis of Faith* (London: SPCK, 1970).

Wheeler, Michael, *Death and the Future Life in Victorian Literature and Theology* (Cambridge: Cambridge University Press, 1990).

12 Visual culture

Armstrong, Nancy, *Fiction in the Age of Photography: The Legacy of British Realism* (Cambridge, Mass.: Harvard University Press, 1999).

Byerly, Alison, *Realism, Representation and the Arts in Nineteenth-Century Literature* (Cambridge: Cambridge University Press, 1997).

Christ, Carol T. and John O. Jordan (eds.), *Victorian Literature and the Visual Imagination* (Berkeley: University of California Press, 1995).

Crary, Jonathan, *Techniques of the Observer: On Vision and Modernity in the Nineteenth Century* (Cambridge, Mass.: MIT Press, 1992).

Flint, Kate, '"Seeing Is Believing": Visuality and Victorian Fiction', in Francis O'Gorman (ed.), *A Concise Companion to the Victorian Novel* (Oxford: Basil Blackwell, 2005), pp. 4–24.

The Victorians and the Visual Imagination (Cambridge: Cambridge University Press, 2000).

Maxwell, Richard (ed.), *The Victorian Illustrated Book* (Charlottesville: University Press of Virginia, 2002).

Meisel, Martin, *Realizations: Narrative, Pictorial, and Theatrical Arts in Nineteenth-Century England* (Princeton: Princeton University Press, 1983).

Schwartz, Vanessa and Jeannene M. Przyblyski (eds.), *The Nineteenth Century Visual Culture Reader* (London: Routledge, 2004).

Smith, Lindsay, *Victorian Photography, Painting and Poetry: The Enigma of Visibility in Ruskin, Morris and the Pre-Raphaelites* (Cambridge: Cambridge University Press, 1995).

Witemeyer, Hugh, *George Eliot and the Visual Arts* (New Haven: Yale University Press, 1979).

Yeazell, Ruth Bernard, *Art of the Everyday: Dutch Painting and the Realist Novel* (Princeton: Princeton University Press, 2007).

13 Empire and nationalism

Anderson, Benedict, *Imagined Communities: Reflections on the Origin and Spread of Nationalism* (rev. edn., London: Verso, 1991).

Azim, Firdous, *The Colonial Rise of the Novel* (New York: Routledge, 1993).

Brantlinger, Patrick, *Dark Vanishings: Discourse on the Extinction of Primitive Races* (Ithaca, NY: Cornell University Press, 2003).
  Rule of Darkness: British Literature and Imperialism, 1830–1914 (Ithaca: Cornell University Press, 1988).
Bratton, J. S., 'British Heroism and the Structure of Melodrama', in Bratton *et al.*, *Acts of Supremacy: The British Empire and the Stage, 1790–1930* (Manchester: Manchester University Press, 1991), pp. 18–61.
Chakravarty, Gautam, *The Indian Mutiny and the British Imagination* (Cambridge: Cambridge University Press, 2005).
Cronin, Sean, *Irish Nationalism: A History of Its Roots and Ideology* (Dublin: Academy Press, 1980).
Mukherjee, Upamanyu Pablo, *Crime and Empire: The Colony in Nineteenth-Century Fictions of Crime* (Oxford: Oxford University Press, 2003).
Rajan, Balanchandra, *Under Western Eyes: India from Milton to Macaulay* (Durham, NC: Duke University Press, 1999).
Reynolds, Matthew, *The Realms of Verse: English Poetry in a Time of Nation-Building* (Oxford: Oxford University Press, 2001).
Richards, Jeffrey (ed.), *Imperialism and Juvenile Literature* (Manchester: Manchester University Press, 1989).
Said, Edward, *Culture and Imperialism* (New York: Knopf, 1993).
Stocking, George, *Victorian Anthropology* (New York: Free Press, 1987).
Trumpener, Katie, *Bardic Nationalism: The Romantic Novel and the British Empire* (Princeton: Princeton University Press, 1997).

14 Transatlantic relations

Claybaugh, Amanda, 'Towards a New Transatlanticism: Dickens in the United States', *Victorian Studies*, 48, 3 (2006), pp. 439–60.
Giles, Paul, *Transatlantic Insurrections: British Culture and the Formation of American Literature, 1730–1860* (Philadelphia: University of Pennsylvania Press, 2001).
Gilroy, Paul, *The Black Atlantic: Modernity and Double Consciousness* (Cambridge, Mass.: Harvard University Press, 1993).
Kohn, Denise, Sarah Meer and Emily B. Todd (eds.), *Transatlantic Stowe: Harriet Beecher Stowe and European Culture* (Iowa City: University of Iowa Press, 2006).
Manning, Susan and Andrew Taylor, *Transatlantic Literary Studies: A Reader* (Edinburgh: Edinburgh University Press, 2007).
Roach, Joseph, *Cities of the Dead: Circum-Atlantic Performance* (New York: Columbia University Press, 1996).
Stevens, Laura M., 'Transatlanticism Now', *American Literary History*, 16, 1 (2004), pp. 93–102.
Weisbuch, Robert, *Atlantic Double-Cross: American Literature and British Influence in the Age of Emerson* (Chicago: University of Chicago Press, 1986).

15 European exchanges

Bullen, J. B., *The Myth of the Renaissance in Nineteenth-Century Writing* (Oxford: Clarendon Press, 1994).

Buzard, James, *The Beaten Track: European Tourism, Literature and the Ways to 'Culture' 1800–1918* (Oxford: Clarendon Press, 1993).

Chapman, Alison and Jane Stabler (eds.), *Unfolding the South: Nineteenth-Century British Women Writers and Artists in Italy* (Manchester: Manchester University Press, 2001).

Churchill, Kenneth, *Italy and English Literature 1764–1930* (Basingstoke: Macmillan, 1980).

Fraser, Hilary, *The Victorians and Renaissance Italy* (Oxford: Blackwell, 1992).

Keirstead, Christopher M., 'A "Bad Patriot"? Elizabeth Barrett Browning and Cosmopolitanism', *Victorian Institute Journal*, 33 (2005), pp. 69–95.

Lootens, Tricia, 'Bengal, Britain, France: The Locations and Translations of Toru Dutt', *Victorian Literature and Culture*, 34 (2006), pp. 573–90.

Maxwell, Richard, *Mysteries of Paris and London* (Charlottesville: University Press of Virginia, 1992).

Millbank, Alison, *Dante and the Victorians* (Manchester: Manchester University Press, 1998).

Moretti, Franco, *Atlas of the European Novel 1800–1900* (London: Verso, 1998).

Morgan, Marjorie, *National Identities and Travel in Victorian Britain* (Basingstoke: Palgrave, 2001).

Simmons, Claire A., *Eyes across the Channel: French Revolutions, Party History, and British Writing, 1830–1882* (Amsterdam: Harwood Academic Publishing, 2000).

INDEX

Cambridge Companions to. . .

AUTHORS

Edward Albee edited by Stephen J. Bottoms

Margaret Atwood edited by Coral Ann Howells

W. H. Auden edited by Stan Smith

Jane Austen edited by Edward Copeland and Juliet McMaster

Beckett edited by John Pilling

Aphra Behn edited by Derek Hughes and Janet Todd

Walter Benjamin edited by David S. Ferris

William Blake edited by Morris Eaves

Brecht edited by Peter Thomson and Glendyr Sacks (second edition)

The Brontës edited by Heather Glen

Frances Burney edited by Peter Sabor

Byron edited by Drummond Bone

Albert Camus edited by Edward J. Hughes

Willa Cather edited by Marilee Lindemann

Cervantes edited by Anthony J. Cascardi

Chaucer, second edition edited by Piero Boitani and Jill Mann

Chekhov edited by Vera Gottlieb and Paul Allain

Kate Chopin edited by Janet Beer

Coleridge edited by Lucy Newlyn

Wilkie Collins edited by Jenny Bourne Taylor

Joseph Conrad edited by J. H. Stape

Dante edited by Rachel Jacoff (second edition)

Daniel Defoe edited by John Richetti

Don DeLillo edited by John N. Duvall

Charles Dickens edited by John O. Jordan

Emily Dickinson edited by Wendy Martin

John Donne edited by Achsah Guibbory

Dostoevskii edited by W. J. Leatherbarrow

Theodore Dreiser edited by Leonard Cassuto and Claire Virginia Eby

John Dryden edited by Steven N. Zwicker

W. E. B. Du Bois edited by Shamoon Zamir

George Eliot edited by George Levine

T. S. Eliot edited by A. David Moody

Ralph Ellison edited by Ross Posnock

Ralph Waldo Emerson edited by Joel Porte and Saundra Morris

William Faulkner edited by Philip M. Weinstein

Henry Fielding edited by Claude Rawson

F. Scott Fitzgerald edited by Ruth Prigozy

Flaubert edited by Timothy Unwin

E. M. Forster edited by David Bradshaw

Benjamin Franklin edited by Carla Mulford

Brian Friel edited by Anthony Roche

Robert Frost edited by Robert Faggen

Elizabeth Gaskell edited by Jill L. Matus

Goethe edited by Lesley Sharpe

Günter Grass edited by Stuart Taberner

Thomas Hardy edited by Dale Kramer

David Hare edited by Richard Boon

Nathaniel Hawthorne edited by Richard Millington

Seamus Heaney edited by Bernard O'Donoghue

Ernest Hemingway edited by Scott Donaldson

Homer edited by Robert Fowler

Horace edited by Stephen Harrison

Ibsen edited by James McFarlane

Henry James edited by Jonathan Freedman

Samuel Johnson edited by Greg Clingham

Ben Jonson edited by Richard Harp and Stanley Stewart

James Joyce edited by Derek Attridge (second edition)

Kafka edited by Julian Preece

Keats edited by Susan J. Wolfson

Lacan edited by Jean-Michel Rabaté

D. H. Lawrence edited by Anne Fernihough

Primo Levi edited by Robert Gordon

Lucretius edited by Stuart Gillespie and Philip Hardie

David Mamet edited by Christopher Bigsby

Thomas Mann edited by Ritchie Robertson

Christopher Marlowe edited by Patrick Cheney

Herman Melville edited by Robert S. Levine

Arthur Miller edited by Christopher Bigsby (second edition)

Milton edited by Dennis Danielson (second edition)

Molière edited by David Bradby and Andrew Calder

Toni Morrison edited by Justine Tally

Nabokov edited by Julian W. Connolly

Eugene O'Neill edited by Michael Manheim

TOPICS